1.95

THIS UNIQUE BOOK

has been designed to reward the general reader and student alike.

When you open it, your eye will light upon two different languages. On the left-hand page you will find the authentic text of nine complete selections from Chaucer's great Middle English classic, *The Canterbury Tales;* on the right, a graceful rendering into modern English.

This Dual-Language Book will enable even those readers with no previous knowledge of Middle English to enjoy all the magnificent poetic splendor of the original. Notes on background material are included as a special aid to the student and reader.

THE AENEID OF VIRGIL Translated by Allen Mandelbaum
THE BROTHERS KARAMAZOV by Fyodor Dostoevsky
BARABBAS by Pär Lagerkvist
CANDIDE by Voltaire
COLLECTED SHORT STORIES by Aldous Huxley
THE COMPLETE SHORT STORIES OF MARK TWAIN
    Edited by Charles Neider
A COUNTRY DOCTOR'S NOTEBOOK by Mikhail Bulgakov
CRIME AND PUNISHMENT by Fyodor Dostoevsky
FAR FROM THE MADDING CROWD by Thomas Hardy
FATHERS AND SONS by Ivan Turgenev
50 GREAT AMERICAN SHORT STORIES Edited by Milton
    Crane
FOUR SHORT NOVELS by Herman Melville
GREEN MANSIONS by W. H. Hudson
GULLIVER'S TRAVELS AND OTHER STORIES by Jonathan
    Swift
HEART OF DARKNESS and THE SECRET SHARER by
    Joseph Conrad
THE HUNCHBACK OF NOTRE DAME by Victor Hugo
THE IDIOT by Fyodor Dostoevsky
THE IMMORALIST by André Gide
LORD JIM by Joseph Conrad
MADAME BOVARY by Gustave Flaubert
THE METAMORPHOSIS AND OTHER STORIES BY FRANZ
    KAFKA Edited by Stanley Corngold
NOTES FROM UNDERGROUND by Fyodor Dostoyevsky
NOTES OF A NATIVE SON by James Baldwin
THE OCTOPUS by Frank Norris
THE ODYSSEY by Homer
SADNESS by Donald Barthelme
75 SHORT MASTERPIECES Edited by Roger Goodman
SISTER CARRIE by Theodore Dreiser
A SPY IN THE HOUSE OF LOVE by Anaïs Nin
THOREAU: WALDEN AND OTHER WRITINGS Edited by
    Joseph Wood Krutch
THREE SHORT NOVELS by Joseph Conrad
WAR AND PEACE by Leo Tolstoy
WE by Yevgeny Zamiatin

A BANTAM DUAL-LANGUAGE BOOK
CHAUCER
CANTERBURY TALES | TALES OF CAUNTERBURY

Edited by A. Kent Hieatt and Constance Hieatt

selected, with translations, a critical introduction,
and notes by the editors

CHAUCER: CANTERBURY TALES

A Bantam Dual-Language Book / May 1964

2nd printing .... August 1965	6th printing .... October 1968
3rd printing .. December 1965	7th printing .. November 1968
4th printing .. November 1966	8th printing ..... August 1969
5th printing .. September 1967	9th printing ..... March 1970

Bantam edition / August 1971

11th printing .... August 1972	14th printing . December 1975
12th printing ..... April 1973	15th printing . December 1976
13th printing ..... April 1975	16th printing . September 1978

Library of Congress Catalog Card Number: 63-19053

ISBN 0-553-12511-7

Published simultaneously in the United States and Canada

Bantam Books are published by Bantam Books, Inc. Its trademark, consisting of the words "Bantam Books" and the portrayal of a bantam, is registered in the United States Patent Office and in other countries. Marca Registrada. Bantam Books, Inc., 666 Fifth Avenue, New York, New York 10019.

PREFACE

This book offers a massive selection from *The Canterbury Tales* together with a facing-page translation designed as both a help to the beginner and as an independently readable entity.

Most people who are acquainting themselves with Chaucer for the first time do so in a class in literature, where the time allotted to the *Tales* must be short. If they use a translation, they may read enough to begin to see how a number of tales illuminate each other and what the whole work is like, but they do not hear Chaucer's voice. This seems a pity, considering how much easier for us his language is than a foreign one. Contrariwise, if they read in the original "The Prologue" and two or three of the tales, they hear the voice but miss the variety and multiple reference.

The present book seeks to overcome this dilemma. We think that what we offer here speeds comprehension, so that more can be read, and provides flexibility, so that parts can be read in the original and parts in translation if necessary.

We think that a facing-page translation will bring understanding of the original faster than do marginal glossing and notes at the bottom of the page, because these latter aids often do not clarify some of the syntactical relationships that leave most beginners at sea. It is true that anyone who has an acquaintance with the syntax of the Revised Version, and with Latin, a Romance language, and one Germanic language besides English, needs little help with Chaucerian English; but any teacher who has attentively put an American undergraduate class through its first weeks or even months with the *Tales* knows that Chaucer is a little more difficult than ripe literary scholars are likely to imagine. Of course, an interlinear translation offers as much help as we do here, but its continual leapfroggings cannot be followed comfortably.

Like most other people who are interested in poetry, we want to help everyone to an understanding of as much Chaucer as possible, as rapidly as possible. We believe that this book offers the way to do it. We know as well as some of our readers the shortcomings of both our theory and our execution, and we are exasperated by them; but we look in vain for a better way. "The dart is set up . . . Cacche who so may, who renneth best lat see." We have already heard the first question of those with classroom experience; our answer is that, for recitation purposes, an opaque object may be interposed. For the rest, if a student shows a comprehension of Chaucer's meaning, we do not think that it makes much difference where he got it.

We have based our text on that of W. W. Skeat (Clarendon Press, 1900), because his spelling is phonetically most consistent. In a beginner's book with translation, the admired alternatives (most nearly modern MS spelling for easiest recognition of words, or attachment to spellings of one MS) make less sense. Where Skeat's reading differs from that of the more modern texts of Robinson or Donaldson, we have made our own choice, generally after consulting the variants listed by Skeat and Robinson. We have departed from the authority of all seniors very infrequently, and at only one notable spot ("Nun's Priest's Tale" 3386, in Robinson's numbering). Something is said about our policy of translation, beginning on p. xxii. Each of our selections is complete, except that only the last eleven lines appear of the "Introduction to the Pardoner's Tale" (not "The Pardoner's Prologue," which is complete).

An asterisk in either text signals an explanatory note which may be located in a glossary at the end of the book. The glossary is arranged alphabetically, in each case under the word immediately preceding the asterisk in the text.

CONTENTS

INTRODUCTION

Geoffrey Chaucer (ca. 1343-1400) and The Canterbury Tales

Little is known about Chaucer personally, although one must be very perverse not to like him after having read his poetry. It is safe to say, at any rate, that he was one of a number of court poets of the later Middle Ages in western Europe. Although such a man would find his place among courts and the nobility, he would probably be a bourgeois or a lesser noble; the high nobility generally had no time for the skills involved. He would often write of love in a long-standing tradition for a class that was publicly and privately much occupied with love's power. "Poet" in the strictly modern sense is not the word for such a writer, for besides short lyrics his output might include almost any of the forms of literature, narrative and otherwise, known to the day; and "court" is deceptive, too, since, aside from courtiers, his audience would probably include some churchmen, civil servants, and students and a growing class of literate bourgeois. Unlike a modern poet, he would almost automatically be held learned, or sage: whether or not his learning went very deep, he belonged to the world of letters, one of whose functions was the transmission of truth and wisdom; he was expected to be a source of information on the world and what was above and below it, to cite ancient saws and instances, and to know what was important in other books, particularly the Latin classics. He might also be (as Chaucer was) a cultural middleman in a more systematic sense —a translator into his own language of works of moral wisdom and the like. However secular or classical his poetic interests might be, these would finally be subordinated to a Christian view of things. But in spite of all this, it was not excluded that he should write both amusingly and satirically, and a liking for compositions so intended easily coexisted with a desire for more solemn kinds of writing in the minds of some of his audience. Finally, there would be something anomalous about his position as a writer per se: in spite of the theoretical respect of the late Middle Ages and the Renaissance for letters, such a man did not have the institutional or economic standing that mass publication has given to later authors. His work did not reach people through printed books but was recited and circulated in manuscript copies, and as a poet pure and simple he would be the kept man of one or a succession of patrons who did not view him as an established limb of the social order. If he did not become some kind of churchman or make himself useful as a kind of civil servant, he was likely to feel self-conscious and uncertain about his own role, as the extreme case of Dante shows.

For Chaucer this problem seems to have solved itself: he served his rulers, probably well, in nonpoetic capacities. From one point of view his career formed only a step in the rise of a bourgeois family. His grandfather and father were London wine merchants. A woman who is almost surely his granddaughter died a duchess. We first find Chaucer himself around age fourteen as, most likely, a page in the household of one of Edward III's daughters-in-law. In his subsequent career he was a trusted emissary to the Continent for Edward III and Richard II, held a number of fairly important administrative positions, and was highly though unevenly rewarded by these kings and by their successor, Henry IV. Part of his good fortune may have been due to his marriage: his sister-in-law was first mistress then wife of John of Gaunt, a powerful son of Edward III and the father of Henry IV.

Chaucer was, then, a widely traveled, substantial citizen with some gift for affairs. In addition, to survive and prosper, however chancily, under three kings and without a fixed place in any ecclesiastical or aristocratic hierarchy, he must have displayed tact, adaptability, and at least occasional hustle. Much beyond that, the known facts simply tantalize, because they can be interpreted in so many different ways. We know that he was well-educated and widely read, but we are not sure how much or in what way. He would naturally speak French, as the ruling classes had done since the Norman Conquest; he is the earliest poet of the first rank to write English since Anglo-Saxon times. His Latin is natural in a bookish man. His knowledge of Italian works, however, is rarer in an Englishman of his time; what part his missions to Italy played in this is not known. Apparently he liked the help of a French translation when he worked with a Latin or Italian manuscript. We do not know to what extent he really had reverses in his career (he very likely had some). We do not know whether he was always scrupulous, what his marriage and family were like, what kind of relationship he had with his closest associates. The innkeeper of the *Tales* describes him as "elvish"—retiring and tending to stare at the ground; and Chaucer describes his regimen at one time as constant reading after he has returned from his work—like a hermit, except that he indulged in little eremitical abstinence. We do not know how much of this is irony.

Before coming to *The Canterbury Tales* in what may have been 1386, Chaucer had written a large number of works, some now lost. Those most read today are an elegy in "dream vision" form for the first wife of John of Gaunt (*The Book of the Duchess*), two other dream visions (*The House of Fame, The Parlement of Foules*), one of the great romances of the Middle Ages (*Troilus and Criseyde*), and a series of "Saints' legends of Cupid" generally called *The Legend of Good Women*. The *Tales* is the culmination of his career. He died while it was still unfinished. According to its "General Prologue," thirty or so people, who happen to represent almost every social type of the late Middle Ages, are to tell two tales each on a pilgrimage from London to the shrine of St. Thomas à Becket in Canterbury and two more tales on the way back. Such a program had nothing unnatural about it: pilgrimages to shrines were mass activities in the Middle Ages, partly because they were as likely to be vacations as religious observances. Wherever Chaucer got his idea for this scheme (there were a number like it in the fourteenth century, including Boccaccio's *Decameron*), what he made of it was different from anything else in literary history. The stories which the pilgrims tell are in widely different literary genres and styles, and almost each of these traditional medieval forms is turned into something surprisingly new. In addition, a story is often so well fitted to a pilgrim's character and opinion that tale and teller illuminate each other; and the interplay between the often very discordant temperaments and views of the pilgrims, both in direct interchanges and in their tales, is a further element in this highly complex and satisfying literary pattern.

Critics have generally praised in the Chaucer of the *Tales* the power to show, not simply people doing things for good or evil, but what those people and their actions are really like, so that their personalities become more vital and individual and life-enriching than those of many people whom we know intimately. Certainly he is the poet with an eye for those essences that make a woman a particular woman or even a rooster a particular rooster; and he is justly acclaimed for his healthy humanity, his joy in people and actions as they are—

not ideally powerful, beautiful, or wise, impotent, ugly, or stupid, good or evil, but fascinating particular creations which, if we are big enough men, we contemplate dispassionately and at the same time with gratitude and gusto. Another aspect of his mastery that is often stressed today is his humorous irony— what might be called manipulation without espousal: he has a great range and precision of feeling for levels of literary style and for the different ways of looking at life which are the springs of individuality, and he uses these to speak to us indirectly and ironically. The reality of a situation and the style in which he presents it may humorously clash, or one atmosphere of ideas and feelings, built up perfectly, may ironically undermine a previous one no less perfect, or a slight twist of expression may put into doubt a whole emotional effect; and the result in each case is a kind of double vision which implies a third thing of value. Admittedly, only very simple-minded people, or none, lack all irony of this kind, for most of us can visualize and even occasionally follow several mutually incompatible sets of reactions to a given situation. And it is true as well that only very single-minded authors do not consciously manipulate stylistic levels with ironic intentions. But Chaucer's virtuosity in this direction is such that one is tempted to say his work perfectly illustrates one view of what art, as contrasted with life, ought to be: where life, to be successful, conceives of event and action only as they subserve intention, belief, and need, art must attend to all aspects of what happens for their own sake, without interest in the attainment of a practical end. Finally, however, it is likely to be an unhistorical exaggeration to push this characterization of Chaucer's work to its conclusion, useful as it is, for many readers still register, behind his exquisite modulations of style and fertile creations of role (even one for himself) a unitary, if complex, personality and viewpoint.

Chaucer lived to complete only "The General Prologue" and twenty-two of his tales (two others are unfinished). There are many signs that he changed his plans as he worked. Since we do not have all the pilgrims' linking speeches between the tales, we are not sure in what order Chaucer wished his work to be read, if he ever completely made up his mind on this subject. The eighty and more sometimes widely differing manuscripts in which all or parts of the *Tales* survive are often contradictory on this point as on much else.

One point about the creative process behind most of these tales probably needs explanation. We are used to modern novelists who use much personal experience in their books, and we do not say they lack invention for doing so; we ask, instead, whether they have formulated the elements of their stories, including, probably, personal experience, in such a way as to give a vision of life which is powerful and serviceable to us. The question is ultimately the same with Chaucer, but the most obvious plot elements which he formulates are likely to be some other author's story rather than personal experience (as is the case, incidentally, with the majority of authors before the nineteenth century). Thus "The Knight's Tale" depends for its plot and much else on a much longer tale by Boccaccio and on some other literary sources; "The Miller's Tale" belongs to a whole family of narratives of which the plots are very similar; and the climactic parts of "The Wife of Bath's Tale," "The Franklin's Tale," and "The Pardoner's Tale" belong, in the same way, to widespread plot families for which Chaucer did not invent the main incidents. "The Prioress's Tale" rests on legendary material. "The Nun's Priest's Tale" is very close in plot to certain previously written examples of the beast fable. Even "The Wife of Bath's Prologue" is an amalgam of literary materials from many quarters. In each case Chaucer was borrowing, sometimes very closely, but what we must ask is how he has developed the borrowed material. "The Knight's Tale," which is closest of these to its main source, is much shorter than Boccaccio's story, transfers the interest from Arcite to Theseus, deploys much less classical mythology, has a much firmer social context, is "philosophical" in a different way, and has, essentially, a different point. The other known instances of the plot of "The Miller's Tale" are, by and large, just dirty stories, without character development or detail. The borrowed plot elements in the tales of the Wife, the Franklin, and the Pardoner share only the most general similarity with their analogues. "The Prioress's Tale" contains more beautiful artifice than any other treatment of the motif of the martyr child. "The Nun's Priest's Tale" is like no other beast fable ever written, whatever the affinities of its plot may be.

"The Knight's Tale," the longest of the selections here, belongs to the flexible genre of the medieval romance—that is to say, it is a story in which men might see idealized images of human behavior, in the persons of the highest social classes behaving according to an exacting code in their special sphere of love and war. Action and language are stylized and formalized to a degree, and both joy and pathos are treated with much rhetorical artifice. One way of looking at this romance is to see its affinities with the later Elizabethan world of Shakespeare, Edmund Spenser, and Sir Philip Sydney: man's soul, the state, and the universe are all viewed in terms of a kind of Christian Platonism, for much of which Chaucer depended upon a work he had translated, Boethius' *Consolation of Philosophy*. The nature of the good ruler, of friendship, and of love receive much attention. As in other tales, one needs to recognize the traditional medieval and Elizabethan embodiment of passionate love in a God of Love, who in one of his manifestations is a jealous and malign tyrant, arousing jealousy and strife among his adherents. As Cupid, he has a classical derivation, and other gods of the classical pantheon play large parts in the narrative. Traditionally, they exercise arbitrary and competitive astrological power from the planets which bear their names, and before these influences (which a modern biologist might call the hereditary and environmental factors) man seems to be helpless. Arrayed against them, however, a supreme power, called here the Prime Mover, works for a harmonious, freely chosen accord (love in its other sense): Theseus is its princely representative and the marriage with which the tale closes is its familial embodiment.

The romance is the most idealistic of the secular story forms of the Middle Ages; the tale told by the drunken and boorish Miller, which directly follows, belongs to the most cynical and earthy one, the fabliau. Examples of this form are generally peopled by the lower social orders. Its main convention is that people are usually (and for the most part cheerfully) motivated by lechery, gluttony, avarice, or sloth; only the very stupid live by any other principles. Uniquely, Chaucer transformed this kind of narrative so that what regularly is the baldly related plot and uproarious point of a lavatory story becomes a marvel of witty *double-entendre*, telling detail, and characterization.

It is worth noting that a pilgrim who had once been a carpenter tries angrily to keep the Miller from telling his tale, in which a carpenter is brought low. After "The Miller's Tale," this pilgrim tells another fabliau (not included here), in which a miller is made ridiculous. There are several such opposing pairs of storytellers in the *Tales;* they usually belong to groups proverbially at odds with each other. Carpenters were not regularly enemies of millers, but reeves, or estate managers, were; and the former carpenter is now the Reeve of the pilgrimage.

Another more subdued pairing of tales is possibly part of the plan in the case of the Monk (a member of the regular clergy) and the Nun's Priest (of the secular clergy). "The Monk's Tale" (not included here) consists of a series of mostly lugubrious, high-flown accounts, starting with Lucifer and Adam, of the fall of the exalted by Fortune's blow or Divine decree. They are capped by the Priest's instance of how someone in high degree fell but was subsequently raised up again (he ends up, in fact, at the top of a tree). Furthermore the story is embellished with modish philosophical reflections on Fortune and Providence, and with high-flown rhetoric and solemnly adduced exemplary tales. The heroic subject of all this is, however, a rooster, and what is more, a rooster who lives high, is subject to concupiscence (being in the pride of life, he is ripe for Fortune's blow), has visions, and suffers marital difficulties—like Adam, he wrongly accepts his wife's advice. This tale is a transformation of yet another medieval literary genre, the beast fable, or beast epic: stories of Renard the fox and his dupes were popular long before and after Chaucer, generally for their social satire. But Chaucer's many-layered, happily toppling pyramid of literary nonsense is an extremely bold, quite unprecedented development of the form.

Chaucer evokes various aspects of marriage through the words of the Knight, the Miller, and the Nun's Priest, but he focuses on this institution in the so-called Marriage Group, represented in this book by three of its most important tales, those of the Wife, the Merchant, and the Franklin. Their interrelationships are too complex to describe here. The last of these tales is, like "The Knight's Tale," a romance (a short variety called the Breton *lai*), and displays the only kind of love relationship which the mature Chaucer was apparently willing to take seriously in this highly serious genre: like the married pair in "The Knight's Tale," the man and wife here are matched in age and background. They are in accord in other respects as well, because only the free choice of love brought them together and because they are mutually forebearing and animated by true *gentilesse*—a key word here, in "The Knight's Tale," in Dante, and in the thirteenth-century French *Roman de la Rose*, which Chaucer translated, as he says.

A just sense of Chaucerian irony and humor is needed to balance this tale against the Wife's and Merchant's contributions. The Wife in a long prologue—a virtuoso piece of female monologue, recognizable to readers of both sexes—and the aged, rich, and lecherous knight January in his behavior with his young wife have something in common. They both claim to know the divinely appointed purpose of marriage, but the actions of both show that they have an eye mainly to their own erotic and other satisfactions. They aim at the domination and manipulation of their consorts, not at a marriage of mutual forebearance and *gentilesse:* January essentially buys his bride, whom he wants to be young and pliable; the Wife defends her practice with the rule that the woman should have the mastery in marriage, and triumphantly enforces it through five marriages. Her tale illustrates her rule: it opens with the most violent act of mastery which a man can commit against a woman, and closes when that man attains his happiness by committing everything into his wife's hands. By a shrewd twist, "The Merchant's Tale," which is neither a romance nor quite a fabliau, but should probably be called a verse novella, shows the defeat of January: the young wife both deceives and masters him with particular grossness. It is a masterstroke of Chaucerian irony that this protagonist, the Merchant ostensibly telling the tale, and the reader find themselves viewing the same events with entirely different feelings.

Of the two remaining tales, the Pardoner's is a swift and deadly exemplum, an illustrative story embedded in a sermon on avarice by this disgustingly avaricious professional preacher; and the Prioress's is a highly formal narrative in the genre of "Miracles of the Virgin" or "Our Lady," having affinities with the Saint's Legend or tale of martyrdom. The simple pathos of its immolation of innocence by villainy represents another side of Chaucer's art, although some readers have suspected an ironical effect even here, in the contrast between the Prioress's approbation of the cruel punishment of the Jews in the tale and her gentleheartedness otherwise.

CHAUCER'S LANGUAGE: Pronunciation, Idiom and Versification

(Information on how to use the translation in this book is given in Sec. 45, 46, below.)

Practically speaking, Chaucer's language is in some respects a foreign one, in others identical with ours. What to do about pronouncing it? One analogy suggests that we should be very exact. We do not enjoy a rendition, no matter how soulful, of Keats' "Ode to a Nightingale" by a man who knows little

English. Yet experience suggests that a poem has a high survival value and that its nascent pattern of sound and meaning can in large part be brought to life by someone whose mode of speech is quite different from the author's. Certainly Shakespeare would be astonished, and probably irritated, at our rendering of his verse, yet we think that we get along fairly well without learning what is known about pronunciation in his time.

If this latter argument appeals, the pronunciation of Chaucer's verse presents little difficulty: in order to preserve his meter, do as Sec. 2, below, directs, and for the rest proceed as in Modern English. Doing so, the reader may gain great satisfaction, like the old gentleman in the Red Cross swimming manual who swam a quarter-mile daily with a rudimentary and lethargic breaststroke.

But the ensuing dislocation of the vowel system and of many consonantal sounds of Chaucer's language stretches his poetry so close to the breaking point that many teachers demand a little more effort so as to preserve most of the music of his poetry as he himself probably heard it. Even so, he would find our reading strange, but perhaps no more so than, say, an Australian's rendering of Keats' ode seems to American ears. Although we are not certain of all features of fourteenth-century sounds, and although the following description simplifies on what we do know, the beginner will be poetically much safer in absorbing as much of it as he can. He may, incidentally, go much faster if he uses a recording of passages from *The Canterbury Tales*. (A reliable one, spoken by H. Kökeritz, is available from the National Council of Teachers of English.)

We call the English of Chaucer's time Middle English (ME): examples printed in *italics* below. He spoke and wrote the London dialect of it—the one which has evolved into Modern English (ModE): examples printed in **bold-face**. In becoming ModE, ME changed the sound of many of its vowels and lost many of its inflexions.

For introductory and review purposes, we may now summarize the rules that appear later below: Unstressed vowels are pronounced as in ModE except that final *e* in certain frequent conditions is pronounced and that the last *e* in words like *peyned* (**pained**) or *gates* must be sounded. Stressed vowels are short or long. Short vowels are pronounced as in modern American except that short *a* and *o* are pronounced in modern British fashion. Long vowels are generally pronounced (less often spelled) like long vowel sounds in Continental languages; these sounds must be remembered. There are two kinds of long *e* and *o.* The sounds of five diphthongs must also be remembered: *ei (ey, ai, ay), au (aw), ew (eu, u) oi (oy), ou (ow,* also *o,* before *gh).* Long and short vowels are identified as such in various ways. Short *i* is so spelled; long *i* is generally spelled *y* in this book. Short *u* is spelled *u* or (next to certain letters) *o;* the long *u* sound is spelled *ou* or *ow. A, e,* and *o,* are long when doubled or in certain kinds of syllables; they are most often short in other situations. Apart from the long-short distinction, the two kinds of long *e* in ME words may be distinguished by the spelling in equivalent ModE words; the two kinds of long *o,* by the sounds in the equivalent ModE words. The diphthong spelled *ou* or *ow* is distinguished from long *u* spelled *ou* or *ow* by the sound of equivalent ModE words. The diphthong *ew* when spelled *u* is similarly distinguished from short *u,* so spelled. Consonants are pronounced as in ModE, except for *ch.* We now proceed to greater detail.

VOWEL SOUNDS

Unstressed vowels. (1) Unstressed (unaccented) vowels all verge on the sound of a in **sofa**, as in ModE. For example, all the vowels except the stressed one in **unaccented** verge on this sound, in natural utterance. In ME such sounds thus take care of themselves. But if the natural main stress, the length of the word, or the slow pace of utterance forces you to stress a vowel, follow the rules about stressed vowels. (2) But regularly give the sound of a in **sofa** to the unstressed *e* at the end of a word or syllable, unless the next word or syllable begins with a vowel or an *h:* Chaucer's *take* has two syllables, but in *take our wey* it has only one. *Semely* (**seemly**) has three syllables. In *looth were him, were* has only one syllable (the *h* of *him* is scarcely sounded, if at all, so that *were* is really followed by a vowel sound). But if these rules do violence to meter in a particular line, they may be abrogated. (3) Sound the unstressed *e* in the endings *-es, -ed,* etc.: *peyned* (**pained**), *bedes* (**beads**) each have two syllables.

Stressed vowels. (4) Such vowels are either long or short. (5) Short *e, i, u* are pronounced as in the following ModE equivalents of the following ME words: *bed* (**bed**), *his* (**his**), *ful* (**full**). (6) Short *a* is like **o** in **lot** as most Americans pronounce it, or like the **a** in German **kann**: ME *sat, that.* (7) Short *o* as in Modern British **hot**, French **coq**: *lot.* Long *a* as in **father**: *maken* (**make**). (9) Long *e.* Two kinds. Close long *e* (tongue close to roof of mouth) is like a in **name**: *teeth, gree* (**favor**). (10) Open long *e* (tongue lower down, to increase opening) is sounded like *ea* in **bear**: *beem* (**beam**), *greet* (**great**). (11) Long *i* (generally spelled *y*) as *i* in **machine**: *ryden* (**ride**), *lyf* (**life**). (12) Long *o*. Two kinds. Close long *o* as in **tone**: *good*. (13) Open long *o* as in **fork** or as *aw* in **raw**: *go, hoom* (**home**). (14) Long *u* (spelled *ou, ow*), sounded as **oo** in **loot**: *you, yow* (**you**).

Diphthongs. (15) *Ei* (spelled *ei, ey, ai, ay*) sounded like **ay** in **day**: *day, weilawey*. (16) *Au* (spelled *au, aw*), sounded like **ou** in **out**: *chaungeth, awe*. (17) *Ew* (spelled *ew, eu, u*) sounded as in **few**: *knew, adieu, accuse, vertu*. (18) *Oi* (spelled *oi, oy*), sounded as in **coy**: *coy, boile*. (19) *Ou* (spelled *ou, ow*, and sometimes *o* before *gh*) sounded as in **thought**, pronounced slowly: *knowed, soule, thoghte*.

SPELLING OF VOWEL SOUNDS

Length of Vowels. (20) Any vowel before a doubled consonant is short: *dradde* (**dreaded**), *bettre* (**better**), *brimme* (**brim**), *pottes*. (21) In this text, *i* is intended to be short and *y* is used for long *i*: *smith, smyte*. But *y* is not long when it appears in the diphthongs *ay, ey, oy*, or when it appears at the end of a word: *many, sobrely*. The pronoun *I* is so written, but it is pronounced as a long *i*. (22) The sound of long *u* is always spelled *ou* or *ow*. (23) The sound of short *u* is spelled *u* or *o*. The *o* spelling occurs only next to letters made (like *u*) with parallel upright strokes in manuscripts: *some, sonne* (**sun**), *come, love, above*. Follow the pronunciation in the equivalent ModE word. (24) *A, e,* and *o* are long when doubled: *caas* (**case**), *beem* (**beam**), *goon* (**go, gone**). (25) *A, e,* or *o* is long in a stressed next-to-last syllable of a longer word, if the *a, e,* or *o* in question is followed by only one consonant or by *th*, and if, also, that consonant or *th* is immediately followed by another vowel: *date, lepe* (**leap**), *brother, fiftene, forbere* (**to forbear**). (26) Apart from Secs. 23, 24, *a, e,* and *o* are most frequently short: *carye* (**carry**; three syllables with stress on first), *hat, men, God*. But note these long vowels: *be, he*.

Close and open long e and o. (27) Regularly, long *e* is close when it corresponds to any spelling except *ea* in the equivalent ModE word: *degree, greete* (**greet**). Exceptions: *heren* (**hear**), *dere* (**dear**), and some other words have close long *e* in spite of modern *ea* spelling. (28) Regularly long *e* is open when it corresponds to the spelling *ea* in the modern form of the word:

heeth (**heath**), *beem* (**beam**). Exceptions: *speche* (**speech**) and a number of other words have open long *e*. (29) Regularly, long *o* is close when it corresponds to the pronunciation of **o** in **food** or **good**: *cook, do, foot, to* (**to, too**). Exceptions: *brother, other, moder* (**mother**) have close long *o* in spite of ModE pronunciation. (30) Regularly, long *o* is open when it corresponds to the pronunciation of **o** in **holy**: *boot* (**boat**), *goon* (**go**), *hoom* (**home**), *to* (**toe**), *rood* (**rode**).

Other distinctions. (31) *Ou* or *ow* signifies the diphthong of Sec. 19 when the ModE equivalent has the vowel sound of ModE **know** or **brought**. Otherwise it signifies long *u*. (32) The diphthong *ew* (Sec. 17) is spelled *u* in words derived from French and Latin: *mute, vertu*. Equivalent ModE words generally maintain the sound. It may thus be distinguished from short *u*, so spelled.

CONSONANTS

(33) Pronounced as in ModE except following cases: *ch* always as in **church**, never as in **machine**: *royalliche* (**royally**). (34) *Gg* may represent the sound of **dg** in **bridge** (*brigge*), as well as the sound in **dagger** (*daggere, frogges*). (35) *Gh* after *ei* or *i* is sounded like **ch** in German **ich**: *sleighte* (**sleight, trick**). (36) *Gh* after *a, o,* or *u* is sounded like **ch** in German **Bach** or Scots **loch**: *ynogh* (**enough**). (37) Both consonants of *gn, kn,* and *wr* are sounded at beginning of word or syllable: *gnawe, knight, know.* (38) Elsewhere *gn* is sounded as *n*: *signe.* (39) *H* is not (or very little) sounded at the beginning of words from French or of short, common words: *humble, his, him, hem* (**them**; cf. colloquial **I got 'em**). (40) Sound *l* in such words as *folk, half.*

GRAMMAR

(41) The possessive case of nouns generally ends in (e)s much as in ModE, but without apostrophe. (24) The pronoun *I* is pronounced with a long *i*. *Thou* or *thow* (nominative case) and *thee* (objective) are the forms for **you**, singular; *ye* (nom.) and *you* or *yow* (obj.) are the forms for **you**, plural. *Thou, thow, you, yow* are all pronounced to rhyme with **you.** Chaucer's form for **his** and **its** is *his;* his word for **their** is *hir* (variously spelled); for **them,** *hem. Who* is never a relative pronoun; it is interrogative, or it means **whoever,** as in *who* (or *who so*) *loveth, he hath peyne and sorwe.* For **those,** Chaucer uses *tho.*

(43) Present tense indicative of verbs: *I love, thou lovest, he loveth, we (ye, they) love(n)*. The translation in this book does not always reveal whether Chaucer's verb is past or present tense, since he frequently shifts from past to present and back again (that is, he uses the historical present more than we do). But the reader can recognize Chaucer's own alternations in the majority of cases. If, for instance, a verb ends in *-eth*, it is present tense (third person singular indicative). Also, one kind of verb (the so-called weak verbs) in both ModE and ME takes the suffix *(e)d* as a sign of the past tense; past tense indicative: *I loved(e), thou lovedest, he loved(e), we (ye, they) loved(e)* or *loveden*. Consequently any verb with these endings is in the past tense. (In a few cases, a verb's original stem contains these letters, as in *bede*, to offer—this word may have other verbal meanings.) But strong verbs do not form their past tense with the *-(e)d* ending; rather, they change their stem vowels. Thus, the past tense of *take(n)* is *I took, thou tooke, he (she, it) took, we (ye, they) tooke(n)*. In the case of this and many other strong verbs, however, the speaker of ModE recognizes the form automatically, because it has survived. Nevertheless a number of past or present forms of ME strong verbs have not survived: *they gonnen* (they began). To distinguish the tense of such unfamiliar strong verbs you will sometimes need help apart from the translation. Past participles preserve much the same distinction between weak and strong; in addition they may have the prefix *y-*: *I have y-loved, I have y-take(n)*. The subjunctive, which is more frequent in ME than in ModE, also uses the *(e)d* sign or the change in stem vowel to distinguish past from present, but, in all persons, its singular ending is *e*, pl. *e(n)*.

The impersonal verb forms **methinks** and **meseems** (instead of **I think**, or the other impersonal form **It seems to me**) are sometimes used in ModE to give a (not very convincing) archaic flavor. ME uses similar forms frequently: *me thinketh, me seemeth, me list* (**I want**), and the like. Double or triple negatives are common in ME. Also, the negative sign is often combined with other words: *nas (ne was), nis (ne is)*. Other such combinations occur: *shaltou (shalt thou), wiltou (wilt thou), criedestou (criedest thou)*, and the like.

(44) Certain connectives are sometimes confusing even after consulting the translation. Observe: *al wente he* (**although** or **even though** he went); *but they comen* (**unless they come**); *for (that) he hire lovede* (**because he loved her**). *That* as a conjunction introducing adverbial clauses is often used where it

would not be appropriate in ModE: the translation **in order that** or **so that** will often come close to the meaning.

VOCABULARY AND SYNTAX

(45) Many ModE words related in form to ME words have changed their meanings. ME *suffre,* for instance, does not mean to experience pain, as **suffer** usually does in ModE; it means to **undergo, endure,** or to **permit, allow,** as in *Suffre thy wyves tonge* or in "Suffer the little children to come unto me," or in **on sufferance.** ME *corage* does not generally mean **courage,** but **disposition, mood, spirits,** in the sense that one may be well or badly disposed, or in good or bad spirits; these meanings, like the modern one, center around the idea "state of heart," for the word is related to Latin *cor* (**heart**). Note that the change in meaning represents a subtle and comprehensible migration, not an arbitrary jump from one meaning to another. Your reading of Chaucer will be much enriched (1) if you can locate the center of meaning in ME words as, in different contexts, they extend in one direction or another to meet a specific need for which we give an equivalent in the translation, and (2) if, in addition, you can see the relation of meaning to a ModE equivalent.

Generally speaking, ME words are much closer in their meanings than ours are to the words from which they have developed or to which they are related by form in other languages. In many cases the other languages are Germanic ones, but the words for abstractions, generally, come from Latin, frequently by way of French. Additionally, and naturally, the meanings of ME words are as a rule more closely related to the meanings of ModE words as these are used in thoughtful written prose rather than as they are in conversational, casual usage, where the words have come to have single, specialized, blunt meanings. This could be easily shown in the case of *suffre* and *corage.*

(46) The loveliness and the force of Chaucer's verse depend in part on the easy, colloquial, but very sensitive movement of his sentences, even his very long ones. But by the standard of modern written prose, the relationship among their parts is often ambiguous, illogical, and awkward. The initial difficulty is something like that with a transcript of a conversation or a news conference. To find the meaning often involves taking the original sentence apart and reasoning about the meaningful relation of its constituents. Just getting the drift will not do. The general drift is usually the most unimportant

aspect of poetry, and you may miss even that if you read Chaucer as you would a newspaper.

Our translation should help you in finding your way through these complexities, because it sticks to the original vocabulary, arrangement, and semantic relationships as much as we have been able to arrange. Sometimes, however, we have not found a way of following Chaucer's sentence construction without doing violence to Modern English. Consider the simple example of line 208 of "The Franklin's Tale," describing the squire Aurelius's love for Dorigen. Students at first glance think that this line means "not knowing about this Dorigen at all." It happens to mean "Dorigen not knowing of this at all," and it would be useful to the student if we could render the sentence as "This squire had loved her for two years and more, Dorigen not knowing of this at all. . . ." Because, however, we think that this is awkward, we have substituted for the construction in question a prepositional phrase: "completely without Dorigen's knowledge." Later in the same sentence the phrase *as was his aventure* comes out "as chanced to fall to his lot." This looks like wilful obscurantism rather than clarification, but it is not: *aventure* is not ModE **adventure**. As you will see if you look up the word, its derivation suggests the concept "what comes to one rather than what one brings about," and one overtone here is that what made the happening come about is not being discussed; it is assumed for present purposes that the happening came by chance (cf. ModE **adventitious**, with much the same ultimate derivation). The squire Aurelius did not try to fall in love with another man's wife, but that was what happened to him. This point is important for an understanding of a certain integrity in this would-be seducer's character and of Chaucer's feeling about some manifestations of love. If we used the modern word **adventure**, we should be making Chaucer say about Aurelius's love, "Such was the thrilling thing that happened to him," but this aspect of the situation Chaucer is not concerned to emphasize here.

A similar chain of reasoning is behind each of our departures from Chaucer's vocabulary and sentence structure, and a little mental agility is sometimes called for to see the connection.

VERSIFICATION

(47) All the verse in this book is regularly iambic pentameter, the usual five-beat line of English poetry. In all but one selection the lines rhyme in couplets. In "The Prioress's Tale"

rhymes organize the verse into a seven-line stanza called rime-royal. To preserve the meter it is important to remember the rules about pronunciation of final -e and of such endings as -ed, -es. But for the sake of his meter Chaucer probably requires us to slur or eliminate many final -e's and to sound others which would ordinarily be silent. Because we know so little about the pattern of the spoken sentence in ME, we are sometimes unsure of how to scan a given line. Note the following (a dot under an e means that it should be dropped or slurred): Jálous/ he wás/ and heéld/ hirę nár/wę in cág/e (trochee in first foot; extra syllable at end); And má/ken ál/ this lá/mentá/tioún (suffixes -ious or -ion almost always have two syllables); Heérę in/ this tém/ple óf/ the gód/dessę Cleménc/e (first foot trochee; but we do not know whether of should receive a strong stress. We do not know which syllable of goddesse should be stressed. Judging from Chaucer's use of the word elsewhere, it was possible to stress either syllable lightly. If the word is stressed on its second syllable, the fourth foot is an anapest; if on the first, the fifth foot is an anapest; there is an extra syllable at the end). Át/ which boók/ he loúgh/ alwéy/ ful fást/e (apparently the first foot is simply at, stressed, which requires a little getting used to; extra syllable at end).

CANTERBURY TALES

THE PROLOGE

Here biginneth the Book of the Tales of Caunterbury

WHAN that Aprill with his shoures sote
The droghte of Marche hath perced to the rote,
And bathed every veyne in swich licour
Of which vertu engendred is the flour;
Whan Zephirus eek with his swete breeth
Inspired hath in every holt and heeth
The tendre croppes, and the yonge sonne
Hath in the Ram his halfe cours y-ronne,
And smale fowles maken melodye,
That slepen al the night with open yĕ   **10**
(So priketh hem Nature in hir corages):
Than longen folk to goon on pilgrimages
And palmers for to seken straunge strondes,
To ferne halwes, couthe in sondry londes;
And specially, from every shires ende
Of Engelond, to Caunterbury they wende,
The holy blisful martir for to seke
That hem hath holpen, whan that they were seke.
    Bifel that in that seson on a day,
In Southwerk at the Tabard as I lay   **20**
Redy to wenden on my pilgrimage
To Caunterbury with ful devout corage,
At night was come into that hostelrye
Wel nyne and twenty in a companye
Of sondry folk, by aventure y-falle
In felawshipe, and pilgrims were they alle,
That toward Caunterbury wolden ryde.
The chambres and the stables weren wyde,
And wel we weren esed atte beste.
And shortly, whan the sonne was to reste,   **30**
So hadde I spoken with hem everichon,
That I was of hir felawshipe anon,
And made forward erly for to ryse,
To take our wey, ther as I yow devyse.
    But natheles, whyl I have tyme and space,
Er that I ferther in this tale pace,

THE PROLOGUE

Here begins the Book of the Canterbury Tales

WHEN April with his sweet showers has
pierced the drought of March to the root,
and bathed every vein in such moisture
as has power to bring forth the flower;
when, also, Zephyrus with his sweet breath
has breathed spirit into the tender new shoots
in every wood and meadow, and the young sun
has run half his course in the sign of the Ram,
and small birds sing melodies and
sleep with their eyes open all the night
(so Nature pricks them in their hearts):
then people long to go on pilgrimages,
and palmers long to seek strange shores
and far-off shrines known in various lands,
and, especially, from the ends of every shire
in England they come to Canterbury,
to seek the holy, blissful martyr*
who helped them when they were sick.

It befell that one day in that season,
as I was in Southwark at the Tabard Inn,
ready to go on my pilgrimage
to Canterbury with a most devout heart,
at night there came into that hostelry
a company of nine-and-twenty people—
all sorts of people, who had met by chance;
and all of them were pilgrims
who were riding toward Canterbury.
The chambers and the stables were spacious,
and we were made most comfortable.
And shortly, when the sun had gone down,
I had spoken with every one of them
so that I had soon become one of their group,
and made an arrangement to rise early
to be on our way, as I shall tell you.

But none the less, while I have time and space,
before I pass further in this tale,

* See Glossary.

3

Me thinketh it acordaunt to resoun,
To telle yow al the condicioun
Of ech of hem, so as it semed me,
And whiche they weren, and of what degree,   40
And eek in what array that they were inne:
And at a knight than wol I first biginne.

A KNIGHT ther was, and that a worthy* man,
That fro the tyme that he first bigan
To ryden out, he loved chivalrye,
Trouthe and honour, fredom and curteisye.
Ful worthy was he in his lordes werre,
And therto hadde he riden, no man ferre,
As wel in Cristendom as hethenesse,
And ever honoured for his worthinesse.   50
At Alisaundre he was, whan it was wonne;
Ful ofte tyme he hadde the bord bigonne
Aboven alle naciouns in Pruce;
In Lettow hadde he reysed and in Ruce,
No Cristen man so ofte of his degree;
In Gernade at the sege eek hadde he be
Of Algezir, and riden in Belmarye;
At Lyeys was he, and at Satalye,
Whan they were wonne; and in the Grete See
At many a noble armee hadde he be.   60
At mortal batailles hadde he been fiftene,
And foughten for our feith at Tramissene
In listes thryes, and ay slayn his fo.
This ilke worthy Knight had been also
Somtyme with the lord of Palatye,
Ageyn another hethen in Turkye:
And evermore he hadde a sovereyn prys.
And though that he were worthy, he was wys,
And of his port as meke as is a mayde.
He never yet no vileinye ne sayde   70
In al his lyf, unto no maner wight.
He was a verray, parfit, gentil* knight.
But for to tellen yow of his array,
His hors were gode, but he was nat gay.
Of fustian he wered a gipoun
Al bismotered with his habergeoun;
For he was late y-come from his viage,
And wente for to doon his pilgrimage.
With him there was his sone, a yong SQUYER,
A lovyere, and a lusty bacheler,   80

it seems to me in order
to tell you all about
each of them, as they seemed to me—
and who they were, and of what rank in life,
and also what they wore—
and with a knight, then, I will begin.

   There was a KNIGHT, a valiant man,
who, from the time when he had first begun
to venture out, had loved chivalry,
truth and honor, liberality and courtesy.
He had proved his worth in his lord's wars,
in which he had ridden as far as any man,
both in Christendom and in heathen lands,
and he had always been honored for his valor.

   He was at Alexandria when it was won;
many times he had sat at the head of the table
in Prussia, above knights of all nations;
he had campaigned in Lithuania, and in Russia,
more often than any other Christian man of his rank;
he had also been in Granada at the siege
of Algeciras, and had fought in Benmarin.
He had been at Lyas and at Attalia
when they were won; and he had sailed upon
the Mediterranean with many a noble host.
He had been in fifteen mortal battles,
and fought for our faith at Tlemcen
three times in tournaments, and always slain his foe.
This same worthy Knight had also been
at one time with the lord of Balat,
against another heathen in Turkey:
and always he had won the highest honor.
Although he was valiant, he was prudent,
and bore himself as meekly as a maiden;
never in all his life had he been
rude to anyone at all.
He was a true, perfect, gentle knight.
But to tell you about his array—
His horses were good, but he was not gaily dressed.
He wore a fustian tunic,
much stained by his hauberk;
for he had just come back from his expedition,
and was on his way to make his pilgrimage.

   With him was his son, a young SQUIRE,
a lover, and a gay youth on his way to knighthood,

Knight in process
Zeal / Prowess / Valor

With lokkes crulle as they were leyd in presse.
Of twenty yeer of age he was, I gesse.
Of his stature he was of evene lengthe,
And wonderly deliver, and of greet strengthe.
And he had been somtyme in chivachye,
In Flaundres, in Artoys, and Picardye,
And born him wel, as of so litel space,
In hope to stonden in his lady grace.
Embrouded was he, as it were a mede
Al ful of fresshe floures, whyte and rede.   90
Singinge he was, or floytinge, al the day;
He was as fresh as is the month of May.
Short was his goune, with sleves longe and wyde.
Wel coude he sitte on hors, and faire ryde.
He coude songes make and wel endyte,
Juste and eek daunce, and well purtreye and wryte.
So hote he lovede, that by nightertale
He slepte namore than dooth a nightingale.
Curteys he was, lowly, and servisable,
And carf biforn his fader at the table.   100

    A YEMAN hadde he, and servaunts namo
At that tyme, for him liste ryde so;
And he was clad in cote and hood of grene;
A sheef of pecok-arwes brighte and kene
Under his belt he bar ful thriftily;
Wel coude he dresse his takel yemanly:
His arwes drouped noght with fetheres lowe;
And in his hand he bar a mighty bowe.
A not-heed hadde he, with a broun visage.
Of wode-craft wel coude he al the usage.   110
Upon his arm he bar a gay bracer,
And by his syde a swerd and a bokeler,
And on that other syde a gay daggere,
Harneised wel, and sharp as point of spere;
A Cristofre on his brest of silver shene;
An horn he bar, the bawdrik was of grene.
A forster was he, soothly, as I gesse.

    Ther was also a Nonne, a PRIORESSE,
That of hir smyling was ful simple and coy.
Hir gretteste ooth was but by Seinte Loy;   120
And she was cleped Madame Eglentyne.
Ful wel she song the service divyne,
Entuned in hir nose ful semely;
And Frensh she spak ful faire and fetisly,

with locks as curly as if they had been pressed.
He was about twenty years old, I guess;
he was of normal height
and wonderfully agile, and of great strength.
He had been on cavalry expeditions for a while—
in Flanders, in Artois, and in Picardy—
and in this short time he had borne himself well,
in the hope of winning his lady's favor.
His clothing was embroidered so as to look like a meadow
all full of fresh flowers, white and red.
He sang or fluted all the day long;
he was as youthful as the month of May.
His gown was short, with long, wide sleeves.
He knew how to sit his horse well, and ride beautifully;
he could compose songs and poems,
joust and dance, too, and draw and write.
So hotly did he love that at night
he slept no more than a nightingale.
He was courteous, humble, and serviceable,
and carved for his father at the table.

   A YEOMAN was also with the Knight, and no other servants
at the time (so it pleased him to ride);
the yeoman was dressed in a coat and hood of green;
beneath his belt he carefully carried a
sheaf of bright, keen peacock-feathered arrows
(well did he know how to take care of his equipment:
his arrows never drooped with tired feathers!)
and in his hand he carried a mighty bow.
He was a brown-faced man, with a close-cropped head.
He knew all there is to know about woodcraft.
On his arm was a fine wrist guard,
and by one side a sword and shield;
on the other, a bright dagger,
well mounted and sharp as the point of a spear.
A silver Christopher medal shone on his breast;
he carried a horn, with a green baldric.
I suppose that he must have been a forester.

   There was also a nun, a PRIORESS, _(simple + coy)_
whose smile was modest and sweet.
Her greatest oath was only "By Saint Loy!"
She was called Madame Eglantine. _- Sweet Briar_
She sang the divine service well,
entuning it in her nose in a most seemly way; _- she is_
and she spoke French well and properly,

pretension in her singing

· she is more wordly/+ worldly than appears

After the scole of Stratford atte Bowe,
For Frensh of Paris was to hir unknowe.
At mete wel y-taught was she withalle;
She leet no morsel from hir lippes falle,
Ne wette hir fingres in hir sauce depe.
Wel coude she carie a morsel, and wel kepe,   130
That no drope ne fille upon hir brest.
In curteisye was set ful muchel hir lest.
Hir over-lippe wyped she so clene
That in hir coppe was no ferthing sene
Of grece, whan she dronken hadde hir draughte.
Ful semely after hir mete she raughte,
And sikerly she was of greet disport,
And ful plesaunt, and amiable of port,
And peyned hir to countrefete chere
Of court, and been estatlich of manere,   140
And to ben holden digne of reverence.
But, for to speken of hir conscience,
She was so charitable and so pitous
She wolde wepe if that she sawe a mous
Caught in a trappe, if it were deed or bledde.
Of smale houndes had she, that she fedde
With rosted flesh, or milk and wastel-breed.
But sore wepte she if oon of hem were deed,
Or if men smoot it with a yerde smerte:
And al was conscience and tendre herte.   150
Ful semely hir wimpel pinched was;
Hir nose tretys; hir eyen greye as glas;
Hir mouth ful smal, and thereto softe and reed.
But sikerly she hadde a fair forheed;
It was almost a spanne brood, I trowe;
For, hardily, she was nat undergrowe.
Ful fetis was hir cloke, as I was war.
Of smal coral aboute hir arm she bar
A peire of bedes, gauded al with grene,
And theron heng a broche of gold ful shene,   160
On which ther was first write a crowned A,
And after, *Amor vincit omnia.*

   Another NONNE with hir hadde she,
That was hir chapeleyne, and PREESTES THREE.

   A MONK ther was, a fair for the maistrye,
An out-rydere, that lovede venerye;
A manly man, to been an abbot able.
Ful many a deyntee hors hadde he in stable:

after the school of Stratford-at-Bow—
for the French of Paris was unknown to her.
Her table manners were admirable:
she never let a morsel fall from her lips,
nor wet her fingers too deeply in the sauce;
daintily she carried a morsel to her lips, taking care
that no drop should fall on her breast:
she took much pleasure in proper etiquette.
She wiped her upper lip so carefully that no
trace of grease could be seen in her cup
when she had taken a drink from it;
she helped herself to food in a very proper way.
And certainly she was very cheerful,
most pleasant, and amiable in bearing,
and took great pains to behave in a well-
bred fashion, to be stately in manner,
and to appear worthy of reverence.
But to speak of her tender feelings:
she was so charitable and so full of pity
that she would weep if she saw a mouse
caught in a trap and dead or bleeding.
She had a few small dogs that she fed
with roast meat, or milk and fine bread;
but she wept indeed if one of them died,
or if someone hit it smartly with a stick—
she was all feeling and tender heart.
Her wimple was suitably pleated;
her nose well-shaped; her eyes bright as glass;
her mouth very small, and soft and red;
and indeed she had a fine forehead—
it was almost a handspan broad, I believe,
for certainly she was not undersized.
I noticed that her cloak was becoming.
Around her arm she wore a rosary of
tiny coral beads, marked off with green,
and on it hung a lovely golden brooch,
on which was written first a crowned *A*,
and then, *Amor* vincit omnia.

　With her she had another NUN,
who was her assistant, and THREE PRIESTS.

　There was a MONK—a splendid sort;
an inspector of his monastery's estates, who loved venery;
a manly man, capable of being an abbot.
He had many a dainty horse in the stable,

And whan he rood men mighte his brydel here
Ginglen in a whistling wind as clere　　　　　　170
And eek as loude as dooth the chapel-belle
Ther as this lord was keper of the celle.
The reule of Seint Maure or of Seint Beneit,
By cause that it was old and somdel streit,
This ilke Monk leet olde thinges pace,
And held after the newe world the space.
He yaf nat of that text a pulled hen
That seith that hunters been nat holy men,
Ne that a monk, whan he is recchelees
Is lykned til a fish that is waterlees;　　　　　180
This is to seyn, a monk out of his cloistre.
But thilke text held he nat worth an oistre;
And I seyde his opinioun was good.
What sholde he studie, and make himselven wood,
Upon a book in cloistre alwey to poure,
Or swinken with his handes and laboure,
As Austin bit? How shal the world be served?
Lat Austin have his swink to him reserved.
Therefore he was a pricasour aright;
Grehoundes he hadde, as swifte as fowel in flight;　　190
Of priking and of hunting for the hare
Was al his lust, for no cost wolde he spare.
I seigh his sleves purfiled at the hond
With grys, and that the fyneste of a lond;
And, for to festne his hood under his chin,
He hadde of gold y-wroght a curious pin:
A love-knotte in the gretter ende ther was.
His heed was balled, that shoon as any glas,
And eek his face, as he had been anoint.
He was a lord ful fat and in good point;　　　　200
His eyen stepe, and rollinge in his heed,
That stemed as a forneys of a leed;
His botes souple, his hors in greet estat.
Now certeinly he was a fair prelat:
He was nat pale as a forpyned goost;
A fat swan loved he best of any roost.
His palfrey was as broun as is a berye.
　A FRERE ther was, a wantown and a merye,
A limitour, a ful solempne man.
In alle the ordres foure is noon that can　　　　210
So muche of daliaunce and fair langage.
He hadde maad ful many a mariage

and when he rode one might hear the
bells on his bridle jingle in the wind as
loud and clear as the chapel bell
in the place where this Monk was in charge.
As for the rule of Saint Maurus* or Saint Benedict:
since it was old and somewhat strict,
this same Monk let old-fashioned things pass away
and held to the ways of the modern world.
He didn't give a plucked hen for that text
which says that hunters are not holy men,
and that a monk, when he is heedless of duty,
is like a fish out of water—
that is to say, a monk out of his cloister;
but he held that text was not worth an oyster.
And I said his opinion was good.
Why should he study and drive himself mad,
always poring over a book in the cloister,
or work with his hands and labor
as Saint Augustine ordered? How shall the world be served?
Let Augustine have his labor to himself.
Therefore he was a really hard-riding horseman.
He had greyhounds as swift as a bird in flight;
riding and hunting the hare
were all his joy; for this he spared no cost.
I saw that his sleeves were edged at the cuff
with gray fur, and that the finest in the land;
and to fasten his hood under his chin
he had a very intricate pin made of gold;
there was a love knot in the bigger end.
His head was bald and shone like glass,
and his face did, too, as if he had been anointed.
He was a fine fat lord, in splendid shape;
his protruding eyes rolled in his head and
glowed like a furnace under a pot;
his boots were supple, his horse well-groomed:
now certainly he was a handsome prelate—
he was not pale, like a wasted ghost;
his favorite roast was a good fat swan;
his palfrey was as brown as a berry.
  There was a FRIAR, who was wanton and merry.
He was one licensed to beg in a limited area—a dignified
man. In all the four orders of friars no one else knew
as much about dalliance and sweet talk.
He had married off many a

Of yonge wommen, at his owene cost.
Unto his ordre he was a noble post.
Ful wel biloved and famulier was he
With frankeleyns overal in his contree,
And eek with worthy wommen of the toun:
For he had power of confessioun,
As seyde himself more than a curat,
For of his ordre he was licentiat.   220
Ful swetely herde he confessioun,
And plesaunt was his absolucioun.
He was an esy man to yeve penaunce
Ther as he wiste to han a good pitaunce;
For unto a povre ordre for to yive
Is signe that a man is wel y-shrive;
For if he yaf, he dorste make avaunt,
He wiste that a man was repentaunt;
For many a man so hard is of his herte,
He may nat wepe althogh him sore smerte.   230
Therefore, in stede of weping and preyeres,
Men moot yeve silver to the povre freres.
His tipet was ay farsed ful of knyves
And pinnes, for to yeven faire wyves.
And certeinly he hadde a mery note;
Wel coude he singe and pleyen on a rote.
Of yeddinges he bar utterly the prys.
His nekke whyt was as the flour-de-lys;
Therto he strong was as a champioun.
He knew the tavernes wel in every toun,   240
And everich hostiler and tappestere
Bet than a lazar or a beggestere;
For unto swich a worthy man as he
Acorded nat, as by his facultee,
To have with seke lazars aqueyntaunce:
It is nat honest, it may nat avaunce
For to delen with no swich poraille,
But al with riche and sellers of vitaille,
And overal, ther as profit sholde aryse,
Curteys he was, and lowly of servyse.   250
Ther nas no man nowher so vertuous.
He was the beste beggere in his hous,
And yaf a certeyn ferme for the graunt;
Noon of his bretheren cam ther in his haunt;
For thogh a widwe hadde noght a sho,
So plesaunt was his *"In principio,"*

young woman at his own expense.
He was a noble pillar of his order!
He was a well-beloved and familiar figure
among the franklins* all over his part of the country,
and among the respectable townswomen, too:
for, as he himself said, he had powers connected with
confession which were greater than those of a curate,
since he was a licentiate of his order.
Most sweetly he heard confession,
and his absolution was pleasant.
He was an easy man in giving penance
where he knew he would gain a good pittance;
for to give to a poor order
is a sign that a man is well shriven;
if one gave, the friar could swear that
he knew that a man was repentant;
many a man is so hardhearted
he cannot weep, although he is very sorrowful.
Therefore, instead of weeping and praying,
men can give silver to the poor friars.
His cape was always stuffed full of knives
and pins, to give to fair young wives;
certainly he could carry a merry tune;
well could he sing and play a fiddle.
His ballads absolutely took the prize.
His neck was as white as the fleur-de-lis;
moreover, he was strong as a champion.
He knew the taverns well in every town,
and every innkeeper and barmaid
better than a leper or a beggarwoman; for
it is not fitting for such a respectable
man as he, in his position,
to be acquainted with sick lepers:
it is not right, there is no profit
in dealing with such paupers;
but with the rich and the sellers of food,
and in general wherever it might be profitable,
he was courteous and humbly serviceable.
There was nowhere a better man.
He was the best beggar in his house
and gave a definite rent for his area;
none of his brethren came into his domain;
For though a widow might not have a shoe,
his *In* principio was so pleasant

Yet wolde he have a ferthing, er he wente.
His purchas was wel bettre than his rente.
And rage he coude, as it were right a whelpe.
In love-dayes ther coude he muchel helpe,   260
For there he was nat lyk a cloisterer,
With a thredbar cope, as is a povre scoler,
But he was lyk a maister or a pope:
Of double worsted was his semi-cope,
That rounded as a belle out of the presse.
Somwhat he lipsed, for his wantownesse,
To make his English swete upon his tonge;
And in his harping, whan that he had songe,
His eyen twinkled in his heed aright
As doon the sterres in the frosty night.   270
This worthy limitour was cleped Huberd.

A MARCHANT was ther with a forked berd,
In mottelee, and hye on horse he sat,
Upon his heed a Flaundrish bever hat,
His botes clasped faire and fetisly.
His resons he spak ful solempnely,
Souninge alway th'encrees of his winning.
He wolde the see were kept for any thing
Bitwixe Middelburgh and Orewelle.
Wel coude he in eschaunge sheeldes selle.   280
This worthy man ful wel his wit bisette;
Ther wiste no wight that he was in dette,
So estatly was he of his governaunce,
With his bargaynes, and with his chevisaunce.
For sothe he was a worthy man withalle;
But, sooth to seyn, I noot how men him calle.

A CLERK ther was of Oxenford also,
That unto logik hadde longe y-go.
As lene was his hors as is a rake,
And he nas nat right fat, I undertake,   290
But loked holwe, and therto soberly.
Ful thredbar was his overest courtepy,
For he hadde geten him yet no benefyce,
Ne was so worldly for to have offyce.
For him was lever have at his beddes heed
Twenty bokes, clad in blak or reed,
Of Aristotle and his philosophye,
Than robes riche, or fithele, or gay sautrye.
But al be that he was a philosophre,
Yet hadde he but litel gold in cofre;   300

that he would still get a farthing before he went.
His takings were a good deal better than his rent.
He could wanton as if he were a puppy.
He was a great help with legal settlements,
at these he did not look like a cloistered monk,
with a threadbare cloak, as a poor scholar does,
but more like a master or a pope:
his robe was made of double worsted
and was rounded like a bell right out of the mold.
He affected somewhat of a lisp
to make his English sweet upon his tongue;
and when he harped at the end of a song,
his eyes twinkled in his head just
like the stars on a frosty night.
This worthy licensed beggar was called Hubert.

There was a MERCHANT with a forked beard;
dressed in motley, he sat high on his horse.
On his head was a Flemish beaver hat;
his boots were clasped handsomely and well.
He delivered his remarks very solemnly,
always emphasizing how his profits grew.
He wanted the sea to be guarded at all costs
between Middelburg* and Orwell.
He did well on the exchange, selling French currency.
This worthy man made good use of his wits;
no one knew he was in debt,
he conducted himself in such a stately way,
with his bargainings and his borrowings.
In any case, he was indeed a worthy man;
but to tell the truth, I don't know what his name is.

There was also a CLERK of Oxford,
who had long since devoted himself to the course of logic.
His horse was as lean as a rake,
and he himself was not exactly fat, I assure you,
but looked hollow and serious.
His outer cloak was very threadbare,
for as yet he had not got himself a benefice,
nor was he worldly enough to hold a secular office.
He would rather have twenty volumes
of Aristotle and his philosophy, bound in
black or red, at the head of his bed than
rich robes, or a fiddle or lively harp.
But although he was a philosopher,
he still had little gold in his coffers;

But al that he mighte of his freendes hente,
On bokes and on lerninge he it spente,
And bisily gan for the soules preye
Of hem that yaf him wherwith to scoleye.
Of studie took he most cure and most hede.
Noght o word spak he more than was nede,
And that was seyd in forme and reverence,
And short and quik, and ful of hy sentence.
Souninge in moral vertu was his speche,
And gladly wolde he lerne, and gladly teche.   310

A SERGEANT OF THE LAWE, war and wys,
That often hadde been at the parvys,
Ther was also, ful riche of excellence.
Discreet he was, and of greet reverence:
He semed swich, his wordes weren so wyse.
Justyce he was ful often in assyse,
By patente, and by pleyn commissioun;
For his science, and for his heigh renoun
Of fees and robes hadde he many oon.
So greet a purchasour was no-wher noon;   320
Al was fee simple to him in effect,
His purchasing mighte nat been infect.
Nowher so bisy a man as he ther nas,
And yet he semed bisier than he was.
In termes hadde he caas and domes alle
That from the tyme of King William were falle.
Therto he coude endyte, and make a thing,
Ther coude no wight pinche at his wryting;
And every statut coude he pleyn by rote.
He rood but hoomly in a medlee cote   330
Girt with a ceint of silk, with barres smale;
Of his array telle I no lenger tale.

A FRANKELEYN was in his companye;
Whyt was his berd, as is the dayesye.
Of his complexioun* he was sangwyn.
Wel loved he by the morwe a sop in wyn.
To liven in delyt was ever his wone,
For he was Epicurus owne sone,
That heeld opinioun that pleyn delyt
Was verray felicitee parfyt.   340
An housholdere, and that a greet, was he;
Seint Julian he was in his contree.
His breed, his ale, was alwey after oon;
A bettre envyned man was nowher noon.

he spent all that he could get from his friends
on books and learning,
and diligently prayed for the souls
of those who gave him money to carry on his studies with.
He gave most of his attention to studying.
He never spoke a word more than was necessary,
and what he did say was in due form, and reverent,
and short and to the point, and full of lofty thought:
his talk tended toward moral qualities,
and gladly would he learn, and gladly teach. ✗

A SERGEANT OF THE LAW, wary and wise,
who had often been in the portal of Saint Paul's*
for consultation, was also there—an excellent man.
He was discreet, and greatly to be respected:
or so he seemed, his words were so wise.
He had often been a justice in assizes,
by appointment and by full commission;
his knowledge and his high renown had
won him many fees and robes.
Nowhere was there a greater buyer of land;
all was fee-simple to him, in effect:
his title could never be found defective.
Nowhere was there a man as busy as he—
and yet he seemed busier than he was.
he knew the exact terms of all the cases and judgments
occurring since the time of King William the Conquerer.
Also, he could write and draw up a deed
so that no man could find fault with his drafts;
and he knew every statute absolutely by heart.
He rode simply dressed in a coat of mixed weave,
gathered with a silk belt with small metal ornaments.
I shall not say any more about his dress.

A FRANKLIN* accompanied him;
his beard was as white as a daisy.
His temperament was sanguine. He dearly
loved a morning sop of bread in wine.
It was always his custom to live pleasurably,
for he was own son to Epicurus,
who believed that complete pleasure
equaled true and perfect happiness.
He was a householder, and a great one:
the patron saint of hospitality of his part of the country.
The quality of his bread and ale never varied;
a man better furnished in his wine cellar did not exist.

Withoute bake mete was never his hous,
Of fish and flesh, and that so plentevous
It snewed in his hous of mete and drinke,
Of alle deyntees that men coude thinke.
After the sondry sesons of the yeer,
So chaunged he his mete and his soper.   350
Ful many a fat partrich hadde he in mewe,
And many a breem and many a luce in stewe.
Wo was his cook but if his sauce were
Poynaunt and sharp, and redy al his gere.
His table dormant in his halle alway
Stood redy covered al the longe day.
At sessiouns ther was he lord and sire;
Ful ofte tyme he was knight of the shire.
An anlas and a gipser al of silk
Heng at his girdel, whyt as morne milk.   360
A shirreve hadde he been, and a countour;
Was nowher such a worthy vavasour.

An HABERDASSHER and a CARPENTER,
A WEBBE, a DYERE, and a TAPICER,
Were with us eek, clothed in o liveree
Of a solempne and greet fraternitee.
Ful fresh and newe hir gere apyked was;
Hir knyves were y-chaped noght with bras,
But al with silver; wroght ful clene and weel
Hir girdles and hir pouches every-deel.   370
Wel semed ech of hem a fair burgeys
To sitten in a yeldhalle on a deys.
Everich, for the wisdom that he can,
Was shaply for to been an alderman;
For catel hadde they ynogh and rente,
And eek hir wyves wolde it wel assente;
And elles certein were they to blame:
It is ful fair to been y-clept *"ma dame,"*
And goon to vigilyës al bifore,
And have a mantel royalliche y-bore.   380
A COOK they hadde with hem for the nones,
To boille the chiknes with the marybones,
And poudre-marchant tart, and galingale.
Wel coude he knowe a draughte of London ale.
He coude roste, and sethe, and broille, and frye,
Maken mortreux, and wel bake a pye.
But greet harm was it, as it thoughte me,
That on his shine a mormal hadde he.

His house was never without baked dishes,
both fish and meat, and these so plenteous
that it seemed to snow food and drink in his house,
with all the delicacies thinkable.
He varied his dinner and supper
according to the various seasons of the year.
He had many a fat partridge in his coop,
and many a carp and pike in his fishpond.
Woe betide his cook unless his sauce was
pungent and sharp, and all his utensils ready.
In his great hall the table stood
always ready, fully set all the day long.
At court sessions he was lord and master.
He was often in Parliament as Knight of the Shire.
A dagger and a purse made of silk
hung at his girdle, white as morning milk.
He had been a sheriff and a county auditor.
Nowhere else was there such a worthy landholder.

A HABERDASHER and a CARPENTER,
a WEAVER, a DYER, and a TAPESTRY MAKER were with us, too,
all clothed in the same livery—
that of a great and dignified guild.
Their gear was all freshly and newly adorned;
Their knives were mounted not with brass,
but entirely with silver; their belts and their
purses were beautifully made in every respect.
Each of them seemed indeed a burgess imposing enough
to sit on the dais in a guildhall;
every one of them, because of his wisdom,
was suited to be an alderman,
for they had enough property and income,
and also their wives would certainly agree to it
(otherwise they would surely be to blame):
it is very nice to be called "Madame,"
to go into church first on feast eves,
and to have your mantle borne right royally.

They had a COOK with them for the occasion,
to boil the chickens with the marrowbones
and tart spices and seasonings.
He could easily recognize a draft of London ale.
He could roast, and boil, and broil, and fry,
make stews, and bake a pie well.
But it was a shame, it seemed to me,
that he had an ulcer on his shin.

For blankmanger, that made he with the beste.
  A SHIPMAN was ther, woning fer by weste: 390
For aught I woot, he was of Dertemouthe.
He rood upon a rouncy, as he couthe,
In a gowne of falding to the knee.
A daggere hanging on a laas hadde he
Aboute his nekke under his arm adoun.
The hote somer had maad his hewe al broun.
And certeinly he was a good felawe;
Ful many a draughte of wyn had he y-drawe
From Burdeux-ward, whyl that the chapman sleep:
Of nyce conscience took he no keep;   400
If that he faught and hadde the hyer hond,
By water he sente hem hoom to every lond.
But of his craft to rekene wel his tydes,
His stremes and his daungers him bisydes,
His herberwe and his mone, his lode-menage,
Ther nas noon swich from Hulle to Cartage.
Hardy he was, and wys to undertake;
With many a tempest hadde his berd been shake.
He knew wel alle the havenes, as they were,
From Gootlond to the cape of Finistere,   410
And every cryke in Britayne and in Spayne;
His barge y-cleped was the Maudelayne.

  With us ther was a DOCTOUR OF PHISYK;
In al this world ne was ther noon him lyk
To speke of phisik and of surgerye.
For he was grounded in astronomye;
He kepte his pacient a ful greet del
In houres by his magik naturel.
Wel coude he fortunen the ascendent
Of his images for his pacient.   420
He knew the cause of everich maladye,
Were it of hoot or cold, or moiste, or drye,
And where engendred, and of what humour;
He was a verray, parfit practisour.
The cause y-knowe, and of his harm the rote,
Anon he yaf the seke man his bote.
Ful redy hadde he his apothecaries
To sende him drogges and his letuaries,
For ech of hem made other for to winne;
Hir frendschipe nas nat newe to biginne.   430
Wel knew he th'olde Esculapius,
And Deiscorides, and eek Rufus,

For making an elegant chicken stew, he was among the best.
A SHIPMAN was there, who lived far in the west;
for all I know, he came from Dartmouth.
In a coarse knee-length woolen gown, he
rode a large nag as best he could.
He had a dagger hanging on a strap
which went about his neck and down under his arm.
The hot summer had tanned him.
And certainly he was a good fellow;
he had drawn many a draft of wine
on the way from Bordeaux while the wine merchant slept.
He paid no mind to fussy conscience;
if he fought and had the upper hand,
he sent his captives home to every land by water.
But when it came to his craft of reckoning his tides,
his currents and the hazards around him,
his anchorage and his moon and his compass work,
there was no other such man from Hull to Cartagena.
He was a hardy man, prudent in his undertakings;
many a tempest had shaken his beard.
He knew all the havens as they appear
from Gotland to the cape of Finisterre,
and every creek in Brittany and Spain;
his ship was called the *Magdalen*.

With us there was a DOCTOR OF MEDICINE;
in all this world there was none other like him
when it comes to medicine and surgery.
For he was grounded in astronomy, and he
tended his patients at the proper astrological
hours through his knowledge of natural magic.
He could tell when the right planet was in
the ascendant for the use of images to help
his patient. He knew the cause of every malady,
be it hot or cold or moist or dry,
and where it is engendered, and from what humor:*
he was a really perfect practitioner.
Having learned the cause and root of the evil,
he gave the sick man a remedy at once.
He had his apothecaries quite ready
to send him drugs and medicines,
for each of them helped the other to profit;
their friendship was not recently begun.
Well did he know ancient Aesculapius,*
Dioscorides, and Rufus, too;

Old Ypocras, Haly, and Galien,
Serapion, Razis, and Avicen,
Averrois, Damascien, and Constantyn,
Bernard, and Gatesden, and Gilbertyn.
Of his diete mesurable was he,
For it was of no superfluitee,
But of greet norissing and digestible.
His studie was but litel on the Bible.   440
In sangwin and in pers he clad was al,
Lyned with taffata and with sendal;
And yet he was but esy of dispence;
He kepte that he wan in pestilence.
For gold in phisik is a cordial,
Therfore he lovede gold in special.
  A good Wyf was ther of bisyde Bathe,
But she was somdel deef, and that was scathe.
Of clooth-making she hadde swiche an haunt
She passed hem of Ypres and of Gaunt.   450
In al the parisshe wyf ne was ther noon
That to th' offring bifore hir sholde goon;
And if ther dide, certeyn so wrooth was she,
That she was out of alle charitee.
Hir coverchiefs ful fyne were of ground:
I dorste swere they weyeden ten pound
That on a Sonday were upon hir heed.
Hir hosen weren of fyn scarlet reed,
Ful streite y-teyd, and shoos ful moiste and newe.
Bold was hir face, and fair, and reed of hewe.   460
She was a worthy womman al hir lyve;
Housbondes at chirche-dore she hadde fyve,
Withouten other companye in youthe;
But therof nedeth nat to speke as nouthe.
And thryes hadde she been at Jerusalem;
She hadde passed many a straunge streem;
At Rome she hadde been, and at Boloigne,
In Galice at Seint Jame, and at Coloigne.
She coude muche of wandring by the weye.
Gat-tothed was she, soothly for to seye.   470
Upon an amblere esily she sat,
Y-wimpled wel, and on hir heed an hat
As brood as is a bokeler or a targe;
A foot-mantel aboute hir hipes large,
And on hir feet a paire of spores sharpe.
In felawschip wel coude she laughe and carpe.

ancient Hippocrates, Hali and Galen, Serapion,
Rhazes, and Avicenna, Averroes,
Damascenus, and Constantine,
Bernard, and Gatesden, and Gilbert.
He was temperate in his diet,
for it did not include anything superfluous,
but was very nourishing and digestible.
His study was but rarely of the Bible.
He was dressed entirely in bright red and blue,
lined with taffeta and finest silk;
and yet he was far from free in his spending;
he kept the money he gained in time of pestilence.
Since gold in medicine is a stimulant,
therefore he loved gold especially.

 A good WIFE was there, from near Bath.
She was somewhat deaf, which was a shame.
She had such a talent for making cloth
that she surpassed the weavers of Ypres and Ghent.
In all the parish there was no wife
entitled to make her offering before her,
and if one did, certainly she was so angry
that she was out of all charity.
Her kerchiefs were of very fine fabric:
I dare say that the ones that were on her head of
a Sunday must have weighed ten pounds.
Her hose were of fine scarlet red,
laced tightly, and her shoes very new and supple.
Her face was bold and handsome and ruddy.
She had been a worthy woman all her life:
she had had five husbands at the church door,
aside from other company in youth;
but of that there is no need to speak now.
And three times had she been at Jerusalem;
she had crossed many a strange river;
she had been at Rome and at Boulogne,
in Galicia at the shrine of Saint James, and at Cologne.
She knew much about wandering by the way.
She was gap-toothed, to tell the truth. — boldness +
                                            sexuality
On an ambling horse she sat easily,
well wimpled; and on her head was a hat
as broad as a buckler or a shield;
a footmantle was about her ample hips,
and on her feet a pair of sharp spurs.
In company she could laugh and gossip well.

Of remedyes of love she knew perchaunce,
For she coude of that art the olde daunce.
    A good man was ther of religioun,
And was a povre PERSOUN of a toun,   480
But riche he was of holy thoght and werk.
He was also a lerned man, a clerk,
That Cristes gospel trewely wolde preche;
His parisshens devoutly wolde he teche.
Benigne he was, and wonder diligent,
And in adversitee ful pacient,
And swich he was y-preved ofte sythes.
Ful looth were him to cursen for his tythes,
But rather wolde he yeven, out of doute,
Unto his povre parisshens aboute   490
Of his offring and eek of his substaunce.
He coude in litel thing han suffisaunce.
Wyd was his parisshe, and houses fer asonder,
But he ne lafte nat, for reyn ne thonder,
In siknes nor in meschief, to visyte
The ferreste in his parisshe, muche and lyte,
Upon his feet, and in his hand a staf.
This noble ensample to his sheep he yaf,
That first he wroghte, and afterward he taughte;
Out of the gospel he tho wordes caughte;   500
And this figure he added eek therto,
That if gold ruste, what shal iren do?
For if a preest be foul, on whom we truste,
No wonder is a lewed man to ruste;
And shame it is, if a preest take keep,
A shiten shepherde and a clene sheep.
Wel oghte a preest ensample for to yive
By his clennesse how that his sheep shold live.
He sette nat his benefice to hyre
And leet his sheep encombred in the myre   510
And ran to London, un-to Seinte Poules,
To seken him a chaunterie for soules,
Or with a bretherhed to been withholde,
But dwelte at hoom and kepte wel his folde,
So that the wolf ne made it nat miscarie;
He was a shepherde and no mercenarie.
And though he holy were, and vertuous,
He was to sinful men nat despitous,
Ne of his speche daungerous ne digne,
But in his teching discreet and benigne.   520

She knew of the remedies of love, as it happened,
for she knew that art's old dance.

There was a good man of religion
who was a poor PARSON of a town;
but he was rich in holy thoughts and works.
He was also a learned man, a clerk,
who would truly preach Christ's gospel;
he would teach his parishioners devoutly.
He was benign, and wonderfully diligent,
and most patient in adversity,
and had been proved to be such many times.
He was loath to excommunicate for his tithes,
but would, without a doubt, rather give
his poor parishioners thereabouts
part of his own offerings and property.
He was satisfied with very little.
His parish was wide and its houses far apart,
but he never neglected—for rain or thunder,
sickness or trouble—to visit on foot,
with a staff in his hand,
the furthest in his parish, great or humble.
He gave this noble example to his sheep:
that he practiced first and preached afterwards.
He took this motto from the Gospel
and further added this saying:
that if gold rusts, what shall iron do?
For if a priest in whom we trust be corrupt,
it is no wonder if an ignorant man go to rust.
And it is indeed shameful (if a priest will but note)
to find a filthy shepherd and a clean sheep.
Surely a priest ought to give an example,
by his own spotlessness, of how his sheep should live.
He did not hire out his benefice
and leave his sheep encumbered in the mire
while he ran off to London, to Saint Paul's,
to find himself a chantry for souls
or be shut up with a religious order,
but stayed at home and kept his fold well,
so that the wolf could not harm it:
he was a shepherd and not a mercenary.
And although he was holy and virtuous,
he was not scornful to sinful men,
or haughty and proud in his speech,
but discreet and benign in his teaching.

To drawen folk to heven by fairnesse
By good-ensample, this was his bisinesse:
But it were any persone obstinat,
What-so he were, of heigh or lowe estat,
Him wolde he snibben sharply for the nones.
A bettre preest I trowe that nowher noon is.
He wayted after no pompe and reverence,
Ne maked him a spyced conscience,
But Cristes lore, and his apostles twelve,
He taughte, and first he folwed it himselve. 530
 With him ther was a PLOWMAN, was his brother,
That hadde y-lad of dong ful many a fother.
A trewe swinker and a good was he,
Livinge in pees and parfit charite;
God loved he best with al his hole herte
At alle tymes, thogh him gamed or smerte,
And thanne his neighebour right as himselve.
He wolde thresshe, and therto dyke and delve,
For Cristes sake, for every povre wight,
Withouten hyre, if it lay in his might. 540
His tythes payed he ful faire and wel,
Bothe of his propre swink and his catel.
In a tabard he rood upon a mere.
 Ther was also a Reve and a Millere,
A Somnour and a Pardoner also,
A Maunciple, and myself; ther were namo.
 The MILLER was a stout carl, for the nones;
Ful big he was of braun, and eek of bones;
That proved wel, for overal ther he cam
At wrastling he wolde have alwey the ram. 550
He was short-sholdred, brood, a thikke knarre.
Ther nas no dore that he nolde heve of harre,
Or breke it, at a renning, with his heed.
His berd as any sowe or fox was reed,
And therto brood, as though it were a spade.
Upon the cop right of his nose he hade
A werte, and theron stood a tuft of heres,
Reed as the bristles of a sowes eres;
His nose-thirles blake were and wyde.
A swerd and bokeler bar he by his syde. 560
His mouth as greet was as a greet forneys.
He was a janglere and a goliardeys;
And that was most of sinne and harlotryes.
Wel coude he stelen corn, and tollen thryes;

To draw folk to heaven by fair behavior
and good example—that was his business.
But if any person were obstinate,
whoever he was, of high or low degree,
he would scold him sharply on that occasion.
I believe there is no better priest anywhere.
He did not look for pomp and reverence,
nor affect an overly scrupulous conscience;
he taught the lore of Christ and his twelve
Apostles—but first he followed it himself.

    With him there was a PLOWMAN, his brother,
who had conducted many a cartload of dung.
He was a good and faithful laborer,
living in peace and perfect charity.
He loved God best with all his heart,
at all times, whether he was pleased or grieved,
and next he loved his neighbor as himself.
He would thresh, and also dig and delve
for Christ's sake, for every poor man,
without pay, if it were in his power.
He paid his tithes fairly and well,
both on his own earnings and on his property.
Wearing a tunic, he rode upon a mare.

    There were also a Reeve and a Miller,
a Summoner and a Pardoner, too,
a Manciple and myself—there were no more.

    The MILLER was a stout fellow indeed;
he was huge—brawny, and large-boned, too;
this was well proved, for wherever he came
he always won the ram at wrestling matches.
He was short-shouldered and broad—a thick-set knave.
There was no door that he could not heave from its hinges
or break at a run with his head.
His beard was as red as a sow or a fox,
and as broad as a spade as well;
right on top of his nose he had
a wart, and on it stood a tuft of hairs,
red as the bristles of a sow's ears;
his nostrils were black and wide.
He bore a sword and buckler by his side.
His mouth was as wide as a great furnace.
He was a chatterer and a teller of tavern tales,
mostly about sin and ribaldry.
He knew well how to steal corn and charge threefold;

And yet he hadde a thombe of gold, pardee.
A whyt cote and a blew hood wered he.
A baggepype wel coude he blowe and sowne,
And therwithal he broghte us out of towne.

    A gentil MAUNCIPLE was ther of a temple,
Of which achatours mighte take exemple   570
For to be wyse in bying of vitaille,
For whether that he payde, or took by taille,
Algate he wayted so in his achat
That he was ay biforn and in good stat.
Now is not that of God a ful fair grace,
That swich a lewed mannes wit shal pace
The wisdom of an heep of lerned men?
Of maistres hadde he mo than thryes ten,
That were of lawe expert and curious,
Of which ther were a doseyn in that hous   580
Worthy to been stiwardes of rente and lond
Of any lord that is in Engelond,
To make him live by his propre good,
In honour dettelees, but he were wood,
Or live as scarsly as him list desire,
And able for to helpen al a shire
In any cas that mighte falle or happe;
And yit this Maunciple sette hir aller cappe.

    The REVE was a sclendre colerik man.
His berd was shave as ny as ever he can;   590
His heer was by his eres round y-shorn;
His top was dokked lyk a preest biforn;
Ful longe were his legges and ful lene,
Ylyk a staf: ther was no calf y-sene.
Wel coude he kepe a gerner and a binne;
Ther was noon auditour coude on him winne.
Wel wiste he, by the droghte and by the reyn,
The yelding of his seed and of his greyn.
His lordes sheep, his neet, his dayerye,
His swyn, his hors, his stoor, and his pultrye,   600
Was hoolly in this reves governing,
And by his covenaunt yaf the rekening,
Sin that his lord was twenty yeer of age;
Ther coude no man bringe him in arrerage.
Ther nas baillif, ne herde, ne other hyne,
That he ne knew his sleighte and his covyne;
They were adrad of him as of the deeth.
His woning was ful fair upon an heeth;

and yet he had a thumb of gold, all right.
He wore a white coat and a blue hood.
He could blow and play a bagpipe well,
and to its tune he brought us out of town.

There was a gentle MANCIPLE of the Inner Temple,
from whom buyers might take an example
of how to be wise in purchasing food supplies;
for whether he paid or bought on account,
he was always so careful in his buying
that he was always ahead and prosperous.
Now, isn't it a fair example of God's favor
that such an ignorant man's wit can surpass
the wisdom of a heap of learned men?
He had more than thirty masters
who were cunning experts in the law
and of whom there were a dozen in that house
worthy to be stewards of the income and land
of any lord in England,
to help him live on his own wealth
honorably and without debt (unless he were out of his wits)
or to live as economically as he might wish—
men who could help a whole county
in any case that might come up:
and yet this Manciple got the best of them all!

The REEVE was a slender, choleric man.
His beard was shaved as close as could be;
his hair was shorn around his ears;
the top of his head was clipped like a priest's in front.
His legs were very long and lean,
like a staff—no calf was visible.
He knew very well how to watch over a granary and a bin;
no auditor could catch him short.
He could calculate, according to droughts and
rains, what the yield of his seed and grain should be.
His lord's sheep, his cattle, his dairy,
his pigs, his horses, his stores, and his poultry
were wholly in this Reeve's power,
and under his contract he had given his reckoning
since his lord was twenty years old.
No man could find him to be in arrears.
There was no bailiff, or shepherd or other laborer
whose tricks and plots were unknown to him;
they were scared to death of him.
His home was a pleasant one, in a meadow;

With grene trees yshadwed was his place.
He coude bettre than his lord purchace;   610
Ful riche he was astored prively.
His lord wel coude he plesen subtilly,
To yeve and lene him of his owne good,
And have a thank, and yet a cote and hood.
In youthe he lerned hadde a good mister;
He was a wel good wrighte, a carpenter.
This reve sat upon a ful good stot
That was al pomely grey and highte Scot.
A long surcote of pers upon he hade,
And by his syde he bar a rusty blade.   620
Of Northfolk was this Reve, of which I telle,
Bisyde a toun men clepen Baldeswelle.
Tukked he was, as is a frere, aboute,
And ever he rood the hindreste of our route.

A SOMNOUR was ther with us in that place,
That hadde a fyr-reed cherubinnes face,
For sawcefleem he was, with eyen narwe.
As hoot he was, and lecherous, as a sparwe,
With scalled browes blake and piled berd;
Of his visage children were aferd.   630
Ther nas quiksilver, litarge, ne brimstoon,
Boras, ceruce, ne oille of tartre noon,
Ne oynement that wolde clense and byte
That him mighte helpen of his whelkes whyte,
Nor of the knobbes sittinge on his chekes.
Wel loved he garleek, oynons, and eek lekes,
And for to drinken strong wyn, reed as blood.
Than wolde he speke, and crye as he were wood.
And whan that he wel dronken hadde the wyn,
Than wolde he speke no word but Latyn.   640
A fewe termes hadde he, two or three,
That he had lerned out of som decree;
No wonder is, he herde it al the day;
And eek ye knowen wel how that a jay
Can clepen "Watte" as well as can the Pope.
But who-so coude in other thing him grope,
Thanne hadde he spent al his philosophye;
Ay "Questio quid iuris" wolde he crye.
He was a gentil harlot and a kinde;
A bettre felawe sholde men noght finde.   650
He wolde suffre, for a quart of wyn,
A good felawe to have his concubyn

his place was shadowed with green trees.
He was a better buyer than his lord;
he had privately laid by considerable riches.
He knew how to please his lord well, underhandedly
giving and lending him the lord's own goods,
and got thanks and a coat and hood besides.
In youth he had learned a good trade;
he was a good craftsman, a carpenter.
He sat on a very good farm horse,
a dappled gray called Scot.
He wore a long blue outer coat,
and he carried a rusty blade by his side.
This Reeve I am telling you about came from Norfolk,
near a town which is called Bawdeswell.
His coat was tucked up around him like a friar's,
and he always rode last in our company.

A SUMMONER was with us there,
who had a fire-red face like a cherub in a painting,
for he was pimply, with narrow eyes.
He was as hot and lecherous as a sparrow,
with scabby black brows and a scanty beard;
his face frightened little children.
There was no quicksilver, lead, or brimstone,
borax, white lead, or oil of tartar,
or any kind of cleansing or astringent ointment,
that could cure him of his white blotches
or of the knobs on his cheeks. ⎫ *phalic symbols*
He loved garlic, onions, and leeks, ⎭
and he liked to drink strong wine as red as blood.
Then he would talk and shout as if he were mad.
And when he had drunk deep of his wine,
then he would not speak a word except Latin.
He knew a few terms—two or three—
that he had learned out of some decree;
which was no wonder, for he heard it all day long,
and, too, you know that a parrot
can say "Walt!" as well as the Pope.
But if anyone wanted to try him further,
he had exhausted his learning;
he would just keep crying, "*Questio* quid juris.*"
He was a gentle, kindly rascal;
no one could find a better fellow.
For a quart of wine he would allow
a good fellow to have his concubine

A twelf-month, and excuse him atte fulle:
Ful prively a finch eek coude he pulle.
And if he fond owher a good felawe,
He wolde techen him to have non awe
In swich cas of the erchedeknes curs,
But if a mannes soule were in his purs;
For in his purs he sholde y-punisshed be.
"Purs is the erchedeknes helle," seyde he.   660
But wel I woot he lyed right in dede;
Of cursing oghte ech gilty man him drede—
For curs wol slee, right as assoilling saveth—
And also war him of a *significavit*.
In daunger hadde he at his owne gyse
The yonge girles of the diocyse,
And knew hir counseil, and was al hir reed.
A gerland hadde he set upon his heed,
As greet as it were for an ale-stake;
A bokeler hadde he maad him of a cake.   670
   With him ther rood a gentil PARDONER
Of Rouncival, his freend and his compeer.
That streight was comen fro the court of Rome.
Ful loude he song, "Com hider, love, to me."
This Somnour bar to him a stiff burdoun:
Was never trompe of half so greet a soun.
This Pardoner hadde heer as yelow as wex,
But smothe it heng as dooth a strike of flex;
By ounces henge his lokkes that he hadde,
And therwith he his shuldres overspradde;   680
But thinne it lay, by colpons oon and oon;
But hood, for jolitee, ne wered he noon,
For it was trussed up in his walet.
Him thoughte he rood al of the newe jet;
Dischevele, save his cappe, he rood al bare.
Swiche glaringe eyen hadde he as an hare.
A vernicle hadde he sowed on his cappe;
His walet lay biforn him in his lappe,
Bretful of pardoun come from Rome al hoot.
A voys he hadde as smal as hath a goot;   690
No berd hadde he, ne never sholde have,
As smothe it was as it were late y-shave;
I trowe he were a gelding or a mare.
But of his craft, fro Berwik into Ware,
Ne was ther swich another pardoner:
For in his male he hadde a pilwe-beer,

for a year, and would excuse him fully:
he could pluck a finch in secrecy himself.
And if he found a good fellow anywhere,
he would teach him not to stand in awe,
in such a case, of the Archdeacon's curse,
unless the man's soul were in his purse;
for it was in his purse that he was to be punished.
"Purse is the Archdeacon's hell," said he.
But I know well that he lied indeed;
every guilty man should dread excommunication—
for it will slay, just as absolution saves—
and beware of a writ of *significavit** (which ends in jail).
He had the young wenches of the diocese
under control, at his own wish,
and knew their secrets, and was their sole advisor.
He had set a garland on his head, as big as the ones
that hang from the ale-stake before a drinking house;
he had made himself a shield out of a cake.

With him there rode a gentle PARDONER
of Rouncivalle;* he was the Summoner's friend and
comrade, who had come straight from the court of
Rome. Loudly he sang, "Come hither, love, to me,"
and the Summoner accompanied him powerfully—
never did a trumpet make half so great a sound.
The Pardoner had hair as yellow as wax,
but it hung as smoothly as a hank of flax;
wisp by wisp his locks hung down,
and he had spread them over his shoulders—
but they lay thinly, in strands, one by one;
however, for sport, he wore no hood;
it was trussed up in his pack.
He thought he rode all in the latest style;
with his hair down, he rode bareheaded except for his cap.
He had staring eyes just like a hare's.
He had sewed a veronica on his cap;
his bag was in his lap before him,
brimful of pardons, all come hot from Rome.
He had a voice as thin as a goat's;
no beard did he have, nor would ever have—
his face was as smooth as if he had just shaved;
I expect he was a gelding or a mare. (homo)
But to speak of his craft, from Berwick to Ware
there was no other such pardoner;
for in his bag he had a pillowcase

Which that, he seyde, was Our Lady veyl;
He seyde he hadde a gobet of the seyl
That Seinte Peter hadde whan that he wente
Upon the see, til Jesu Crist him hente; 700
He hadde a croys of latoun, ful of stones,
And in a glas he hadde pigges bones—
But with thise relikes, whan that he fond
A povre person dwelling upon lond,
Upon a day he gat him more moneye
Than that the person gat in monthes tweye.
And thus, with feyned flaterye and japes,
He made the person and the peple his apes.
But trewely to tellen atte laste,
He was in chirche a noble ecclesiaste. 710
Wel coude he rede a lessoun or a storie,
But alderbest he song an offertorie;
For wel he wiste whan that song was songe
He moste preche, and wel affyle his tonge
To winne silver, as he ful wel coude;
Therefore he song the murierly and loude.

Now have I told you shortly, in a clause,
Th'estat, th'array, the nombre, and eek the cause
Why that assembled was this companye
In Southwerk, at this gentil hostelrye 720
That highte the Tabard, faste by the Belle.
But now is tyme to yow for to telle
How that we baren us that ilke night
Whan we were in that hostelrye alight,
And after wol I telle of our viage
And al the remenaunt of our pilgrimage.
But first I pray yow, of your curteisye,
That ye n'arette it nat my vileinye,
Thogh that I pleynly speke in this matere,
To telle yow hir wordes and hir chere, 730
Ne thogh I speke hir wordes properly;
For this ye knowen also wel as I,
Who-so shal telle a tale after a man,
He moot reherce, as ny as ever he can,
Everich a word, if it be in his charge,
Al speke he never so rudeliche and large;
Or elles he moot telle his tale untrewe,
Or feyne thing, or finde wordes newe.
He may nat spare, althogh he were his brother;
He moot as wel seye o word as another. 740

which, he said, was Our Lady's veil;
he said he had a piece of the sail
Saint Peter had when he sailed
on the sea, until Jesus Christ took him;
he had a cross of brass, set with stones,
and in a glass he had pigs' bones;
but with these "relics," whenever he found
a poor country parson,
he in one day got himself more money
than the parson got in two months.
And thus, with false flattery and tricks,
he made monkeys of the parson and the people.
But in the end, to do him justice,
in church he was a noble ecclesiastic.
He could read a lesson or a history beautifully,
but best of all he sang an offertory;
for well he knew that when that song was sung
he must preach and smooth his tongue
to win silver, as he indeed could do—
therefore he sang the more merrily and the louder.

Now I have told you truthfully, in a few words,
the condition, the clothing and display, the number, and
the reason for the gathering of this company
in Southwark, at the fine hostelry
that is called the Tabard, right near the Bell.
But now it is time to tell you
what we did that same night,
when we had alighted at that hostelry,
and afterwards I will tell you about our trip,
and all the rest of our pilgrimage.
But first I pray you, by your courtesy,
not to interpret it as my vulgarity
even though I speak plainly in this matter,
in telling you their words and behavior—
not even though I give you their exact words;
for you know as well as I do
that whoever repeats a man's story
is obligated to report, as nearly as he can,
every word that is within the area he has been charged with,
however rudely and broadly he may speak;
otherwise, he would have to falsify his tale,
or invent new matter, or find new words.
He may not forbear, even if his brother told the tale;
he must speak one word as well as another.

Crist spak himself ful brode in Holy Writ,
And wel ye woot no vileinye is it.
Eek Plato seith, who-so that can him rede,
The wordes mote be cosin to the dede.
Also I prey yow to foryeve it me
Al have I nat set folk in hir degree
Here in this tale, as that they sholde stonde;
My wit is short, ye may wel understonde.

  Greet chere made our Hoste us everichon,
And to the soper sette us anon,   750
And served us with vitaille at the beste.
Strong was the wyn, and wel to drinke us leste.
A semely man our Hoste was withalle
For to han been a marshal in an halle;
A large man he was, with eyen stepe,
A fairer burgeys is ther noon in Chepe:
Bold of his speche, and wys, and wel y-taught,
And of manhod him lakkede right naught.
Eek therto he was right a mery man,
And after soper pleyen he bigan,   760
And spak of mirthe amonges othere thinges—
Whan that we hadde maad our rekeninges—
And seyde thus: "Now, lordinges, trewely,
Ye been to me right welcome hertely:
For by my trouthe, if that I shal nat lye,
I saugh nat this yeer so mery a companye
At ones in this herberwe as is now.
Fayn wolde I doon yow mirthe, wiste I how.
And of a mirthe I am right now bithoght,
To doon yow ese, and it shal coste noght.   770
  Ye goon to Caunterbury; God yow spede,
The blisful martir quyte yow your mede.
And wel I woot as ye goon by the weye
Ye shapen yow to talen and to pleye;
For trewely, confort ne mirthe is noon
To ryde by the weye doumb as a stoon;
And therfore wol I maken yow disport,
As I seyde erst, and doon yow som confort.
And if yow lyketh alle, by oon assent,
Now for to stonden at my jugement,   780
And for to werken as I shal yow seye,
Tomorwe, whan ye ryden by the weye,
Now, by my fader soule that is deed,
But ye be merye, I wol yeve yow myn heed.

Christ himself spoke very broadly in Holy Writ,
and you well know that that isn't vulgarity;
also Plato says (as whoever can read him knows)
the words must be cousin to the deed.
Also I pray you to forgive me
if I have not presented people according to their
proper ranks in this account:
my wit is short, as you can easily understand.

  Our Host made each one of us welcome,
and he set us down to supper at once
and served us with the best of food.
The wine was strong, and we were glad to drink.
Our Host was indeed a seemly enough man
to have been a master of ceremonies in a hall;
he was a large man, with prominent eyes;
there isn't a more imposing burgher in all Cheapside:
he was bold in his speech, prudent, and well taught;
and he lacked no manly quality.
Besides that, he was indeed a merry man.
After supper he began to joke,
and spoke of amusements among other things—
when we had all paid our bills—
and said as follows: "Now, my lords, truly
you are right welcome here, with all my heart.
For on my word, to tell the truth,
I haven't seen all year so merry a company
all at one time in this inn as now.
I would be glad to give you some amusement, if I knew how.
And just now a way to please you
has occurred to me, and it shall cost nothing.

  "You are going to Canterbury—God speed you;
may the blissful martyr give you your reward.
Well I know that as you go along the way
you plan to tell tales and amuse yourselves,
for surely there is no consolation or mirth
in riding along the way dumb as a stone;
and therefore I wish to amuse you,
as I said before, and give you pleasure.
If you all agree, with one accord,
to abide by my judgment
and to do as I shall direct you
tomorrow when you ride on your way,
then, by the soul of my dead father,
I swear I shall give you my own head unless you are amused!

Hold up your hond, withouten more speche."
　　Our counseil was nat longe for to seche;
Us thoughte it was noght worth to make it wys,
And graunted him withouten more avys,
And bad him seye his verdit, as him leste.
　　"Lordinges," quod he, "now herkneth for the beste;　　790
But tak it not, I prey yow, in desdeyn;
This is the poynt, to speken short and pleyn,
That ech of yow, to shorte with your weye
In this viage, shal telle tales tweye—
To Caunterbury-ward, I mene it so—
And homward he shal tellen othere two
Of aventures that whylom han bifalle;
And which of yow that bereth him best of alle,
That is to seyn, that telleth in this cas
Tales of best sentence and most solas,　　　　　　　　800
Shal have a soper at our aller cost
Here in this place, sitting by this post,
Whan that we come agayn fro Caunterbury.
And for to make yow the more mery,
I wol myselven goodly with yow ryde,
Right at myn owne cost, and be your gyde.
And who-so wol my jugement withseye
Shal paye al that we spenden by the weye.
And if ye vouche-sauf that it be so,
Tel me anon, withouten wordes mo,　　　　　　　　　810
And I wol erly shape me therfore."
　　This thing was graunted, and our othes swore
With ful glad herte, and preyden him also
That he wold vouche-sauf for to do so,
And that he wolde been our governour
And of our tales juge and reportour,
And sette a soper at a certeyn prys;
And we wold reuled been at his devys,
In heigh and lowe; and thus, by oon assent,
We been acorded to his jugement.　　　　　　　　　820
And therupon the wyn was fet anon;
We dronken, and to reste wente echon,
Withouten any lenger taryinge.
　　A-morwe whan that day bigan to springe,
Up roos our Host, and was our aller cok,
And gadrede us togidre alle in a flok,
And forth we riden, a litel more than pas,
Unto the watering of Seint Thomas;

Hold up your hands, without any more talk."

Our decision was not long in forthcoming;
it did not seem worth a long consultation;
we granted what he asked without further conferring
and told him to give whatever verdict he pleased.

"Lords," said he, "now listen carefully;
but don't, I pray you, take what I say amiss.
This is the point, to speak shortly and plainly:
that each of you, for something to shorten our way with
on this trip, shall tell two tales—
that is, on the way to Canterbury, I mean—
and on the homeward way, two more,
about adventures that happened formerly;
and whichever one of you acquits himself the best—
that is to say, whoever tells in this case
the most instructive and amusing tales—
shall have a supper at the cost of all the rest of us,
right here by this pillar,
when we come back again from Canterbury.
And to make you all the merrier,
I will patiently ride with you myself
(completely at my own cost) and be your guide.
And whoever shall gainsay my judgment
shall pay all that we spend on the way.
If you agree that it be so done,
tell me at once, without more words,
and I will prepare myself early for the purpose."

This was granted, and we gladly took our oaths,
and also prayed him
that he would agree to do so,
and that he would be our governor,
and be judge of our tales and keep count of them,
and set a supper at a certain price;
we would be ruled at his command
in large and small matters. Thus with one accord
we agreed to his judgment.
Thereupon the wine was fetched at once;
we drank and went to rest, every one of us,
without any further tarrying.

The next day, when it began to lighten,
our Host got up and like a cock aroused us,
and gathered us together in a flock.
We rode forth at a little more than footpace,
as far as the watering place of Saint Thomas.

And there our Host bigan his hors areste,
And seyde: "Lordinges, herkneth, if yow leste. 830
Ye woot your forward, and I it yow recorde.
If even-song and morwe-song acorde,
Lat see now who shal telle the firste tale.
As ever mote I drinke wyn or ale,
Who-so be rebel to my jugement
Shal paye for al that by the weye is spent.
Now draweth cut, er that we ferrer twinne;
He which that hath the shortest shal biginne.
Sire Knight," quod he, "my maister and my lord,
Now draweth cut, for that is myn acord. 840
Cometh neer," quod he, "my lady Prioresse;
And ye, sir Clerk, lat be your shamfastnesse,
Ne studieth noght; ley hond to, every man."

  Anon to drawen every wight bigan,
And shortly for to tellen, as it was,
Were it by aventure, or sort, or cas,
The sothe is this, the cut fil to the Knight,
Of which ful blythe and glad was every wight;
And telle he moste his tale, as was resoun,
By forward and by composicioun, 850
As ye han herd; what nedeth wordes mo?
And whan this gode man saugh it was so,
As he that wys was and obedient
To kepe his forward by his free assent,
He seyde: "Sin I shal beginne the game,
What, welcome be the cut, a Goddes name!
Now lat us ryde, and herkneth what I seye."

  And with that word we riden forth our weye;
And he bigan with right a mery chere
His tale anon, and seyde in this manere. 860

There our Host checked his horse
and said, "Lords, listen if you will:
you know your agreement, and I remind you of it;
If evening song and morning song agree,
let's see now who shall tell the first tale.
As sure as ever I drink either wine or ale,
whoever is rebellious toward my judgment
shall pay for all that is spent by the way.
Now draw a lot before we go any further:
he who gets the shortest shall begin.
Sir Knight," said he, "my master and my lord,
now draw your lot, for that is my decision.
Come near," said he, "my lady Prioress;
and you, sir Clerk, leave off your bashfulness,
don't deliberate; lay a hand to, everyone!"

    At once each one drew,
and to tell you in short what happened,
whether it was by luck, or fate, or chance,
the truth is that the lot fell to the Knight,
for which everyone was very glad;
he had to tell his tale, as was right,
according to the agreement and the treaty,
as you have heard. What need is there to say more?
When this good man saw that it was so,
then as a man who was prudent and obedient
in keeping his agreement without being urged,
he said, "Since I shall begin the game,
well, welcome be the lot, in God's name!
Now let us ride, and listen to what I say."

    And with these words we rode forth on our way.
He began his tale at once most cheerfully,
and spoke as follows.

THE KNIGHTES TALE

Iamque domos patrias, Scithice post aspera gentis Prelia, laurigero,
&c. [Statius, *Thebaid*, xii, 519-520.]

WHYLOM, as olde stories tellen us,
Ther was a duk that highte Theseus;
Of Athenes he was lord and governour,
And in his tyme swich a conquerour
That gretter was ther noon under the sonne.
Ful many a riche contree hadde he wonne;
What with his wisdom and his chivalrye,
He conquered al the regne of Femenye,
That whilom was y-cleped Scithia,
And weddede the quene Ipolita,   10
And broghte hir hoom with him in his contree
With muchel glorie and greet solempnitee,
And eek hir yonge suster Emelye.
And thus with victorie and with melodye
Lete I this noble duk to Athenes ryde,
And al his hoost in armes him bisyde.

  And certes, if it nere to long to here,
I wolde han told yow fully the manere,
How wonnen was the regne of Femenye
By Theseus, and by his chivalrye;   20
And of the grete bataille for the nones
Bitwixen Athenes and Amazones;
And how asseged was Ipolita,
The faire, hardy quene of Scithia;
And of the feste that was at hir weddinge,
And of the tempest at hir hoom-cominge;
But al that thing I moot as now forbere.
I have, God woot, a large feeld to ere,
And wayke been the oxen in my plough.
The remenant of the tale is long y-nough.   30
I wol nat letten eek noon of this route;
Lat every felawe telle his tale aboute.
And lat see now who shal the soper winne;
And ther I lefte, I wol ageyn biginne.
  This duk, of whom I make mencioun,
When he was come almost unto the toun,

THE KNIGHT'S TALE

*And now Theseus, approaching his native land in laurelled chariot
after fierce battles with the Scythians, etc.*

[Statius, *Thebaid*, xii, 519-520]

ONCE UPON A TIME, as ancient stories tell us,
there was a duke who was named Theseus.
He was lord and ruler of Athens,
and such a conqueror in his day
that there was no greater under the sun.
He had won many a rich country
by virtue of his wisdom and his knightly prowess.
He conquered the whole realm of the Amazon women,
which formerly was called Scythia,
and took in marriage Queen Hippolyta
and brought her home with him to his country
with much glory and great pomp;
and he brought as well her young sister Emily.
And thus, with victory and the sound of music,
I leave this noble duke riding to Athens
and, with him, all his force in arms.

And, indeed, if it were not too long to listen to,
I would have wanted to tell you fully the way
in which the realm of the Amazons was won
by Theseus and his knightly company;
and of the singularly great battle
between the Athenians and the Amazons;
and how siege was laid to Hippolyta,
the fair bold queen of Scythia;
and of the feast that there was at their wedding,
and of the tempest at their homecoming.
But for now I must shun all that matter.
I have, God knows, a broad field to till,
and the oxen pulling my plow are weak;
the rest of the tale is long enough.
Besides, I don't want to hinder any in this company;
let each of our companions tell his tale in turn,
and let us see, now, who is to win the supper.
Where I left off, I'll begin again.

The duke of whom I speak,
when he had come almost to the town

43

In al his wele and in his moste pryde,
He was war, as he caste his eye asyde,
Wher that ther kneled in the hye weye
A companye of ladies, tweye and tweye,   40
Ech after other, clad in clothes blake;
But swich a cry and swich a wo they make,
That in this world nis creature livinge,
That herde swich another weymentinge;
And of this cry they nolde nevere stenten,
Til they the reynes of his brydel henten.

   "What folk ben ye, that at myn hoom-cominge
Perturben so my feste with cryinge?"
Quod Theseus, "have ye so greet envye
Of myn honour, that thus compleyne and crye?   50
Or who hath yow misboden or offended?
And telleth me if it may been amended,
And why that ye ben clothed thus in blak."

   The eldeste lady of hem alle spak,
When she hadde swowned with a deedly chere,
That it was routhe for to seen and here.
She seyde: "Lord, to whom Fortune hath yiven
Victorie, and as a conquerour to liven,
Nat greveth us your glorie and your honour;
But we biseken mercy and socour.   60
Have mercy on our wo and our distresse.
Some drope of pitee, thurgh thy gentilesse,*
Upon us wrecched wommen lat thou falle.
For certes, lord, ther nis noon of us alle,
That she nath been a duchesse or a quene;
Now be we caitifs, as it is wel sene:
Thanked be Fortune, and hir false wheel,
That noon estat assureth to be weel.
And certes, lord, t'abyden your presence,
Here in this temple of the goddesse Clemence   70
We han ben waytinge al this fourtenight;
Now help us, lord, sith it is in thy might.

   I wrecche, which that wepe and waille thus,
Was whylom wyf to king Capaneus,
That starf at Thebes, cursed be that day!
And alle we, that been in this array
And maken al this lamentacioun,
We losten alle our housbondes at that toun,
Whyl that the sege ther-aboute lay.
And yet now th'olde Creon, weylaway!   80

in all his felicity and in his fullest glory,
became conscious, as he cast his eye to one side,
that in the highway there was kneeling
a company of ladies, two by two,
each pair behind another, dressed in black.
They made such an outcry and grieved so
that no creature living in this world
has heard such another lamentation.
They would not leave off this shrieking
until they had grasped his bridle reins.

"What people are you, who at my homecoming
thus disturb my celebration with your cries?"
said Theseus. "Have you such great envy
of my honor that you thus complain and cry out?
Or who has mistreated or offended you?
Tell me if your wrong can be righted,
and why you are thus clothed in black."

The eldest lady of them all spoke
(after she had reeled faintly, with a look of death about her,
so that it was pitiable to see and hear her),
"My lord, to whom Fortune has given
victory and the life due a conqueror,
your glory and honor do not grieve us at all.
Rather, we beg for mercy and aid.
Have mercy on our woe and our distress!
By reason of your gentleness let some drop of pity fall
upon us wretched women.
For indeed, my lord, there is not one of us all
who has not been a duchess or a queen.
Now we are wretches, as is evident:
thanks to Fortune and her false wheel—
her who assures happiness to no condition of man.
Indeed, my lord, to wait for your presence
we have been attending here in
the temple of the goddess Clemency for a fortnight.
Now help us, lord, since it is in your power.

Wretch that I am, thus weeping and wailing,
I was formerly the wife of King Capaneus,
who died at Thebes, cursed be the day!
All of us, who are dressed as you see
and uttering all this lamentation—
we all lost our husbands at that city
while it was being besieged.
And just recently, alas, old Creon—

That lord is now of Thebes the citee,
Fulfild of ire and of iniquitee,
He, for despyt, and for his tirannye,
To do the dede bodyes vileinye,
Of alle our lordes, whiche that ben y-slawe,
Hath alle the bodyes on an heep y-drawe,
And wol nat suffren hem, by noon assent,
Neither to been y-buried nor y-brent,
But maketh houndes ete hem in despyt."
And with that word, withouten more respyt,   90
They fillen gruf, and cryden pitously,
"Have on us wrecched wommen som mercy,
And lat oure sorwe sinken in thyn herte."

This gentil duk doun from his courser sterte
With herte pitous, whan he herde hem speke.
Him thoughte that his herte wolde breke,
Whan he saugh hem so pitous and so mat,
That whylom weren of so greet estat.
And in his armes he hem alle up hente,
And hem conforteth in ful good entente;   100
And swoor his ooth, as he was trewe knight,
He wolde doon so ferforthly his might
Upon the tyraunt Creon hem to wreke,
That al the peple of Grece sholde speke
How Creon was of Theseus y-served,
As he that hadde his deeth ful well deserved.
And right anoon, withouten more abood,
His baner he desplayeth, and foorth rood
To Thebes-ward, and al his host bisyde;
No neer Athenes wolde he go ne ryde,   110
Ne take his ese fully half a day,
But onward on his wey that night he lay;
And sente anoon Ipolita the quene,
And Emelye hir yonge suster shene,
Unto the toun of Athenës to dwelle;
And forth he rit; ther is namore to telle.

The rede statue of Mars, with spere and targe,
So shyneth in his whyte baner large,
That alle the feeldes gliteren up and doun;
And by his baner born is his penoun   120
Of gold ful riche, in which ther was y-bete
The Minotaur, which that he slough in Crete.
Thus rit this duk, thus rit this conquerour,
And in his host of chivalrye the flour,

who is now lord of the city of Thebes
and is full of wrath and evil—
out of his spitefulness and tyranny
has piled all the corpses in a heap
in order to do an ungentle deed to the dead bodies
of all our husbands, who have been slain.
He will not allow them, by any agreement,
either to be buried or to be burned,
but for spite has dogs eat them."
With that word and without further pause,
the women fell prostrate and cried out piteously,
"Have some mercy on us wretched women
and let our sorrow sink into your heart."

The gentle duke jumped down from his horse
with pitying heart as he heard them speak.
He thought that his heart would break
when he saw how pitiable and dejected they were,
who formerly were of such high estate.
He took up each of them in his arms
and comforted them with a good will
and swore, as he was a faithful knight,
that he would perform what was in his power
in order to avenge them upon the tyrant Creon
to such an extent that all the people of Greece would talk
of how Creon was treated by Theseus
as a villain who had fully deserved death.
And immediately, without further delay,
he displayed his banner and rode forth
toward Thebes with all his army.
He would not walk or ride any nearer to Athens,
nor would he rest for half a day,
but lodged that night further along on his route.
He sent Queen Hippolyta
and Emily, her fair young sister,
to stay in the city of Athens.
And he rode off; there is no more to say.

The red image of Mars, with spear and shield,
so gleamed in Theseus' broad white banner
that all the fields roundabout glistened.
Beside his banner was borne his pennon
of richest cloth of gold, on which was embroidered
an image of the Minotaur, which he had slain in Crete.
Thus rode this duke and conqueror,
with the flower of knighthood in his host,

Til that he cam to Thebes, and alighte
Faire in a feeld, ther as he thoghte to fighte.
But shortly for to speken of this thing,
With Creon, which that was of Thebes king,
He faught, and slough him manly as a knight
In pleyn bataille, and putte the folk to flight;   130
And by assaut he wan the citee after,
And rente adoun bothe wal, and sparre, and rafter;
And to the ladyes he restored agayn
The bones of hir housbondes that were slayn,
To doon obséquies as was tho the gyse.
But it were al to long for to devyse
The grete clamour and the waymentinge
That the ladyes made at the brenninge
Of the bodyes, and the grete honour
That Theseus, the noble conquerour,   140
Doth to the ladyes, whan they from him wente;
But shortly for to telle is myn entente.

Whan that this worthy duk, this Theseus,
Hath Creon slayn, and wonne Thebes thus,
Stille in that feeld he took al night his reste,
And dide with al the contree as him leste.

To ransake in the tas of bodyes dede,
Hem for to strepe of harneys and of wede,
The pilours diden bisinesse and cure,
After the bataille and disconfiture.   150
And so bifel, that in the tas they founde,
Thurgh-girt with many a grevous blody wounde,
Two yonge knightes ligginge by and by,
Bothe in oon armes, wroght ful richely,
Of whiche two, Arcita highte that oon,
And that other knight highte Palamon.
Nat fully quike, ne fully dede they were,
But by hir cote-armures, and by hir gere,
The heraudes knewe hem best in special
As they that weren of the blood royal   160
Of Thebes, and of sustren two y-born.
Out of the tas the pilours han hem torn,
And han hem caried softe unto the tente
Of Theseus, and he ful sone hem sente
To Athenes, to dwellen in prisoun
Perpetuelly; he nolde no raunsoun.
And whan this worthy duk hath thus y-don,
He took his host, and hoom he rit anon

until he came to Thebes and lighted down
in splendor in a field where he intended to wage battle.
But to make a long story short:
he fought with Creon, king of Thebes,
and slew him in manly and knightly fashion
in open battle and put Creon's people to flight.
Thereafter he won the city by assault
and tore down wall and beam and rafter.
To the ladies he returned
their slain husbands' bones, so that
the funeral rites might be celebrated in the way that was
then the custom. But it would take all too long to describe
the great clamor and lamentation
that the ladies made at the burning
of the bodies and the great honor
that the noble conqueror Theseus
paid to the ladies when they departed from him;
to narrate briefly is my intent.

When this valiant Duke Theseus
had killed Creon and thus won Thebes,
he took his rest all night upon that same field
and dealt with all the country as he wished.

Searching in the pile of dead bodies
in order to strip them of armor and clothes,
the pillagers worked hard and carefully
after the battle and defeat.
It so happened that they found in the pile,
thrust through with many a grievous bloody wound,
two young knights lying side by side,
both in identical arms, which were made most richly.
Of the two, one was named Arcite
and the other knight was called Palamon.
They were neither fully alive nor fully dead,
but by their coats of arms and other equipment
the heralds knew them especially well
as the ones who were of the royal line
of Thebes, and sons of two sisters.
The pillagers pulled them from the heap of bodies
and carried them gently to the tent
of Theseus. He immediately sent them
to Athens, to remain in prison
forever; he would not take ransom for them.
When the valiant duke had thus taken action,
he took his army and soon rode home,

With laurer crowned as a conquerour;
And there he liveth, in joye and in honour,   170
Terme of his lyf; what nedeth wordes mo?
And in a tour, in angwish and in wo,
Dwellen this Palamoun and his felawe Arcite,
For evermore; ther may no gold hem quyte.

This passeth yeer by yeer, and day by day,
Til it fil ones, in a morwe of May,
That Emelye, that fairer was to sene
Than is the lilie upon his stalke grene,
And fressher than the May with floures newe—
For with the rose colour stroof hir hewe,   180
I noot which was the fairer of hem two—
Er it were day, as was hir wone to do,
She was arisen, and al redy dight;
For May wol have no slogardye a-night.
The sesoun priketh every gentil herte,
And maketh him out of his sleep to sterte,
And seith, "Arys, and do thyn observaunce."
This maked Emelye have remembraunce
To doon honour to May, and for to ryse.
Y-clothed was she fresh, for to devyse;   190
Hir yelow heer was broyded in a tresse,
Bihinde hir bak, a yerde long, I gesse.
And in the gardin, at the sonne upriste,
She walketh up and doun, and as hir liste
She gadereth floures, party whyte and rede,
To make a subtil gerland for hir hede,
And as an aungel hevenly she song.

The grete tour, that was so thikke and strong,
Which of the castel was the chief dongeoun,
(Ther as the knightes weren in prisoun,   200
Of whiche I tolde yow, and tellen shal)
Was evene joynant to the gardin-wal,
Ther as this Emelye hadde hir pleyinge.
Bright was the sonne, and cleer that morweninge,
And Palamon, this woful prisoner,
As was his wone, by leve of his gayler,
Was risen, and romed in a chambre on heigh,
In which he al the noble citee seigh,
And eek the gardin, ful of braunches grene,
Theras this fresshe Emelye the shene   210
Was in hire walk, and romed up and doun.
This sorweful prisoner, this Palamoun,

crowned with laurel as a conqueror.
And there he lived in joy and honor
to the end of his life; what more need be said?
And in a tower, in anguish and woe,
Palamon and Arcite remain
for evermore; no amount of gold might pay for their release.

This went on day after day and year after year,
until it once happened, of a May morning,
that Emily—who was lovelier to look at
than the lily is upon its green stalk,
and fresher than May with its spring flowers
(for her complexion vied with the color of roses;
I do not know which of the two was fairer)—
this Emily was up and already dressed
before daybreak, as it was her wont to be,
for May won't stand for slug-a-beds:
the season arouses every gentle heart,
and makes him start up from his sleep,
and says, "Get up, pay me your due homage."
All this made Emily take thought
to do honor to May and to arise.
Her clothes were bright and new in appearance;
her blond hair was twined in a braid
down her back—a yard long, by my guess.
In the garden at sunrise
she walked up and down; according to her fancy,
she gathered flowers, some white, some red,
to make an artful garland for her head;
and she sang in a voice as heavenly as an angel's.

The great tower, very thick and strong,
which was the chief dungeon of the castle
(where those knights of whom I told you,
and shall tell you more, were in prison)
adjoined the wall of the garden
where Emily took her amusement.
The sun was bright and the morning fair;
Palamon, the woeful prisoner,
as was his wont by his jailer's leave,
was up and was walking to and fro in a chamber high in the
tower, from which he saw all of the noble city
and the garden, too, full of green branches,
where lively Emily the fair
was at her walk, roaming up and down.
The sorrowful prisoner, this Palamon,

Goth in the chambre, rominge to and fro,
And to himself compleyning of his wo;
That he was born, ful ofte he seyde, "alas!"
And so bifel, by aventure or cas,
That thurgh a window, thikke of many a barre
Of yren greet and square as any sparre,
He caste his eye upon Emelya,
And therwithal he bleynte, and cryde "A!"   220
As though he stongen were unto the herte.
And with that cry Arcite anon up-sterte,
And seyde, "Cosin myn, what eyleth thee,
That art so pale and deedly on to see?
Why crydestow? who hath thee doon offence?
For Goddes love, tak al in pacience
Oure prisoun, for it may non other be;
Fortune hath yeven us this adversitee.
Som wikke aspect or disposicioun
Of Saturne, by sum constellacioun,   230
Hath yeven us this, although we hadde it sworn;
So stood the heven whan that we were born;
We moste endure it: this is the short and pleyn."
    This Palamon answerde, and seyde ageyn,
"Cosyn, for sothe, of this opinioun
Thou hast a veyn imaginacioun.
This prison caused me nat for to crye.
But I was hurt right now thurghout myn yë
Into myn herte; that wol my bane be.
The fairnesse of that lady that I see   240
Yond in the gardin romen to and fro,
Is cause of al my crying and my wo.
I noot wher she be womman or goddesse;
But Venus is it, soothly, as I gesse."
And therwithal on kneës doun he fil,
And seyde: "Venus, if it be thy wil
Yow in this gardin thus to transfigure
Bifore me, sorweful, wrecche creature,
Out of this prisoun help that we may scapen.
And if so be my destinee be shapen   250
By eterne word to dyen in prisoun,
Of oure linage have som compassioun,
That is so lowe y-broght by tirannye."
And with that word Arcite gan espye
Wheras this lady romed to and fro.
And with that sighte hir beautee hurte him so,

walked to and fro in the chamber
and complained to himself of his woe.
Often he said, "Alas!" that he was born.
It so happened, by chance or luck,
that through a window (thick with many an iron bar
as large and squared as any beam)
he cast his eye on Emily.
Therewith he paled and cried out, "Ah!"
as though he had been stung to the heart.
At that cry Arcite at once jumped up
and said, "My cousin, what ails you?
You are so pale and deathlike to look at.
Why did you cry out? Who has done you wrong?
For the love of God, resign yourself in all patience to
our prison, for it may not be otherwise;
Fortune has given us this adversity.
Some unfavorable aspect or disposition
of Saturn, through some arrangement of the heavenly bodies,
has bestowed this on us; it would have been so even if we
    had taken oath to do the opposite.
The heavens stood thus when we were born;
we must endure it: this is the brief, plain truth."

    Palamon answered, "In fact, cousin, in this opinion of
what is wrong you are harboring vain imaginings.
It was not this prison that made me cry out,
but I was hurt just now through my eyes and
to my heart—the hurt will be my destruction.
The beauty of the lady whom I see
wandering yonder in the garden
is the cause of all my cries and my woe.
I do not known whether she is a woman or a goddess,
but my guess is that she is in truth Venus."
With that he fell down on his knees
and said, "Venus, if it be your will
thus to take this shape upon yourself in this garden
before me, sorrowful, wretched creature,
then help us to escape from this prison.
And if it be that my destiny is fashioned,
by eternal decree, to die in prison,
have some compassion on our family,
which is brought so low by tyranny."
At that word Arcite espied
where that lady was wandering to and fro,
and at the sight her beauty touched him so

That, if that Palamon was wounded sore,
Arcite is hurt as muche as he, or more.
And with a sigh he seyde pitously:
"The fresshe beautee sleeth me sodeynly   260
Of hir that rometh in the yonder place;
And, but I have hir mercy and hir grace,
That I may seen hir atte leeste weye,
I nam but deed; ther nis namore to seye."

This Palamon, whan he tho wordes herde,
Dispitously he loked, and answerde:
"Whether seistow this in ernest or in pley?"

"Nay," quod Arcite, "in ernest, by my fey!
God help me so, me list ful yvele pleye."

This Palamon gan knitte his browes tweye: 270
"It nere," quod he, "to thee no greet honour
For to be fals, ne for to be traytour
To me, that am thy cosin and thy brother
Y-sworn ful depe, and ech of us til other,
That nevere, for to dyen in the peyne,
Til that the deeth departe shal us tweyne,
Neither of us in love to hindre other,
Ne in non other cas, my leve brother;
But that thou sholdest trewely forthren me
In every cas, as I shal forthren thee: 280
This was thyn ooth, and myn also, certeyn;
I wot right wel, thou darst it nat withseyn.
Thus artow of my counseil, out of doute.
And now thou woldest falsly been aboute
To love my lady, whom I love and serve,
And evere shal, til that myn herte sterve.
Nay, certes, fals Arcite, thou shalt nat so.
I loved hir first, and tolde thee my wo
As to my counseil, and my brother sworn
To forthre me, as I have told biforn.   290
For which thou art y-bounden as a knight
To helpen me, if it lay in thy might,
Or elles artow fals, I dar wel seyn."

This Arcite ful proudly spak ageyn,
"Thou shalt," quod he, "be rather fals than I;
And thou art fals, I telle thee utterly;
For *par amour* I loved hir first er thow.
What wiltow seyn? thou wistest nat yet now
Whether she be a womman or goddesse!
Thyn is affeccioun of holinesse,   300

that, if Palamon was sorely wounded,
Arcite was hurt as much or more.
With a sigh he said pitiably,
"The lively beauty of her who wanders in that
place yonder works sudden death upon me;
unless I have mercy and favor from her,
so that I may at least see her,
I am but dead; there is no more to say."

Palamon, hearing these words,
gave an angry look and answered,
"Do you say this in earnest or as a joke?"

"No," said Arcite, "in earnest, on my honor!
God help me, I have little desire to joke."

Palamon knitted his brows;
"It would not," he said, "be any great honor for you
to be false, or to be a traitor
to me, who am your cousin and your sworn brother,
bound most solemnly by oath (as each of us is to the other)
to the pact that never—even under pain of torture to death,
and never until death shall part us two—
shall either of us hinder the other in love,
or in any other case, my dear brother.
Rather that you should faithfully help me
in every situation, and that I should help you:
this was your oath, and mine, too, in certainty.
I know quite well that you dare not deny this.
Thus, without a doubt, you belong to my side.
And now you would treacherously plan
to love my lady, whom I love and serve,
and ever shall do, until my heart perishes.
Now, false Arcite, indeed you shall not do so.
I loved her first and told my sorrow to you
as to my helper and my brother, sworn
to aid me, as I said before.
For which cause you are bound as a knight
to help me, if it lies in your power.
Otherwise you are false: I dare to say it."

Arcite replied, in all his pride,
"You will be false sooner than I;
and you *are* false: I tell you straight out;
for, before you, I loved her first as a woman.
What can you say? Even now you don't know
whether she is a woman or a goddess!
Your emotion pertains to religion;

And myn is love, as to a creature;
For which I tolde thee myn aventure
As to my cosin, and my brother sworn.
I pose, that thou lovedest hir biforn;
Wostow nat wel the olde clerkes sawe,
That 'who shal yeve a lover any lawe?'
Love is a gretter lawe, by my pan,
Than may be yeve to any erthely man.
And therefore positif lawe and swich decree
Is broken al-day for love, in ech degree.   310
A man moot nedes love, maugree his heed.
He may nat fleen it, thogh he sholde be deed,
Al be she mayde, or widwe, or elles wyf.
And eek it is nat lykly, al thy lyf,
To stonden in hir grace; namore shal I;
For wel thou woost thyselven, verraily,
That thou and I be dampned to prisoun
Perpetuelly; us gayneth no rausoun.
We stryve as dide the houndes for the boon:
They foughte al day, and yet hir part was noon;   320
Ther cam a kyte, whyl that they were so wrothe,
And bar awey the boon bitwixe hem bothe.
And therfore, at the kinges court, my brother,
Ech man for himself, ther is non other.
Love if thee list; for I love and ay shal;
And soothly, leve brother, this is al.
Here in this prisoun mote we endure,
And everich of us take his aventure."
  Greet was the stryf and long bitwixe hem tweye,
If that I hadde leyser for to seye;   330
But to th'effect. It happed on a day,
(To telle it yow as shortly as I may)
A worthy duk that highte Perotheus,
That felawe was unto duk Theseus
Sin thilke day that they were children lyte,
Was come to Athenes, his felawe to visyte,
And for to pleye, as he was wont to do.
For in this world he loved no man so:
And he loved him als tendrely ageyn.
So wel they loved, as olde bokes seyn,   340
That whan that oon was deed, sothly to telle,
His felawe wente and soghte him doun in helle;
But of that story list me nat to wryte.
  Duk Perotheus loved well Arcite,

mine is love of a created being.
For which reason I told you what had happened to me—
I told it to you as my cousin and my sworn brother.
Even if I suppose that you loved her first,
don't you know the old proverb of learned men,
'All's fair in love'?
On my head I swear, love is a greater law
than any other that may be given to any earthly man.
Therefore man-made law, and decrees like that,
are broken every day for love, among all classes of men.
A man must needs love, in spite of himself.
He may not flee love, even if he dies for not doing it,
whether his object is maid, or widow, or wife.
Besides, it is not likely that at any time in your life
you will be in her grace, and no more shall I.
For well you yourself know, in fact,
that you and I are condemned to prison
for ever; no ransom will recover us.
We vie like dogs fighting for the bone:
they fought all day, and yet had no part of it;
while they were raging, a kite came
and bore off the bone from between the two of them.
Therefore, at the king's court, my brother, it is
every man for himself; there's no other way.
Love if you like; for I love her and ever shall do so,
and truthfully, dear brother, that's all.
We must endure this prison here,
and each of us must take his chance."
    The strife between the two of them was great and lasting,
as I could describe if I had leisure;
but on to the outcome: it happened one day
(to tell it to you as briefly as I can)
that a valiant duke who was named Pirithous,
and who had been a friend of Duke Theseus
since the day they had been little children,
had come to Athens to visit his friend
and enjoy himself, as he was accustomed to do;
for he loved no other man in the world as much,
and Theseus, in turn, loved him just as strongly.
They loved each other so well, as ancient books say,
that when one of them was dead, to tell the truth
his friend went to look for him in hell—
but I don't want to write about that story.
    Duke Pirithous held Arcite in high esteem

And hadde him knowe at Thebes yeer by yere;
And fynally, at requeste and preyere
Of Perotheus, withouten any raunsoun,
Duk Theseus him leet out of prisoun,
Freely to goon, wher that him liste overal,
In swich a gyse as I you tellen shal.   350
This was the forward, pleynly for t'endyte,
Bitwixen Theseus and him Arcite:
That if so were that Arcite were y-founde
Ever in his lyf, by day or night, o stounde
In any contree of this Theseus,
And he were caught, it was acorded thus,
That with a swerd he sholde lese his heed;
Ther nas non other remedye ne reed,
But taketh his leve, and homward he him spedde;
Let him be war, his nekke lyth to wedde!   360
    How greet a sorwe suffreth now Arcite!
The deeth he feleth thurgh his herte smyte;
He wepeth, wayleth, cryeth pitously;
To sleen himself he wayteth prively.
He seyde, "Allas that day that I was born!
Now is my prison worse than biforn;
Now is me shape eternally to dwelle
Noght in purgatorie, but in helle.
Allas! that evere knew I Perotheus!
For elles hadde I dwelled with Theseus   370
Y-fetered in his prisoun evermo.
Than hadde I been in blisse, and nat in wo.
Only the sighte of hir, whom that I serve,
Though that I never hir grace may deserve,
Wolde han suffised right ynough for me.
O dere cosin Palamon," quod he,
"Thyn is the victorie of this aventure,
Ful blisfully in prison maistow dure;
In prison? certes nay, but in paradys!
Wel hath fortune y-turned thee the dys,   380
That hast the sighte of hir, and I th'absence.
For possible is, sin thou hast hire presence,
And art a knight, a worthy and an able,
That by som cas, sin fortune is chaungeable,
Thou mayst to thy desyr sometime atteyne.
But I, that am exyled, and bareyne
Of alle grace, and in so greet despeir,
That ther nis erthe, water, fyr, ne eir,

and had known him at Thebes for many years.
Finally, at the request and supplication
of Pirithous, Duke Theseus let Arcite
out of prison, without any ransom,
to go freely anywhere that he pleased,
subject to such a special arrangement as I shall describe.
   This was the agreement, to relate plainly,
between Theseus and Arcite:
if it happened that Arcite were found
ever in his life—for a single hour by day or by night—
within any country belonging to Theseus,
and if Arcite were then caught, it was agreed
that he should lose his head by the sword.
There was no other remedy or plan,
except to take his leave and hurry homeward.
Let him beware; his head is in pawn!
   What great sorrow Arcite now suffered!
He felt death smiting his heart.
He wept, he wailed, he cried out pitiably;
he sought occasion to kill himself secretly.
He said, "Alas the day that I was born!
Now my prison is worse than before;
now I am destined to dwell eternally,
not in Purgatory, but in Hell.
Alas, that I ever knew Pirithous!
Otherwise I would have stayed with Theseus,
fettered in his prison evermore.
Then I would have been in bliss, and not in woe.
Just the sight of her whom I serve,
even though I might never deserve her favor,
would have been quite enough for me.
Oh, dear cousin Palamon," he said,
"the victory is yours in this adventure;
most happily you may stay in prison.
In prison? Indeed, no, but in Paradise!
Fortune has well set the dice for you,
who have sight of Emily, while I am absent from her.
For it is possible—since you are near her,
and are a valiant and able knight—
that by some chance, since Fortune is changeable,
you may some time attain your desire.
But I, that am exiled and out
of all favor, and am in such great despair
that there is neither earth, water, fire, nor air,

Ne creature, that of hem maked is,
That may me helpe or doon confort in this:　　390
Wel oughte I sterve in wanhope and distresse;
Farwel my lyf, my lust, and my gladnesse!
　Allas, why pleynen folk so in commune
Of purveyaunce of God, or of Fortune,
That yeveth hem ful ofte in many a gyse
Wel bettre than they can hemself devyse?
Som man desyreth for to han richesse,
That cause is of his mordre or greet siknesse.
And som man wolde out of his prison fayn,
That in his hous is of his meynee slayn.　　400
Infinite harmes been in this matere;
We witen nat what thing we preyen here.
We faren as he that dronke is as a mous;
A dronke man wot wel he hath an hous,
But he noot which the righte wey is thider;
And to a dronke man the wey is slider.
And certes, in this world so faren we;
We seken faste after felicitee,
But we goon wrong ful often, trewely.
Thus may we seyen alle, and namely I,　　410
That wende and hadde a greet opinioun,
That, if I mighte escapen from prisoun,
Than hadde I been in joye and perfit hele,
Ther now I am exyled fro my wele.
Sin that I may nat seen yow, Emelye,
I nam but deed; ther nis no remedye."
　Upon that other syde Palamon,
Whan that he wiste Arcite was agon,
Swich sorwe he maketh that the grete tour
Resouneth of his youling and clamour.　　420
The pure fettres on his shines grete
Weren of his bittre salte teres wete.
"Allas!" quod he, "Arcita, cosin myn,
Of al oure stryf, God woot, the fruyt is thyn.
Thow walkest now in Thebes at thy large,
And of my wo thou yevest litel charge.
Thou mayst, sin thou hast wisdom and manhede,
Assemblen alle the folk of oure kinrede,
And make a werre so sharp on this citee
That by som aventure, or som tretee,　　430
Thou mayst have hir to lady and to wyf,
For whom that I moste nedes lese my lyf.

nor creature made from them,
that can help or comfort me in this affair—
I ought indeed to perish in hopelessness and distress.
Farewell my life, my desire, and my joy!
    Alas, why do people so commonly complain
over God's providence, or over Fortune,
which often gives them, in many a fashion,
something much better than they themselves can devise?
One man desires to have wealth, which becomes
the cause of his being murdered or greatly diseased.
Another man would willingly get out of his prison,
who in his home will be slain by one of his household.
There are infinite evils under this heading;
we do not know what we pray for in this connection;
we turn out to be like the man who is drunk as a mouse:
a drunken man knows that he has a house,
but he does not know which is the right way to it;
and for a drunken man any path is slippery.
Certainly we all prosper in this same way in the world:
we continually seek felicity,
but, truly, we often go far astray.
We may all say so, and chiefly may I,
who imagined and was perfectly convinced
that, if I might have escaped from prison,
then I would have been in joy and perfect satisfaction
in the situation where I am now exiled from my happiness.
Since I may not see you, Emily,
I am as good as dead; there is no help for it."
    On the other hand, Palamon,
having learned that Arcite was gone,
made such lamentation that the great tower
echoed with his howls and clamor.
The very fetters on his powerful shins
were wet with his bitter, salt tears.
"Alas!" he said, "Arcite, my cousin,
God knows you have the best of our quarrel.
You now walk at liberty in Thebes,
and you take small account of my sorrow.
Since you have shrewdness and valor, you can
assemble all our kindred
and make so sharp an attack on this city
that, by some chance or some treaty,
you may have for lady and for wife her
for whom I must needs lose my life.

For, as by wey of possibilitee,
Sith thou art at thy large, of prison free,
And art a lord, greet is thyn avauntage,
More than is myn, that sterve here in a cage.
For I mot wepe and wayle, whyl I live,
With al the wo that prison may me yive,
And eek with peyne that love me yiveth also,
That doubleth al my torment and my wo." 440
Therwith the fyr of jelousye up-sterte
Withinne his brest, and hente him by the herte
So woodly, that he lyk was to biholde
The box-tree, or the asshen dede and colde.
Thanne seyde he, "O cruel goddes, that governe
This world with binding of your word eterne,
And wryten in the table of athamaunt
Youre parlement, and youre eterne graunt,
What is mankinde more unto yow holde
Than is the sheep that rouketh in the folde? 450
For slayn is man right as another best,
And dwelleth eek in prison and arest,
And hath siknesse, and greet adversitee,
And ofte tymes giltelees, pardee!
    "What governaunce is in this prescience,
That giltelees tormenteth innocence?
And yet encreseth this al my penaunce,
That man is bounden to his observaunce,
For Goddes sake, to letten of his wille,
Ther as a beest may al his lust fulfille. 460
And whan a beest is deed, he hath no peyne;
But man after his deeth moot wepe and pleyne,
Though in this world he have care and wo:
Withouten doute it may stonden so.
Th' answere of this I lete to divynis,
But wel I woot, that in this world gret pyne is.
Allas! I see a serpent or a theef,
That many a trewe man hath doon mescheef,
Goon at his large, and wher him list may turne.
But I mot been in prison thurgh Saturne, 470
And eek thurgh Juno, jalous and eek wood,
That hath destroyed wel ny al the blood
Of Thebes, with his waste walles wyde.
And Venus sleeth me on that other syde
For jelousye, and fere of him Arcite."
    Now wol I stinte of Palamon a lyte,

In terms of what is possible
(since you are at large, freed from prison,
and are a ruler), your chance of success is great—
greater than I have, who perish here in a cage.
I must weep and wail as long as I live,
with all the woe that prison can give me
and, also, the pain which love, too, gives me,
and which doubles all my torment and sorrow."
With that the fire of jealousy leaped up
within his breast and caught his heart
so madly that, to look at, he was like
the white boxtree or the ashes that are dead and cold.
Then he said, "Oh, cruel gods, who govern
this world by the constraint of your eternal decree
and inscribe upon a tablet of adamant
your decision and eternally unchanging allotment,
in what way is mankind more esteemed by you
than is the sheep that cowers in the fold?
For man is slain like any other beast,
and also remains in prison and detention,
and suffers sickness and other great adversity;
often, in fact, these things happen to a guiltless man!
How much reason is in this divine foreknowledge
that torments innocence, all guiltless?
And yet another point increases my suffering:
that man is bound to his moral duty,
so as to restrain his own desire for the sake of God,
where a beast may fulfill all its desire.
And when an animal is dead, it feels no more pain;
but man must weep and sorrow after his death,
even though he has had care and woe on earth:
beyond doubt, this is the way it all may be.
I leave the final question to the theologians,
but well I know there is great suffering in this world.
Alas, I see a serpent or a thief,
who has done mischief to many a true man,
allowed to go at large; he may go where he pleases.
But I must stay in prison, by the will of Saturn*
and also of Juno,* the jealous and wrathful;
she has destroyed nearly all the royal blood
of Thebes, with its wide walls laid waste.
And Venus slays me on the other hand
for jealousy and fear of Arcite."
Now I wish to stop talking about Palamon for a while

And lete him in his prison stille dwelle,
And of Arcita forth I wol yow telle.

The somer passeth, and the nightes longe
Encresen double wyse the peynes stronge   480
Bothe of the lovere and the prisoner.
I noot which hath the wofuller mester.
For, shortly for to seyn, this Palamoun
Perpetuelly is dampned to prisoun,
In cheynes and in fettres to ben deed;
And Arcite is exyled upon his heed
For evermo, as out of that contree,
Ne nevere mo he shal his lady see.

Yow loveres axe I now this questioun,
Who hath the worse, Arcite or Palamoun?   490
That oon may seen his lady day by day,
But in prison he moot dwelle alway.
That other wher him list may ryde or go,
But seen his lady shal he nevere mo.
Now demeth as yow liste, ye that can,
For I wol telle forth as I bigan.

II

Whan that Arcite to Thebes comen was,
Ful ofte a day he swelte and seyde "allas,"
For seen his lady shal he never-mo.
And shortly to concluden al his wo,   500
So muche sorwe had never creature
That is, or shal, whyl that the world may dure.
His sleep, his mete, his drink is him biraft,
That lene he wex, and drye as is a shaft.
His eyen holwe, and grisly to biholde;
His hewe falwe, and pale as asshen colde,
And solitarie he was, and ever allone,
And wailling al the night, making his mone.
And if he herde song or instrument,
Then wolde he wepe, he mighte nat be stent;   510
So feble eek were his spirits, and so lowe,
And chaunged so, that no man coude knowe
His speche nor his vois, though men it herde.
And in his gere, for al the world he ferde
Nat oonly lyk the loveres maladye
Of Hereos, but rather lyk manye

and leave him dwelling quietly in his prison;
I want to tell you further of Arcite.
  The summer passed, and the long nights
increased with doubled strength the extreme tortures
of both the lover and the prisoner.
I don't know which one had the more sorrowful lot.
To put it briefly, Palamon
is condemned forever to prison,
to die in chains and fetters;
and Arcite is exiled, on pain of death,
from that country forever;
and he is supposed nevermore to see his lady.
  I ask this question of you lovers:
which has the worse part, Arcite or Palamon?
The one may see his lady daily,
but always has to stay in prison.
The other may ride or walk wherever he pleases,
but is never supposed to see his lady again.
Now decide as you like—you who can—
and I shall go on narrating as I began.

II

  When Arcite had come to Thebes
he swooned and said, "Alas" many times a day,
for he was nevermore to see his lady.
To sum up his woe briefly,
so much sorrow never came to any other created being
which is or shall be as long as the world endures.
His sleep, his food, his drink were banished from him
so that he grew lean and dry as the shaft of a spear.
His eyes were hollow and frightening to look at;
his complexion was sallow and pale as dead ashes.
He was given to solitude and ever alone,
and wailing all night as he uttered his complaint.
If he heard song, or an instrument being played,
he would weep so that he could not be stopped.
Also his spirits were so feeble, low,
and changed that no one could recognize
his speech or his voice, even if one were listening to it.
In his moodiness he behaved for all the world
not only like one afflicted with the lovers' malady
called "hereos,"* but also rather more as having the mania

Engendred of humour malencolyk,
Biforen, in his celle fantastyk.
And shortly, turned was al up-so-doun
Bothe habit and eek disposicioun   520
Of him, this woful lovere daun Arcite.
   What sholde I al-day of his wo endyte?
Whan he endured hadde a yeer or two
This cruel torment, and this peyne and wo,
At Thebes, in his contree, as I seyde,
Upon a night in sleep as he him leyde,
Him thoughte how that the winged god Mercurie
Biforn him stood and bad him to be murye.
His slepy yerde in hond he bar uprighte;
An hat he werede upon his heres brighte.   530
Arrayed was this god (as he took keep)
As he was whan that Argus took his sleep;
And seyde him thus: "To Atthenes shaltou wende;
Ther is thee shapen of thy wo an ende."
And with that word Arcite wook and sterte.
"Now trewely, how sore that me smerte,"
Quod he, "To Atthenes right now wol I fare;
Ne for the drede of deeth shal I nat spare
To see my lady, that I love and serve;
In hir presence I recche nat to sterve."   540
   And with that word he caughte a greet mirour,
And saugh that chaunged was al his colour,
And saugh his visage al in another kinde.
And right anoon it ran him in his minde,
That, sith his face was so disfigured
Of maladye, the which he hadde endured,
He mighte wel, if that he bar him lowe,
Live in Athenes evermore unknowe,
And seen his lady wel ny day by day.
And right anon he chaunged his array,   550
And cladde him as a povre laborer,
And al allone, save oonly a squyer,
That knew his privetee and al his cas,
Which was disgysed povrely, as he was,
To Atthenes is he goon the nexte way.
And to the court he wente upon a day,
And at the gate he profreth his servyse,
To drugge and drawe, what so men wol devyse.
And shortly of this matere for to seyn,
He fil in office with a chamberleyn,   560

caused by the humor of melancholy
in the front cell of his brain, where fantasy resides.
Briefly, both the habits and the state of mind
of this woeful lover, Lord Arcite,
were turned completely upside down.

Why should I continually relate his woe?
When for a year or two he had endured
this cruel torment and this pain and woe,
then (in Thebes, in his country, as I said)
one night as he was lying asleep
it seemed to him that the winged god Mercury
stood before him and told him to be of good cheer.
Mercury held his sleep-inducing staff upright in his hand
and wore a hat upon his shining hair.
This god was dressed (as Arcite noticed)
as he had been when Argus* had his slumber.
He said to Arcite, "You are to go to Athens;
the end of your woe is destined for you there."
At those words Arcite awoke and jumped up.
"Now truly, no matter how much I suffer for it,"
he said, "I shall go to Athens at once,
and I shall not hesitate for dread of death
to see my lady, whom I love and serve.
In her presence I care not if I die."

With these words he caught up a large mirror
and saw that his complexion was completely changed
and that his face looked entirely different.
Instantly it came into his mind
that, since his face was so disfigured
with the sickness which he had undergone,
he might well, if he bore himself humbly,
live unknown in Athens ever after
and see his lady nearly every day.
Immediately he changed his clothes
and dressed himself as a poor laborer.
All alone, except for a squire
who knew his secret and his whole situation
and who was disguised, like Arcite, as a poor man,
he traveled the shortest way to Athens.
He went one day to the court
and at the gate offered his services
to fetch and carry at whatever kind of labor anyone devised.
To speak shortly of this matter,
he got employment with a chamberlain

The which that dwelling was with Emelye;
For he was wys, and coude soon aspye
Of every servaunt, which that serveth here.
Wel coude he hewen wode, and water bere,
For he was yong and mighty for the nones,
And therto he was strong and big of bones
To doon that any wight can him devyse.
A yeer or two he was in this servyse,
Page of the chambre of Emelye the brighte;
And "Philostrate" he seide that he highte.   570
But half so wel biloved a man as he
Ne was ther never in court, of his degree;
He was so gentil of condicioun,
That thurghout al the court was his renoun.
They seyden that it were a charitee
That Theseus wolde enhauncen his degree,
And putten him in worshipful servyse,
Ther as he mighte his vertu excercyse.
And thus, with-inne a whyle, his name is spronge,
Bothe of his dedes and his goode tonge,   580
That Theseus hath taken him so neer
That of his chambre he made him a squyer,
And yaf him gold to mayntene his degree;
And eek men broghte him out of his contree
From yeer to yeer, ful prively, his rente;
But honestly and slyly he it spente,
That no man wondred how that he it hadde.
And three yeer in this wyse his lyf he ladde,
And bar him, so in pees and eek in werre,
Ther was no man that Theseus hath derre.   590
And in this blisse lete I now Arcite,
And speke I wol of Palamon a lyte.

   In derknesse and horrible and strong prisoun
This seven yeer hath seten Palamoun,
Forpyned, what for wo and for distresse;
Who feleth double soor and hevinesse
But Palamon that love destreyneth so,
That wood out of his wit he gooth for wo?
And eek therto he is a prisoner
Perpetuelly, noght oonly for a yeer.   600
Who coude ryme in English proprely
His martirdom? for sothe, it am nat I;
Therefore I passe as lightly as I may.
   It fel that in the seventhe yeer, in May,

who attended upon Emily,
for Arcite was shrewd and could soon find out
which of all the servants served her.
He could hew wood and carry water handily,
for he was young and really strong,
and also big and powerfully boned
enough to do whatever anyone could devise for him.
He was in this service for a year or two
as page of the chamber of lovely Emily;
he said that he was called Philostrato.
There was never a man of his rank who was
half so well liked in the court:
he was so gentle in his manners
that his fame ran throughout the court.
They said it would be a good deed
for Theseus to raise his rank
and put him into honorable service
where he might exercise his ability.
Thus in a little while his reputation,
both for his deeds and his speech, had spread
to the point that Theseus took him so near him
as to make him a squire of his chamber
and gave him money to maintain his station.
Also there was brought to him from his country
(yearly, and very privately) his income;
but he spent it suitably and discreetly
so that no one wondered how he got it.
He led his life in this fashion for three years
and conducted himself in peace—and in war, too—
so that Theseus held no one else dearer.
And I now leave Arcite in this bliss
and will speak a little of Palamon.

   In darkness, in the horror of a strong prison,
Palamon had sat these seven years,
wasted away, what with sorrow and distress.
Who but Palamon felt twofold sorrow and grief?
Love afflicted him so
that for grief he was completely out of his mind.
And, besides, he was a prisoner
forever, not simply for a year.
Who could properly tell his martyrdom
in English verse? Indeed, I am not the one;
therefore I pass over as lightly as I may.
   It happened in the seventh year that on

The thridde night, (as olde bokes seyn,
That al this storie tellen more pleyn,)
Were it by aventure or destinee
(As, whan a thing is shapen, it shal be)
That, sone after the midnight, Palamoun,
By helping of a freend, brak his prisoun,   610
And fleeth the citee, faste as he may go;
For he had yive his gayler drinke so
Of a clarree, maad of a certeyn wyn,
With nercotikes and opie of Thebes fyn,
That al that night, thogh that men wolde him shake,
The gayler sleep, he mighte nat awake;
And thus he fleeth as faste as ever he may.
The night was short, and faste by the day,
That nedes-cost he moste himselven hyde,
And til a grove, faste ther besyde,   620
With dredeful foot than stalketh Palamoun.
For shortly, this was his opinioun,
That in that grove he wolde him hyde al day,
And in the night than wolde he take his way
To Thebes-ward, his freendes for to preye
On Theseus to helpe him to werreye;
And shortly, outher he wolde lese his lyf,
Or winnen Emelye unto his wyf;
This is th'effect and his entente pleyn.
    Now wol I torne to Arcite ageyn,   630
That litel wiste how ny that was his care,
Til that Fortune had broght him in the snare.
    The bisy larke, messager of day,
Saluëth in hir song the morwe gray;
And fyry Phebus ryseth up so bright,
That al the orient laugheth of the light,
And with his stremes dryeth in the greves
The silver dropes hanging on the leves.
And Arcita, that in the court royal
With Theseus is squyer principal,   640
Is risen, and loketh on the myrie day.
And, for to doon his observaunce to May,
Remembring on the poynt of his desyr,
He on a courser, startlynge as the fyr,
Is riden into the feeldes, him to pleye,
Out of the court, were it a myle or tweye;
And to the grove, of which that I yow tolde,
By aventure, his wey he gan to holde,

the third night of May (as ancient books say,
which tell all this story more fully),
whether it was by chance or destiny
(as, when a thing is fated, it shall be),
Palamon, soon after midnight and
with the help of a friend, broke out of prison
and fled the city as fast as he could go.
He had given his jailer so much to drink
of a spiced, honied potion made of a certain wine
with narcotics and refined opium of Thebes
that all that night, even if the jailer were shaken,
he slept and could not wake up.
And thus Palamon fled as fast as he could.
The night was short and the dawn close by,
when (as need was) he would have to hide.
With fearful footstep, then, Palamon crept
to a grove close by.
Briefly, it was his expectation
that he would hide himself in that grove all day
and then take his way during the night
in the direction of Thebes, in order to ask his friends
to help him make war on Theseus.
To put it in a few words, either he would lose his life
or he would win Emily to wife:
this was his aim and full intention.

Now I shall return to Arcite,
who little knew how near trouble was
until Fortune had brought him into the snare.

The busy lark, the messenger of day,
saluted the bright morning with her song,
and fiery Phoebus rose up so bright
that all the east laughed with his light;
among the branches he dried with his rays
the silver drops hanging on the leaves.
Arcite, who was in the royal court
as chief squire to Theseus,
rose and looked out upon the merry day.
In order to pay his respects to May,
and bringing to mind the object of his longing,
he rode out into the fields on a courser as spirited
as fire in order to amuse himself
outside the court, perhaps a mile or two away.
To the grove that I told you of
he by chance took his way

To maken him a gerland of the greves,
Were it of wodebinde or hawethorn-leves,   650
And loude he song ageyn the sonne shene:
"May, with alle thy floures and thy grene,
Welcome be thou, faire fresshe May,
In hope that I som grene gete may."
And from his courser, with a lusty herte,
Into the grove ful hastily he sterte,
And in a path he rometh up and doun,
Theras, by aventure, this Palamoun
Was in a bush, that no man mighte him see,
For sore afered of his deeth was he.   660
Nothing ne knew he that it was Arcite:
God wot he wolde have trowed it ful lyte.
But sooth is seyd, go sithen many yeres,
That "feeld hath eyen, and the wode hath eres."
It is ful fair a man to bere him evene,
For al-day meteth men at unset stevene.
Ful litel woot Arcite of his felawe,
That was so ny to herknen al his sawe,
For in the bush he sitteth now ful stille.

Whan that Arcite hadde romed al his fille,   670
And songen al the roundel lustily,
Into a studie he fil sodeynly,
As doon thise loveres in hir queynte geres,
Now in the croppe, now doun in the breres,
Now up, now doun, as boket in a welle.
Right as the Friday, soothly for to telle,
Now it shyneth, now it reyneth faste,
Right so can gery Venus overcaste
The hertes of hir folk; right as hir day
Is gereful, right so chaungeth she array.   680
Selde is the Friday al the wowke ylike.

Whan that Arcite had songe, he gan to syke,
And sette him doun withouten any more:
"Alas!" quod he, "that day that I was bore!
How longe, Juno, thurgh thy crueltee,
Woltow werreyen Thebes the citee?
Allas! y-broght is to confusioun
The blood royal of Cadme and Amphioun;
Of Cadmus, which that was the firste man
That Thebes bulte, or first the toun bigan,   690
And of the citee first was crouned king,
Of his linage am I, and his ofspring

to make himself a garland of the branches,
whether they were woodbine or hawthorn,
and he loudly sang this song in the face of the shining sun:
"May, with all your flowers and green—
be welcome, fair, fresh May;
in hope that I may get some green."
And with a happy heart he sprang
from his courser and into the grove,
and walked up and down in a path
where Palamon by chance
was in a bush where no one could see him;
he was terribly afraid that he would be killed.
He had no idea that the intruder was Arcite; God knows
there is small chance that he would have imagined it.
But it has been said truthfully, for many years past,
"The field has eyes and the wood has ears."
It is very fitting for a man to behave coolly,
for one is faced every day with unexpected meetings.
Little did Arcite know of his friend,
who was so near as to hear all that he said,
for Palamon now sat in the bush in complete silence.

When Arcite had had his fill of roaming
and had gaily sung all the roundel,
he suddenly began to brood,
as lovers do, in their curious moods:
sometimes in the treetop, other times in the briars,
now up, now down, like a bucket in a well.
To tell truly, just as on Friday (Venus's day)
it sometimes shines and at other times rains continually,
just so, changeable Venus overcasts
the hearts of her followers; just as her day
is changeable, so she changes her arrangements.
Seldom is Friday like the rest of the week.

When Arcite had sung, he began to sigh
and sat down without further ado.
He said, "Alas, the day that I was born!
How long, Juno, in your cruelty
will you make war on the city of Thebes?
Alas! brought to confusion is
the royal blood of Cadmus* and Amphion—
of Cadmus, who was the first man
to build Thebes, the first to begin it,
and was first crowned king of the city:
I am of his lineage, and am his offspring

By verray ligne, as of the stok royal:
And now I am so caitif and so thral,
That he, that is my mortal enemy,
I serve him as his squyer povrely.
And yet doth Juno me wel more shame,
For I dar noght biknowe myn owne name;
But ther as I was wont to highte Arcite,
Now highte I Philostrate, noght worth a myte.　　　700
Allas! thou felle Mars, allas! Juno,
Thus hath your ire our lynage al fordo,
Save only me, and wrecched Palamoun,
That Theseus martyreth in prisoun.
And over al this, to sleen me outrely,
Love hath his fyry dart so brenningly
Y-stiked thurgh my trewe careful herte,
That shapen was my deeth erst than my sherte.
Ye sleen me with your eyen, Emelye;
Ye been the cause wherefore that I dye.　　　710
Of al the remenant of myn other care
Ne sette I nat the mountaunce of a tare,
So that I coude don aught to youre plesaunce!"
And with that word he fil doun in a traunce
A longe tyme; and after he up-sterte.

This Palamoun, that thoughte that thurgh his herte
He felte a cold swerd sodeynliche glyde,
For ire he quook, no lenger wolde he byde.
And whan that he had herd Arcites tale,
As he were wood, with face deed and pale,　　　720
He sterte him up out of the buskes thikke,
And seyde: "Arcite, false traitour wikke,
Now artow hent, that lovest my lady so,
For whom that I have al this peyne and wo,
And art my blood, and to my counseil sworn,
As I ful ofte have told thee heer-biforn,
And hast by-japed here duk Theseus,
And falsly chaunged hast thy name thus;
I wol be deed, or elles thou shalt dye.
Thou shalt nat love my lady Emelye,　　　730
But I wol love hir only, and namo;
For I am Palamoun, thy mortal fo.
And though that I no wepene have in this place,
But out of prison am astert by grace,
I drede noght that outher thou shalt dye,
Or thou ne shalt nat loven Emelye.

by the true line, being of the royal stock.
And now, I am so wretched and enslaved
that the man who is my mortal enemy
I serve meanly as his squire.
And Juno does me yet more shame,
in that I dare not declare my own name;
whereas I was accustomed to be called Arcite,
I am now called Philostrato, worth nothing.
Alas, cruel Mars, alas, Juno:
thus your wrath has destroyed all our line
except for me, and wretched Palamon,
whom Theseus torments in prison.
And on top of all this, so as to slay me utterly,
Love has so ardently thrust his fiery dart
through my faithful, troubled heart that it seems that my
death was prepared for me before my first clothes were made.
You slay me with your eyes, Emily;
you are the cause of my dying.
On all the rest of my cares
I would not set the worth of one weed,
if I could do anything that would please you!"
At that he fell down in a trance
for a long time; then he got up.

Palamon, who thought that he felt
a cold sword suddenly gliding through his heart,
quaked with wrath; he would wait no longer.
When he had heard what Arcite said,
he jumped from the thick bushes
as if he were mad, with a face of deadly pallor;
he said, "Arcite, false and wicked traitor,
now you are caught, you who so love my lady
(for whom I have all this pain and sorrow),
you who are of my blood, and are sworn to be on my side
(as I have often told you before this),
you who have deceived Duke Theseus here
and thus falsely changed your name,
either you shall die, or I will.
You shall not love my lady Emily,
for only I, and no others, shall love her.
I am Palamon, your mortal foe.
Though I have no weapon here,
but have just escaped by luck from prison,
let there be no fear: either you shall die
or you shall not love Emily.

Chees which thou wolt for thou shalt nat asterte."
  This Arcite, with ful despitous herte,
Whan he him knew, and hadde his tale herd,
As fiers as leoun pulled out a swerd,   740
And seyde thus: "by God that sit above,
Nere it that thou are sik, and wood for love,
And eek that thou no wepne hast in this place,
Thou sholdest never out of this grove pace,
That thou ne sholdest dyen of myn hond.
For I defye the seurtee and the bond
Which that thou seyst that I have maad to thee.
What, verray fool, think wel that love is free,
And I wol love hir, maugre al thy might!
But, for as muche thou art a worthy knight,   750
And wilnest to darreyne hir by batayle,
Have heer my trouthe, to-morwe I wol nat fayl
Withoute witing of any other wight,
That here I wol be founden as a knight,
And bringen harneys right ynough for thee;
And chees the beste, and leef the worste for me
And mete and drinke this night wol I bringe
Ynough for thee, and clothes for thy beddinge.
And, if so be that thou my lady winne,
And slee me in this wode ther I am inne,   760
Thou mayst wel have thy lady, as for me."
This Palamon answerd, "I graunte it thee."
And thus they been departed til a-morwe,
Whan ech of hem had leyd his feith to borwe.
  O Cupide, out of alle charitee!
O regne, that wolt no felawe have with thee!
Ful sooth is seyd that love ne lordshipe
Wol noght, his thankes, have no felaweshipe;
Wel finden that Arcite and Palamoun.
Arcite is riden anon unto the toun,   770
And on the morwe, er it were dayes light,
Ful prively two harneys hath he dight,
Bothe suffisaunt and mete to darreyne
The bataille in the feeld bitwix hem tweyne.
And on his hors, allone as he was born,
He carieth al the harneys him biforn;
And in the grove, at tyme and place y-set,
This Arcite and this Palamon ben met.
Tho chaungen gan the colour in hir face;
Right as the hunter in the regne of Trace,   780

Choose which you want, for you shall not escape."
  With scornful heart, Arcite,
when he recognized Palamon and had heard what he said,
pulled out a sword; he was fierce as a lion.
He said, "By God who sits above,
if it were not that you are sick and crazed through love,
and also that you have no weapon here,
you should never go from this grove
without dying at my hand.
I spurn the covenant and the bond
which you say I have entered into with you.
Why, you absolute fool, recall that love is free,
and that I will love her, in spite of all you can do!
Yet, as you are a valiant knight,
and desire to decide the claim to her by battle,
take here my promise: tomorrow, without anyone's
knowing of it, I shall not fail
to be found here, on my faith as a knight,
and to bring quite enough armor for you;
you choose the better and leave the worse for me.
Tonight I shall bring food and drink
enough for you, and bedding;
if it be that you win my lady
and kill me in this wood where I am now,
you are welcome to your lady, for all of me."
Palamon answered, "I agree to this plan."
Thus they parted until the next day,
for which time each had faithfully pledged himself.
  O Cupid, beyond all charity!
O sovereignty that wants none equal with yourself!
It is said most truly that neither love nor rule
will willingly endure a shared role.
Arcite and Palamon indeed discovered this.
Arcite then rode to town,
and before daylight the next day
he very secretly provided two suits of armor,
both of them sufficient and suitable for deciding
the lonely battle between them.
On his horse, utterly alone,
he carried all the armor before him;
in the thicket, at the set time and place,
Arcite and Palamon were met.
Then their complexions began to change color;
just as the Thracian hunter, who stands at the gap with a

That stondeth at the gappe with a spere,
Whan hunted is the leoun or the bere,
And hereth him come russhing in the greves,
And breketh bothe bowes and the leves,
And thinketh, "heer cometh my mortel enemy,
Withoute faile, he moot be deed, or I;
For outher I mot sleen him at the gappe,
Or he mot sleen me, if that me mishappe":
So ferden they, in chaunging of hir hewe,
As fer as everich of hem other knewe.   790
Ther nas no good day, ne no saluing;
But streight, withouten word or rehersing,
Everich of hem halp for to armen other,
As freendly as he were his owne brother;
And after that, with sharpe speres stronge
They foynen ech at other wonder longe.
Thou mightest wene that this Palamoun
In his fighting were a wood leoun,
And as a cruel tygre was Arcite:
As wilde bores gonne they to smyte,   800
That frothen whyte as foom for ire wood.
Up to the ancle foghte they in hir blood.
And in this wyse I lete hem fighting dwelle;
And forth I wol of Theseus yow telle.
     The destinee, ministre general,
That executeth in the world over-al
The purveyaunce, that God hath seyn biforn,
So strong it is, that, though the world had sworn
The contrarie of a thing, by ye or nay,
Yet somtyme it shal fallen on a day   810
That falleth nat eft with-inne a thousand yere.
For certeinly, our appetytes here,
Be it of werre, or pees, or hate, or love,
Al is this reuled by the sighte above.
This mene I now by mighty Theseus,
That for to hunten is so desirous,
And namely at the grete hert in May,
That in his bed ther daweth him no day,
That he nis clad, and redy for to ryde
With hunte and horn, and houndes him bisyde.   820
For in his hunting hath he swich delyt,
That it is al his joye and appetyt
To been him-self the grete hertes bane:
For after Mars he serveth now Diane.

spear, when the lion or the bear is being hunted,
and hears the beast come rushing among the branches,
breaking both branches and leaves,
thinks, "Here comes my mortal enemy;
without fail either he or I must die,
for either I must slay him at this gap
or he must kill me, if I do badly";
just so they fared, as their complexions changed
as soon as each recognized the other.
There was no "Good day" or other greeting,
but straightway, without speech or rehearsal of their
agreement, each helped to arm the other,
as friendly as if one were the other's brother.
After that, with sharp, strong spears,
they thrust at each other a very long time.
You might have thought that Palamon
in his fighting was a wrathful lion,
and that Arcite was a cruel tiger;
they smote each other like wild boars
which froth themselves white as foam in their wild wrath.
They fought up to the ankles in their blood.
And I leave them continuing the fight in this manner;
I shall go on to tell about Theseus.

Destiny, the governor general
who executes everywhere in this world
the providence that God has foreseen,
is so strong that, even if the world had sworn,
by yea or nay, the contrary of an event,
still yet one day that event should befall,
though it should not happen again in a thousand years.
For certainly, our desires here below,
be it for war or peace, or hate or love,
are all ruled by the providence above.
I intend all this now in reference to mighty Theseus,
who was so fond of hunting—
especially for the great hart in May—
that no day dawned upon him
when he was not dressed and ready to ride
with hunt and horn, and hounds beside him.
He had such delight in hunting
that all his joy and longing was
to be, himself, the scourge of the great hart;
for, after Mars, he now served Diana the huntress.

Cleer was the day, as I have told er this,
And Theseus, with alle joye and blis,
With his Ipolita, the fayre quene,
And Emelye, clothed al in grene,
On hunting be they riden royally.
And to the grove, that stood ful faste by,   830
In which ther was an hert, as men him tolde,
Duk Theseus the streighte wey hath holde.
And to the launde he rydeth him ful right,
For thider was the hert wont have his flight,
And over a brook, and so forth on his weye.
This duk wol han a cours at him, or tweye,
With houndes, swiche as that him list comaunde.

And whan this duk was come unto the launde,
Under the sonne he loketh, and anon
He was war of Arcite and Palamon,   840
That foughten breme, as it were bores two;
The brighte swerdes wenten to and fro
So hidously, that with the leeste strook
It seemed as it wolde felle an ook;
But what they were, nothing he ne woot.
This duk his courser with his spores smoot,
And at a stert he was bitwix hem two,
And pulled out a swerd and cride, "Ho!
Namore, up peyne of lesing of your heed.
By mighty Mars, he shal anon be deed,   850
That smyteth any strook, that I may seen!
But telleth me what mister men ye been,
That been so hardy for to fighten here
Withouten juge or other officere,
As it were in a listes royally?"
This Palamon answerde hastily
And seyde: "Sire, what nedeth wordes mo?
We have the deeth deserved bothe two.
Two woful wrecches been we, two caytyves,
That been encombred of our owne lyves;   860
And as thou art a rightful lord and juge,
Ne yeve us neither mercy ne refuge,
But slee me first, for seynte charitee;
But slee my felawe eek as wel as me.
Or slee him first; for, though thou knowest it lyte,
This is thy mortal fo, this is Arcite,
That fro thy lond is banished on his heed,
For which he hath deserved to be deed.

The day was clear, as I have said before,
and with joy Theseus,
with his fair queen Hippolyta
and with Emily—all dressed in green—
had ridden royally to the hunt.
He went straight to the grove,
which stood nearby and
in which there was a hart, as he was told.
He rode right to the glade among the trees,
for the hart in his flight was likely to go there,
and then across a brook, and forth on his way.
The duke wanted to have him in chase once or twice
with such dogs as it pleased him to direct.

When the duke had come to the glade,
he squinted below the low-lying sun and
immediately became aware of Arcite and Palamon,
who were fighting as furiously as if they were two boars.
The bright swords went to and fro
so hideously that with the least of their strokes
it seemed as if they would fell an oak.
He had no idea, however, who they were.
The duke struck spurs to his courser
and at a lunge he was between the two of them;
he pulled out a sword and cried "Halt!
No more, on pain of losing your heads!
By mighty Mars, the man shall be instantly dead
who gives another stroke that I can see!
Tell me what kind of men you are
who are so rash as to fight here
without judge or other officer
just as though you were in the lists under royal control?"

Palamon hastily answered,
"Sire, what need is there for further words?
We have both deserved death.
We are two woeful wretches, two captives,
whose lives are an encumbrance to us;
and as you are a just lord and judge,
do not give us mercy or refuge,
but kill me first, for holy charity,
but kill my companion too, as well as me.
Or kill him first; for though you little know it,
this is your mortal enemy; this is Arcite,
who was banished from your land on pain of death,
for which reason he has deserved to die.

For this is he that cam unto thy gate,
And seyde that he highte Philostrate. 870
Thus hath he japed thee ful many a yeer,
And thou hast maked him thy chief squyer:
And this is he that loveth Emelye.
For sith the day is come that I shal dye,
I make pleynly my confessioun,
That I am thilke woful Palamoun,
That hath thy prison broken wikkedly.
I am thy mortal fo, and it am I
That loveth so hote Emelye the brighte,
That I wol dye present in hir sighte. 880
Wherfore I axe deeth and my juwyse;
But slee my felawe in the same wyse,
For both han we deserved to be slayn."

This worthy duk answerde anon agayn,
And seyde, "This is a short conclusioun:
Youre owene mouth, by youre confessioun,
Hath dampned you, and I wol it recorde;
It nedeth noght to pyne yow with the corde.
Ye shal be deed, by mighty Mars the rede!"

The quene anon, for verray wommanhede, 890
Gan for to wepe, and so dide Emelye,
And alle the ladies in the companye.
Gret pitee was it, as it thoughte hem alle,
That evere swich a chaunce sholde falle;
For gentil men they were, of greet estat,
And nothing but for love was this debat;
And sawe hir blody woundes wyde and sore;
And alle crieden bothe lasse and more,
"Have mercy, lord, upon us wommen alle!"
And on hir bare knees adoun they falle, 900
And wolde have kist his feet theras he stood,
Til at the laste aslaked was his mood;
For pitee renneth sone in gentil herte.
And though he first for ire quook and sterte,
He hath considered shortly, in a clause,
The trespas of hem bothe, and eek the cause:
And although that his ire hir gilt accused
Yet in his reson he hem bothe excused;
As thus: he thoghte wel, that every man
Wol helpe himself in love, if that he can, 910
And eek delivere himself out of prisoun;
And eek his herte hadde compassioun

For he is the one that came to your gate
and said his name was Philostrato.
Thus he has deceived you many a year
and you have made him your chief squire;
and this is one who loves Emily.
And since the day has come when I shall die,
I fully make my confession
that I am that same woeful Palamon
who has wickedly broken from your prison.
I am your mortal enemy, and I am one
who loves lovely Emily so ardently
that I wish to die in her sight.
Therefore I ask for my punishment and for death;
but on the same principle kill my companion,
for we have both deserved to be slain."

    The valiant duke answered immediately,
"This is a quick settlement:
by your confession your own mouth
has condemned you, and I will remember it;
there is no need to make you confess by torture.
You shall be slain, by mighty Mars the red!"

    Then for very womanhood the queen
began to weep, and so did Emily
and all the other ladies of the company.
It seemed to all of them a great pity
that such a chance should ever befall;
for the young men were gentle and of high station,
and their quarrel was for nothing but love;
the ladies saw their bloody wounds, great and painful,
and all of the ladies, both least and greatest, cried out,
"Have mercy, lord, upon all us women!"
They fell down on their knees
and would have kissed his feet where he stood,
until at last his anger was slaked,
for pity* soon arises in the gentle heart.
Though at first he quaked and shook with anger,
he gave brief, concise consideration
to the misdeeds of the two, and to the cause of these as
well: and although his anger affirmed their guilt,
he still excused both of them in his reason,
thus: he well considered that every man
will help himself in love, if he can,
and also will escape from prison;
and, besides, his heart took pity

Of wommen, for they wepen ever in oon;
And in his gentil herte he thoghte anoon,
And softe unto himself he seyde: "Fy
Upon a lord that wol have no mercy,
But been a leoun, bothe in word and dede,
To hem that been in repentaunce and drede
As wel as to a proud despitous man
That wol maynteyne that he first bigan!   920
That lord hath litel of discrecioun,
That in swich cas can no divisioun,
But weyeth pryde and humblesse after oon."
And shortly, whan his ire is thus agoon,
He gan to loken up with eyen lighte,
And spak thise same wordes al on highte:
"The god of love, a! *benedicite*,
How mighty and how greet a lord is he!
Ayeins his might ther gayneth none obstacles,
He may be cleped a god for his miracles;   930
For he can maken at his owene gyse
Of everich herte, as that him list devyse.
Lo heer, this Arcite and this Palamoun,
That quitly weren out of my prisoun,
And mighte han lived in Thebes royally,
And witen I am hir mortal enemy,
And that hir deeth lyth in my might also;
And yet hath love, maugree hir eyen two,
Broght hem hider bothe for to dye!
Now loketh, is nat that an heigh folye?   940
Who may been a fool, but if he love?
Bihold, for Goddes sake that sit above,
Se how they blede! be they noght well arrayed?
Thus hath hir lord, the god of love, y-payed
Hir wages and hir fees for hir servyse!
And yet they wenen for to been ful wyse
That serven love, for aught that may bifalle!
But this is yet the beste game of alle,
That she, for whom they han this jolitee,
Can hem therefore as muche thank as me;   950
She woot namore of al this hote fare,
By God, than woot a cokkow or an hare!
But al mot been assayed, hoot and cold;
A man mot been a fool, or yong or old;
I woot it by myself ful yore agoon:
For in my tyme a servant was I oon.

on the women, for they continued to weep.
And in that gentle heart he now considered,
and said silently to himself, "Shame
upon a ruler that will have no mercy
but be a ravening lion, both in word and deed,
to those who are repentant and fearful
as much as to a proud, scornful man
who will persist in the same course of action that he began
with. That ruler has little discernment
who knows no dividing line in such a case,
but weighs pride and humility by one measure."
Shortly, when his anger had thus passed off,
he looked up with cheerful eyes
and pronounced the following in a loud voice:
"The god of love—ah, bless us all—
how great and mighty a ruler he is!
No obstacles withstand his might;
he may be called a god for his miracles,
for according to his own desire he can make
whatever he pleases of every heart.
Look at this Arcite and Palamon here,
who were clean out of my prison
and might have lived as kings in Thebes,
and who know that I am their mortal enemy
and that their death, too, lies within my power;
yet Love, in spite of what they can do, has
brought both of them here to die!
Consider now; isn't that the height of folly?
Who may be a real fool unless he is in love?
For the sake of God who sits above,
see how they bleed! Aren't they in good shape?
Thus their lord, the god of love, has paid
their wages and fees for their service!
And yet those think themselves very wise
who serve love, no matter what may happen!
But the best joke of all is
that the lady for whom they are having this diversion
knows as little to thank them for in it as I do;
she knows no more of these hot-blooded goings-on,
by God, than a cuckoo or a hare does!
But everything has to be tried, hot or cold;
a man must be a fool, either young or old;
I know that from very long ago through my own experience,
for in my time I was one of those servants of Love.

And therfore, sin I knowe of loves peyne,
And woot how sore it can a man distreyne,
As he that hath ben caught ofte in his las,
I yow foryeve al hoolly this trespas,   960
At requeste of the quene that kneleth here,
And eek of Emelye, my suster dere.
And ye shul bothe anon unto me swere,
That nevere mo ye shul my contree dere,
Ne make werre upon me night ne day,
But been my freendes in al that ye may;
I yow foryeve this trespas every del."
And they him swore his axing fayre and wel,
And him of lordshipe and of mercy preyde,
And he hem graunteth grace, and thus he seyde: 970
  "To speke of royal linage and richesse,
Though that she were a quene or a princesse,
Ech of yow bothe is worthy, doutelees,
To wedden whan tyme is, but nathelees
I speke as for my suster Emelye,
For whom ye have this stryf and jalousye.
Ye woot yourself she may not wedden two
At ones, though ye fighten evermo:
That oon of yow, al be him looth or leef,
He moot go pypen in an ivy-leef;   980
This is to seyn, she may nat now han bothe,
Al be ye never so jalouse ne so wrothe.
And for-thy I yow putte in this degree,
That ech of yow shal have his destinee
As him is shape; and herkneth in what wyse;
Lo heere your ende of that I shal devyse.
  My wil is this, for plat conclusioun,
Withouten any replicacioun—
If that yow lyketh, tak it for the beste,
That everich of yow shal gon wher him leste   990
Frely, withouten raunson or daunger;
And this day fifty wykes, fer ne ner,
Everich of you shal bringe an hundred knightes,
Armed for listes up at alle rightes,
Al redy to darreyne hir by bataille.
And this bihote I yow, withouten faille,
Upon my trouthe, and as I am a knight,
That whether of yow bothe that hath might—
This is to seyn, that whether he or thou
May with his hundred, as I spak of now,   1000

Therefore, since I know of the pain of Love,
and realize, as one who has often been caught in his net,
how sorely this pain can constrain a man,
I wholly forgive you this misdeed,
at the request of the queen, who kneels here,
and also of my dear sister, Emily.
You must both swear to me at once
that you will never harm my country,
or make war upon me by night or day,
but be my friends in every matter that you can;
I forgive you every bit of this misdeed."
They swore to him fairly and well what he had asked for
and sued for his patronage and mercy.
He granted them favor and spoke thus:
    "In the matter of royal lineage and wealth,
even if the lady were a queen or princess,
each of you is no doubt worthy
to marry when the time comes, but all the same
I am speaking for my sister Emily,
for whose sake you sustain this conflict and jealousy.
You yourselves know that she may not marry two
at the same time, even if you fight forever:
one of you, whether he likes it or not,
must be left out in the cold;
that is to say, she may not now have you both,
no matter how jealous or angry you are.
Therefore I am placing you in the following position
so that each of you shall have his destiny
as it is shaped for him. Listen to how;
see, here is your solution in terms of what I devise:
    My will is as follows, as a flat conclusion to the matter
without any arguing; if it pleases you, take it willingly:
each of you shall go where he wishes,
freely and without reason or control,
and fifty weeks from this day, neither more nor less,
each of you shall bring here a hundred knights,
armed properly for the lists
and ready to decide the claim to her by battle.
I promise you without fail,
on my faith and as I am a knight,
that whichever of you two has the might—
that is to say, whichever, he or you,
can, with the hundred knights I spoke of,

Sleen his contrarie, or out of listes dryve—
Him shal I yeve Emelya to wyve,
To whom that Fortune yeveth so fair a grace.
The listes shal I maken in this place,
And God so wisly on my soule rewe,
As I shal evene juge been and trewe.
Ye shul non other ende with me maken,
That oon of yow ne shal be deed or taken.
And if yow thinketh this is wel y-sayd,
Seyeth your avys, and holdeth yow apayd.   1010
This is youre ende and youre conclusioun."

    Who loketh lightly now but Palamoun?
Who springeth up for joye but Arcite?
Who couthe telle, or who couthe it endyte,
The joye that is maked in the place
Whan Theseus hath doon so fair a grace?
But doun on knees wente every maner wight,
And thanked him with al hir herte and might,
And namely the Thebans often sythe.
And thus with good hope and with herte blythe   1020
They taken hir leve, and hom-ward gonne they ryde
To Thebes, with his olde walles wyde.

III

    I trowe men wolde deme it necligence.
If I foryete to tellen the dispence
Of Theseus, that goth so bisily
To maken up the listes royally,
That swich a noble theatre as it was,
I dar wel seyn that in this world ther nas.
The circuit a myle was aboute,
Walled of stoon, and diched al withoute.   1030
Round was the shap, in maner of compas,
Ful of degrees, the heighte of sixty pas,
That, whan a man was set on o degree,
He letted nat his felawe for to see.

    Estward ther stood a gate of marbel whyt,
Westward, right swich another in the opposit.
And shortly to concluden, swich a place
Was noon in erthe, as in so litel space;
For in the lond ther nas no crafty man,
That geometrie or ars-metrike can,   1040

kill his opponent or drive him from the lists—
then to him, to whom Fortune gives such fair favor,
I shall give Emily in marriage.
I shall set up the lists in this spot;
and, as God shall have pity on my soul,
I shall be a fair and faithful judge;
you shall not come to terms with me
unless one of you is dead or captured.
If you think this is a good plan,
say so, and consider yourselves well treated.
This is your settlement and decision."
    Who but Palamon now looks happy?
Who but Arcite jumps for joy?
Who could say or sing
the joy that was made in that spot
when Theseus had performed so fair a favor?
Every kind of person present went down on his knees
and thanked him with all his heart and might,
and especially the Thebans thanked him many times.
Thus with good hope and happy heart
they took their leave and began to ride homeward
to Thebes, with its ancient wide walls.

III

    I imagine that it would be considered negligence
if I forgot to tell of the outlay
of Theseus, who went so hard to work
to construct the lists in royal fashion
that there was not, I may well say, anywhere else
in the world such a noble amphitheater as it was.
The distance around it was a mile;
it was walled with stone and provided with a moat on the
outside. The shape was round, an exact circle,
and it was filled with tiered seats, to the height of sixty feet,
so that when a man sat on one tier
he did not keep his neighbor from seeing.
    To the east there stood a gate of white marble;
and to the west just such another opposite it.
To conclude briefly, there was not such another place
in all the earth arranged in so little space.
For in all the land there was no skilled workman
who knew geometry or arithmetic,

Ne purtreyour, ne kerver of images,
That Theseus ne yaf him mete and wages
The theatre for to maken and devyse.
And for to doon his ryte and sacrifyse,
He estward hath, upon the gate above,
In worship of Venus, goddesse of love,
Don make an auter and an oratorie;
And on the gate westward, in memorie
Of Mars, he maked hath right swich another,
That coste largely of gold a fother.   1050
And northward, in a touret on the wal,
Of alabastre whyt and reed coral
An oratorie riche for to see,
In worship of Dyane of chastitee,
Hath Theseus doon wroght in noble wyse.
    But yet hadde I foryeten to devyse
The noble kerving and the portreitures,
The shap, the countenaunce, and the figures,
That weren in thise oratories three.
    First in the temple of Venus maystow see   1060
Wroght on the wal, ful pitous to biholde,
The broken slepes, and the sykes colde;
The sacred teres, and the waymentynge,
The fyry strokes of the desirynge
That Loves servaunts in this lyf enduren;
The othes that hir covenants assuren;
Plesaunce and Hope, Desyr, Foolhardinesse,
Beautee and Youthe, Bauderie, Richesse,
Charmes and Force, Lesinges, Flaterye,
Dispense, Bisynesse, and Jelousye,   1070
That wered of yelwe goldes a gerland,
And a cokkow sitting on hir hand;
Festes, instruments, caroles, daunces,
Lust and Array, and alle the circumstaunces
Of love, whiche that I rekne and rekne shal,
By ordre weren peynted on the wal,
And mo than I can make of mencioun.
For soothly al the mount of Citheroun,
Ther Venus hath hir principal dwellynge,
Was shewed on the wal in portreyynge,   1080
With al the gardin and the lustinesse.
Nat was foryeten the porter Ydelnesse,
Ne Narcisus the faire of yore agon,
Ne yet the folye of king Salamon,

nor any painter or sculptor,
to whom Theseus did not give food and wages
to plan and construct the amphitheater.
For conducting his rites and making his sacrifices
he had an altar and an oratory made
at the east end, above the gate,
in honor of Venus, the goddess of love;
and over the gate to the west, in memory
of Mars, he made just such another,
which cost a generous pile of gold.
To the north, in a turret on the wall,
Theseus caused to be constructed in noble fashion
an oratory, richly adorned,
of white alabaster and red coral,
in worship of chaste Diana.

But I have yet forgotten to describe
the noble sculptures and paintings,
the shape, the appearance, and the markings
of these three oratories.

First, in the temple of Venus you may see
depicted on the wall (and very pitiable to look at)
interrupted slumbers, sad sighs,
devoted tears, and lamentation,
the fiery strokes of desire
which the servants of Love endure in this life;
the pledges that seal their covenants;
Pleasure and Hope, Desire, Foolhardiness,
Beauty and Youth, Bawdry, Riches,
Enchantments and Force, Lies, Flattery,
Extravagance, Anxious Labor, and Jealousy,
who wore a garland of marigolds
and had a cuckoo sitting on her hand;
banquets, musical instruments, carols, dances,
Joy and Adornment, and all the circumstances
of love which I have reckoned and shall reckon up
were painted in order on the wall—
and others more than I can mention.
For in fact all the mountain of Cithaeron,*
where Venus has her principal dwelling,
was portrayed on the wall,
with all its garden and its pleasures.
The porter Idleness* was not forgotten,
nor Narcissus the fair of long ago,
nor yet the folly of King Solomon,

Ne yet the grete strengthe of Hercules—
Th'enchauntements of Medea and Circes—
Ne of Turnus, with the hardy fiers corage,
The riche Cresus, caytif in servage.
Thus may ye seen that wisdom ne richesse,
Beautee ne sleighte, strengthe, ne hardinesse,   1090
Ne may with Venus holde champartye;
For as hir list the world than may she gye,
Lo, alle thise folk so caught were in hir las,
Til they for wo ful ofte seyde "allas!"
Suffyceth heer ensamples oon or two,
And though I coude rekne a thousand mo.

The statue of Venus, glorious for to see,
Was naked fleting in the large see,
And fro the navele doun all covered was
With wawes grene, and brighte as any glas.   1100
A citole in hir right hand hadde she,
And on hir heed, ful semely for to see,
A rose gerland, fresh and wel smellinge;
Above hir heed hir dowves flikeringe.
Biforn hir stood hir sone Cupido,
Upon his shuldres winges hadde he two;
And blind he was, as it is often sene;
A bowe he bar and arwes brighte and kene.

Why sholde I noght as wel eek telle yow al
The portreiture that was upon the wal   1110
Withinne the temple of mighty Mars the rede?
Al peynted was the wal, in lengthe and brede,
Lyk to the estres of the grisly place,
That highte the grete temple of Mars in Trace,
In thilke colde, frosty regioun,
Theras Mars hath his sovereyn mansioun.

First on the wal was peynted a forest,
In which ther dwelleth neither man ne best,
With knotty, knarry, bareyn treës olde
Of stubbes sharpe and hidous to biholde;   1120
In which ther ran a rumbel in a swough,
As though a storm sholde bresten every bough.
And downward from an hille, under a bente,
Ther stood the temple of Mars armipotente,
Wroght al of burned steel, of which the entree
Was long and streit, and gastly for to see.
And therout cam a rage and such a vese,
That it made al the gates for to rese.

the great strength of Hercules,*
the enchantments of Medea* and Circe,
Turnus* with his brave, fierce disposition,
rich Croesus, captive in servitude.
Thus you may see that neither wisdom nor riches,
beauty nor trickery, strength nor boldness
may share power equally with Venus,
for as she wishes she may guide the world.
Behold, all these people were caught in her snare
until for sorrow they often said, "Alas!"
One or two examples suffice here,
although I could reckon up a thousand more.

    The statue of Venus, glorious to behold,
was naked, floating in the sea,
and from the navel down was covered
with green waves, glittering like glass.
She had a stringed instrument in her right hand
and on her head a garland of roses,
handsome, fresh, and fragrant;
above her head her doves were fluttering.
Before her stood her son Cupid;
he had two wings upon his shoulders,
and he was blind, as is often seen;
he carried a bow and shining, keen arrows.

    Why should I not tell you as well of all
the pictures upon the wall
within the temple of mighty Mars the red?
The wall was covered with pictures just as was
the interior of the grisly place
which is called the great temple of Mars in Thrace,
in that cold and frosty region
where Mars has his principal seat.

    First on the wall was depicted a forest
in which dwelled neither man nor beast,
with knotty, gnarled, barren old trees
having splintered stubs of branches, hideous to see.
In it there ran a rumbling sound and a soughing
as though a storm would break every branch.
Down a hill, at the bottom of the slope,
stood the temple of Mars the powerful in arms;
it was made entirely of burnished steel; the entry
was long, narrow and ghastly to look at.
From it came such a blast and rush of wind
that it made all the gates tremble.

The northren light in at the dores shoon,
For windowe on the wal ne was ther noon,   1130
Thurgh which men mighten any light discerne.
The dore was alle of adamant eterne,
Y-clenched overthwart and endelong
With iren tough; and, for to make it strong,
Every piler, the temple to sustene,
Was tonne-greet, of iren bright and shene.
  Ther saugh I first the derke imagining
Of Felonye, and al the compassing;
The cruel Ire, reed as any glede;
The pykepurs, and eek the pale Drede;   1140
The smyler with the knyf under the cloke;
The shepne brenning with the blake smoke;
The treson of the mordring in the bedde;
The open werre, with woundes al bibledde;
Contek, with blody knyf and sharp manace;
Al ful of chirking was that sory place.
The sleere of himself yet saugh I ther;
His herte-blood hath bathed al his heer;
The nayl y-driven in the shode a-night;
The colde Deeth, with mouth gaping upright.   1150
Amiddes of the temple sat Meschaunce,
With disconfort and sory contenaunce.
Yet saugh I Woodnesse laughing in his rage;
Armed Compleint, outhees, and fiers Outrage.
The careyne in the bush, with throte y-corve:
A thousand slayn, and nat of qualm y-storve;
The tiraunt, with the prey by force y-raft;
The toun destroyed, ther was nothing laft.
Yet saugh I brent the shippes hoppesteres;
The hunte strangled with the wilde beres;   1160
The sowe freten the child right in the cradel;
The cook y-scalded, for al his longe ladel.
Noght was foryeten by th'infortune of Marte;
The carter overriden with his carte,
Under the wheel ful lowe he lay adoun.
Ther were also, of Martes divisioun,
The barbour, and the bocher, and the smith,
That forgeth sharpe swerdes on his stith.
And al above, depeynted in a tour,
Saw I Conquest sittinge in greet honour,   1170
With the sharpe swerde over his heed
Hanginge by a sotil twynes threed.

The northern lights shone in at the doors;
there was no window in the wall
through which one could discern any light.
All the doors were of eternal adamant,
clamped together crosswise and lengthwise
with hard iron; and, to make the temple strong,
every pillar supporting the temple
was as big as a cask, and made of bright, glittering iron.

There I first saw the dark plannings
of Treachery, and all the execution of the plan;
cruel Ire, red as a glowing coal;
the pickpurse, and pale Dread;
the smiler with the knife beneath his cloak;
the stable burning with its black smoke;
the treason of the murder in the bed;
open warfare, with wounds covered with gore;
Strife, with bloody knife and sharp menace;
the whole sorry place was full of strident noise.
More, I saw there the suicide
(his heart's blood had soaked his hair);
the nail driven by night into a man's temple; and
cold Death, on his back with his mouth gaping.
In the midst of the temple sat Misfortune
with discouraged and sorry countenance.
I further saw Madness, laughing in his rage;
armed Grievance, Outcry, and fierce Outrage;
the corpse in the bush, with his throat cut;
a thousand slain, not dead of the plague;
the tyrant, with his prey snatched by force; and
the town so destroyed that nothing was left.
I saw further the ships being burned as they danced on the
waves, the hunter strangled by the wild bears,
the sow devouring the child right in the cradle,
the cook scalded in spite of the length of his ladle.
Nothing was forgotten of the ill fortune caused by Mars;
the carter run over by his cart,
beneath the wheel he lay right low.
Also there, of Mars' people, were
the barber-surgeon and the butcher and the smith,
who forges sharp swords on his anvil.
I saw at the top, depicted in a tower,
Conquest sitting in great honor,
with the sharp sword hanging over his head
by a thin thread of twine.

Depeynted was the slaughtre of Julius,
Of grete Nero, and of Antonius;
Al be that thilke tyme they were unborn,
Yet was hir deeth depeynted ther-biforn,
By manasinge of Mars, right by figure;
So was it shewed in that portreiture,
As is depeynted in the sterres above
Who shal be slayn or elles deed for love. 1180
Suffyceth oon ensample in stories olde,
I may not rekne hem alle though I wolde.

The statue of Mars upon a carte stood,
Armed, and loked grim as he were wood;
And over his heed ther shynen two figures
Of sterres, that been cleped in scriptures,
That oon Puella, that other Rubeus.
This god of armes was arrayed thus:
A wolf ther stood biforn him at his feet
With eyen rede, and of a man he eet; 1190
With sotil pencel depeynted was this storie,
In redoutinge of Mars and of his glorie.

Now to the temple of Diane the chaste
As shortly as I can I wol me haste,
To telle yow al the descripcioun.
Depeynted been the walles up and doun
Of hunting and shamefast chastitee.
Ther saugh I how woful Calistopee,
Whan that Diane agreved was with here,
Was turned from a womman til a bere, 1200
And after was she maad the lode-sterre;
Thus was it peynt, I can say yow no ferre;
Hir sone is eek a sterre, as men may see.
Ther saugh I Dane, y-turned til a tree—
I mene nat the goddesse Diane,
But Penneus doughter, which that highte Dane.
Ther saugh I Attheon an hert y-maked,
For vengeaunce that he saugh Diane al naked;
I saugh how that his houndes have him caught,
And freten him, for that they knewe him naught. 1210
Yet peynted was a litel forther moor,
How Atthalante hunted the wilde boor,
And Meleagre, and many another mo,
For which Diane wroghte him care and wo.
Ther saugh I many another wonder storie,
The which me list nat drawen to memorie.

Depicted there were the murders of Julius Caesar,
of great Nero, and of Caracalla;*
although they were not born at that time,
their deaths were depicted beforehand, by the menacing
of Mars, according to astrological calculation.
Thus were they revealed in those paintings
as in the stars above is delineated
who is to be killed or to die for love.
One example is enough in ancient stories;
I may not reckon up all of them even if I wanted to.

The statute of Mars stood armed upon a chariot
and looked as fierce as if he were mad with anger;
over his head there shone two constellations,
of which, in writings on the subject,
one is called *Puella,** the other *Rubeus*.
This god of arms was thus equipped:
before him at his feet there stood a wolf,
red-eyed, who was eating at a man;
with skillful brush this history was depicted
in fearful reverence of Mars and of his glory.

Now, as short a way as I can, I shall hasten to
the temple of Diana the chaste
to describe it to you fully.
The walls were covered from top to bottom with pictures
of hunting and modest chastity.
There I saw how woeful Callisto,*
when Diana was offended by her,
was changed from a woman into a bear,
and how, afterwards, she was made into the North Star;
thus it was painted; I can say no more;
her son is also a star, as may be seen.
I saw there Daphne,* turned into a tree
(I do not mean the goddess Diana,
but the daughter of Peneus, who was called Daphne).
I saw there Actaeon,* turned into a hart
in vengeance for his having seen Diana naked;
I saw how his dogs caught
and ate him, because they did not recognize him.
In addition there was painted a little further along
how Atalanta and Meleager* and many another
hunted the wild boar,
for which reason Diana gave Meleager care and sorrow.
I saw there many another marvelous story
which I do not want to bring to memory.

This goddesse on an hert ful hye seet,
With smale houndes al aboute hir feet;
And undernethe hir feet she hadde a mone,
Wexing it was, and sholde wanie sone.   1220
In gaude grene hir statue clothed was,
With bowe in honde, and arwes in a cas.
Hir eyen caste she ful lowe adoun,
Ther Pluto hath his derke regioun.
A womman travailinge was hir biforn,
But, for hir child so longe was unborn,
Ful pitously Lucyna gan she calle,
And seyde, "Help, for thou mayst best of alle."
Wel couthe he peynten lyfly that it wroghte;
With many a florin he the hewes boghte.   1230
  Now been thise listes maad, and Theseus,
That at his grete cost arrayed thus
The temples and the theatre every del,
Whan it was doon, him lyked wonder wel.
But stinte I wol of Theseus a lyte,
And speke of Palamon and of Arcite.
  The day approcheth of hir retourninge,
That everich sholde an hundred knightes bringe,
The bataille to darreyne, as I yow tolde;
And til Athenes, hir covenant for to holde,   1240
Hath everich of hem broght an hundred knightes
Wel armed for the werre at alle rightes.
And sikerly ther trowed many a man
That nevere, sithen that the world bigan,
As for to speke of knighthod of hir hond,
As fer as God hath maked see or lond,
Nas, of so fewe, so noble a companye.
For every wight that lovede chivalrye,
And wolde, his thankes, han a passant name,
Hath preyed that he mighte ben of that game;   1250
And wel was him, that therto chosen was.
For if ther fille to-morwe swich a cas,
Ye knowen wel that every lusty knight
That loveth paramours, and hath his might,
Were it in Engelond, or elleswhere,
They wolde, hir thankes, wilnen to be there.
To fighte for a lady, *ben'cite!*
It were a lusty sighte for to see.
  And right so ferden they with Palamon.
With him ther wenten knightes many oon;   1260

On high the goddess sat upon a hart
and had small hounds about her feet;
beneath her feet she had a moon;
it was waxing, but should soon wane.
Her statue was clothed in bright green;
she had a bow in hand and arrows in a quiver.
She was casting her eyes far down
to where Pluto* holds his dark region.
A woman in labor was before her,
but, because childbirth was so long delayed,
the woman called upon Lucina* piteously,
saying, "Help me, for you may do it best of all."
He who made the picture could indeed paint to the life;
he bought the paints with many a florin.

Now the lists were constructed, and Theseus,
who at great cost had thus arranged
every part of the temples and the amphitheater,
liked the work marvelously well when it was done.
But I shall cease for a while on the subject of Theseus
and speak of Palamon and Arcite.

The day approached for their return,
when each of them should bring a hundred knights
to decide the battle, as I told you;
to keep their agreement, each of them brought
a hundred knights to Athens,
well armed in all respects for the battle.
And, indeed, many a man believed
that never since the world began,
as far as God extended sea or land,
had there been concentrated in such a small number of men
such a noble company in respect of knightly valor.
For every man that loved chivalry
and wanted, for his part, to have a surpassing reputation
had asked that he might take part in that affair;
and happy was he who was chosen for it.
For, if such a matter came up tomorrow,
you well know that every lusty knight
who loves in the manner of man and woman and has his
strength would, whether in England or elsewhere,
desire for his part to be there.
To fight for a lady, Lord bless us,
would be a joyous sight to see.

And so it was for those who were with Palamon.
Many a knight went with him;

Som wol ben armed in an habergeoun,
And in a brestplate and a light gipoun;
And somme wol have a peyre plates large;
And somme wol have a Pruce sheld or a targe;
Somme wol ben armed on hir legges weel,
And have an ax, and somme a mace of steel;
Ther is no newe gyse that it nas old;
Armed were they, as I have you told,
Everich after his opinioun.

   Ther maistow seen coming with Palamoun   1270
Ligurge himself, the grete king of Trace;
Blak was his berd, and manly was his face.
The cercles of his eyen in his heed,
They gloweden bitwixen yelow and reed,
And lyk a griffon loked he aboute,
With kempe heres on his browes stoute;
His limes grete, his braunes harde and stronge,
His shuldres brode, his armes rounde and longe.
And as the gyse was in his contree,
Ful hye upon a char of gold stood he,   1280
With foure whyte boles in the trays.
Instede of cote-armure over his harnays,
With nayles yelwe and brighte as any gold
He hadde a beres skin, col-blak for old.
His longe heer was kembd bihinde his bak;
As any ravenes fether it shoon for blak;
A wrethe of gold, arm-greet, of huge wighte,
Upon his heed, set ful of stones brighte,
Of fyne rubies and of dyamaunts.
Aboute his char ther wenten whyte alaunts,   1290
Twenty and mo, as grete as any steer,
To hunten at the leoun or the deer,
And folwed him, with mosel faste y-bounde,
Colered of gold, and torets fyled rounde.
An hundred lordes hadde he in his route
Armed ful wel, with hertes sterne and stoute.

   With Arcita, in stories as men finde,
The grete Emetreus, the king of Inde,
Upon a stede bay, trapped in steel,
Covered in cloth of gold diapred weel,   1300
Cam ryding lyk the god of armes, Mars.
His cote-armure was of cloth of Tars,
Couched with perles whyte and rounde and grete.
His sadel was of brend gold newe y-bete;

some preferred to be armed in a coat of mail,
a breast plate, and a light tunic;
some would wear two steel plates, front and back,
and some would have a Prussian shield or a round one;
some wanted to be well armed on their legs,
and have an ax, and some wanted a steel mace:
there is no new fashion which is not also old.
They were armed, as I have told you,
each one according to his own idea.

There you might see coming with Palamon
Lycurgus himself, the great king of Thrace;
his beard was black and his face manly.
The pupils of his eyes
glowed between yellow and red,
and he looked about him like a griffin,
with thick hair on his strong brows;
his limbs were large, his muscles hard and strong,
his shoulders broad, his arms long and rounded.
As the custom was in his country,
he sat high upon a golden chariot
with four white bulls in the traces.
Instead of a coat of arms over his battle dress
he had a bearskin, coal-black with age,
its yellow claws glittering like gold.
His long hair was combed down his back;
it shone like a raven's feather in its blackness;
a gold wreath, as thick as an arm and of huge weight,
was upon his head and shone with bright stones—
fine rubies and diamonds.
About his chariot moved white wolfhounds,
twenty and more, and large as steers,
for hunting lion or deer;
they followed him, with their muzzles tightly bound
and gold collars with leash holes filed round.
He had a hundred lords in his company,
well armed, with stern, proud spirits.

With Arcite, as we find in histories,
came riding, like Mars, god of arms,
the great Emetreus, king of India,
upon a bay steed; its trappings were of steel
and it was covered with cloth-of-gold patterned skillfully.
His coat of arms was of cloth of Tartary,
set with pearls that were white and smooth and large.
His saddle was of burnished gold newly hammered;

A mantelet upon his shuldre hanginge,
Bret-ful of rubies rede, as fyr sparklinge.
His crispe heer lyk ringes was y-ronne,
And that was yelow, and glitered as the sonne.
His nose was heigh, his eyen bright citryn,
His lippes rounde, his colour was sangwyn,   1310
A fewe fraknes in his face y-spreynd,
Betwixen yelow and somdel blak y-meynd,
And as a leoun he his loking caste.
Of fyve and twenty yeer his age I caste.
His berd was wel bigonne for to springe;
His voys was as a trompe thunderinge.
Upon his heed he wered of laurer grene
A gerland fresh and lusty for to sene.
Upon his hand he bar, for his deduyt,
An egle tame, as eny lilie whyt.   1320
An hundred lordes hadde he with him there,
Al armed, save hir heddes, in al hir gere,
Ful richely in alle maner thinges.
For trusteth wel that dukes, erles, kinges,
Were gadered in this noble companye,
For love, and for encrees of chivalrye.
Aboute this king ther ran on every part
Ful many a tame leoun and lepart.
And in this wyse thise lordes, alle and some,
Ben on the Sonday to the citee come   1330
Aboute pryme, and in the toun alight.
     This Theseus, this duk, this worthy knight,
Whan he had broght hem into his citee,
And inned hem, everich in his degree,
He festeth hem, and dooth so greet labour
To esen hem, and doon hem al honour,
That yet men wenen that no mannes wit
Of noon estat ne coude amenden it.
The minstralcye, the service at the feste,
The grete yiftes to the meeste and leste,   1340
The riche array of Theseus paleys,
Ne who sat first ne last upon the deys,
What ladies fairest been or best daunsinge,
Or which of hem can dauncen best and singe,
Ne who most felingly speketh of love;
What haukes sitten on the perche above,
What houndes liggen on the floor adoun:
Of al this make I now no mencioun;

a short mantle hanging upon his shoulders
was brimful of rubies, sparkling like fire.
His curly hair was clustered in ringlets;
it was yellow and glittered like the sun.
His nose was highly arched, his eyes bright citron-colored,
his lips rounded, his color sanguine.
A few freckles were sprinkled in his face,
mixed between yellow and something near black,
and he cast his glance forth like a lion.
I estimate his age to have been twenty-five.
His beard had made a good beginning;
his voice was like a trumpet thundering.
Upon his head he wore a garland
of green laurel, fresh and pleasant to the eye.
Upon his hand he bore for his pleasure
a tame falcon, white as a lily.
He had a hundred lords there with him,
all armed, except for their heads, in all their gear,
very richly in all respects.
For you can be sure that dukes, earls, and kings
were gathered together in this noble company
for love and for the glory of chivalry.
There ran about this king on every side
many a tame lion and leopard.
And in this fashion these lords, one and all,
came to the city on the Sunday
about nine in the morning, and lighted down in the town.

   Theseus, the duke and valiant knight,
after having escorted them into his city,
and lodged them, each according to his rank,
feasted them, and expended so much energy
to make them comfortable and do them all honor
that people still think the wit of no man of any rank
could improve on what he did.
The music, the service at the feast,
the noble gifts for the great and small,
the rich adornment of Theseus' palace,
who sat highest or lowest on the dais,
which ladies were the most beautiful or danced best,
or which of them could both sing and dance best,
or who talked most feelingly of love;
what hawks sat above on the perch,
or what dogs lay below on the floor:
all these things I do not mention now,

But al th'effect, that thinketh me the beste;
Now comth the poynt, and herkneth if yow leste.   1350
⸗ The Sonday night, er day bigan to springe,
When Palamon the larke herde singe,
(Although it nere nat day by houres two,
Yet song the larke), and Palamon right tho,
With holy herte, and with an heigh corage
He roos, to wenden on his pilgrimage
Unto the blisful Citherea benigne—
I mene Venus, honurable and digne.
And in hir houre he walketh forth a pas
Unto the listes, ther hire temple was,   1360
And doun he kneleth, and with humble chere
And herte soor, he seyde as ye shul here:
"Faireste of faire, o lady myn, Venus,
Doughter to Jove and spouse of Vulcanus,
Thou glader of the mount of Citheroun,
For thilke love thou haddest to Adoun,
Have pitee of my bittre teres smerte,
And tak myn humble preyer at thyn herte.
Allas, I ne have no langage to telle
Th'effectes ne the torments of myn helle;   1370
Myn herte may myne harmes nat biwreye;
I am so confus, that I can noght seye
But, 'mercy, lady bright, that knowest weele
My thought, and seest what harmes that I feele.'
Considere al this, and rewe upon my sore,
As wisly as I shal for evermore,
Emforth my might, thy trewe servant be,
And holden werre alwey with chastitee;
That make I myn avow, so ye me helpe.
I kepe noght of armes for to yelpe,   1380
Ne I ne axe nat tomorwe to have victorie,
Ne renoun in this cas, ne veyne glorie
Of pris of armes blowen up and doun;
But I wolde have fully possessioun
Of Emelye, and dye in thy servyse.
Find thou the maner how and in what wyse:
I recche nat but it may bettre be
To have victorie of hem, or they of me,
So that I have my lady in myne armes.
For though so be that Mars is god of armes,   1390
Youre vertu is so greet in hevene above
That, if yow list, I shal wel have my love.

but only what resulted; that seems to be best;
now comes the point, and listen if you will.

That Sunday night,* before daybreak,
When Palamon heard the lark singing
(although it was not yet light by two hours,
the lark nevertheless sang), he immediately rose
with reverent heart and exalted mind
to go on his pilgrimage
to blissful and benign Cytherea—
that is to say, Venus, worthy of honor and reverence.
In her hour* he went forth at a footpace
to where her temple was in the lists,
and kneeled down, and with humility
and a troubled heart spoke as you shall hear:

"Fairest of fair ones, my lady Venus,
daughter to Jove and spouse of Vulcan,
giver of joy on Mount Cithaeron:*
for the sake of the love you felt for Adonis,
have pity on my bitter, painful tears
and take my humble prayer to your heart.
Alas, I have no speech to describe
the causes or the torments of my hell;
my heart may not disclose my sufferings;
I am so abashed that I can ask nothing
but, 'Mercy, fair lady, who know well
my thought and see what wounds I feel.'
Consider all this and take pity on my pain,
as surely as I shall for evermore
be your true servant to the extent of my strength
and always be a foe to continence;
I make that my vow, if you help me.
I do not care to boast of arms,
and I do not ask to have the victory tomorrow,
or renown in this matter, or vain glory
of reputation in arms rumored to and fro;
But I would have full possession
of Emily, and die in your service;
I implore you, find how and by what means to do this.
I do not care whether it may be better
to have victory over them or for them to have it over me,
if I may have my lady in my arms.
Though it is true that Mars is god of arms,
your power is so great in heaven above
that, if you desire it, I shall indeed have my love.

Thy temple wol I worshipe evermo,
And on thyn auter, wher I ryde or go,
I wol don sacrifice and fyres bete.
And if ye wol nat so, my lady swete,
Than preye I thee, tomorwe with a spere
That Arcita me thurgh the herte bere.
Thanne rekke I noght, whan I have lost my lyf,
Though that Arcita winne hir to his wyf.   1400
This is th'effect and ende of my preyere:
Yif me my love, thou blisful lady dere."

     Whan th'orisoun was doon of Palamon,
His sacrifice he dide, and that anon,
Ful pitously, with alle circumstaunces,
Al telle I noght as now his observaunces.
But atte laste the statue of Venus shook,
And made a signe, wherby that he took
That his preyere accepted was that day.
For thogh the signe shewed a delay,   1410
Yet wiste he wel that graunted was his bone;
And with glad herte he wente him hoom ful sone.

     The thridde houre inequal that Palamon
Bigan to Venus temple for to goon,
Up roos the sonne, and up roos Emelye,
And to the temple of Diane gan hye.
Hir maydens, that she thider with hire ladde,
Ful redily with hem the fyr they hadde,
Th'encens, the clothes, and the remenant al
That to the sacrifyce longen shal;   1420
The hornes fulle of meth, as was the gyse;
Ther lakked noght to doon hir sacrifyse.
Smoking the temple, ful of clothes faire,
This Emelye, with herte debonaire.
Hir body wessh with water of a welle;
But how she dide hir ryte I dar nat telle,
But it be any thing in general.
And yet it were a game to heren al;
To him that meneth wel, it were no charge;
But it is good a man ben at his large.   1430
Hir brighte heer was kempt, untressed al;
A coroune of a grene ook cerial
Upon hir heed was set ful fair and mete.
Two fyres on the auter gan she bete,
And dide hir thinges, as men may biholde
In Stace of Thebes, and thise bokes olde.

I will worship your temple for ever,
and wherever I ride or walk, I will do sacrifice
and make fires upon your altar.
And if, my sweet lady, you do not wish it so,
then I pray to you that tomorrow Arcite
pierce me through the heart with a spear.
Then, when I have lost my life, I shall not care
even if Arcite wins her to his wife.
This is the point and purpose of my prayer:
give me my love, dear and blissful lady."

When Palamon's prayer was done,
he made his sacrifice; he did it immediately,
very pitiably, and with all attendant ceremonies,
although for now I do not relate his observances.
At last the statue of Venus shook
and made a sign, by which he gathered
that his prayer that day was accepted.
For though the sign showed a delay,
he well knew that his request was granted;
with happy heart he went quickly home.

In the third unequal hour* after Palamon
had started for Venus' temple,
the sun rose, and so did Emily,
and started out for the temple of Diana.
Her maidens, whom she took there with her,
had ready with them the fire,
the incense, the vestments, and all the rest
that must go with the sacrifice—
the horns full of mead, as was the custom;
nothing lacked to make sacrifice to Diana.
When the temple was smoking with incense and full of fair
vestments, Emily, with a pious heart,
washed her body with water of the well;
but how she performed her rite I dare not tell,
except in general.
Yet it would be a satisfaction to hear all of it;
for him that means well it would be no burden;
but it is good for a man to be free to omit what he wants.
Her shining hair was combed, completely loose;
a crown of evergreen oak
was set fairly and becomingly on her head.
She began to make two fires upon the altar
and performed her duties as we may read
in Statius' *Thebaid** and other ancient books.

Whan kindled was the fyr, with pitous chere
Unto Diane she spak, as ye may here:
"O chaste goddesse of the wodes grene,
To whom bothe heven and erthe and see is sene,   1440
Quene of the regne of Pluto derk and lowe,
Goddesse of maydens, that myn herte hast knowe
Ful many a yeer, and woost what I desire,
As keep me fro thy vengeaunce and thyn ire,
That Attheon aboughte cruelly.
Chaste goddesse, wel wostow that I
Desire to been a mayden al my lyf,
Ne nevere wol I be no love ne wyf.
I am, thou woost, yet of thy companye
A mayde, and love hunting and venerye,   1450
And for to walken in the wodes wilde,
And noght to been a wyf and be with childe.
Noght wol I knowe companye of man.
Now help me, lady, sith ye may and can,
For tho thre formes that thou hast in thee.
And Palamon, that hath swich love to me,
And eek Arcite, that loveth me so sore,
This grace I preye thee withoute more,
As sende love and pees bitwixe hem two;
And from me turne awey hir hertes so,   1460
That al hir hote love and hir desyr,
And al hir bisy torment and hir fyr
Be queynt, or turned in another place.
And if so be thou wolt not do me grace,
Or if my destinee be shapen so,
That I shal nedes have oon of hem two,
As sende me him that most desireth me.
Bihold, goddesse of clene chastitee,
The bittre teres that on my chekes falle.
Sin thou are mayde, and keper of us alle,   1470
My maydenhede thou kepe and wel conserve,
And whyl I live, a mayde I wol thee serve."
     The fyres brenne upon the auter clere,
Whyl Emelye was thus in hir preyere;
But sodeinly she saugh a sighte queynte,
For right anon oon of the fyres queynte,
And quiked agayn, and after that anon
That other fyr was queynt, and al agon;
And as it queynte it made a whistelinge,
As doon thise wete brondes in hir brenninge,   1480

When the fire was kindled, with a piteous countenance
she spoke to Diana as you may hear:

"O chaste goddess of the green wood,
to whom both heaven and earth and sea are visible,
queen of the dark, deep kingdom of Pluto,
goddess of virgins, who have known my heart
for many a year, and who know what I desire,
keep me from your vengeance and your anger,
which Actaeon paid for painfully.
Chaste goddess, well you know
that I desire to be a maiden all my life;
I never want to be either a beloved or a wife.
You know that I am still one of your company,
a virgin, and love hunting
and roaming in the wild wood,
and do not desire to be a wife and to be with child.
I do not want to know the company of man.
Now help me lady, since you may and can,
by virtue of the three forms which you possess.
As for Palamon, who bears such love to me,
and Arcite, too, who loves me so strongly
(this boon I beg without another),
send love and peace between the two of them;
and so turn away their hearts from me
that all their fervent love and their desire,
and all their vexatious torment and their ardor
is quenched or turned in another direction.
And if it be that you will not grant me this favor,
or if my destiny is so shaped
that I must have one of the two,
send me the one that most desires me.
Behold, goddess of pure chastity,
the bitter tears that fall upon my cheeks.
Since you are a maid and the preserver of us all,
keep and preserve my maidenhood,
and as long as I live I will serve you as a maiden."

The fires burned upon the splendid altar
while Emily was thus engaged in her prayer;
but suddenly she saw a strange vision,
for just then one of the fires was quenched,
and then caught again, and after that
the other fire was quenched and completely extinguished;
and as it was quenched, it crackled
as wet wood does as it burns,

And at the brondes ende out-ran anoon
As it were blody dropes many oon;
For which so sore agast was Emelye,
That she was wel ny mad, and gan to crye;
For she ne wiste what it signifyed,
But only for the fere thus hath she cryed,
And weep, that it was pitee for to here.
And therwithal Diane gan appere,
With bowe in hond, right as an hunteresse,
And seyde: "Doghter, stint thyn hevinesse.   1490
Among the goddes hye it is affermed,
And by eterne word write and confermed,
Thou shalt ben wedded unto oon of tho
That han for thee so muchel care and wo;
But unto which of hem I may nat telle.
Farwel, for I ne may no lenger dwelle.
The fyres which that on myn auter brenne
Shulle thee declaren, er that thou go henne,
Thyn aventure of love, as in this cas."
And with that word, the arwes in the cas   1500
Of the goddesse clateren faste and ringe,
And forth she wente, and made a vanisshinge;
For which this Emelye astoned was,
And seyde, "What amounteth this, allas?
I putte me in thy proteccioun,
Diane, and in thy disposicioun."
And hoom she gooth anon the nexte weye.
This is th'effect, ther is namore to seye.

    The nexte houre of Mars folwinge this,
Arcite unto the temple walked is   1510
Of fierse Mars, to doon his sacrifyse,
With alle the rytes of his payen wyse.
With pitous herte and heigh devocioun,
Right thus to Mars he seyde his orisoun:
    "O stronge god, that in the regnes colde
Of Trace honoured art and lord yholde,
And hast in every regne and every lond
Of armes al the brydel in thyn hond,
And hem fortunest as thee list devyse,
Accept of me my pitous sacrifyse.   1520
If so be that my youthe may deserve,
And that my might be worthy for to serve
Thy godhede, that I may been oon of thyne,
Than preye I thee to rewe upon my pyne

and at the end of the firebrands then ran out
many of what seemed bloody drops;
Emily was so terribly frightened at this
that she was very nearly out of her wits, and cried out.
She did not know what the meaning of all this was;
it was only for shock that she cried out
and wept, so that it was pitiable to hear her.
At that, Diana appeared
with bow in hand, clad as a huntress,
and said, "Daughter, stop your sorrow.
Among the high gods it is declared
and by eternal word written and confirmed
that you shall be wedded to one of them
who have had so much care and trouble for you;
but which of them I may not tell.
Farewell, for I may stay no longer.
The fires that burn on my altar
shall declare to you, before you go hence,
your fortune in love, in this present situation."
With that word, the arrows in the quiver
of the goddess clattered and rang loudly,
and she went forth and disappeared;
Emily was astonished at this
and said, "Alas, what does this mean?
Diana, I put myself under your protection,
to be disposed of as you wish."
Then she went home the nearest way.
This is what happened; there is no more to say.

The hour* of Mars next followed this:
Arcite proceeded to the temple
of fierce Mars to make his sacrifice
with all the rites of his pagan custom.
With piteous heart and exalted devotion
he thus said his prayer to Mars:

"O strong god, who are honored and held
a lord in the cold realm of Thrace,
and who have, in every realm and land,
the whole bridle of war in your hand
and destine it as you desire to contrive,
accept from me my piteous sacrifice.
If it be that my youth deserves it,
and that my strength is worthy to serve
your godhead, so that I may be one of your own,
then I pray you to take pity upon my pain

For thilke peyne, and thilke hote fyr
In which thou whylom brendest for desyr,
Whan that thou usedest the beautee
Of fayre, yonge, fresshe Venus free,
And haddest hir in armes at thy wille—
Although thee ones on a tyme misfille   1530
Whan Vulcanus had caught thee in his las,
And fond thee ligging by his wyf, allas.
For thilke sorwe that was in thyn herte,
Have routhe as wel upon my peynes smerte.
I am yong and unkonning, as thou wost,
And, as I trowe, with love offended most
That evere was any lyves creature;
For she that dooth me al this wo endure,
Ne reccheth never wher I sinke or flete.
And wel I woot, er she me mercy hete,   1540
I moot with strengthe winne hir in the place;
And wel I woot, withouten help or grace
Of thee ne may my strengthe noght availle.
Than help me, lord, tomorwe in my bataille,
For thilke fyr that whylom brende thee,
As well as thilke fyr now brenneth me,
And do that I tomorwe have victorie.
Myn be the travaille, and thyn be the glorie.
Thy soverein temple wol I most honouren
Of any place, and alwey most labouren   1550
In thy plesaunce and in thy craftes stronge,
And in thy temple I wol my baner honge,
And all the armes of my companye;
And everemo unto that day I dye
Eterne fyr I wold biforn thee finde.
And eek to this avow I wol me binde:
My berd, myn heer, that hongeth long adoun,
That nevere yet ne felte offensioun
Of rasour nor of shere, I wol thee yive,
And been thy trewe servant whyl I live.   1560
Now, lord, have routhe upon my sorwes sore:
Yif me victorie, I aske thee namore."
    The preyere stinte of Arcita the stronge,
The ringes on the temple dore that honge,
and eek the dores, claftereden ful faste,
Of which Arcita somwhat him agaste.
The fyres brende upon the auter brighte,
That it gan al the temple for to lighte;

for the sake of the same pain and same ardent fire
in which you once burned for desire,
when you enjoyed the beauty
of the fair, young, fresh, and gracious Venus,
and had her at your will in your arms—
even though misfortune once befell you,
when Vulcan had caught you in his net
and found you, alas, lying by his wife.
For the sake of the pain which was in your heart,
take pity upon my exceeding pain as well.
I am young and inexperienced, as you know,
and, as I think, more injured by love
than was ever any other living creature;
for she that makes me endure all this woe
never cares whether I sink or swim.
Well I know that before she offers me mercy
I must win her by force on the spot;
and well I know that without help or favor
from you, my strength may not avail.
Then, lord, help me tomorrow in my battle,
for the sake of that fire that once burned you
as much as that fire now burns me,
and arrange it that I shall have victory tomorrow.
Mine be the pains, and yours the glory.
I will honor your sovereign temple above
any other place, and always labor most
for your pleasure and in your mighty skills,
and in your temple I will hang my banner
and all the arms of my company;
and from now on until the day I die
I will provide eternal fire before you.
I will bind myself to this vow also:
I will give to you my beard and my hair that hangs
far down my back and that never yet has felt the injury
of razor or shears,
and I will be your faithful servant while I live.
Now, lord, take pity upon my bitter sorrows:
give me victory, I ask no more of you."
     The prayer of Arcite the strong having ended,
the rings that hung on the temple door,
and the doors, too, set up a loud clattering,
at which Arcite was somewhat afraid.
The fires so burned upon the splendid altar
that they lighted up all the temple;

A swete smel anon the ground up yaf;
And Arcita anon his hand up haf, 1570
And more encens into the fyr he caste,
With othere rytes mo; and atte laste
The statue of Mars bigan his hauberk ringe.
And with that soun he herde a murmuringe
Ful lowe and dim, that sayde thus, "Victorie";
For which he yaf to Mars honour and glorie.
And thus with joye and hope wel to fare
Arcite anon unto his inne is fare,
As fayn as fowel is of the brighte sonne.
  And right anon swich stryf ther is bigonne, 1580
For thilke graunting, in the hevene above,
Bitwixe Venus, the goddesse of love,
And Mars, the sterne god armipotente,
That Jupiter was bisy it to stente;
Til that the pale Saturnus the colde,
That knew so manye of aventures olde,
Fond in his olde experience an art,
That he ful sone hath plesed every part.
As sooth is sayd, elde hath greet avantage;
In elde is bothe wisdom and usage; 1590
Men may the olde at-renne, and noght at-rede.
Saturne anon, to stinten stryf and drede,
Al be it that it is agayn his kynde,
Of al this stryf he gan remedie fynde.
  "My dere doghter Venus," quod Saturne,
"My cours, that hath so wyde for to turne,
Hath more power than wot any man.
Myn is the drenching in the see so wan;
Myn is the prison in the derke cote;
Myn is the strangling and hanging by the throte, 1600
The murmure and the cherles rebelling,
The groyning, and the pryvee empoysoning:
I do vengeance and pleyn correccioun
Whyl I dwelle in the signe of the Leoun.
Myn is the ruine of the hye halles,
The falling of the toures and of the walles
Upon the mynour or the carpenter.
I slow Sampsoun, shaking the piler;
And myne be the maladyes colde,
The derke tresons, and the castes olde; 1610
My loking is the fader of pestilence.
Now weep namore, I shal doon diligence

then the floor gave off a sweet smell,
and Arcite lifted up his hand
and cast more incense into the fire,
performing other rites; at last
the statue of Mars began to make its coat of mail jingle.
With that sound he heard a murmuring,
very low and indistinct, which said, "Victory";
for this he gave honor and glory to Mars.
And thus with joy and hope of faring well
Arcite then went to his inn,
as happy as a bird is for the bright sun.

 Immediately, on account of this grant, such strife
began in heaven above
between Venus, the goddess of love,
and Mars, the stern god powerful in arms,
that Jupiter strove to stop it;
until pale Saturn the cold,
who had known so many ancient turns of fortune,
thought of a trick from his aged experience
so that he had very soon pleased all sides.
It is truly said, age has a great advantage;
in age there is both wisdom and practice;
one may outrun the old and still not surpass them in
 counsel,
Saturn, then, to stop strife and fear
(although such action is against his nature),
began to find a remedy for all this strife.

 "My dear daughter Venus," said Saturn,
"my planetary course, which has to make so wide an orbit,
has more astrological power than any man knows. Mine is
the drowning in the pale sea;
mine is the prison in the dark hut;
mine is the strangling and hanging by the throat,
mine is the uproar and the revolt of the underlings,
the discontent and the poisoning;
I take vengeance and do full chastisement
while I dwell in the zodiacal sign of the Lion.
Mine is the collapse of the lofty halls,
the falling of the towers and of the walls
upon the miner and the carpenter.
I slew Samson, shaking the pillar;
and mine are the chilling sicknesses,
the hidden treasons, and the hoariest plots.
My look is the father of pestilence.
Now weep no more; I shall see to it carefully

That Palamon, that is thyn owene knight,
Shal have his lady, as thou hast him hight.
Though Mars shal helpe his knight, yet nathelees
Bitwixe yow ther moot be som tyme pees,
Al be ye noght of o complexioun,*
That causeth al day swich divisioun.
I am thyn aiel redy at thy wille;
Weep thou namore, I wol thy lust fulfille."   1620
  Now wol I stinten of the goddes above,
Of Mars, and of Venus, goddesse of love,
And telle yow as pleynly as I can
The grete effect, for which that I bigan.

IV

  Greet was the feeste in Athenes that day,
And eek the lusty seson of that May
Made every wight to been in swich plesaunce
That al that Monday justen they and daunce,
And spenden it in Venus heigh servyse.
But by the cause that they sholde ryse   1630
Erly, for to seen the grete fight,
Unto hir reste wente they at night.
And on the morwe whan that day gan springe,
Of hors and harneys noyse and clateringe
Ther was in hostelryes al aboute;
And to the paleys rood ther many a route
Of lordes upon stedes and palfreys.
Ther maystow seen devysing of herneys
So uncouth and so riche, and wroght so weel
Of goldsmithrie, of browding, and of steel;   1640
The sheeldes brighte, testers, and trappures;
Gold-hewen helmes, hauberks, cote-armures;
Lordes in paraments on hir courseres;
Knightes of retenue, and eek squyeres
Nailinge the speres and helmes bokelinge,
Gigginge of sheeldes, with layneres lacinge—
Ther as need is they weren no thing ydel—
The fomy stedes on the golden brydel
Gnawinge, and faste the armurers also
With fyle and hamer prikinge to and fro;   1650
Yemen on fote and communes many oon
With shorte staves, thikke as they may goon;

that Palamon, who is your own knight,
shall have his lady as you have promised him.
Although Mars shall help his knight, nevertheless
there must some time be peace between you,
even if the two of you are not of one humor,
which fact causes such argument continually.
I am your grandfather, ready at your will;
now weep no more, I will fulfill your desire."

Now I will stop talking about the gods above—
about Mars and about Venus, goddess of love—
and tell you, as plainly as I can,
the great climax for the sake of which I began.

IV

There was a great festival in Athens that day,
and, besides, the joyful season of May
made all of them so happy
that they jousted and danced all of Monday
and spent it in the noble service of Venus.
But because they were to get up
early the next day to see the great battle,
they went to bed at nightfall.
At daybreak the next day
there was noise and rattling of horse and battle gear
in inns on all sides;
many a train of lords on chargers and palfreys
rode to the palace.
Thereabouts you might see contrivances of battle gear
that were very strange, rich, and well-made
in goldsmith's work, embroidery, and steel;
you might see glittering shields, head armor, and horse
armor; gold-hued helmets, coats of mail, coats of arms;
lords in clothes of state upon their coursers;
knights in service, and squires, too,
fastening points on spearshafts and buckles on helmets,
putting straps on shields, inserting thongs in the rings—
where need was, they were by no means idle—
the foam-flecked horses gnawing on their golden bridles,
and the armorers also continually
riding hard to and fro with file and hammer;
yeomen on foot and many commoners
with short staves, as crowded together as they could be and

Pypes, trompes, nakers, clariounes,
That in the bataille blowen blody sounes;
The paleys ful of peples up and doun—
Heer three, ther ten, holding hir questioun,
Divyninge of thise Thebane knightes two.
Somme seyden thus, somme seyde it shall be so;
Somme helden with him with the blake berd,
Somme with the balled, somme with the thikke-herd;   1660
Somme sayde he loked grim and he wolde fighte;
"He hath a sparth of twenty pound of wighte."
Thus was the halle ful of divyninge
Longe after that the sonne gan to springe.

The grete Theseus, that of his sleep awaked
With minstralcye and noyse that was maked,
Heeld yet the chambre of his paleys riche,
Til that the Thebane knightes, bothe yliche
Honoured, were into the paleys fet.
Duk Theseus was at a window set,   1670
Arrayed right as he were a god in trone.
The peple preesseth thiderward ful sone
Him for to seen and doon heigh reverence,
And eek to herkne his heest and his sentence.

An heraud on a scaffold made an "Oo!"
Til al the noyse of peple was ydo;
And whan he saugh the peple of noyse al stille,
Thus shewed he the mighty dukes wille:
"The lord hath of his heigh discrecioun
Considered that it were destruccioun   1680
To gentil blood to fighten in the gyse
Of mortal bataille now in this empryse;
Wherfore, to shapen that they shul nought dye,
He wol his firste purpos modifye.
No man therfor, up peyne of los of lyf,
No maner shot, ne pollax, ne short knyf
Into the listes sende, or thider bringe;
Ne short swerd for to stoke with poynt bytinge,
No man ne drawe, ne bere it by his syde.
Ne no man shal unto his felawe ryde   1690
But o cours with a sharp y-grounde spere;
Foyne, if him list, on fote, himself to were.
And he that is at meschief shal be take,
And noght slayn, but be broght unto the stake
That shal ben ordeyned on either syde;
But thider he shal by force, and ther abyde.

still walk; pipes, trumpets, kettledrums, clarions
that blow the bloody sounds of battle;
the palace full of people up and down,
here three, there ten, discussing and
conjecturing about these two Theban knights. Some said
it would be thus and such, others said that was the way
it would be; some chose the one with the black beard,
others the one that was bald, still others, the one with thick
hair; others said that one looked grim: he would fight;
"He has a battle-axe that weighs twenty pounds."
Thus the hall was full of guesses
long after the sun had come up.

    Great Theseus, who woke from his sleep
because of the music and noise that was being made,
still stayed in the bedchamber of his rich palace
until the Theban knights, both alike
honored, were brought into the palace.
Duke Theseus then sat at a window,
situated and adorned as if he were a god upon his throne.
The people crowded that way very quickly
to see him and to show him high respect,
and also to listen to his bidding and announced intention.

    A herald on a scaffold cried out, "Hear ye!"
until the noise of the crowd was done;
and when he saw that the people were completely quiet,
he thus disclosed the mighty duke's will:

    "Our lord in his noble discretion
has considered that it would be destruction
of gentle blood to fight in the manner
of mortal combat in this present enterprise;
wherefore, to arrange things so that the contestants shall not
die, it is his will to modify his first plan.
Therefore, no man, on pain of losing his life,
shall send into the lists, or bring there,
any kind of missile, or battle-axe, or dagger;
no man shall draw, or bear at his side,
any short sword with a piercing point to thrust with.
No man shall ride more than one course against
his fellow with a spear ground to sharpness; he may
parry with it, if he wishes, on foot, to defend himself.
And anyone who is in trouble shall be taken prisoner,
not killed, and be brought to the stake
which shall be placed on each side;
there he shall be conveyed by force, and there he shall stay.

And if so falle the chieftayn be take
On either syde, or elles slee his make,
No lenger shal the turneyinge laste.
God spede yow: goth forth and ley on faste.   1700
With long swerd and with maces fight your fille.
Goth now your wey. This is the lordes wille."
  The voys of peple touchede the hevene,
So loude cride they with mery stevene,
"God save swich a lord, that is so good:
He wilneth no destruccioun of blood!"
Up goon the trompes and the melodye,
And to the listes rit the companye,
By ordinaunce, thurghout the citee large,
Hanged with cloth of gold, and nat with sarge.   1710
  Ful lyk a lord this noble duk gan ryde,
Thise two Thebanes upon either syde;
And after rood the quene and Emelye,
And after that another companye
Of oon and other, after hir degree.
And thus they passen thurghout the cittee,
And to the listes come they by tyme—
It nas not of the day yet fully pryme.
Whan set was Theseus ful riche and hye,
Ipolita the quene and Emelye,   1720
And othere ladies in degrees aboute,
Unto the seetes preesseth al the route.
And westward, thurgh the gates under Marte,
Arcite and eek the hundred of his parte,
With baner reed, is entred right anon;
And in that selve moment Palamon
Is under Venus, estward in the place,
With baner whyt, and hardy chere and face.
In al the world, to seken up and doun,
So evene withouten variacioun,   1730
Ther nere swiche companyes tweye;
For ther was noon so wys that coude seye
That any hadde of other avauntage
Of worthinesse, ne of estaat, ne age,
So evene were they chosen, for to gesse.
And in two renges faire they hem dresse.
  Whan that hir names rad were everichoon,
That in hir nombre gyle were ther noon,
Tho were the gates shet, and cryed was loude,
"Do now youre devoir, yonge knightes proude!"   1740

And if it happens that the chieftain is captured
on either side, or else if he kills his opposite,
then the tourney shall last no longer.
God speed you: go out and hit hard.
Fight your fill with the long sword and with maces.
Now go your way. This is our lord's will."
   The people's voice reached the heavens,
so loud they cried out with joyful voice,
"God save such a lord, who is so good;
he wills that there be no loss of blood!"
Up start the trumpets and the music,
and the company rides to the lists
in order through the large city,
which was hung with cloth of gold, not with dark serge.
   In very lordly fashion this noble duke rode,
one of these two Thebans on either side;
next rode the queen and Emily,
and after them another company
of various people according to their rank.
In this way they passed through the city
and arrived in good time at the lists—
it was not yet quite nine o'clock.
When Theseus was seated in a noble and lofty position,
Queen Hippolyta, Emily,
and other ladies being in tiers about him,
all the crowd pressed to the seats.
On the west, through the gates under Mars,
Arcite and also the hundred on his side
entered immediately with their red banner;
and in the same moment Palamon
entered under Venus, on the east of the field,
with his white banner and with a bold bearing.
Nowhere, no matter where you searched,
where there two such companies
so evenly matched, without differentiation.
For there was none so wise as to be able to say
that any of them had an advantage over another
in respect to valor, nobility, or age,
so evenly were they chosen, as far as one could guess.
They drew themselves up fairly in two ranks.
   When each of their names had been read, so that
there would be no deception in the total on each side,
then the gates were shut, and the cry was loudly given,
"Do now what you ought, proud young knights!"

The heraudes lefte hir priking up and doun;
Now ringen trompes loude and clarioun;
Ther is namore to seyn, but west and est
In goon the speres ful sadly in arest;
In goth the sharpe spore into the syde.
Ther seen men who can juste and who can ryde;
Ther shiveren shaftes upon sheeldes thikke;
He feleth thurgh the herte-spoon the prikke.
Up springen speres twenty foot on highte;
Out goon the swerdes as the silver brighte;   1750
The helmes they to-hewen and to-shrede;
Out brest the blood with sterne stremes rede;
With mighty maces the bones they to-breste;
He thurgh the thikkeste of the throng gan threste;
Ther stomblen stedes stronge, and doun goth al;
He rolleth under foot as dooth a bal;
He foyneth on his feet with his tronchoun,
And he him hurtleth with his hors adoun;
He thurgh the body is hurt and sithen take,
Maugree his heed, and broght unto the stake: 1760
As forward was, right ther he moste abyde;
Another lad is on that other syde.

And som tyme dooth hem Theseus to reste,
Hem to refresshe and drinken if hem leste.
Ful ofte a day han thise Thebanes two
Togidre y-met and wroght his felawe wo;
Unhorsed hath ech other of hem tweye.
Ther nas no tygre in the vale of Galgopheye,
Whan that hir whelp is stole whan it is lyte,
So cruel on the hunte as is Arcite   1770
For jelous herte upon this Palamoun;
Ne in Belmarye ther nis so fel leoun,
That hunted is, or for his hunger wood,
Ne of his praye desireth so the blood,
As Palamon to sleen his fo Arcite.
The jelous strokes on hir helmes byte;
Out renneth blood on both hir sydes rede.

Som tyme an ende ther is of every dede:
For er the sonne unto the reste wente,
The stronge king Emetreus gan hente   1780
This Palamon, as he faught with Arcite,
And made his swerd depe in his flesh to byte;
And by the force of twenty is he take
Unyolden, and y-drawe unto the stake.

The heralds left off their spurring up and down;
now the loud trumpets and clarions ring out;
there is no more to say; but east and west
the spears go firmly into the spear rests;
the sharp spurs go into the horses' sides.
There they see who can joust and ride;
there spear shafts shatter on thick shields;
one feels the thrust through the breastbone.
Up spring the spears twenty feet in the air;
out come the swords glittering like silver;
they hew and cut to pieces the helmets;
out bursts the blood in violent streams;
the knights break bones with strong maces;
that one thrusts through the thickest of the press;
there strong steeds stumble, and down go horse and man;
this one rolls under foot like a ball;
that one, on foot, parries with the shaft of his spear;
another crashes down with his horse.
Another is wounded through the body and then captured,
in spite of all he can do, and brought to the stake:
as the rule said, he must stay right there;
another is led to the stake on the other side.

At times Theseus has them rest,
to refresh themselves and to drink if they wish.
The two Thebans have very often
met together, and each has caused the other pain;
each has unhorsed the other twice.
In the vale of Gargaphia no tiger
whose whelp has been stolen when it was young
is as cruel to the hunter as Arcite is
for the jealousy of his heart against Palamon;
and in Benmarin there is no lion
hunted or maddened with hunger which is so cruel
or so desires the blood of his prey
as Palamon desires to kill his foe Arcite.
The jealous strokes bite into their helmets;
the blood runs red down the sides of both.

There is an end some time for every action:
before the sun went down
strong King Emetreus caught
Palamon as he fought with Arcite;
the king's sword bit deeply into Palamon's flesh;
and by the strength of twenty men he was captured,
without having surrendered, and was pulled to the stake.

And in the rescous of this Palamoun
The stronge king Ligurge is born adoun;
And king Emetreus, for al his strengthe,
Is born out of his sadel a swerdes lengthe,
So hitte him Palamon er he were take;
But al for noght, he was broght to the stake.   1790
His hardy herte mighte him helpe naught;
He moste abyde, whan that he was caught,
By force, and eek by composicioun.

Who sorweth now but woful Palamoun,
That moot namore goon agayn to fighte?
And whan that Theseus hadde seyn this sighte,
Unto the folk that foghten thus echoon
He cryde, "Ho! namore, for it is doon!
I wol be trewe juge, and no partye.
Arcite of Thebes shal have Emelye,
That by his fortune hath hir faire y-wonne."   1800
Anon ther is a noyse of peple bigonne
For joye of this, so loude and heigh withalle,
It seemed that the listes sholde falle.

What can now faire Venus doon above?
What seith she now? what dooth this quene of love?
But wepeth so, for wanting of hir wille,
Til that hir teres in the listes fille;
She seyde, "I am ashamed, doutelees."
Saturnus seyde, "Doghter, hold thy pees.   1810
Mars hath his wille, his knight hath al his bone,
And, by myn heed, thou shalt ben esed sone."

The troumpours, with the loude minstralcye,
The heraudes that ful loude yelle and crye
Been in hir wele for joye of daun Arcite—
But herkneth me, and stinteth now a lyte,
Which a miracle ther bifel anon.

This fierse Arcite hath of his helm y-don,
And on a courser, for to shewe his face,
He priketh endelong the large place,   1820
Loking upward upon this Emelye;
And she agayn him caste a freendlich yë
(For wommen, as to speken in comune,
They folwen al the favour of fortune),
And she was al his chere, as in his herte.
Out of the ground a furie infernal sterte,
From Pluto sent at requeste of Saturne,
For which his hors for fere gan to turne,

In the attempt to rescue him
strong King Lycurgus was borne down;
and King Emetreus, in spite of all his strength,
was carried a sword's length out of his saddle,
Palamon hit him so hard before being captured;
but all this was for nothing; he was brought to the stake.
His brave heart could not help him;
he had to stay there, when he was captured,
by force and also by the rules.

   Who sorrows now more than woeful Palamon,
who may no longer resume the fight?
And when Theseus had seen this sight,
he cried out to the people, each of whom was thus fighting,
"Stop! No more; it's finished!
I will be a faithful judge, not a friend of one party.
Arcite of Thebes shall have Emily;
by his good fortune he has won her fairly."
Then such a clamor arose—
for joy at this—so loud and high
that it seemed the lists should collapse.

   What could fair Venus do now in heaven?
What did she say now? What did the queen of love do?
She only wept, for not having her way—but so hard
that her tears fell in the lists;
she said, "I am put to shame, beyond a doubt."
Saturn said, "Daughter, stop complaining and wait.
Mars has his wish, his knight has all his request,
and, by my head, you shall soon be comforted."

   The trumpeters with their loud music,
the heralds, who loudly cried and shouted,
were in a bliss of joy for Sir Arcite.
But listen to me, and stop your noises for a little
to hear what a miracle then befell there.

   Fierce Arcite had taken off his helmet,
and to show his face he spurred on a courser along
the length of the large field,
looking up at Emily;
and she cast a friendly eye toward him
(for, to speak in general, women
all follow the favor of fortune),
and she was the source of all the happiness in his heart.
A Fury from the infernal regions started up from the
ground, sent by Pluto at the request of Saturn,
which made his horse turn

And leep asyde, and foundred as he leep;
And, er that Arcite may taken keep, 1830
He pighte him on the pomel of his heed,
That in the place he lay as he were deed,
His brest to-brosten with his sadel-bowe.
As blak he lay as any cole or crowe,
So was the blood y-ronnen in his face.
Anon he was y-born out of the place,
With herte soor, to Theseus paleys.
Tho was he corven out of his harneys,
And in a bed y-brought ful faire and blyve,
For he was yet in memorie and alyve, 1840
And alway crying after Emelye.

Duk Theseus, with al his companye,
Is comen hoom to Athenes his citee,
With alle blisse and greet solempnitee;
Al be it that this aventure was falle,
He nolde noght disconforten hem alle.
Men seyde eek that Arcite shal nat dye;
He shal ben heled of his maladye.
And of another thing they were as fayn:
That of hem alle was ther noon y-slayn, 1850
Al were they sore y-hurt, and namely oon,
That with a spere was thirled his brest-boon.
To othere woundes and to broken armes
Some hadden salves, and some hadden charmes;
Fermacies of herbes and eek save
They dronken, for they wolde hir limes have.
For which this noble duk, as he wel can,
Conforteth and honoureth every man,
And made revel al the longe night
Unto the straunge lordes, as was right. 1860
Ne ther was holden no disconfitinge,
But as a justes or a tourneyinge;
For soothly ther was no disconfiture:
For falling nis nat but an aventure;
Ne to be lad with fors unto the stake
Unyolden, and with twenty knightes take,
O persone allone, withouten mo,
And haried forth by arme, foot, and to,
And eek his stede driven forth with staves,
With footmen, bothe yemen and eek knaves— 1870
It nas aretted him no vileinye;
Ther may no man clepen it cowardye.

and leap to the side, and he foundered as he leaped;
and, before Arcite could take heed,
the horse pitched him on the pommel of the saddle and
over his head so hard that he lay in the field as if dead,
his breast crushed in with his saddle bow.
He lay looking as black as a coal or a crow,
blood had so suffused his face.
He was immediately borne out of the field,
with a painful heart, to Theseus' palace.
Then he was cut out of his armor
and put into a bed easily and quickly,
for he was still alive and in his senses,
and always he cried out for Emily.

Duke Theseus with all his company
came home to his city of Athens
with all joy and ceremony;
in spite of this mischance
he did not want to disconcert them all.
Also it was said that Arcite would not die;
that he would be healed of his sickness.
For another matter they were just as glad:
that none of them all was killed,
although they were badly wounded, and especially one of
them whose breastbone was pierced with a spear.
For other wounds and for broken arms
some had salves, others had incantations;
they drank herb medicines and decoctions,
for they wanted to keep their limbs.
For their sakes the noble duke (as he well could)
gave comfort and honor to every man
and feasted the foreign lords the long
night through, as it was right to do.
And there was held to have been no vanquishing in this
affair, except as in a joust or tourney;
for in fact there was no defeat:
falling is a result of nothing but luck;
likewise, to be led by force to the stake,
without surrendering, and having been captured by twenty
knights—one person by himself, without more—
and dragged on by arm, foot, and toe,
and also his horse driven on with staves
by footmen—both yeomen and servants—
all this was not reckoned a disgrace to Palamon;
no one could call it cowardice.

For which anon duk Theseus leet crye,
To stinten alle rancour and envye,
The gree as wel of o syde as of other,
And either syde ylik, as otheres brother;
And yaf hem yiftes after hir degree,
And fully heeld a feste dayes three;
And conveyed the kinges worthily
Out of his toun a journee largely.   1880
And hoom wente every man the righte way.
Ther was namore, but "Fare wel, have good day."
Of this bataille I wol namore endyte,
But speke of Palamon and of Arcite.
   Swelleth the brest of Arcite, and the sore
Encreesseth at his herte more and more.
The clothered blood, for any lechecraft,
Corrupteth and is in his bouk y-laft,
That neither veyne-blood, ne ventusinge,
Ne drinke of herbes may ben his helpinge.   1890
The vertu expulsif or animal
Fro thilke vertu cleped natural
Ne may the venim voyden, ne expelle.
The pypes of his longes gonne to swelle,
And every lacerte in his brest adoun
Is shent with venim and corrupcioun.
Him gayneth neither, for to gete his lyf,
Vomyt upward, ne dounward laxatif;
Al is to-brosten thilke regioun,
Nature hath now no dominacioun,   1900
And certeinly, ther nature wol nat wirche,
Farewel, phisyk: go ber the man to chirche.
This al and som, that Arcita moot dye,
For which he sendeth after Emelye,
And Palamon, that was his cosin dere;
Than seyde he thus, as ye shal after here:
   "Naught may the woful spirit in myn herte
Declare o poynt of alle my sorwes smerte
To yow, my lady, that I love most;
But I biquethe the service of my gost   1910
To yow aboven every creature,
Sin that my lyf may no lenger dure.
Allas the wo, allas the peynes stronge,
That I for yow have suffred, and so longe;
Allas the deeth, allas myn Emelye;
Allas, departing of our companye;

For these reasons Duke Theseus caused to be publicly
announced, in order to prevent all rancor and envy,
the success of each side as well as the other,
and either side alike as though they had been brothers;
he gave them gifts according to their rank,
and held a feast for fully three days,
and conveyed the kings nobly
out of his town the distance of a generous day's journey.
Every màn went home the direct way.
There was nothing further but "Farewell! Good-bye!"
I shall not write any more of this battle,
but speak of Palamon and Arcite.

The breast of Arcite swelled, and the pain
at his heart increased more and more.
No matter what medical skill was tried, the clotted blood
corrupted and remained in his body,
so that neither bleeding nor cupping
nor herb decoctions could help him.
The expulsive,* or animal, power
could not void or expel the poison
from that power named the natural one.
The tubes of his lungs began to swell,
and every muscle down in his breast
was damaged with venom and corruption.
Nothing helped to save his life, neither
vomiting upward nor laxative downward;
that region was completely shattered.
Nature now had no dominion,
and, certainly, where nature will not work,
farewell, medicine: go bear the man to church.
In a word, Arcite had to die,
for which reason he sent for Emily,
and for Palamon, who was his dear cousin;
then he spoke thus, as you shall hear:

"The woeful spirit within me
cannot declare the smallest part of the pain of my sorrow
to you, my lady, whom I most love;
but I bequeath the service of my spirit
to you above any other creature,
since my life may last no longer.
Alas, the woe, alas, the bitter pains
that I have suffered for you, and for so long;
alas, death, and alas, my Emily;
alas, the parting of our company;

Allas, myn hertes quene, allas, my wyf,
Myn hertes lady, endere of my lyf!
What is this world? what asketh men to have?
Now with his love, now in his colde grave,   1920
Allone, withouten any companye.
Fare wel, my swete fo, myn Emelye,
And softe tak me in your armes tweye,
For love of God, and herkneth what I seye.
    I have heer with my cosin Palamon
Had stryf and rancour many a day agon,
For love of yow, and for my jalousye;
And Juppiter so wis my soule gye—
To speken of a servant proprely,
With alle circumstaunces trewely,   1930
That is to seyn, trouthe, honour, knighthede,
Wisdom, humblesse, estaat, and heigh kinrede,
Fredom, and al that longeth to that art—
So Juppiter have of my soule part,
As in this world right now ne knowe I non
So worthy to ben loved as Palamon,
That serveth yow, and wol doon al his lyf.
And if that evere ye shul been a wyf,
Foryet nat Palamon, the gentil man."
And with that word his speche faille gan,   1940
For from his feet up to his brest was come
The cold of deeth, that hadde him overcome;
And yet more over, for in his armes two
The vital strengthe is lost and al ago.
Only the intellect withouten more,
That dwelled in his herte syk and sore,
Gan faillen whan the herte felte deeth:
Dusked his eyen two, and failled breeth.
But on his lady yet caste he his yë.
His laste word was, "Mercy, Emelye."   1950
His spirit chaunged hous and wente ther
As I cam never, I can nat tellen wher.
Therfor I stinte, I nam no divinistre;
Of soules finde I nat in this registre,
Ne me ne list thilke opiniouns to telle
Of hem, though that they wryten wher they dwelle.
Arcite is cold, ther Mars his soule gye.
Now wol I speken forth of Emelye.
    Shrighte Emelye, and howleth Palamon,
And Theseus his suster took anon   1960

alas, heart's queen, alas, my wife,
lady of my heart, ender of my life!
What is this world? What does man ask to have?
One instant with his love, the next in his cold grave,
alone, and without company.
Farewell, my sweet foe, my Emily,
and softly take me in your two arms,
for the love of God, and listen to what I say.
　　With my cousin Palamon here
I have had strife and rancor for much past time,
for the love of you, and for my jealousy.
Jupiter so wise, guide my soul—
to speak properly of a servant of love,
faithfully with all his qualities—
that is to say, faithfulness, honor, chivalry,
wisdom, humility, nobility, high descent,
magnanimity, and all else that belongs to that calling—
as I hope Jupiter will take my soul,
I know at this very moment none in this world
so worthy to be loved as Palamon,
who serves you, and will do so all his life.
And if you are ever to be a wife,
forget not Palamon, the gentle man."
At those words his speech began to fail,
for from his feet up to his breast had come
the cold of death that had overcome him;
and, yet more, in his two arms
the vital strength was lost and gone.
Without the other powers, the intellect, last and alone,
which dwelt in his sick and painful heart,
began to fail when the heart felt death:
his two eyes darkened, and his breath failed.
But yet he cast his eye on his lady.
His last word was, "Mercy, Emily."
His spirit changed its house and went where
I have never gone; I cannot say where.
Therefore I cease; I am no theologian;
I find nothing about souls in my book,
and I do not wish to relate the opinions
of theologians, even if they write where souls dwell.
Arcite is dead; may Mars guide his soul thither.
Now I would continue to speak of Emily.
　　Emily shrieked and Palamon howled,
and Theseus soon took his sister

Swowninge, and bar hir fro the corps away.
What helpeth it to tarien forth the day
To tellen how she weep, bothe eve and morwe?
For in swich cas wommen have swich sorwe,
Whan that hir housbondes been from hem ago,
That for the more part they sorwen so,
Or elles fallen in swich maladye,
That at the laste certeinly they dye.

  Infinite been the sorwes and the teres
Of olde folk and folk of tendre yeres,   1970
In al the toun for deeth of this Theban;
For him ther wepeth bothe child and man;
So greet weping was ther noon, certayn,
Whan Ector was y-broght, al fresh y-slayn,
To Troye; allas, the pitee that was ther,
Cracching of chekes, renting eek of heer;
"Why woldestow be deed," thise wommen crye,
"And haddest gold ynough, and Emelye?"
No man mighte gladen Theseus,
Savinge his olde fader Egeus,   1980
That knew this worldes transmutacioun,
As he had seyn it chaungen bothe up and doun—
Joye after wo, and wo after gladnesse,
And shewed hem ensamples and lyknesse:
  "Right as ther deyed nevere man," quod he,
"That he ne livede in erthe in som degree,
Right so ther livede nevere man," he seyde,
"In al this world, that some tyme he ne deyde.
This world nis but a thurghfare ful of wo,
And we been pilgrimes, passinge to and fro;   1990
Deeth is an ende of every worldly sore."
And over al this yet seyde he muchel more
To this effect, ful wisely to enhorte
The peple, that they sholde hem reconforte.
  Duk Theseus, with al his bisy cure,
Caste now wher that the sepulture
Of good Arcite may best y-maked be,
And eek most honurable in his degree.
And at the laste he took conclusioun,
That ther as first Arcite and Palamoun   2000
Hadden for love the bataille hem bitwene,
That in that selve grove swote and grene,
Ther as he hadde his amourouse desires,
His compleynt, and for love his hote fires,

swooning and bore her away from the corpse.
What good is it to spend time
in telling how she wept, both evening and morning?
For in such cases women feel such sorrow—
when their husbands are gone from them—
that for the most part they mourn thus,
or else fall into such sickness
that in the end they certainly die.
    The sorrows and tears
of old and young were endless
in all the town for the death of this Theban;
both child and adult wept for him;
there was not such great weeping, certainly,
when Hector, only just killed, was brought
into Troy; alas, the pity here:
scratching of cheeks, and also tearing of hair.
"Why would you be dead," these women cry,
"when you had money enough, and Emily?"
No one could raise the spirits of Theseus
except his old father Aegeus,
who had come to know the mutability of this world
as he had seen it changing, both up and down—
joy after sorrow, and sorrow after happiness;
he expounded precedents and analogies to Theseus:
    "Just as no man," he said, "ever died
who did not in some condition live on earth,
so," he said, "there never lived a man
in all this world who did not some time die.
This world is but a highway full of sorrow,
and we are pilgrims, passing to and fro;
death is an end of every earthly pain."
And besides this he said much more still
to this effect, in order to exhort
the people to take comfort.
    Duke Theseus with all diligent care
now planned where the funeral
of good Arcite might be best held
in a manner honorable to his rank.
In the end he decided
that in the place where Arcite and
Palamon first battled for love—
in the same fresh, green grove
where Arcite showed his amorous desires,
his plaint, and the ardent fires of love—

He wolde make a fyr in which the office
Funeral he mighte al accomplice;
And leet comaunde anon to hakke and hewe
The okes olde, and leye hem on a rewe
In colpons wel arrayed for to brenne.
His officers with swifte feet they renne   2010
And ryde anon at his comaundement.
And after this, Theseus hath y-sent
After a bere, and it al over-spradde
With cloth of gold, the richeste that he hadde.
And of the same suyte he cladde Arcite;
Upon his hondes hadde he gloves whyte,
Eek on his heed a coroune of laurer grene,
And in his hond a swerd ful bright and kene.
He leyde him, bare the visage, on the bere.
Therwith he weep that pitee was to here.   2020
And for the peple sholde seen him alle,
Whan it was day he broghte him to the halle,
That roreth of the crying and the soun.
    Tho cam this woful Theban Palamoun,
With flotery berd and ruggy, asshy heres,
In clothes blake, y-dropped al with teres;
And, passing othere of weping, Emelye,
The rewfulleste of al the companye.
In as muche as the service sholde be
The more noble and riche in his degree,   2030
Duk Theseus leet forth three stedes bringe,
That trapped were in steel al gliteringe,
And covered with the armes of daun Arcite.
Upon thise stedes, that weren grete and whyte,
Ther seten folk, of which oon bar his sheeld,
Another his spere up in his hondes heeld,
The thridde bar with him his bowe Turkeys—
Of brend gold was the caas, and eek the harneys;
And riden forth a paas with sorweful chere
Toward the grove, as ye shul after here.   2040
The nobleste of the Grekes that ther were
Upon hir shuldres carieden the bere,
With slakke paas, and eyen rede and wete,
Thurghout the citee by the maister-strete,
That sprad was al with blak, and wonder hye
Right of the same is the strete y-wrye.
Upon the right hond wente old Egeus,
And on that other syde duk Theseus,

a fire would be built, in which the funeral
rites might be wholly-accomplished;
Theseus then had the order given to lop and cut down
the old oaks and lay them in rows
of piles well arranged for burning.
His officers then ran swiftly
and rode at his command.
After this Theseus sent for
a bier and covered it completely
with cloth of gold, the richest that he had.
He clothed Arcite correspondingly;
he had white gloves on his hands;
also, upon his head he had a crown of green laurel,
and in his hand a bright, keen sword.
Theseus laid him with his face bare upon the bier,
at the same time he wept so that it was a pity to hear him.
And, in order that all the people should see him,
Theseus brought him into the hall when daylight came;
it resounded with the weeping and the noise.

Then came the woeful Theban Palamon,
with fluttering beard and wild hair covered with ashes,
in black dress, all sprinkled with tears;
and Emily, surpassing all others in weeping,
the saddest of all the company.
So that the service would be
the more noble and rich of its kind,
Duke Theseus had three steeds brought forth,
which were furnished with trappings of glittering steel
and covered with the arms of Lord Arcite.
On these steeds (which were large and white)
there sat men of whom one bore his shield,
a second held up Arcite's spear in his hands,
and the third carried his Turkish bow—
the quiver and the trappings were of burnished gold;
they rode forth sorrowfully at footpace
toward the grove, as you shall hereafter hear.
The noblest there of the Greeks
carried the bier on their shoulders,
at a slow pace and with reddened eyes,
through the city by the main street,
which was wholly spread with black cloth; and all
the street fronts to a great height were hung with the same.
On the right hand walked old Aegeus,
and on the other side Duke Theseus

With vessels in hir hand of gold ful fyn,
Al ful of hony, milk, and blood, and wyn;   2050
Eek Palamon, with ful greet companye;
And after that cam woful Emelye,
With fyr in honde, as was that tyme the gyse,
To do the office of funeral servyse.

Heigh labour and ful greet apparaillinge
Was at the service and the fyr-makinge,
That with his grene top the heven raughte,
And twenty fadme of brede the armes straughte—
This is to seyn, the bowes were so brode.
Of stree first ther was leyd ful many a lode.   2060
But how the fyr was maked up on highte,
And eek the names how the treës highte—
As ook, firre, birch, asp, alder, holm, popler,
Wilow, elm, plane, ash, box, chasteyn, lind, laurer,
Mapul, thorn, beech, hasel, ew, whippel-tree—
How they weren feld shal nat be told for me;
Ne how the goddes ronnen up and doun,
Disherited of hir habitacioun,
In which they woneden in reste and pees—
Nymphes, faunes, and amadrides;   2070
Ne how the bestes and the briddes alle
Fledden for fere, whan the wode was falle;
Ne how the ground agast was of the light,
That was nat wont to seen the sonne bright;
Ne how the fyr was couched first with stree,
And than with drye stikkes cloven a three,
And than with grene wode and spycerye,
And than with cloth of gold and with perrye,
And gerlandes hanging with ful many a flour,
The mirre, th'encens, with al so greet odour;   2080
Ne how Arcite lay among al this,
Ne what richesse aboute his body is;
Ne how that Emelye, as was the gyse,
Putte in the fyr of funeral servyse;
Ne how she swowned whan men made the fyr,
Ne what she spak, ne what was hir desyr;
Ne what jeweles men in the fire caste,
Whan that the fyr was greet and brente faste;
Ne how some caste hir sheeld and some hir spere,
And of hir vestiments, whiche that they were,   2090
And cuppes ful of wyn, and milk, and blood,
Into the fyr, that brente as it were wood;

with vessels of fine gold in hand,
all filled with honey, milk, blood, and wine;
Palamon also came, with a great company,
and after them came sad Emily,
with fire in hand, as was then the custom,
to perform the funeral rite.

   Noble activity and great preparation
were given to the service and the making of the pyre,
which reached the heavens with its green top;
its sides stretched out twenty fathoms in breadth
(that is to say, the boughs were so broad).
There was first laid many a load of straw.
But how the pyre was constructed above,
and also what were the names of the trees—
such as oak, fir, birch, aspen, alder, holm-oak, poplar,
willow, elm, plane, ash, box, chestnut, linden, laurel,
maple, thorn, beech, hazel, yew, dogwood—
and how they were felled shall not be told as far as I am
concerned; nor how the divinities ran up and down,
disinherited of their habitation,
in which they had lived in calm and peace—
nymphs, fauns, hamadryads;
nor how the beasts and birds all
fled for fear when the woods were felled;
nor how at the light the ground was aghast,
not being accustomed to see the bright sun;
nor how the fire was first laid with straw,
and then with dry sticks split into threes,
and then with green wood and spices,
and then with cloth of gold and jewels
and hanging garlands with many a flower,
and myrrh and incense with so strong a fragrance;
nor how Arcite lay among all this,
nor what riches lay about his body;
nor how Emily, as was the custom,
put in the ceremonial funeral fire;
nor how she swooned when the fire was made up,
nor what she said, nor what was her desire;
nor what jewels were cast into the fire
when it had grown and was burning hard;
nor how some cast their shields, and some their spears
and part of the clothes they wore,
and cups full of wine, milk, and blood
into the fire, which burned like mad;

Ne how the Grekes with an huge route
Thryës riden al the fyr aboute
Upon the left hand with a loud shoutinge,
And thryës with hir speres clateringe;
And thryës how the ladies gonne crye;
Ne how that lad was homward Emelye;
Ne how Arcite is brent to asshen colde;
Ne how that liche-wake was y-holde   2100
Al thilke night; ne how the Grekes pleye
The wake-pleyes, ne kepe I nat to seye—
Who wrastleth best naked, with oille enoynt,
Ne who that bar him best, in no disjoynt;
I wol nat tellen eek how that they goon
Hoom til Athenes whan the pley is doon;
But shortly to the poynt than wol I wende,
And maken of my longe tale an ende.
   By processe and by lengthe of certeyn yeres
Al stinted is the moorning and the teres   2110
Of Grekes, by oon general assent.
Than semed me ther was a parlement
At Athenes, upon certeyn poynts and cas;
Among the whiche poynts y-spoken was
To have with certeyn contrees alliaunce,
And have fully of Thebans obeisaunce:
For which this noble Theseus anon
Leet senden after gentil Palamon,
Unwist of him what was the cause and why;
But in his blake clothes sorwefully   2120
He cam at his comaundement in hye.
Tho sente Theseus for Emelye.
Whan they were set, and hust was al the place,
And Theseus abiden hadde a space
Er any word cam from his wyse brest,
His eyen sette he ther as was his lest,
And with a sad visage he syked stille,
And after that right thus he seyde his wille:
   "The Firste Moevere of the cause above,
Whan he first made the faire cheyne of love,   2130
Greet was th'effect, and heigh was his entente—
Wel wiste he why and what therof he mente:
For with that faire cheyne of love he bond
The fyr, the eyr, the water, and the lond
In certeyn boundes, that they may nat flee;
That same Prince and that Moevere," quod he,

nor how the Greeks in a huge troop
rode thrice around the fire
leftward, with loud shouting,
and thrice rattled their spears;
nor how the ladies thrice cried out;
nor how Emily was led homeward;
nor how Arcite was burned to cold ashes;
nor how the funeral wake was held
all that night; nor how the Greeks performed
the funeral games, I do not care to say—
who wrestled best naked and anointed with oil,
nor who bore himself best, not getting into any predicament.
I don't wish to tell, either, how they went
home to Athens when the games were finished;
I will move briefly to the point
and make an end of my long tale.

By course of time and elapse of a certain number of years
the mourning and tears wholly ceased.
Then, it seems to me, there was, by a general agreement,
a meeting of the Greeks
at Athens on certain questions and affairs,
among which questions it was proposed
to have alliance with certain countries
and to have the Thebans fully in submission:
for which purpose noble Theseus then
had gentle Palamon sent for,
without the latter's knowing the matter or the reason.
But Palamon came sorrowfully in his black clothes
at Theseus' high command.
Then Theseus sent for Emily.
When they had sat down, and all the place was quiet,
and Theseus had waited for a time
before any word came from his wise breast,
he set his eyes there where he wished
and sighed quietly with a sad face;
after that he said his will just thus:

"When the First* Mover of the supernal Cause
first made the fair chain of love,
great was the outcome, and his plan was exalted;
he well knew why and what he intended by it;
for with that fair chain of love he bound
the fire, the air, the water, and the earth
within sure limits, so that they might not flee.
That same Prince and Mover," said Theseus,

"Hath stablissed in this wrecched world adoun
Certeyne dayes and duracioun
To al that is engendred in this place,
Over the whiche day they may nat pace, 2140
Al mowe they yet tho dayes wel abregge:
Ther needeth non auctoritee t'allegge,
For it is preved by experience,
But that me list declaren my sentence.
Thanne may men by this ordre wel discerne
That thilke Moevere stable is and eterne:
Wel may men knowe, but it be a fool,
That every part deryveth from his hool,
For nature hath nat take his beginning
Of no partie ne cantel of a thing, 2150
But of a thing that parfit is and stable,
Descending so, til it be corrumpable.
And therfore, of his wyse purveyaunce,
He hath so wel biset his ordinaunce
That speces of thinges and progressiouns
Shullen enduren by successiouns,
And nat eterne, withouten any lyë:
This maistow understonde and seen at yë.
   Lo the ook, that hath so long a norisshinge
From tyme that it first biginneth springe, 2160
And hath so long a lyf, as we may see,
Yet at the laste wasted is the tree;
Considereth eek how that the harde stoon
Under oure feet, on which we trede and goon,
Yit wasteth it as it lyth by the weye;
The brode river somtyme wexeth dreye;
The grete tounes see we wane and wende—
Than may ye see that al this thing hath ende.
   Of man and womman seen we wel also,
That nedeth, in oon of thise termes two— 2170
This is to seyn, in youthe or elles age—
He moot ben deed, the king as shal a page:
Som in his bed, som in the depe see,
Some in the large feeld, as men may se;
Ther helpeth noght, al goth that ilke weye.
Thanne may I seyn that al this thing moot deye.
What maketh this but Juppiter the king,
That is prince and cause of alle thing,
Converting al unto his propre welle
From which it is deryved, sooth to telle? 2180

"has established down in this wretched world
certain periods and durations
for all that is engendered here,
beyond which limits they may not pass,
although they may well shorten their days;
it is not necessary to cite any authority;
for this is proved by experience;
but I desire to make my meaning clear.
We may well discern, then, by this orderliness
that that Mover is immovable and eternal.
Anyone but a fool may easily see
that every part derives from the whole to which it belongs,
for nature did not take its beginning
from a mere part or portion of a thing,
but from a thing that is complete and unchangeable,
descending until the point where it is subject to destruction.
And therefore in his wise providence
he has beyond doubt so well arranged his scheme
that particular things and happenings
are to last by succeeding themselves
and not by being individually eternal:
this you may comprehend and perceive at a glance.

   Look at the oak, that has so long a period of growth
from the time it first begins to sprout,
and has so long a life, as we may see:
yet at last the tree is destroyed.
Consider also beneath our feet the stone
on which we tread and travel,
hard as it is, yet wastes away as it lies by the road.
The broad river at some time goes dry.
We see great towns diminish and pass away.
You may see, then, that all these things have an end.

   In the case of man and woman also, we see
that necessarily in one of two periods—
that is to say, in youth or else in age—
the king as well as the page must die:
one in his bed, another in the deep sea,
another in the broad field, as one may perceive;
nothing helps; all go that same way.
I may then say that everything around us must die.
What causes this but Jupiter the ruler,
who, truthfully, is prince and cause of all things,
converting everything into its proper source
from which it was derived?

And here-agayns no creature on lyve,
Of no degree, availleth for to stryve.
    Thanne is it wisdom, as it thinketh me,
To maken vertu of necessitee,
And take it wel, that we may nat eschue,
And namely that to us alle is due.
And whoso gruccheth ought, he dooth folye,
And rebel is to him that al may gye.
And certeinly a man hath most honour
To dyen in his excellence and flour,   2190
Whan he is siker of his gode name;
Thanne hath he doon his freend, ne him, no shame.
And gladder oghte his freend ben of his deeth
Whan with honour up-yolden is his breeth,
Than whan his name apalled is for age,
For al forgeten is his vasselage.
Thanne is it best, as for a worthy fame,
To dyen whan that he is best of name.
    The contrarie of al this is wilfulnesse.
Why grucchen we? why have we hevinesse,   2200
That good Arcite, of chivalrye flour,
Departed is with duetee and honour
Out of this foule prison of this lyf?
Why grucchen heer his cosin and his wyf
Of his welfare that loved hem so weel?
Can he hem thank?—nay, God wot, never a deel—
That bothe his soule and eek hemself offende,
And yet they mowe hir lustes nat amende.
    What may I conclude of this longe serie,
But after wo I rede us to be merie   2210
And thanken Juppiter of al his grace?
And, er that we departen from this place,
I rede that we make of sorwes two
O parfyt joye, lasting everemo;
And loketh now, wher most sorwe is herinne,
Ther wol we first amenden and biginne.
    "Suster," quod he, "this is my fulle assent,
With al th'avys heer of my parlement,
That gentil Palamon, your owne knight,
That serveth yow with wil and herte and might,   2220
And evere hath doon sin ye first him knewe,
That ye shul of your grace upon him rewe,
And taken him for housbonde and for lord:
Lene me youre hond, for this is our acord.

Against this no living creature
of any condition succeeds in striving.
    Then it is wisdom, as it seems to me,
to make a virtue of necessity,
and to accept willingly what we may not avoid,
and particularly what happens to all of us.
Whoever complains at all is guilty of folly
and is rebellious against the one who has power to
control all. And, certainly, a man gains most honor
in dying in his excellence and flower,
when he is sure of his good name;
then he has done no shame to his friend, or to himself.
And his friend ought to be happier for his death
when his breath is given up with honor,
than when his name is faded with age;
for then his prowess is all forgotten.
Then it is best, for the sake of a worthy reputation,
for a man to die when his name is most esteemed.
    To deny all this is willfulness.
Why do we grumble? Why are we sad
that good Arcite, the flower of chivalry,
has departed with duty and honor
from the foul prison of this life?
Why do his cousin and his bride here complain
about the good fortune of him who loved them so well?
Can he thank them for it? No, God knows, not a bit—
not them, who offer offense to both his soul and themselves,
and still cannot cheer themselves up.
    What may I conclude from this long chain of reasoning
except that, after woe, I advise us to be merry
and thank Jupiter for all his favor?
And, before we leave this place,
I advise that we make out of two sorrows
one complete joy, lasting evermore;
and consider now, where there is most sorrow in this matter,
there will we first start the improvement.
    "Sister," he said, "this is my final opinion,
with the advice of my councillors here,
concerning Palamon, your own knight,
who serves you with will and heart and strength,
and has always done so since you first knew him:
that you should by your favor take pity on him
and accept him as husband and lord:
give me your hand, for this is our agreement.

Lat see now of your wommanly pitee.
He is a kinges brother sone, pardee;
And though he were a povre bacheler,
Sin he hath served yow so many a yeer,
And had for yow so greet adversitee,
It moste been considered, leveth me;   2230
For gentil mercy oghte to passen right."
    Than seyde he thus to Palamon the knight:
"I trowe ther nedeth litel sermoning
To make yow assente to this thing.
Com neer, and taak youre lady by the hond."
Bitwixen hem was maad anon the bond
That highte matrimoine or mariage,
By al the counseil and the baronage.
And thus with alle blisse and melodye
Hath Palamon y-wedded Emelye.   2240
And God, that al this wyde world hath wroght,
Sende him his love, that hath it dere aboght.
For now is Palamon in alle wele,
Living in blisse, in richesse, and in hele;
And Emelye him loveth so tendrely,
And he hir serveth al so gentilly,
That nevere was ther no word hem bitwene
Of jalousie, or any other tene.
Thus endeth Palamon and Emelye;
And God save al this faire companye.—Amen.   2250

Now let's see your womanly sympathy.
By heaven, he is son to the brother of a king;
and if he were nothing but a poor youth not yet a knight,
his service to you for so many a year,
and the great adversity he has suffered for you
would have to be considered, believe me; for gentle mercy
ought to be more esteemed than standing on one's rights."
　　Then he spoke thus to Palamon, the knight:
"I imagine that little preaching is needed
to make you agree to this.
Come near and take your lady by the hand."
Between them was then made the bond
that is called matrimony or marriage,
in the presence of all the council and nobility.
And thus with full bliss and melody
Palamon married Emily.
And God, Who has wrought all this wide world,
send him his love who has paid for it dearly.
Now is Palamon in complete happiness,
living in bliss, in riches, and in health;
and Emily loves him so tenderly,
and he serves her just so gently,
that there has never been between them a word
of jealousy or any other vexation.
Thus ends the story of Palamon and Emily,
and God save all this fair company. —Amen.

THE MILLERE

Wordes bitwene the Host and the Millere

WHAN that the Knight had thus his tale y-told,
In al the route nas ther yong ne old
That he ne seyde it was a noble storie,
And worthy for to drawen to memorie,
And namely the gentils everichoon.
Our Hoste lough and swoor, "So moot I goon,
This gooth aright: unbokeled is the male.
Lat see now who shal tell another tale,
For trewely the game is well bigonne.
Now telleth ye, sir Monk, if that ye conne,   10
Sumwhat to quyte with the Knightes tale."
The Miller, that for dronken was all pale,
So that unnethe upon his hors he sat,
He nolde avalen neither hood ne hat,
Ne abyde no man for his curteisye,
But in Pilates vois he gan to crye,
And swoor, "By armes and by blood and bones,
I can a noble tale for the nones,
With which I wol now quyte the Knightes tale!"
    Our Hoste saugh that he was dronke of ale,   20
And seyde, "Abyd, Robin, my leve brother;
Som bettre man shal telle us first another.
Abyd, and lat us werken thriftily."
    "By Goddes soul," quod he, "that wol nat I;
For I wol speke or elles go my wey."
Our Hoste answerde, "Tel on, a devel wey!
Thou art a fool, thy wit is overcome."
    "Now herkneth," quod the Miller, "alle and some.
But first I make a protestacioun
That I am dronke, I knowe it by my soun;   30
And therefore if that I misspeke or seye,
Wyte it the ale of Southwerk, I yow preye;
For I wol tell a legende and a lyf
Bothe of a carpenter and of his wyf,
How that a clerk hath set the wrightes cappe."
    The Reve answerde and seyde, "Stint thy clappe!

THE MILLER

Words between the Host and the Miller

WHEN the Knight had thus told his tale,
in all that company there was no one, young or old,
who did not say it was a noble story,
and worthy to be remembered,
particularly the gentlefolk, each and every one.
Our Host laughed, and swore, "As I may walk,
this goes well: the pouch is unbuckled.
Now let's see who shall tell another tale,
for the game is indeed well begun.
Now, sir Monk, if you can, tell
something to repay the Knight's tale."
The Miller, who was all pale with drunkenness,
so that he could hardly sit on his horse,
was not minded to doff his hood or hat
nor wait on any man for courtesy's sake,
but began to cry out in a voice like Pilate's,*
and swore, "By God's arms and blood and bones,
I know a splendid tale for the occasion,
with which I'll now match the Knight's tale!"

Our Host saw that he was drunk with ale,
and said, "Wait, Robin, my dear brother;
first some better man shall tell us another.
Wait, and let us do things properly."

"By God's soul," said he, "that I will not;
for I will speak or else go on my way."
Our Host answered, "Tell on, in the devil's name!
You are a fool; your wits are drowned."

"Now listen," said the Miller, "everyone.
But first I will proclaim that
I am drunk; I know it by the sound of my voice.
And therefore, if I speak amiss,
blame it on the ale of Southwark, I pray you;
for I am going to tell a legend, a history,
of both a carpenter and his wife,
and how a clerk* made a fool of the carpenter."

The Reeve answered and said, "Stop your gabble!

Lat be thy lewed dronken harlotrye.
It is a sinne and eek a greet folye
To apeiren any man or him diffame,
And eek to bringen wyves in swich fame.   40
Thou mayst ynogh of othere thinges seyn."
   This dronken Miller spak ful sone ageyn
And seyde, "Leve brother Osewold,
Who hath no wyf, he is no cokewold.
But I sey nat therfore that thou art oon;
Ther been ful gode wyves many oon,
And ever a thousand gode ayeyns oon badde;
That knowestow wel thyself, but if thou madde.
Why artow angry with my tale now?
I have a wyf, pardee, as well as thou;   50
Yet nolde I, for the oxen in my plogh,
Take upon me more than ynogh
As demen of myself that I were oon;
I wol beleve wel that I am noon.
An housbond shal nat been inquisitif
Of Goddes privetee, nor of his wyf.
So he may finde Goddes foyson there,
Of the remenant nedeth nat enquere."
   What sholde I more seyn but this Millere
He nolde his wordes for no man forbere,   60
But tolde his cherles tale in his manere,
M'athinketh that I shal reherce it here,
And therfore every gentil wight I preye,
For Goddes love, demeth nat that I seye
Of evel entent, but for I moot reherce
Hir tales alle, be they bettre or werse,
Or elles falsen some of my matere.
And therfore, whoso list it nat y-here,
Turne over the leef and chese another tale,
For he shal finde ynowe, grete and smale,   70
Of storial thing that toucheth gentillesse,
And eek moralitee and holinesse.
Blameth nat me if that ye chese amis.
The Miller is a cherl, ye knowe wel this;
So was the Reve, and othere mo,
And harlotrye they tolden bothe two.
Avyseth yow and putte me out of blame;
And eek men shal nat make ernest of game.

Leave off your stupid, drunken obscenity.
It is sinful and very foolish
to injure any man or defame him,
and also to bring wives into such repute.
You can say enough about other things."

This drunken Miller replied at once,
and said, "Dear brother Oswald,
he who has no wife is no cuckold.
But I don't say that therefore you are one;
there are a great many good wives,
and always a thousand good ones to one bad one;
you know that perfectly well yourself, unless you're crazy.
Why are you angry with my story now?
I have a wife, by God, just as you do;
yet I wouldn't, for the oxen in my plow,
take more than enough on myself so
as to think that I am a cuckold;
I will believe firmly that I am none.
A husband should not be inquisitive
about God's secrets—or his wife's.
Just so I can find God's plenty there,
there's no need to inquire about the rest."

What more should I say but that this Miller
would not spare his words for any man,
but told his churl's tale in his own way.
I regret that I must repeat it here,
and therefore I ask every well-bred person,
for God's love, don't think that I speak
with evil intentions; but I must repeat
all their tales, be they better or worse,
or else be false to some of my material.
And therefore whoever does not wish to hear it,
turn over the leaf and choose another tale;
for he shall find enough, long and short,
of narratives that deal with nobility,
and also morality and holiness.
Don't blame me if you choose amiss.
The Miller is a churl, you know this well;
so was the Reeve, and some of the others.
Both of them recited ribaldry.
Take heed, and don't put the blame on me;
and then, too, one should not take a game seriously.

Here biginneth the Millere his tale

WHYLOM ther was dwellinge at Oxenforde
A riche gnof, that gestes heeld to borde,
And of his craft he was a carpenter.
With him ther was dwellinge a poure scoler,
Hadde lerned art, but al his fantasye
Was turned for to lerne astrologye,
And coude a certeyn of conclusiouns
To demen by interrogaciouns,
If that men axed him in certein houres
Whan that men sholde have droghte or elles shoures,   10
Or if men axed him what sholde bifalle
Of every thing—I may nat rekene hem alle.
    This clerk was cleped hende* Nicholas;
Of derne love he coude, and of solas;
And therto he was sleigh and ful privee,*
And lyk a mayden meke for to see.
A chambre hadde he in that hostelrye
Allone, withouten any companye,
Ful fetisly y-dight with herbes swote;
And he himself as swete as is the rote
Of licorys or any cetewale.
His Almageste and bokes grete and smale,
His astrelabie, longinge for his art,
His augrim-stones layen faire apart
On shelves couched at his beddes heed;
His presse y-covered with a falding reed;
And al above ther lay a gay sautrye,
On which he made a-nightes melodye
So swetely that al the chambre rong;
And *Angelus ad virginem* he song;   30
And after that he song the kinges note;
Ful often blessed was his myrie throte.
And thus this swete clerk his tyme spente
After his freendes finding and his rente.
    This carpenter had wedded newe a wyf
Which that he lovede more than his lyf;
Of eightetene yeer she was of age.
Jalous he was, and heeld hire narwe in cage,
For she was wilde and yong, and he was old,
And demed himself ben lyk a cokewold.   40
He knew nat Catoun, for his wit was rude,
That bad man sholde wedde his similitude:

Here begins the Miller's tale

ONCE upon a time there lived at Oxford
a rich churl who boarded paying guests;
he was a carpenter by trade.
At his house lived a poor scholar
who had completed part of his arts* course, but his whole
imagination was directed to learning astrology.
He knew a number of propositions
by which to make a decision in astrological analyses
in certain hours if you asked him
when you would have drought or else showers,
or if you asked him what should come
of all sorts of things; I can't mention all of them.
     This clerk was named pleasant Nicholas;
he knew all about secret love and pleasurable consolations,
and, besides, he was sly and very discreet
and looked as meek as a maiden.
In that boarding house he had a room,
alone, without further company,
and nicely decked with fragrant herbs;
and he himself was as sweet and clean as the root
of licorice or any ginger.
His *Almagest* and books large and small,
his astrolabe, proper to his art,
and his counters for arithmetic lay neatly separated
on shelves set at the head of his bed;
his storage chest was covered with a red woolen cloth.
At the top there lay a pretty psaltery
on which by night he made melody
so sweetly that all the room rang with it;
he sang *Angelus* ad virginem,
and after that he sang the King's Tune;
people often blessed his merry voice.
And thus this sweet clerk spent his time,
depending upon his friends' support and his income.
     This carpenter had recently married a wife
whom he loved more than his life;
she was eighteen years of age.
He was jealous and kept her on a short leash,
for she was wild and young, and he was old,
and judged himself near to being a cuckold.
He did not know (for his understanding was crude) Cato's*
saying that a man should marry someone like himself:

Men sholde wedden after hir estaat,
For youthe and elde is often at debaat.
But sith that he was fallen in the snare,
He moste endure, as other folk, his care.
   Fair was this yonge wyf, and therwithal
As any wesele hir body gent and smal.
A ceynt she werede barred al of silk,
A barmclooth eek as whyt as morne milk   50
Upon hir lendes, ful of many a gore.
Whyt was hir smok and broyden al bifore
And eek bihinde, on hir coler aboute,
Of col-blak silk, withinne and eek withoute.
The tapes of hir whyte voluper
Were of the same suyte of hir coler;
Hir filet brood of silk, and set ful hye;
And sikerly she hadde a likerous yë.
Ful smale y-pulled were hir browes two,
And tho were bent and blake as any sloo.   60
She was ful more blisful on to see
Than is the newe pere-jonette tree;
And softer than the wolle is of a wether.
And by hir girdel heeng a purs of lether,
Tasseld with silk, and perled with latoun.
In al this world, to seken up and doun,
There nis no man so wys that coude thenche
So gay a popelote or swich a wenche.
Ful brighter was the shyning of hir hewe
Than in the tour the noble y-forged newe.   70
But of hir song, it was as loude and yerne
As any swalwe sitting on a berne.
Therto she coude skippe and make game
As any kide or calf folwinge his dame.
Hir mouth was swete as bragot or the meeth,
Or hord of apples leyd in hey or heeth.
Winsinge she was as is a joly colt,
Long as a mast, and upright as a bolt.
A brooch she baar upon hir lowe coler
As brood as is the bos of a bocler.
Hir shoes were laced on hir legges hye.
She was a prymerole, a pigges-nye,
For any lord to leggen in his bedde,
Or yet for any good yeman to wedde.
   Now sire, and eft sire, so bifel the cas,
That on a day this hende Nicholas

people should wed according to their condition,
for youth and age are often at odds.
But since he had fallen into the trap,
he had to endure his trouble, like other people.
    This young wife was lovely;
her body was as graceful and slim as a weasel's.
She wore a sash threaded with silk,
and around her loins a flared apron
white as morning-fresh milk;
her smock was white, and embroidered with
black silk around the collar,
inside and outside, front and back.
The ribbons of her cap
matched her collar,
and her broad silk headband sat well back from her face.
And—certainly—she had a wanton eye.
Her eyebrows were closely plucked,
and they arched gracefully and were black as a sloe.
She was more of a treat to look at
than a peartree, just come into bloom,
and she was softer to touch than the wool of a sheep.
At her waist hung a leather purse,
tasseled with silk and beaded in bright metal.
In all this world, if you search up and down,
you can find no man clever enough to imagine
so gay a poppet or such a wench. The brilliance
of her coloring was better than the gleam of a
gold noble* newly minted in the Tower of London.
As for her singing, it was as clear and lively
as the notes of a barn swallow.
Besides all this, she could gambol and play
like any kid or calf following his mother.
Her mouth was as sweet as drinks made from honey,
or as a hoard of apples laid away in hay or heather.
She was skittish as a colt,
tall as a mast, and straight as an arrow.
On her low collar she wore a brooch
as broad as the boss of a buckler.
Her shoes were laced far up her legs.
She was a morning glory, she was a daisy,
fit for any lord to lay in his bed,
or yet for any good yeoman to marry.
    Now sir, and again sir, the case so befell
that one day this pleasant Nicholas

Fil with this yonge wyf to rage and pleye,
Whyl that hir housbond was at Oseneye,
As clerkes ben ful subtile and ful queynte;
And prively he caughte hir by the queynte,   90
And seyde, "y-wis, but if ich have my wille,
For derne love of thee, lemman, I spille."
And heeld hir harde by the haunche-bones,
And seyde, "lemman, love me al at-ones,
Or I wol dyen, also God me save!"
And she sprong as a colt doth in the trave,
And with hir heed she wryed faste awey,
And seyde, "I wol nat kisse thee, by my fey.
Why, lat be," quod she, "lat be, Nicholas!
Or I wol crye 'out, harrow' and 'allas.'   100
Do wey your handes, for your curteisye!"

   This Nicholas gan mercy for to crye,
And spak so faire, and profred hir so faste,
That she hir love him graunted atte laste,
And swoor hir ooth, by Seint Thomas of Kent,
That she wol been at his comandement,
Whan that she may hir leyser wel espye.
"Myn housbond is so ful of jalousye
That, but ye wayte wel and been privee,
I woot right wel I nam but deed," quod she.   110
"Ye moste been ful derne, as in this case."

   "Nay, therof care thee noght," quod Nicholas,
"A clerk hadde litherly biset his whyle,
But if he coude a carpenter bigyle."
And thus they been acorded and y-sworn
To wayte a tyme, as I have told biforn.
Whan Nicholas had doon thus everydeel,
And thakked hir aboute the lendes weel,
He kist hir swete, and taketh his sautrye,
And pleyeth faste, and maketh melodye.   120

   Thanne fil it thus, that to the parissh chirche,
Cristes owne werkes for to wirche,
This gode wyf wente on an haliday:
Hir forheed shoon as bright as any day,
So was it wasshen whan she leet hir werk.

   Now was ther of that chirche a parissh clerk,
The which that was y-cleped Absolon.
Crul was his heer, and as the gold it shoon,
And strouted as a fanne large and brode;
Ful streight and even lay his joly shode.   130

happened to flirt and play with this young wife
while her husband was at Osney
(these clerks are very subtle and sly),
and privily he grabbed her where he shouldn't
and said, "Unless I have my will of you,
sweetheart, I'm sure to die for suppressed love."
And he held her hard by the hips
and said, "Sweetheart, love me right away
or I'll die, so God help me!"
She jumped like a colt imprisoned in a shoeing frame
and twisted her head away hard
and said, "I won't kiss you, on my faith;
why let be," she said, "let be, Nicholas,
or I'll cry 'Help!' and 'Alas!'
Take away your hands; where are your manners!"

   This Nicholas started begging for mercy
and spoke so prettily and pushed himself so hard
that she finally granted him her love
and made her oath, by Saint Thomas à Becket,
that she would be his to command —
when she could see her opportunity.
"My husband is so filled with jealousy
that, unless you are on guard and keep it a secret,
I know for sure that I'm as good as dead," she said.
"You must be very discreet in this matter."

   "No, don't bother about that," said Nicholas,
"A clerk would certainly have spent his time poorly
if he couldn't fool a carpenter."
And thus they agreed and promised
to look out for an occasion, as I told before.
When Nicholas had accomplished all this,
and patted her thoroughly about the loins,
he kissed her sweetly, and took his psaltery
and played it hard and made music.

   Then it happened that this good wife
went to the parish church on a holy day
to perform Christ's own works:
her forehead shone as bright as day,
it had been washed so thoroughly when she left her work.

   Now, there was a parish clerk of that church
who was called Absalom.
His hair was curly and shone like gold
and spread out like a big, wide fan;
the pretty parting of his hair lay straight and even.

His rode was reed, his eyen greye as goos;
With Powles window corven on his shoos,
In hoses rede he wente fetisly.
Y-clad he was ful smal and proprely,
Al in a kirtel of a light wachet—
Ful faire and thikke been the poyntes set.
And therupon he hadde a gay surplys
As whyt as is the blosme upon the rys.
A merye child he was, so God me save.
Wel coude he laten blood and clippe and shave,   140
And maken a chartre of lond, or acquitaunce.
In twenty manere coude he trippe and daunce,
After the scole of Oxenforde tho,
And with his legges casten to and fro,
And pleyen songes on a small rubible;
Therto he song somtyme a loud quinible,
And as wel coude he pleye on a giterne.
In al the toun nas brewhous ne taverne
That he ne visited with his solas,
Ther any gaylard tappestere was.   150
But sooth to seyn, he was somdel squaymous
Of farting, and of speche daungerous.

   This Absolon, that jolif was and gay,
Gooth with a sencer on the haliday,
Sensinge the wyves of the parish faste;
And many a lovely look on hem he caste,
And namely on this carpenteres wyf:
To loke on hir him thoughte a merye lyf,
She was so propre and swete and likerous.
I dar wel seyn, if she had been a mous,   160
And he a cat, he wolde hire hente anon.
This parissh clerk, this joly Absolon,
Hath in his herte swich a love-longinge
That of no wyf ne took he noon offringe;
For curteisye, he seyde, he wolde noon.

   The mone, whan it was night, ful brighte shoon,
And Absolon his giterne hath y-take,
For paramours he thoghte for to wake.
And forth he gooth, jolif and amorous,
Til he cam to the carpenteres hous   170
A litel after cokkes hadde y-crowe,
And dressed him up by a shot-windowe
That was upon the carpenteres wal.
He singeth in his vois gentil and smal,

his complexion was red, his eyes as gray as a goose;
he went very elegantly in red hose,
with St. Paul's window* tooled into his shoes.
He was dressed very properly and with a close fit
in a light blue tunic;
its laces were set in neatly and close together.
In addition he had a handsome surplice
as white as a blossom on the bough.
He was a merry lad, God help me.
He well knew how to let blood, to clip hair, and to shave,
and how to draw up a charter of land or a release.
He could trip and dance twenty different ways — *good*
according to the then manner of Oxford   *dancer*
and prance to and fro on his legs,
and play song tunes on a small fiddle
(he sometimes sang the high treble loudly);
and he could play as well on his guitar.
There wasn't a beer house or tavern in the whole town
that he didn't visit with his entertainment,
if there was any gay barmaid there.
But, to tell the truth, he was a little squeamish
about farting and prim in his speech.

  This Absalom, who was lively and playful,
went with a censer on the holy day
censing the wives of the parish zealously,
and many a loving look he cast upon them,
particularly on the carpenter's wife:
looking at her seemed a merry life to him,
she was so neat and sweet and appetizing.
I daresay that if she had been a mouse
and he a cat, he would have grabbed her right away.
Jolly Absalom, this parish clerk,
had such love longing in his heart
that he accepted no offering from any wife;
he said that he wouldn't for the sake of his manners.

  When night came, the moon shone brightly
and Absalom took his guitar,
for he planned to stay up as lovers do.
Forth he went, lusty and amorous,
until he came to the carpenter's house
a little after cockcrow,
and took his stand by a hinged window
in the carpenter's wall.
He sang in his refined, dainty voice,

"Now, dere lady, if thy wille be,
I preye yow that ye wol rewe on me,"
Ful wel acordaunt to his giterninge.
This carpenter awook and herde him singe,
And spak unto his wyf, and seyde anon,
"What, Alison, herestow nat Absolon   180
That chaunteth thus under our boures wal?"
And she answerde hir housbond therwithal,
"Yis, god wot, John, I here it every-del."
      This passeth forth. what wol ye bet than wel?
Fro day to day this joly Absolon
So woweth hire, that him is wo-bigon:
He waketh the night and al the day;
He kempte hise lokkes brode and made him gay;
He woweth hir by menes and brocage,
And swoor he wolde been hir owne page;   190
He singeth, brokkinge as a nightingale;
He sente hir piment, meeth, and spyced ale,
And wafres, pyping hote out of the glede;
And, for she was of toune, he profred mede.
For som folk wol ben wonnen for richesse,
And som for strokes, and som for gentillesse.
      Somtyme to shewe his lightnesse and maistrye,
He pleyeth Herodes upon a scaffold hye.
But what availleth him as in this cas?
She loveth so this hende Nicholas   200
That Absolon may blowe the bukkes horn;
He ne hadde for his labour but a scorn;
And thus she maketh Absolon hir ape,
And al his ernest turneth til a jape.
Ful sooth is this proverbe, it is no lye;
Men seyn right thus, "Alwey the nye slye
Maketh the fere leve to be looth."
For though that Absolon be wood or wrooth,
By cause that he fer was from hir sighte,
This nye Nicholas stood in his lighte.   210
      Now bere thee wel, thou hende Nicholas,
For Absolon may waille and singe "Allas."
And so bifel it on a Saterday
This carpenter was goon til Osenay;
And hende Nicholas and Alisoun
Acorded been to this conclusioun,
That Nicholas shal shapen him a wyle
This sely jalous housbonde to bigyle;

"Now, dear lady, if it be your will,
I pray you to take pity on me,"
nicely in tune with his playing.
The carpenter woke up and heard him sing
and spoke to his wife saying,
"Why, Alison, don't you hear Absalom
singing that way below our chamber wall?"
And she thereupon answered her husband,
"Yes; God knows, John, I hear every bit of it."

So things went on. What do you want better than good
enough? From day to day this pretty Absalom
wooed her until he was woebegone:
he stayed awake all night and all day;
he combed his wide-spreading locks and made himself look
pretty; he wooed her by go-betweens and proxy
and swore he would be her own page;
he sang quaveringly, like a nightingale;
he sent her sweetened wine, mead, spiced ale,
and pastries piping hot out of the coals;
and (since she was a townswoman) he offered bribes.
For some will be won with riches,
some with blows, and some with kindness.

Once, to show his agility and skill,
he played Herod* on a high scaffold.
But what use was anything to him in this case?
She loved pleasant Nicholas so much
that Absalom could go whistle to the wind;
he earned nothing but scorn for his labors;
thus she made a monkey of Absalom
and turned all his seriousness into a joke.
There's no doubt that this proverb is very true;
men say just this: "Always the nearby sly one
makes the distant dear one to be hated."
Though Absalom may be raging and furious
because he was far from her sight,
this nearby Nicholas stood in his light.

Now play your part well, you pleasant Nicholas,
for Absalom may wail and sing "Alas."
And so it happened on a Saturday
that this carpenter had gone to Osney;
and pleasant Nicholas and Alison
agreed to this effect,
that Nicholas should invent himself a trick
to fool this simple-minded, jealous husband;

And if so be the game wente aright,
She sholde slepen in his arm al night, 220
For this was his desyr and hir also.
And right anon, withouten wordes mo,
This Nicholas no lenger wolde tarie,
But doth ful softe unto his chambre carie
Bothe mete and drinke for a day or tweye,
And to hir housbonde bad hire for to seye,
If that he axed after Nicholas,
She sholde seye she niste where he was—
Of al that day she saugh him nat with yë;
She trowed that he was in maladye, 230
For for no cry hir mayde coude him calle;
He nolde answere, for nothing that mighte falle.

This passeth forth al thilke Saterday
That Nicholas stille in his chambre lay,
And eet, and sleep, or dide what him leste,
Til Sonday that the sonne gooth to reste.

This sely carpenter hath greet merveyle
Of Nicholas, or what thing mighte him eyle,
And seyde, "I am adrad, by Seint Thomas,
It stondeth nat aright with Nicholas. 240
God shilde that he deyde sodeynly!
This world is now ful tikel, sikerly:
I saugh today a cors y-born to chirche
That now, on Monday last, I saugh him wirche.
Go up," quod he unto his knave anoon;
"Clepe at his dore, or knokke with a stoon.
Loke how it is, and tel me boldely."

This knave gooth him up ful sturdily,
And at the chambre-dore, whyl that he stood,
He cryde and knokked as that he were wood, 250
"What! how! what do ye, maister Nicholay?
How may ye slepen al the longe day?"

But al for noght; he herde nat a word.
An hole he fond, ful lowe upon a bord,
Ther as the cat was wont in for to crepe;
And at that hole he looked in ful depe,
And at the laste he hadde of him a sighte.
This Nicholas sat evere caping uprighte,
As he had kyked on the newe mone.
Adoun he gooth, and tolde his maister sone 260
In what array he saugh this ilke man.

This carpenter to blessen him bigan,

and if the game went right,
she would sleep in his arms all night,
for this was his desire, and hers, too.
Right away, without another word,
Nicholas wouldn't stand for further tarrying
but very quietly carried to his room
both food and drink for a day or two,
and told her to say to her husband
if he asked for Nicholas
that she didn't know where he was—
that she hadn't laid eyes on him all that day;
and that she imagined he was sick,
for her maid couldn't rouse him, no matter how she shouted;
he wouldn't answer, no matter what happened.

It followed that all that Saturday
and until sundown on Sunday
Nicholas stayed quiet in his room
and ate and slept, or did whatever he wanted.

This foolish carpenter was astonished
at Nicholas and wondered what ailed him;
he said, "By St. Thomas, I am afraid
that things aren't right with Nicholas.
God forbid that he should die suddenly!
This world now is very ticklish, in truth:
I saw a corpse being borne to church today,
and just last Monday I saw the man going about his business.
Go up," he said then to his servant,
"call at his door or knock with a stone.
See how matters stand, and tell me straight out."

This servant went up sturdily,
and as he stood at the chamber door
he shouted and knocked like mad.
"How now, what are you doing, Master Nicholas?
How can you sleep all day long?"

But all for nothing; he heard not a word.
He found a hole low down on one of the boards
where the cat was accustomed to creep in,
and he looked far in there;
at last he had a sight of him.
Nicholas sat there, continuously gaping up in the air,
as though he were gazing at the new moon.
The servant went down and soon told his master
in what state he had seen this man.

The carpenter set to crossing himself

And seyde, "Help us, Seinte Frideswyde!
A man woot litel what him shal bityde.
This man is falle, with his astromye,
In som woodnesse or in som agonye;
I thoghte ay wel how that it sholde be!—
Men sholde nat knowe of Goddes privetee.
Ye, blessed be alwey a lewed man,
That noght but only his bileve can.   270
So ferde another clerk with astromye:
He walked in the feeldes for to prye
Upon the sterres, what ther sholde bifalle,
Til he was in a marle-pit y-falle—
He saugh nat that. But yet, by Seint Thomas,
Me reweth sore of hende Nicholas.
He shal be rated of his studying,
If that I may, by Jesus, hevene king!
Get me a staf, that I may underspore,
Whyl that thou, Robin, hevest up the dore.   280
He shal out of his studying, as I gesse."
And to the chambre-dore he gan him dresse.
His knave was a strong carl for the nones,
And by the haspe he haf it up atones:
Into the floor the dore fil anon.
This Nicholas sat ay as stille as stoon,
And ever caped upward into the eir.
This carpenter wende he were in despeir,
And hente him by the sholdres mightily,
And shook him harde, and cryde spitously,   290
"What, Nicholay! what, how! what! loke adoun!
Awaak, and thenk on Cristes passioun!
I crouche thee from elves and fro wightes."
Therwith the night-spel seyde he anon-rightes
On foure halves of the hous aboute,
And on the threshfold of the dore withoute:
    "Jesu Crist and seinte Benedight,
    Blesse this hous from every wikked wight;
    For nightes nerye the White Pater Noster.*
    Where wentestow, seynt Petres soster?"   300
And atte laste this hende Nicholas
Gan for to syke sore, and seyde, "Allas,
Shal al the world be lost eftsones now?"
    This carpenter answerde, "What seystow?
What! thenk on God, as we don, men that swinke."
    This Nicholas answerde, "Fecche me drinke,

and said, "Help us, Saint Frideswide!
A man little knows what is going to happen to him.
This man has fallen, with his astromy,
into some madness or fit;
I always thought it would be this way!—
men shouldn't pry into the secret things of God.
Yea, ever blessed be an unschooled man
who knows nothing but his creed.
Another clerk fared the same way with astromy:
he walked in the fields to pry
upon the stars and find out what was to occur
until he fell into a pit of fertilizer—
he didn't see that. And yet, by St. Thomas,
I sorely pity pleasant Nicholas.
He shall be scolded for his studying
if I can do it, by Jesus, heaven's king!
Get me a staff, so that I can pry underneath
while you, Robin, heave up the door.
He shall come out of his studying, I'll bet."
And he began to apply himself to the chamber door.
His servant was a strong fellow for the purpose,
and he heaved it up at once by the hasp:
the door then fell on the floor.
Nicholas continued to sit as still as stone
and kept gaping up in the air.
The carpenter thought that Nicholas was in a fit,
and seized him strongly by the shoulders
and shook him hard, crying roughly,
"What! Nicholas, what! Look down!
Awake, and think on Christ's Passion!
I sign you with the cross against elves and evil creatures."
Then he immediately said the night charm
toward the four quarters of the house
and on the threshold of the outside door:
  "Jesus Christ and Saint Benedict,
  bless this house against every wicked creature;
  let the White Pater Noster defend us by night.
  Where did you go, Saint Peter's sister?"
At last pleasant Nicholas
began to sigh sorely and said, "Alas,
shall all this world now be lost again?"
  The carpenter answered, "What are you saying?
How now! Think on God, as we do—we men that work."
  Nicholas answered, "Bring me something to drink,

And after wol I speke in privetee
Of certeyn thing that toucheth me and thee;
I wol telle it non other man, certeyn."
    This carpenter goth doun and comth ageyn,   310
And broghte of mighty ale a large quart;
And whan that ech of hem had dronke his part,
This Nicholas his dore faste shette,
And doun the carpenter by him he sette.
    He seyde, "John, myn hoste lief and dere,
Thou shalt upon thy trouthe swere me here
That to no wight thou shalt this conseil wreye;
For it is Cristes conseil that I seye,
And if thou telle it man, thou are forlore,
For this vengeaunce thou shalt han therfore,   320
That if thou wreye me, thou shalt be wood."
"Nay, Crist forbede it, for his holy blood!"
Quod tho this sely man, "I nam no labbe;
Ne, though I seye, I nam nat lief to gabbe.
Sey what thou wolt, I shal it nevere telle
To child ne wyf, by Him that harwed helle."
    "Now John," quod Nicholas, "I wol nat lye;
I have y-founde in myn astrologye,
As I have loked in the mone bright,
That now a Monday next, at quarter night,   330
Shal falle a reyn, and that so wilde and wood,
That half so greet was never Noës flood.
This world," he seyde, "in lasse than an hour
Shal al be dreynt, so hidous is the shour;
Thus shal mankynde drenche, and lese hir lyf."
    This carpenter answerde, "Allas, my wyf!
And shal she drenche? allas, myn Alisoun!"
For sorwe of this he fil almost adoun,
And seyde, "Is ther no remedie in this cas?"
    "Why, yis, for Gode," quod hende Nicholas,   340
"If thou wolt werken after lore and reed—
Thou mayst nat werken after thyn owene heed;
For thus seith Salomon, that was ful trewe,
'Werk al by conseil, and thou shalt nat rewe.'
And if thou werken wolt by good conseil,
I undertake, withouten mast and seyl,
Yet shal I saven hir and thee and me.
Hastow nat herd how saved was Noë,
Whan that oure Lord hadde warned him biforn
That al the world with water sholde be lorn?"   350

and afterwards I want to speak in private
of a certain thing that concerns you and me;
I won't tell it to another man, for sure."

The carpenter went down and came up again,
bringing a generous quart of strong ale;
and when each of them had drunk his share,
Nicholas shut his door tight
and sat the carpenter down beside him.

He said, "John, my beloved and esteemed host,
you shall swear to me here on your word of honor
that you will not betray this secret to any creature;
for it is Christ's secret that I am going to utter,
and if you tell it to anyone, you are lost,
because for doing so you shall suffer this vengeance:
if you betray me, you shall go mad."
"No, Christ forbid it for the sake of his holy blood!"
said this simple man, "I am no blabber;
no, though I say it myself, I don't like to gossip.
Say what you will, I shall never tell it
to child or wife, by Him Who harrowed hell."

"Now, John," said Nicholas, "I won't lie;
I have discovered in my astrology,
as I was looking at the bright moon,
that on Monday next, when a quarter of the night is still
to go, there shall fall a rain, so wild and furious
that Noah's flood was never half so great.
In less than an hour," he said, "this world
shall be drowned, so hideous will be the downpour;
thus all mankind shall drown and lose their lives."

The carpenter answered, "Alas, my wife!
Shall she drown? Alas, my Alison!"
For his sorrow at this he almost collapsed,
and said, "Is there no remedy in this matter?"

"Why, yes, indeed, by God," said pleasant Nicholas,
"if you will act according to learning and advice—
you may not act according to your own idea;
for thus says Solomon, who was very truthful,
'Do everything according to advice and you will not be sorry.'
And if you will act on good advice,
I promise that, without mast or sail,
I shall yet save her and you and myself.
Haven't you heard how Noah was saved
when our Lord had forewarned him
that all the world should be lost by water?"

"Yis," quod this carpenter, "ful yore ago."
"Hastow nat herd," quod Nicholas, "also
The sorwe of Noë with his felaweshipe,
Er that he mighte gete his wyf to shipe?
Him hadde be lever, I dar wel undertake,
At thilke tyme, than alle hise wetheres blake
That she hadde had a ship hirself allone.
And therfore, wostou what is best to done?
This asketh haste, and of an hastif thing
Men may nat preche or maken tarying.   360

Anon go gete us faste into this in
A kneding-trogh or elles a kimelin
For ech of us, but loke that they be large,
In whiche we mowe swimme as in a barge,
And han ther-inne vitaille suffisant
But for a day—fy on the remenant!
The water shal aslake and goon away
Aboute pryme upon the nexte day.

But Robin may nat wite of this, thy knave,
Ne eek thy mayde Gille I may nat save;   370
Axe nat why, for though thou aske me,
I wol nat tellen Goddes privetee.
Suffiseth thee, but if thy wittes madde,
To han as greet a grace as Noë hadde.
Thy wyf shal I wel saven, out of doute.
Go now thy wey, and speed thee heer-aboute.

But whan thou hast, for hir and thee and me,
Y-geten us thise kneding-tubbes three,
Thanne shaltow hange hem in the roof ful hye,
That no man of oure purveyaunce spye.   380
And whan thou thus hast doon as I have seyd,
And hast our vitaille faire in hem y-leyd,
And eek an ax to smyte the corde atwo
When that the water comth, that we may go,
And broke an hole an heigh upon the gable
Unto the gardin-ward, over the stable,
That we may frely passen forth our way
Whan that the grete shour is goon away—
Than shaltow swimme as myrie, I undertake,
As doth the whyte doke aftir hir drake.   390
Than wol I clepe, 'how, Alison! how, John!
Be myrie, for the flood wol passe anon.'
And thou wolt seyn, 'Hayl, maister Nicholay!
Good morwe, I se thee wel, for it is day!'

"Certainly," said the carpenter, "long ago."

"Haven't you heard also," said Nicholas,
"of the anxiety of Noah and his companions
until he could get his wife* on board?
I'll bet that that time he would rather have
had her have a ship to herself
than keep all his fine black wethers.
And do you know what's best to do for all this?
This requires haste, and about an urgent matter
you mayn't preach or make delay.

Go promptly and bring right into this inn
a kneading trough, or else a shallow tub,
for each of us, but be sure they are large ones,
in which we can float as in a ship,
and have in them victuals enough
for a day only—fie on the rest!
The water shall diminish and go away
about nine in the morning the next day.

But Robin, your servant, may not know of this,
and I mayn't save Jill, your maid, either;
don't ask why, for even if you do,
I won't reveal God's private affairs.
It is enough for you, unless you are mad,
to have as great grace as Noah had.
I shall indeed save your wife, beyond a doubt.
Now go your way, and hurry about our business.

But when, for her and yourself and me, you have
got us these three kneading tubs,
then you are to hang them high up in the roof,
so that no one will spy out our preparations.
And when you've done as I have said,
and have stowed our victuals in them safely,
and an axe, too, to cut the rope in two
when the water comes, so that we may float,
and when you've broken a hole high up on the gable
toward the garden and over the stable,
so that we can get out freely on our way
when the great rain is over—
then you'll float as merrily, I promise,
as the white duck does after her drake.
Then I'll call out, 'How now, Alison! How now, John!
Cheer up; the flood will go away soon,'
and you will say, 'Hail, Master Nicholas!
Good morning, I see you well, it's light.'

And thanne shul we be lordes al oure lyf
Of al the world, as Noë and his wyf.
   But of o thyng I warne thee ful right:
Be wel avysed on that ilke night
That we ben entred into shippes bord
That noon of us ne speke nat a word,   400
Ne clepe, ne crye, but been in his preyere,
For it is Goddes owne heste dere.
   Thy wyf and thou mote hange fer a-twinne,
For that bitwixe yow shal be no sinne—
Namore in looking than ther shal in dede.
This ordinance is seyd; go, God thee spede.
Tomorwe at night, whan men ben alle aslepe,
Into oure kneding-tubbes wol we crepe,
And sitten ther, abyding Goddes grace.
Go now thy wey, I have no lenger space   410
To make of this no lenger sermoning.
Men seyn thus, 'send the wyse, and sey nothing';
Thou art so wys it nedeth thee nat teche:
Go, save our lyf, and that I thee biseche."
   This sely carpenter goth forth his wey.
Ful ofte he seide "Allas" and "Weylawey,"
And to his wyf he tolde his privetee;
And she was war, and knew it bet than he,
What al this queynte cast was for to seye.
But nathelees she ferde as she wolde deye,   420
And seyde, "Allas! go forth thy wey anon,
Help us to scape, or we been dede echon.
I am thy trewe verray wedded wyf:
Go, dere spouse, and help to save oure lyf."
   Lo! which a greet thyng is affeccioun:
Men may dyen of imaginacioun,
So depe may impressioun be take.
This sely carpenter biginneth quake;
Him thinketh verraily that he may see
Noës flood come walwing as the see   430
To drenchen Alisoun, his hony dere.
He wepeth, weyleth, maketh sory chere;
He syketh with ful many a sory swogh;
He gooth and geteth him a kneding-trogh,
And after that a tubbe and a kimelin,
And prively he sente hem to his in,
And heng hem in the roof in privetee.
His owne hand he made laddres three

And then we shall be lords for all our lives
of all the world, like Noah and his wife.
 But I caution you about one thing for sure:
be well forewarned that on that same night
when we have gone on shipboard,
none of us speak a word,
or call, or cry out, but be in prayer,
for it is God's own precious command.
 Your wife and you must hang far apart
so that there shall be no sin between you,
any more in looking than in deed.
Our arrangement has been described; go, Godspeed.
Tomorrow night, when everyone is asleep,
we'll creep into our kneading tubs
and sit there, awaiting God's grace.
Now go on your way, I have no more time
to make a longer sermon of this.
People speak thus, 'Send the wise and say nothing';
you are so wise that there is no need to teach you:
go, save our lives, I beseech you."
 The foolish carpenter went his way.
Often he said, "Alas" and "Alack,"
and he told his secret to his wife;
she was aware of it, and knew better than he
what all this elaborate contrivance amounted to.
Nevertheless, she behaved as though she would die,
and said, "Alas! Go your way immediately,
help us to escape, or we are lost, each one of us.
I am your faithful, true, wedded wife:
go, dear spouse, and help to save our lives."
 Look what a great thing emotion is!
one may die by force of imagining things,
so deeply may a notion be imprinted.
This foolish carpenter began to shake;
he thinks in truth that he can see
Noah's flood come surging like the sea
to drown Alison, his honey-dear.
He weeps, wails, looks mournful;
he sighs with many a sorry gust;
he went and got himself a kneading trough,
and after that two tubs,
and secretly he sent them to his inn
and hung them under the roof in privacy.
With his own hand he made three ladders

To climben by the ronges and the stalkes
Unto the tubbes hanginge in the balkes,   440
And hem vitailled, bothe trogh and tubbe,
With breed and chese, and good ale in a jubbe,
Suffysinge right ynogh as for a day.
But er that he hadde maad al this array,
He sente his knave, and eek his wenche also,
Upon his nede to London for to go.
And on the Monday whan it drow to night,
He shette his dore withouten candel-light,
And dressed alle thing as it sholde be.
And shortly, up they clomben alle three;   450
They sitten stille wel a furlong wey.
    "Now, *Pater-noster,* clom," seyde Nicholay,
And "Clom," quod John, and "Clom," seyde Alisoun.
This carpenter seyde his devocioun,
And stille he sit and biddeth his preyere,
Awaytinge on the reyn, if he it here.
    The dede sleep, for wery bisinesse,
Fil on this carpenter right, as I gesse,
Aboute corfew-tyme, or litel more;
For travail of his goost he groneth sore,   460
And eft he routeth, for his heed mislay.
Doun of the laddre stalketh Nicholay,
And Alisoun ful softe adoun she spedde;
Withouten wordes mo they goon to bedde
Ther as the carpenter is wont to lye.
Ther was the revel and the melodye,
And thus lyth Alison and Nicholas
In bisinesse of mirthe and of solas
Til that the belle of Laudes gan to ringe
And freres in the chauncel gonne singe.   470
    This parissh clerk, this amorous Absolon,
That is for love alwey so wo-bigon,
Upon the Monday was at Oseneye,
With companye him to disporte and pleye,
And axed upon cas a cloisterer
Ful prively after John the carpenter;
And he drough him apart out of the chirche,
And seyde, "I noot, I saugh him here nat wirche
Sin Saterday; I trow that he be went
For timber ther oure abbot hath him sent,   480
For he is wont for timber for to go
And dwellen at the grange a day or two—

on which they might climb by the rungs and uprights
to the tubs hanging in the rafters,
and victualed both trough and tub
with bread and cheese and good ale in a jug,
quite sufficient for a day.
But before he installed all this array,
he sent his manservant, and also the girl,
to go to London on an errand for him.
On Monday, when night drew on,
he shut his door without lighting any candles
and arranged everything as it was supposed to be.
And, shortly, they climbed up all three;
they sat still for the time it takes to go a furlong.

"Now, *Pater Noster,* hush!" said Nicholas,
and "Hush," said John, and "Hush," said Alison.
The carpenter recited his devotions,
and sat still, offering his prayers
and waiting to see whether he might hear the rain.

Wearied by his own diligence, the carpenter
fell into a dead sleep—as I judge, just
about curfew* time, or a little later.
He groaned painfully for the affliction of his spirit,
and then he snored, for his head lay uncomfortably.
Nicholas crept down from the ladder
and Alison hurried down very softly;
without more words they went to bed
where the carpenter was wont to lie.
There was the revel and the harmony,
and thus lay Alison and Nicholas
in diligence of mirth and pleasure
until the bell of Lauds began to ring
and friars began to sing in the chancel.

The parish clerk, this amorous Absalom,
who was always so woebegone for love,
was at Osney on Monday
to have a good time with company;
he chanced to ask a member of the order
very secretly about John the carpenter;
the man drew him apart, out of the church,
and said, "I don't know, I haven't seen him doing anything
here since Saturday; I imagine that he went
for timber where our abbot sent him,
for he is accustomed to go for timber
and stay at the farm for a day or two;

Or elles he is at his hous, certeyn;
Where that he be I can nat sothly seyn."
  This Absolon ful joly was and light,
And thoghte, "Now is tyme to wake al night,
For sikirly I saugh him nat stiringe
Aboute his dore sin day bigan to springe.
So moot I thryve, I shal, at cokkes crowe,
Ful prively knokken at his windowe   490
That stant ful lowe upon his boures wal.
To Alison now wol I tellen al
My love-longing, for yet I shal nat misse
That at the leste wey I shal hir kisse.
Som maner confort shal I have, parfay.
My mouth hath icched al this longe day;
That is a signe of kissing atte leeste.
Al night me mette eek I was at a feeste.
Therfor I wol go slepe an houre or tweye,
And al the night thanne wol I wake and pleye."   500
  Whan that the firste cok hath crowe, anon
Up rist this joly lover Absolon,
And him arrayeth gay, at point-devys.
But first he cheweth greyn and lycorys,
To smellen swete, er he hadde kembd his heer.
Under his tonge a trewe-love he beer,
For therby wende he to ben gracious.
He rometh to the carpenteres hous,
And stille he stant under the shot-windowe—
Unto his brest it raughte, it was so lowe—
And softe he cougheth with a semi-soun.
"What do ye, hony-comb, swete Alisoun,
My faire brid, my swete cinamome?
Awaketh, lemman myn, and speketh to me.
Wel litel thenken ye upon my wo,
That for your love I swete ther I go.
No wonder is thogh that I swelte and swete:
I moorne as doth a lamb after the tete.
Ywis, lemman, I have swich love-longinge
That lyk a turtel trewe is my moorninge;   520
I may nat ete na more than a mayde."
  "Go fro the window, Jakke fool," she sayde.
"As help me, God, it wol nat be 'com-pa-me.'
I love another—and elles I were to blame—
Wel bet than thee, by Jesu, Absolon.
Go forth thy wey or I wol caste a ston,

or else he's certainly at home;
I cannot truthfully say where he is."
    This Absalom grew frolicsome and lighthearted,
and thought, "Now is the time to stay up all night,
for surely I haven't seen him stirring
about his door since dawn.
As I may thrive, at cockcrow I shall
knock very secretly at the window
that is quite low in the wall of his bedchamber.
Now I'll tell Alison all
my love-sickness, for still it won't fail
at the very least that I'll kiss her.
I shall have some kind of comfort, for sure.
My mouth has itched all this livelong day;
that is a sign of kissing, at least.
Besides, I dreamed all night that I was at a feast.
Therefore, I'll go sleep for an hour or two,
and then I'll stay up and amuse myself all night."
    When the first cock had crowed, then
rose up this lusty lover Absalom,
and dressed himself handsomely to perfection.
But first he chewed cardamon and licorice,
in order to smell sweet, before he combed his hair.
He carried a sprig of clover under his tongue,
for by its means he expected to be pleasing.
He strolled to the carpenter's house
and stood quietly under the hinged window—
it reached only to his chest, it was so low—
and he coughed softly with a small sound.
"What do you, honeycomb, sweet Alison?
My fair bird, sweet cinnamon,
awake, my sweetheart, and speak to me.
Little do you think of my woe, which is
so great that I sweat upon the ground as I walk.
It is no wonder though I melt and sweat:
I yearn as does the lamb for the teat.
Indeed, sweetheart, I have such love-sickness
that my mourning is like that of the faithful turtledove;
I may not eat any more than a girl."
    "Go away from the window, Jack-fool," she said.
"So help me God, it won't be 'come-kiss-me.'
By Jesus, Absalom, I love another a lot better
than you, and otherwise I'd be to blame.
Go your way or I'll throw a stone,

And lat me slepe, a twenty devel wey!"

"Allas," quod Absolon, "and weylawey,
That trewe love was ever so yvel biset.
Thanne kisse me, sin it may be no bet,   530
For Jesus love and for the love of me."

"Wiltow thanne go thy wey therwith?" quod she.

"Ye, certes, lemman," quod this Absolon.

"Thanne make thee redy," quod she, "I come anon."
And unto Nicholas she seyde stille,
"Now hust, and thou shalt laughen al thy fille."

This Absolon doun sette him on his knees,
And seyde, "I am a lord at alle degrees,
For after this I hope ther cometh more.
Lemman, thy grace, and swete brid, thyn ore!"   540

The window she undooth, and that in haste.
"Have do," quod she, "com of and speed thee faste,
Lest that our neighebores thee espye."

This Absolon gan wype his mouth ful drye:
Derk was the night as pich or as the cole,
And at the window out she putte hir hole,
And Absolon, him fil no bet ne wers,
But with his mouth he kiste hir naked ers,
Ful savoury, er he was war of this.

Abak he sterte, and thoghte it was amis,   550
For wel he wiste a womman hath no berd:
He felte a thing al rough and long y-herd,
And seyde, "Fy! allas! what have I do?"

"Tehee," quod she, and clapte the window to;
And Absolon goth forth a sory pas.

"A berd, a berd!" quod hende Nicholas,
"By Goddes corpus, this goth faire and weel."

This sely Absolon herde every deel,
And on his lippe he gan for anger byte,
And to himself he seyde, "I shal thee quyte!"   560

Who rubbeth now, who froteth now his lippes
With dust, with sond, with straw, with clooth, with chippes,
But Absolon, that seith ful ofte, "Allas"?
"My soule bitake I unto Sathanas,
But me were levere than al this toun," quod he,
"Of this despyt awroken for to be.
Allas," quod he "allas, I ne hadde y-bleynt!"
His hote love was cold and al y-queynt,
For fro that tyme that he had kiste hir ers
Of paramours he sette nat a kers,   570

and let me sleep, in the name of twenty devils!"
　"Alas," said Absalom, "and alack
that ever true love was so ill-used.
Kiss me, then—since it may be no better—
for Jesus' love and love of me."
　"Will you go your way then?" she said.
　"Yes, certainly, sweetheart," said Absalom.
"Then get ready," she said, "I'm coming right away."
And she said quietly to Nicholas,
"Now keep quiet, and you shall laugh your fill."
　Absalom got down on his knees,
and said, "I am a lord in every way,
for after this I expect more will be coming.
Your favor, beloved; and sweet bird, your mercy!"
　She undid the window quickly.
"Finish up," she said, "come on and do it quickly,
so that our neighbors won't see you."
　Absalom wiped his mouth very dry;
the night was dark as pitch or coal,
and she stuck her hole out the window,
and Absalom fared neither better nor worse
than with his mouth to kiss her naked arse
with much relish, before he knew what he was doing.
　He started back and thought that something was wrong,
for he well knew that a woman doesn't have a beard;
he felt something that was all rough and long-haired,
and said, "Fie, alas, what have I done?"
　"Teehee," she said, and slammed the window shut;
and Absalom went forth with sorry step.
　"A beard, a beard," said pleasant Nicholas,
"by God's body, this goes nicely."
　Feckless Absalom heard it all,
and he bit his lip for anger
and said to himself, "I'll pay you back!"
　Who now rubs, who wipes, his lips
with dust, with sand, with straw, with cloth, with chips,
but Absalom; who says "Alas" again and again?
"I'll give my soul to Satan,
if I wouldn't rather be revenged for this insult
than have all this town," he said.
"Alas," he said, "alas, that I didn't turn aside!"
His hot love had grown cold and was all quenched,
for from the time that he had kissed her arse,
he didn't give a cress for woman's love,

For he was heled of his maladye.
Ful ofte paramours he gan deffye,
And weep as dooth a child that is y-bete.
A softe paas he wente over the strete
Until a smith men cleped daun Gerveys,
That in his forge smithed plough-harneys:
He sharpeth shaar and cultour bisily.
This Absolon knokketh al esily,
And seyde, "Undo, Gerveys, and that anon."
    "What, who artow?" "It am I, Absolon."   580
"What, Absolon! for Cristes swete tree!
Why ryse ye so rathe? Ey, *benedicite*,
What eyleth yow? som gay gerl, God it woot,
Hath broght yow thus upon the viritoot:
By Seynte Note, ye woot wel what I mene."
    This Absolon ne roghte nat a bene
Of al his pley. No word agayn he yaf:
He hadde more tow on his distaf
Than Gerveys knew, and seyde, "Freend so dere,
That hote cultour in the chimenee here,   590
As lene it me, I have therwith to done,
And I wol bringe it thee agayn ful sone."
    Gerveys answerde, "Certes, were it gold,
Or in a poke nobles alle untold,
Thou sholdest have, as I am trewe smith.
Ey, Cristes foo, what wol ye do therwith?"
    "Therof," quod Absolon, "be as be may;
I shal wel telle it thee to-morwe day,"
And caughte the cultour by the colde stele.
Ful softe out at the dore he gan to stele,   600
And wente unto the carpenteres wal:
He cougheth first, and knokketh therewithal
Upon the windowe, right as he dide er.
    This Alison answerde, "Who is ther
That knokketh so? I warante it a theef."
    "Why, nay," quod he, "God woot, my swete leef,
I am thyn Absolon, my dereling.
Of gold," quod he, "I have thee broght a ring—
My moder yaf it me, so God me save;
Ful fyn it is and thereto wel y-grave;   610
This wol I yeve thee if thou me kisse."
    This Nicholas was risen for to pisse,
And thoughte he wolde amenden al the jape:
He sholde kisse his ers er that he scape.

for he was cured of his sickness.
He renounced love over and over,
and wept like a child that is beaten.
He crossed the street softly
to a smith called Master Gervase,
who was shaping plowing equipment in his forge:
he was busily sharpening plowshares and colters.
Absalom knocked quietly
and said, "Open up, Gervase, right away."
   "What, who are you?" "It's me, Absalom."
"How now, Absalom! Christ's cross!
Why do you rise so early, eh, bless us!
What's wrong with you? Some gay girl, God knows,
has got you on the prowl this way:
by Saint Neot, you well know what I mean."
   Absalom didn't care a bean
for all his joking. He replied not a word:
he had more wool on his distaff
than Gervase knew, and said, "Dear friend,
that hot colter in the chimney there—
lend it to me, I have something to do with it
and I'll return it to you very soon."
   Gervase answered, "Certainly, if it were gold
or uncounted gold nobles in a bag,
you should have it, as I am an honest smith;
eh, the devil, what will you do with it?"
   "Concerning that," said Absalom, "let it be as it may;
I'll tell you indeed tomorrow,"
and he grabbed the colter by its cool handle.
He stole out softly at the door
and walked to the carpenter's wall:
first he coughed and then knocked
on the window, just as he had done before.
   Alison answered, "Who's there
knocking so hard? It's a thief, I warrant."
   "Why, no," he said, "God knows, sweet love,
I am your Absalom, my darling.
I have brought you a gold ring," he said—
"my mother gave it to me, God save me;
it's very fine, and well engraved, too;
I'll give it to you if you'll kiss me."
   Nicholas had risen to urinate,
and thought he would improve on the joke:
Absalom should kiss his arse before getting off.

And up the windowe dide he hastily,
And out his ers he putteth prively
Over the buttok to the haunche-bon;
And therwith spak this clerk, this Absolon,
"Spek, swete brid, I noot nat wher thou art."
This Nicholas anon leet flee a fart,   620
As greet as it had been a thonder-dent,
That with the strook he was almost y-blent;
And he was redy with his iren hoot,
And Nicholas amidde the ers he smoot:
Of gooth the skin an hande-brede aboute;
The hote cultour brende so his toute
That for the smert he wende for to dye.
As he were wood for wo he gan to crye,
"Help! water! water! help, for Goddes herte!"
This carpenter out of his slomber sterte,   630
And herde oon cryen "Water!" as he were wood,
And thoughte, "Allas, now comth Nowélis flood!"
He sit him up withouten wordes mo,
And with his ax he smoot the corde a-two,
And doun goth al; he fond neither to selle
Ne breed ne ale, til he cam to the celle
Upon the floor; and ther aswowne he lay.
Up sterte hire Alison, and Nicholay,
And cryden "Out" and "Harrow" in the strete.
The neighebores, bothe smale and grete,   640
In ronnen, for to gauren on this man,
That yet aswowne lay bothe pale and wan,
For with the fal he brosten hadde his arm;
But stonde he moste unto his owne harm,
For whan he spak he was anon bore doun
With hende Nicholas and Alisoun:
They tolden every man that he was wood—
He was agast so of "Nowélis flood,"
Thurgh fantasye, that of his vanitee
He hadde y-boght him kneding-tubbes three,   650
And hadde hem hanged in the roof above;
And that he preyed hem, for Goddes love,
To sitten in the roof, *par compaignye.*
The folk gan laughen at his fantasye.
Into the roof they kyken and they cape,
And turned al his harm unto a jape,
For what so that this carpenter answerde,
It was for noght: no man his reson herde;

He raised the window quickly
and quietly stuck his arse out
beyond the buttocks, as far back as the thigh bone;
then this clerk Absalom said,
"Speak, sweet bird, I don't know where you are."
     Nicholas then let fly a fart
as strong as a thunderclap,
so that Absalom was almost blinded with its force;
but he was ready with his hot iron
and struck Nicholas in the middle of his arse:
off went the skin a handsbreadth on each side;
the hot colter burned his buttocks so badly
that he thought he would die with the pain.
He began to cry out as if he were mad,
"Help! Water! Help, for God's heart!"
     The carpenter started out of his slumber
and heard someone crying "Water!" like mad,
and he thought, "Alas, now Noel's flood is coming!"
He sat up without another word
and hacked the rope in two with his axe,
and down went all; he didn't find time to sell
either bread or ale before he hit the flooring
at ground level; and there he lay in a faint.
     Alison and Nicholas jumped up
and cried "Alas" and "Help" in the street.
The neighbors high and low
ran in to gape at this man
who still lay in a faint, pale and wan,
for he had broken his arm with the fall;
but he had to take the blame for his own mishap,
for when he spoke he was soon borne down
by pleasant Nicholas and Alison:
they told everyone that he was mad—
he was so afraid of "Noel's flood"
through hallucination that in his folly
he had bought himself three kneading tubs
and had hanged them up under the roof;
and that he had asked them for God's love
to sit under the roof for company's sake.
     The people set to laughing at his delusion.
They peered and gaped up at the roof
and turned all his misfortune into a joke,
for whatever the carpenter said in answer,
it did no good: no one listened to his explanation;

With othes grete he was so sworn adoun,
That he was holden wood in al the toun,   660
For every clerk anon-right heeld with other:
They seyde "The man is wood, my leve brother";
And every wight gan laughen of this stryf.
    Thus swyved was the carpenteres wyf,
For al his keping and his jalousye;
And Absolon hath kist hir nether yë;
And Nicholas is scalded in the toute:
This tale is doon, and God save al the route!

he was so sworn down with strong avowals
that he was considered mad through all the town,
for every clerk immediately stuck with the other's story.
They said, "The man is mad, dear brother";
and everyone laughed at this fuss.

    Thus plumbed was the carpenter's wife,
in spite of all his guard and jealousy;
and Absalom has kissed her lower eye;
and Nicholas is scalded in the bum:
this tale is done, and God save all the company!

THE WYF OF BATHE

The Prologe of the Wyves Tale of Bathe

"EXPERIENCE, though noon auctoritee
Were in this world, were right ynough to me
To speke of wo that is in mariage;
For, lordinges, sith I twelf yeer was of age,
Thonked be God that is eterne on lyve,
Housbondes at chirche dore I have had fyve—
If I so ofte myghte have wedded be;
And alle were worthy men in hir degree.
But me was told certeyn, nat longe agon is,
That sith that Crist ne wente never but onis   10
To wedding in the Cane of Galilee,
That by the same ensample taughte he me
That I ne sholde wedded be but ones.
Herke eek, lo! which a sharp word for the nones
Besyde a welle Jesus, God and man,
Spak in repreve of the Samaritan:
'Thou hast y-had fyve housbondes,' quod He,
'And thilke man, the which that hath now thee,
Is noght thyn housbond'; thus seyde He certeyn;
What that He mente therby, I can nat seyn.   20
But that I axe, why that the fifthe man
Was noon housbond to the Samaritan?
How manye mighte she have in mariage?
Yet herde I never tellen in myn age
Upon this nombre diffinicioun.
Men may devyne and glosen up and doun,
But wel I woot, expres, withoute lye,
God bad us for to wexe and multiplye;
That gentil text can I wel understonde.
Eek wel I woot He seyde myn housbonde   30
Sholde lete fader and moder, and take me;
But of no nombre mencioun made He
Of bigamye or of octogamye;
Why sholde men speke of it vileinye?
Lo, here the wyse king, dan Salomon;
I trowe he hadde wyves mo than oon;

182

THE WIFE OF BATH

The Prologue of the Wife of Bath's Tale

"EXPERIENCE, even if there were no other authority
in this world, would be grounds enough for me
to speak of the woe that is in marriage;
for, my lords, since I was twelve years old,
thanks be to eternal God,
I have had five husbands at the church door—
if I may have been legally married so often;
and all were worthy men in their different ways.
But I was definitely told, not long ago,
that since Christ went but once
to a wedding, in Cana of Galilee,
by that example he taught me
that I should not be married more than once.
Also, consider what sharp words
Jesus, God and man, spoke beside a
well in reproof of the Samaritan:
'Thou hast had five husbands,' he said,
'and he whom thou now hast
is not thy husband'; thus he spoke, certainly;
what he meant by it, I cannot say.
But I ask this, why was the fifth man
no husband to the Samaritan?
How many was she allowed to have in marriage?
Never yet in my life have I heard
this number defined.
People may guess and interpret the text up and down,
but I know well, without a doubt, God bade
us expressly to increase and multiply;
that pleasant text I can well understand.
And also I well know that He said my husband
should leave father and mother, and take me;
but He made no mention of number—
of bigamy or of octogamy;
why should men speak evil of it?
    Look at the wise king, Lord Solomon;
I think he had more than one wife;

As, wolde god, it leveful were to me
To be refresshed half so ofte as he!
Which yifte of God hadde he for alle his wyvis!
No man hath swich that in this world alyve is.   40
God woot, this noble king, as to my wit,
The firste night had many a mery fit
With ech of hem, so wel was him on lyve!
Blessed be God that I have wedded fyve!
Welcome the sixte, whan that ever he shal.
For sothe, I wol nat kepe me chast in al;
Whan myn housbond is fro the world y-gon,
Som Cristen man shal wedde me anon;
For thanne th'Apostle seith that I am free
To wedde, a Goddes half, wher it lyketh me.   50
He seith that to be wedded is no sinne;
Bet is to be wedded than to brinne.
What rekketh me, thogh folk seye vileinye
Of shrewed Lameth and his bigamye?
I woot wel Abraham was an holy man,
And Jacob eek, as ferforth as I can;
And ech of hem hadde wyves mo than two,
And many another holy man also.
Wher can ye seye in any maner age,
That hye God defended mariage   60
By expres word? I pray you, telleth me;
Or wher comanded he virginitee?
I woot as wel as ye, it is no drede,
Th'Apostle, whan he speketh of maydenhede,
He seyde, that precept thereof hadde he noon.
Men may conseille a womman to been oon,
But conseilling is no comandement;
He putte it in our owene jugement.
For hadde God comanded maydenhede,
Thanne hadde He dampned wedding with the dede;   70
And certes, if ther were no seed y-sowe,
Virginitee, whereof than sholde it growe?
Poul dorste nat comanden atte leste
A thing of which his maister yaf noon heste.
The dart is set up for virginitee;
Cacche who so may, who renneth best lat see.
    But this word is nat take of every wight,
But ther as God list give it of His might.
I woot wel that th'Apostel was a mayde;
But natheless, thogh that he wroot and sayde   80

I would to God I could
be refreshed half so often as he!
What a gift from God he had with all his wives!
No man living in this world has such.
God knows this noble king to my thinking
had many a merry bout with each of them
the first night; he had a good life.
Blessed be God that I have married five!
Welcome the sixth, whenever he comes along.
For indeed, I don't want to keep myself entirely chaste;
when my husband has gone from the world,
some Christian man shall wed me soon.
for the Apostle* says that then I am free
to marry in God's name where I please.
He says it's no sin to be married;
it is better to marry than to burn.
What do I care if folk speak evil
of cursed Lamech* and his bigamy?
I know very well that Abraham was a holy man,
and Jacob too, as far as I can see;
and each of them had more than two wives,
and so did many another holy man.
Tell me, where, in any time,
did God on high expressly prohibit marriage?
I pray you, tell me;
or where did he command virginity?
I know as well as you do—not a doubt!—
that the Apostle, when he spoke of maidenhood,
said that he had no commandment for it.
One may counsel a woman to be a virgin,
but counseling is not commandment;
he left it to our own judgment.
For if God had decreed maidenhood, then
he would have condemned marriage in effect;
and certainly if there were no seed sown,
then where should virginity grow from?
Paul did not dare in the least to decree
a thing for which his master gave no order.
The prize is set up for virginity;
grab it who may, let's see who wins the race.

But this saying does not apply to every man,
but only where it pleases God to give it, of His might.
I very well know that the Apostle was a virgin;
but nevertheless, although he wrote and said

He wolde that every wight were swich as he,
Al nis but conseil to virginitee;
And for to been a wyf, he yaf me leve
Of indulgence; so it is no repreve
To wedde me, if that my make dye,
Withoute excepcioun of bigamye—
Al were it good no womman for to touche
(He mente as in his bed or in his couche),
For peril is bothe fyr and tow t'assemble—
(Ye knowe what this ensample may resemble).   90
This is al and som: he heeld virginitee
More parfit than wedding in freletee.
Freeltee clepe I, but if that he and she
Wolde leden al hir lyf in chastitee.
   I graunte it wel, I have noon envye,
Thogh maydenhede preferre bigamye.
Hem lyketh to be clene, body and goost;
Of myn estaat I nil nat make no boost.
For wel ye knowe a lord in his household,
He hath nat every vessel al of gold;   100
Somme been of tree, and doon hir lord servyse.
God clepeth folk to him in sondry wyse,
And everich hath of God a propre yifte.
Som this, som that, as him lyketh shifte.
   Virginitee is greet perfeccioun,
And continence eek with devocioun,
But Crist, that of perfeccioun is welle,
Bad nat every wight he sholde go selle
All that he hadde, and give it to the pore,
And in swich wyse folwe Him and His fore;   110
He spak to hem that wolde live parfitly:
And lordinges, by your leve, that am nat I.
I wol bistowe the flour of al myn age
In th' actes and in fruit of mariage.
   Telle me also, to what conclusioun
Were membres maad of generacioun,
And of so parfit wys a wight y-wroght?
Trusteth right wel, they were nat maad for noght.
Glose whoso wole, and seye bothe up and doun,
That they were maked for purgacioun   120
Of urine, and our bothe thinges smale
Were eek to knowe a femele from a male,
And for noon other cause: sey ye no?
The experience woot wel it is noght so;

that he wished that everyone were such as he,
all this is only advice in favor of virginity;
and he gave me, as an indulgence, leave
to be a wife; so it is no reproach
for me to marry if my mate dies;
it is without any taint of bigamy—
although it may be good not to touch a woman
(he meant in a bed or couch;
for it is dangerous to assemble fire and tow—
you know what this example means).
This is the sum of the matter, he held virginity to be
more perfect than marrying in the frailty of the flesh.
It is frailty, that is, unless the man and woman
intend to live all their lives in chastity.

I grant it freely; I'm not envious,
although maidenhood be preferred to bigamy.
It pleases some to be pure, body and soul;
I won't make any boast about my own estate.
As you well know, a lord doesn't have every
vessel in his household made of gold;
some are made of wood, and are serviceable to their lord.
God calls people to him in sundry ways,
and each one has an appropriate gift of God,
some this, some that—as it pleases Him to provide.

Virginity is a great perfection,
and also devoted continence,
but Christ, who is the well of perfection,
did not bid every man to go and sell
all that he had and give it to the poor,
and in that way to follow in His footsteps;
He spoke to them that wished to live perfectly:
and by your leave, my lords, that isn't me.
I will bestow the flower of my whole life
in the acts and fruits of marriage.

Tell me also, to what end
were reproductive organs made,
why are people made so perfectly?
Believe me, they were not made for nothing.
whoever wants to, let him enlarge on the matter and argue to
and fro that they were made for the purgation
of urine, and that both our private parts
were made to distinguish a female from a male,
and for no other cause—do you say no?
Experience knows well it is not so;

So that the clerkes be nat with me wrothe,
I sey this, that they maked been for bothe;
This is to seye, for office, and for ese
Of engendrure, ther we nat God displese.
Why sholde men elles in hir bokes sette,
That man shal yelde to his wyf hir dette?   130
Now wherwith sholde he make his payement
If he ne used his sely instrument?
Than were they maad upon a creature
To purge uryne, and eek for engendrure.
    But I seye noght that every wight is holde,
That hath swich harneys as I to yow tolde,
To goon and usen hem in engendrure;
Than sholde men take of chastitee no cure.
Crist was a mayde, and shapen as a man,
And many a seint, sith that the world bigan,   140
Yet lived they ever in parfit chastitee.
I nil envye no virginitee;
Lat hem be breed of pured whete seed
And lat us wyves hoten barly breed;
And yet with barly breed, Mark telle can,
Our Lord Jesu refresshed many a man.
In swich estaat as God hath cleped us
I wol persevere, I nam nat precious.
In wyfhode I wol use myn instrument
As frely as my Maker hath it sent.   150
If I be daungerous, God yeve me sorwe!
Myn housbond shal it have bothe eve and morwe,
Whan that him list com forth and paye his dette.
An housbonde I wol have, I nil nat lette,
Which shal be bothe my dettour and my thral,
And have his tribulacioun withal
Upon his flessh, whyl that I am his wyf.
I have the power duringe al my lyf
Upon his propre body, and noght he.
Right thus th'Apostel tolde it unto me,   160
And bad our housbondes for to love us weel.
Al this sentence me lyketh every deel"—
Up sterte the Pardoner, and that anon,
"Now dame," quod he, "by God and by Seint John,
Ye been a noble prechour in this cas!
I was aboute to wedde a wyf; allas!
What sholde I bye it on my flesh so dere?
Yet hadde I lever wedde no wyf to-yere!"

so that the clerics won't be angry with me,
I'll say this: they were made for both;
that is to say, for necessary business and for pleasure
in engendering, when we do not displease God.
Why else should men set it down in their books
that a man shall yield his wife her debt?
Now how shall he make his payment
unless he uses his simple instrument?
Then, they were given to creatures
for purging urine and also for propagation.
    But I don't say that everyone who has
such equipment as I mentioned is bound
to go and use it in engendering;
then we wouldn't care about chastity.
Christ, who was formed as a man, was a virgin,
and many a saint since the world began
lived always in perfect chastity.
I won't envy them virginity:
let them be white bread of finest wheat,
and let us wives be called barley bread;
and yet, with barley bread, as Mark tells us,
Our Lord Jesus refreshed many a man.
In such estate as God has called us to
I'll persevere; I'm not particular.
In marriage I'll use my equipment
as freely as my maker sent it.
If I should be grudging, God give me sorrow!
My husband shall have it both evening and morning,
whenever he wants to come forth and pay his debt.
I'll have a husband—I won't make it difficult—
who shall be both my debtor and my slave,
and have his trouble
in the flesh while I'm his wife.
All through my life I have the power
over his own body, and not he.
Just so the Apostle explained it to me,
and he bade our husbands to love us well.
Every bit of this lesson pleases me—"
Just then the Pardoner started up;
"Now, dame," he said, "by God and by Saint John,
you are a noble preacher in this matter!
I was about to wed a wife; alas,
why should I purchase it so dearly with my flesh?
I'd rather not wed a wife this year!"

"Abyde!" quod she, "my tale is nat bigonne;
Nay, thou shalt drinken of another tonne   170
Er that I go, shal savoure wors than ale.
And whan that I have told thee forth my tale
Of tribulacioun in mariage,
Of which I am expert in al myn age—
This to seyn, myself have been the whippe—
Than maystow chese whether thou wolt sippe
Of thilke tonne that I shal abroche.
Be war of it, er thou to ny approche;
For I shal telle ensamples mo than ten.
Whoso that nil be war by othere men,   180
By him shul othere men corrected be.
The same wordes wryteth Ptholomee;
Rede in his Almageste, and take it there."

    "Dame, I wolde praye yow, if your wil it were,"
Seyde this Pardoner, "as ye bigan,
Telle forth your tale; spareth for no man,
And teche us yonge men of your praktike."

    "Gladly," quod she, "sith it may yow lyke.
But yet I praye to al this companye,
If that I speke after my fantasye,   190
As taketh not agrief of that I seye;
For myn entente nis but for to pleye.

    Now sires, now wol I telle forth my tale.—
As ever mote I drinken wyn or ale,
I shal seye sooth, tho housbondes that I hadde,
As three of hem were gode and two were badde.
The three men were gode, and riche, and olde;
Unnethe mighte they the statut holde
In which that they were bounden unto me—
Ye woot wel what I mene of this, pardee!   200
As help me God, I laughe whan I thinke
How pitously a-night I made hem swinke;
And by my fey, I tolde of it no stoor.
They had me yeven hir lond and hir tresoor;
Me neded nat do lenger diligence
To winne hir love, or doon hem reverence.
They loved me so wel, by God above,
That I ne tolde no deyntee of hir love!
A wys womman wol sette hir ever in oon
To gete hir love, ye, ther as she hath noon;   210
But sith I hadde hem hoolly in myn hond,
And sith they hadde me yeven all hir lond,

"Wait," said she, "my tale is not begun;
no, you'll drink from another barrel
before I am through—one that shall taste worse than ale.
And when I have told you my tale
of the tribulation of marriage,
in which I have been an expert all my life—
that is to say, I myself have been the whip—
then you may choose whether you wish to sip
of the tun that I shall broach.
Be wary of it, before you approach too near;
for I shall tell more than ten examples.
By him who won't be warned by other men
shall other men be warned.
These same words were written by Ptolemy;
read in his *Almagest,** and find it there."

"Dame, I pray you, if it be your will,"
said this Pardoner, "tell your tale
as you began; leave off for no man,
and teach us young men some of your practice."

"Gladly," said she, "since it may please you.
But yet I pray all this company
that if I speak according to my fancy,
you do not take what I say amiss;
for I only intend to amuse you.

Now, sirs, I'll go on with my tale.—
As ever I hope to drink wine or ale,
I'll tell the truth; of those husbands that I had,
three of them were good and two were bad.
The first three men were good, and rich, and old;
they were scarcely able to keep the statute
by which they were bound to me—
you know quite well what I mean by this, by heaven!
So help me God, I laugh when I think
how pitifully I made them work at night;
and by my faith I set no store by it.
They had given me their land and their treasure;
I no longer needed to be diligent
to win their love, or show them reverence.
They loved me so well, by God above,
that I didn't prize their love!
A wise woman will concentrate on getting
that love which she doesn't possess;
but since I had them wholly in my hand,
and since they had given me all their land,

What sholde I taken hede hem for to plese,
But it were for my profit and myn ese?
I sette hem so a-werke, by my fey,
That many a night they songen 'weilawey!'
The bacoun was nat fet for hem, I trowe,
That som men han in Essex at Dunmowe.
I governed hem so well, after my lawe,
That ech of hem ful blisful was and fawe   220
To bringe me gaye thinges fro the fayre.
They were ful glad whan I spak to hem fayre;
For God it woot, I chidde hem spitously.
   Now herkneth, how I bar me proprely,
Ye wyse wyves, that can understonde.
Thus sholde ye speke and bere hem wrong on honde;
For half so boldely can ther no man
Swere and lyen as a womman can.
I sey nat this by wyves that ben wyse,
But if it be whan they hem misavyse.   230
A wys wyf, if that she can hir good,
Shal bere him on hond the cow is wood,
And take witnesse of hir owene mayde
Of hir assent; but herkneth how I sayde.
   'Sir olde kaynard, is this thyn array?
Why is my neighebores wyf so gay?
She is honoured overal ther she goth;
I sitte at hoom, I have no thrifty cloth.
What dostow at my neighebores hous?
Is she so fair? Artow so amorous?   240
What rowne ye with our mayde, *ben'cite!*
Sir olde lechour, lat thy japes be!
And if I have a gossib or a freend,
Withouten gilt, thou chydest as a feend,
If that I walke or pleye unto his hous!
Thou comest hoom as dronken as a mous,
And prechest on thy bench, with yvel preef!
Thou seist to me it is a greet meschief
To wedde a povre womman, for costage;
And if that she be riche, of heigh parage,   250
Than seistow that it is a tormentrye
To suffre hir pryde and hir malencolye.
And if that she be fair, thou verray knave,
Thou seyst that every holour wol hir have:
She may no whyle in chastitee abyde,
That is assailled upon ech a syde.

why should I take pains to please them,
unless it should be for my own profit and pleasure?
I so set them to work, by my faith,
that many a night they sang 'alas!'
The prize of bacon some people have in
Essex at Dunmow* was never brought to them, I know.
I governed them so well in my way
that each of them was most happy and eager
to bring me gay things from the fair.
They were glad indeed when I spoke pleasantly to them;
for God knows I chided them cruelly.

    Now hear how suitably I behaved myself,
you wise wives who can understand.
You should speak thus and put them in the wrong;
for no man can perjure himself and lie
half so boldly as a woman can.
I don't say this for wives that are wise,
except when they have made a mistake.
A wise wife, if she knows what is good for her,
will convince her husband that the chough* is mad,
and call as a witness her own maid,
who conspires with her; but listen to how I spoke.

    'Old sluggard, is this the way you dress me?
Why is my neighbor's wife so smart?
She is honored everywhere she goes;
I sit at home, I have no decent clothes.
What do you do at my neighbor's house?
Is she so fair? Are you so amorous?
What are you whispering to our maid, for heaven's sake?
Old sir, lecher, stop your tricks!
Why, if I have a friend or acquaintance
in all innocence, you chide like a fiend
if I walk to his house and visit!
You come home as drunk as a mouse
and preach from your bench, bad luck to you!
You tell me it is a great misfortune
to marry a poor woman, as far as cost is concerned;
and if she is rich and of high lineage,
then you say that it is a torment
to suffer her pride and her melancholy.
And if she is fair, you knave,
you say that every lecher wants to have her;
she who is assaulted on every side
can't remain chaste very long.

Thou seyst som folk desyre us for richesse,
Som for our shap, and som for our fairnesse;
And som, for she can outher singe or daunce,
And som, for gentillesse and daliaunce;   260
Som, for hir handes and hir armes smale;
Thus goth al to the devel by thy tale.
Thou seyst men may nat kepe a castel wal,
It may so longe assailled been overal.

And if that she be foul, thou seist that she
Coveiteth every man that she may see;
For as a spaynel she wol on him lepe,
Til that she finde som man hir to chepe;
Ne noon so grey goos goth ther in the lake,
As, seistow, that wol been withoute make;   270
And seyst it is an hard thing for to welde
A thing that no man wol, his thankes, helde.
Thus seistow, lorel, whan thow goost to bedde,
And that no wys man nedeth for to wedde,
Ne no man that entendeth unto hevene.
With wilde thonder-dint and firy levene
Mote thy welked nekke be tobroke!

Thow seyst that dropping houses, and eek smoke,
And chyding wyves, maken men to flee
Out of hir owene hous; a, *ben'cite!*   280
What eyleth swich an old man for to chyde?
Thow seyst we wyves wol our vyces hyde
Til we be fast, and than we wol hem shewe;
Wel may that be a proverbe of a shrewe!
Thou seist that oxen, asses, hors, and houndes,
They been assayed at diverse stoundes;
Bacins, lavours, er that men hem bye,
Spones and stoles, and al swich housbondrye,
And so been pottes, clothes, and array;
But folk of wyves maken noon assay   290
Til they be wedded; olde dotard shrewe!
And than, seistow, we wol oure vices shewe.

Thou seist also that it displeseth me
But if that thou wolt preyse my beautee,
And but thou poure alwey upon my face,
And clepe me "faire dame" in every place;
And but thou make a feste on thilke day
That I was born, and make me fresh and gay,
And but thou do to my norice honour,
And to my chamberere withinne my bour,   300

You say some men desire us for wealth,
some for our shapeliness, and some for our beauty;
some want a woman because she can sing or dance,
some because she is well-bred and flirtatious;
some like her hands and her graceful arms;
thus we all go to the devil by your account.
You say no one can keep a castle wall
when it is assailed all around for so long a time.

And if she is ugly, you say that she
covets every man she sees;
for she will leap on him like a spaniel
until she finds some man who will buy her wares;
there is no goose swimming in the lake, you say,
that is so gray it cannot find a mate.
And you say it is very hard to manage
a thing that no man will willingly keep.
You say this, you wretch, as you go to bed,
and that no wise man needs to marry,
nor any man who aspires to heaven.
May wild thunderbolts and fiery lightning
break your withered neck!

You say that leaking houses and smoke
and nagging wives make men flee
out of their own houses; bless us,
what ails such an old man to scold so?
You say we wives will hide our vices
until we are safely married, and then we will show them;
that's certainly a fit proverb for a scolding curmudgeon!
You say that oxen, asses, horses, and hounds
are tested at various times;
and so are basins and washbowls, before people buy them—
spoons and stools and all such household goods,
and so are pots, clothes and adornments;
but men don't try out wives
until they are married; scolding old dotard!
And then, you say, we'll show our vices.

You also say that I am displeased
unless you praise my beauty,
and pore constantly on my face,
and call me "fair dame" everywhere;
and unless you hold a feast on my
birthday, and give me gay new clothing,
and unless you honor my nurse
and my chambermaid,

And to my fadres folk and his allyes;—
Thus seistow, olde barel ful of lyes!
    And yet of our apprentice Janekyn,
For his crisp heer, shyninge as gold so fyn,
And for he squiereth me bothe up and doun,
Yet hastow caught a fals suspecioun;
I wol hym noght, thogh thou were deed tomorwe.
    But tel me this, why hydestow, with sorwe,
The keyes of thy cheste awey fro me?
It is my good as wel as thyn, pardee.   310
What, wenestow make an idiot of our dame?
Now by that lord that called is Seint Jame,
Thou shalt nat bothe, thogh that thou were wood,
Be maister of my body and of my good;
That oon thou shalt forgo, maugree thyne yën.
What helpeth it of me to enquere or spyën?
I trowe, thou woldest loke me in thy cheste!
Thou sholdest seye, "Wyf, go wher thee leste;
Tak your disport; I wol nat leve no talis.
I knowe yow for a trewe wyf, dame Alis."   320
We love no man that taketh kepe or charge
Wher that we goon; we wol ben at our large.
    Of alle men y-blessed moot he be
The wyse astrologien Dan Ptholome,
That seith this proverbe in his Almageste:
"Of alle men his wisdom is the hyeste
That rekketh never who hath the world in honde."
By this proverbe thou shalt understonde,
Have thou ynough, what thar thee recche or care
How merily that othere folkes fare?   330
For certeyn, olde dotard, by your leve,
Ye shul have queynte right ynough at eve.
He is to greet a nigard that wol werne
A man to lighte his candle at his lanterne;
He shal have never the lasse light, pardee;
Have thou ynough, thee thar nat pleyne thee.
    Thou seyst also that if we make us gay
With clothing and with precious array
That it is peril of our chastitee;
And yet, with sorwe, thou most enforce thee,   340
And seye thise wordes in the Apostles name:
"In habit maad with chastitee and shame
Ye wommen shul apparaille yow," quod he,
"And noght in tressed heer and gay perree,

and my father's relatives and connections;—
you say all this, old barrel full of lies!

Moreover, you have caught a false
suspicion of our apprentice Jankin,
because he has curly hair, shining like purest gold,
and squires me everywhere;
I wouldn't want him even if you died tomorrow.

But tell me this, why do you hide—sorrow to you!—
the keys of your chest away from me?
It is my property as well as yours, by heaven.
Do you think you can make an idiot of the mistress of the
house? Now by the lord who is called Saint James,
you shall not be master of both my body and my goods,
even if you rage with anger;
you'll go without one of them, like it or not.
What use is it to snoop and spy on me?
I think you'd like to lock me in your chest!
You should say, "Wife, go where you like;
amuse yourself, I won't believe any gossip.
I know you for a true wife, Dame Alice."
We don't love a man who carefully watches
where we go; we want to be at large.

Beyond all other men, may the wise
astrologer Lord Ptolemy be blessed,
for in his *Almagest* he speaks this proverb:
"The wisest of all men is he
that never cares who has the world in his hand."
You should understand by this proverb
that if you have enough, why should you care
how merrily other folks fare?
For certainly, old dotard, by your leave,
you'll have quite sex enough at night.
He who forbids another man to light a candle
at his lantern is too great a niggard;
he'll have none the less light, by heaven;
if you have enough, you needn't complain.

You also say that if we make ourselves attractive
with fine clothing and adornments
it imperils our chastity;
and further—sorrow take you—you must back yourself up
by saying these words in the Apostle's name:
"You women shall adorn yourselves
in shamefastness and sobriety," said he,
"and not in braided hair and gay jewels,

As perles, ne with gold, ne clothes riche."
After thy text, ne after thy rubriche,
I wol nat wirche as muchel as a gnat.
Thou seydest this, that I was lyk a cat;
For whoso wolde senge a cattes skin,
Thanne wolde the cat wel dwellen in his in;   350
And if the cattes skin be slyk and gay,
She wol nat dwelle in house half a day,
But forth she wole, er any day be dawed,
To shewe hir skin and goon a-caterwawed;
This is to seye, if I be gay, sir shrewe,
I wol renne out, my borel for to shewe.
　　Sire olde fool, what helpeth thee to spyën?
Thogh thou preye Argus, with his hundred yën,
To be my warde-cors, as he can best,
In feith, he shal nat kepe me but me lest;   360
Yet coude I make his berd, so moot I thee.
　　Thou seydest eek, that ther ben thinges three,
The whiche thinges troublen al this erthe,
And that no wight may endure the ferthe;
O leve sir shrewe, Jesu shorte thy lyf!
Yet prechestow, and seyst an hateful wyf
Y-rekened is for oon of thise meschances.
Been ther none othere maner resemblances
That ye may lykne your parables to,
But if a sely wyf be oon of tho?   370
　　Thou lykenest wommanes love to helle,
To bareyne lond, ther water may not dwelle.
Thou lyknest it also to wilde fyr:
The more it brenneth, the more it hath desyr
To consume every thing that brent wol be.
Thou seyst right as wormes shende a tree,
Right so a wyf destroyeth hir housbonde;
This knowe they that been to wyves bonde.'
　　Lordinges, right thus, as ye have understonde,
Bar I stifly myne olde housbondes on honde,   380
That thus they seyden in hir dronkenesse;
And al was fals, but that I took witnesse
On Janekin and on my nece also.
O Lord, the peyne I dide hem and the wo,
Ful giltelees, by Goddes swete pyne!
For as an hors I coude byte and whyne;
I coude pleyne, thogh I were in the gilt,
Or elles often tyme hadde I ben spilt.

as pearls or gold, or rich array";
I won't conform to this text and
rubric one gnat's worth!
You said this: that I was like a cat;
for if someone singes a cat's fur,
then the cat will stay in its dwelling;
and if the cat's fur is sleek and attractive,
she won't stay in the house half a day,
but out she'll go, before the break of day,
to show her fur and go a-caterwauling;
this is to say, sir grouch, that if I'm gaily dressed,
I'll run out to show off my clothes.

    You old fool, what use is it for you to spy?
Even if you ask Argus, with his hundred eyes,
to be my bodyguard (as he can do it best),
in faith, he can't guard me unless I please;
I still could deceive him, as I hope to thrive.

    You also said that there are three things
which trouble all this earth,
and that no man can endure a fourth;
O dear sir tartar, Jesus shorten your life!
Still you preach and say that a hateful wife
is reckoned as one of these misfortunes.
Are there no other kind of comparisons
you can apply your parables to—
must a poor wife be one of them?

    You compare a woman's love to hell,
to barren land where water can't remain.
You compare it also to wild fire:
the more it burns, the more it wants
to consume everything that will burn.
You say that just as worms destroy a tree,
just so a wife destroys her husband; and
that all who are bound to wives know this.'

    My lords, just so, as you have learned,
I boldly accused my old husbands
of speaking in their drunkenness;
and all was false, but I called on
Jankin and my niece as witnesses.
Oh Lord, the pain and woe I gave them,
though they were guiltless, by God's sweet suffering!
For I could bite and whinny like a horse;
I could complain, though I was the guilty one;
else many time I would have been ruined.

Whoso that first to mille comth, first grint;
I pleyned first, so was our werre y-stint.   390
They were ful glad t'excusen hem ful blyve
Of thing of which they never agilte hir lyve.
  Of wenches wolde I beren hem on honde,
Whan that for syk unnethes mighte they stonde.
Yet tikled it his herte, for that he
Wende that I hadde of him so greet chiertee.
I swoor that al my walkinge out by nighte
Was for t'espye wenches that he dighte;
Under that colour hadde I many a mirthe.
For al swich wit is yeven us in our birthe;   400
Deceite, weping, spinning God hath yive
To wommen kindely, whyl they may live.
And thus of o thing I avaunte me,
Atte ende I hadde the bettre in ech degree,
By sleighte, or force, or by som maner thing,
As by continuel murmur or grucching;
Namely abedde hadden they meschaunce,
Ther wolde I chyde and do hem no plesaunce;
I wolde no lenger in the bed abyde,
If that I felte his arm over my syde,   410
Til he had maad his raunson unto me;
Than wolde I suffre him do his nycetee.
And therfore every man this tale I telle,
Winne whoso may, for al is for to selle:
With empty hand men may none haukes lure;
For winning wolde I al his lust endure,
And make me a feyned appetyt;
And yet in bacon hadde I never delyt—
That made me that ever I wolde hem chyde.
For thogh the Pope had seten hem bisyde,   420
I wolde nat spare hem at hir owene bord;
For by my trouthe, I quitte hem word for word.
As help me verray God omnipotent,
Thogh I right now sholde make my testament,
I ne owe hem nat a word that it nis quit.
I broghte it so aboute by my wit
That they moste yeve it up, as for the beste;
Or elles hadde we never been in reste.
For thogh he loked as a wood leoun,
Yet sholde he faille of his conclusioun.   430
  Thanne wolde I seye, 'Gode lief, tak keep
How mekely loketh Wilkin oure sheep;

Whoever comes first to the mill, grinds first;
I complained first, and so our fight was ended.
They were quite glad to excuse themselves quickly
for things they had never been guilty of in their lives.
    I would accuse them about wenches
when they were so sick they could hardly stand.
Yet it tickled a husband's heart, since he
thought I showed such great fondness for him.
I swore that all my walking out by night
was to spy out the wenches he lay with;
under this pretense I had many a merry time,
for all such wit is given us at our birth;
God has given women by nature deceit, weeping,
and spinning, as long as they live.
And thus I can boast of one thing:
in the end I got the better of them in every case,
by trick, or force, or by some kind of method,
such as continual complaining or grouching;
in particular, they had misfortune in bed,
where I would chide and give them no pleasure;
I would no longer stay in the bed
if I felt my husband's arm over my side
until he had paid his ransom to me;
then I'd allow him to do his bit of business.
Therefore I tell this moral to everyone—
profit whoever may, for all is for sale:
you cannot lure a hawk with an empty hand;
for profit I would endure all his lust,
and pretend an appetite myself;
and yet I never had a taste for aged meat—
that's what made me scold them all the time.
For even if the Pope had sat beside them,
I wouldn't spare them at their own board;
I swear I requited them word for word.
So help me almighty God,
even if I were to make my testament right now,
I don't owe them a word which has not been repaid.
I brought it about by my wit
that they had to give up, as the best thing to do,
or else we would never have been at rest.
For though he might look like a raging lion,
yet he would fail to gain his point.
    Then I would say, 'Dear friend, notice
the meek look on Wilkin, our sheep;

Com neer, my spouse, let me ba thy cheke!
Ye sholde been al pacient and meke,
And han a swete spyced conscience,
Sith ye so preche of Jobes pacience.
Suffreth alwey, sin ye so wel can preche;
And but ye do, certein we shal yow teche
That it is fair to have a wyf in pees.
Oon of us two moste bowen, doutelees;   440
And sith a man is more resonable
Than womman is, ye moste been suffrable.
What eyleth yow to grucche thus and grone?
Is it for ye wolde have my queynte allone?
Why taak it al, lo, have it everydeel;
Peter! I shrewe yow but ye love it weel!
For if I wolde selle my *bele chose*,
I coude walke as fresh as is a rose;
But I wol kepe it for your owene tooth.
Ye be to blame, by God, I sey yow sooth.'   450
    Swiche maner wordes hadde we on honde.
Now wol I speken of my fourthe housbonde.
    My fourthe housbonde was a revelour—
This is to seyn, he hadde a paramour;
And I was yong and ful of ragerye,
Stiborn and strong, and joly as a pye.
How coude I daunce to an harpe smale,
And singe, ywis, as any nightingale,
Whan I had dronke a draughte of swete wyn!
Metellius, the foule cherl, the swyn,   460
That with a staf birafte his wyf hir lyf
For she drank wyn, thogh I hadde been his wyf,
He sholde nat han daunted me fro drinke;
And after wyn on Venus moste I thinke:
For al so siker as cold engendreth hayl,
A likerous mouth moste han a likerous tayl.
In womman vinolent is no defence;
This knowen lechours by experience.
    But, Lord Crist! whan that it remembreth me
Upon my yowthe and on my jolitee,   470
It tikleth me aboute myn herte rote;
Unto this day it dooth myn herte bote
That I have had my world as in my tyme.
But age, allas! that al wol envenyme,
Hath me biraft my beautee and my pith;
Lat go, farewel, the devel go therwith!

come near, my spouse, let me kiss your cheek!
You should be quite patient and meek,
and have a scrupulous conscience,
since you preach so of the patience of Job.
Always be patient, since you preach so well;
for unless you do, we shall certainly teach you
that it is a fine thing to have a wife in peace.
One of us two must bend, without a doubt;
and since a man is more reasonable
than a woman is, you must be patient.
What ails you to grumble and groan so?
Is it because you want to have my thing to yourself?
Why take it all, then, have every bit of it!
Peter! I swear you love it well!
Now if I would sell my *belle chose*,
I could walk as fresh as a rose;
but I will keep it for your own taste.
You're to blame, by God, I tell you the truth.'
   We would have words like this.
Now I will speak of my fourth husband.
   My fourth husband was a reveller—
that is to say, he had a paramour;
and I was young and full of wantonness,
stubborn and strong and merry as a magpie.
How gracefully I could dance to a harp,
and sing just like a nightingale,
when I had drunk a draught of sweet wine!
Metellius, the foul churl, the swine,
who took his wife's life with a staff
because she drank wine—if I had been his wife
he wouldn't have daunted me from drink;
and after wine I must needs think of Venus:
for just as surely as cold brings hail,
a lickerish mouth must have a lecherous tail.
A drunken woman has no defense;
this, lechers know by experience.
   But Lord Christ! When I remember
my youth and my gaity,
it tickles me to the bottom of my heart;
to this day it does my heart good
that I have had my world in my time.
But age, alas, that poisons everything,
has robbed me of my beauty and my pith;
let it go, farewell, the devil with it!

The flour is goon, ther is namore to telle:
The bren, as I best can, now moste I selle;
But yet to be right mery wol I fonde.
Now wol I tellen of my fourthe housbonde. 480

    I seye, I hadde in herte greet despyt
That he of any other had delyt.
But he was quit, by God and by Seint Joce!
I made him of the same wode a croce;
Nat of my body in no foul manere,
But, certeinly, I made folk swich chere,
That in his owene grece I made him frye
For angre and for verray jalousye.
By God, in erthe I was his purgatorie,
For which I hope his soule be in glorie. 490
For God it woot, he sat ful ofte and song
Whan that his shoo ful bitterly him wrong.
Ther was no wight, save God and he, that wiste,
In many wyse, how sore I him twiste.
He deyde whan I cam fro Jerusalem,
And lyth y-grave under the rode-beem,
Al is his tombe noght so curious
As was the sepulcre of him Darius,
Which that Appelles wroghte subtilly;
It nis but wast to burie him preciously. 500
Lat him fare wel, God yeve his soule reste!
He is now in the grave and in his cheste.

    Now of my fifthe housbond wol I telle:
God lete his soule never come in helle!
And yet was he to me the moste shrewe;
That fele I on my ribbes al by rewe,
And ever shal, unto myn ending day.
But in our bed he was so fresh and gay,
And therwithal so wel coude he me glose
Whan that he wolde han my *bele chose*, 510
That thogh he hadde me bet on every boon
He coude winne agayn my love anoon.
I trowe I loved him beste for that he
Was of his love daungerous to me.
We wommen han, if that I shal nat lye,
In this matere a queynte fantasye;
Wayte what thing we may nat lightly have,
Therafter wol we crye al day and crave.
Forbede us thing, and that desyren we;
Prees on us faste, and thanne wol we flee. 520

The flour is gone, there is no more to say:
now I must sell the bran, as best I can;
but still I will contrive to be right merry.
Now I'll tell about my fourth husband.

    I tell you I was angry in my heart
that he had delight in any other.
But he was repaid, by God and by Saint Joce!
I made him a staff of the same wood—
not with my body in a filthy way,
but indeed my manner with other men was such
that I made him fry in his own grease
for anger and pure jealousy.
By God, I was his purgatory on earth,
by which help I hope his soul is in glory.
For God knows he often sat and sang out
when his shoe pinched him bitterly.
No one but God and he knew
how sorely I wrung him in many ways.
He died when I came back from Jerusalem,
and lies buried under the rood-beam,*
although his tomb is not so elaborate
as the sepulchre of that Darius was
which Apelles wrought so skillfully;
it would have been just a waste to bury him expensively.
Farewell to him, may God rest his soul;
he is now in his grave and in his coffin.

    Now I will tell of my fifth husband:
God never let his soul go down to hell!
And yet he was the most brutal to me;
that I can feel on my ribs, all down the row,
and always shall, to my dying day.
But in our bed he was so tireless and wanton,
and moreover he could cajole me so well
when he wanted to have my *belle chose*,
that even if he had beaten me on every bone,
he could soon win my love again.
I think I loved him best because
he was so cool in his love to me.
We women have, to tell the truth,
an odd fancy in this matter;
whatever we cannot easily get
we will cry after and crave all day.
Forbid us a thing, and we desire it;
press it upon us, and then we will flee.

With daunger oute we al our chaffare;
Greet prees at market maketh dere ware,
And to greet cheep is holde at litel prys;
This knoweth every womman that is wys.

My fifthe housbonde, God his soule blesse,
Which that I took for love and no richesse,
He somtyme was a clerk of Oxenford,
And had left scole, and wente at hoom to bord
With my gossib, dwellinge in oure toun:
God have hir soule! Hir name was Alisoun.   530
She knew myn herte and eek my privetee
Bet than our parisshe preest, so moot I thee!
To hir biwreyed I my conseil al.
For had myn housebonde pissed on a wal
Or doon a thing that sholde han cost his lyf,
To hir, and to another worthy wyf,
And to my nece, which that I loved weel,
I wolde han told his conseil every deel.
And so I dide ful often, God it woot,
That made his face ful often reed and hoot   540
For verray shame, and blamed himself for he
Had told to me so greet a privetee.

    And so bifel that ones, in a Lente.—
So often tymes I to my gossib wente,
For ever yet I lovede to be gay,
And for to walke, in March, Averille, and May,
Fro hous to hous, to here sondry talis—
That Jankin clerk and my gossib dame Alis
And I myself into the feldes wente.
Myn housbond was at London al that Lente;   550
I hadde the bettre leyser for to pleye,
And for to see, and eek for to be seye
Of lusty folk; what wiste I wher my grace
Was shapen for to be, or in what place?
Therefore I made my visitaciouns
To vigilies and to processiouns,
To preching eek and to thise pilgrimages,
To pleyes of miracles and to mariages,
And wered upon my gaye scarlet gytes:
Thise wormes ne thise motthes ne thise mytes,   560
Upon my peril, frete hem never a deel;
And wostow why? For they were used weel.

    Now wol I tellen forth what happed me.
I seye that in the feeldes walked we,

Faced with coyness we bring out all our wares;
a great crowd at the market makes wares expensive,
and what is too cheap is held to be worth little;
every wise woman knows this.

My fifth husband, God bless his soul,
whom I took for love and not money,
was at one time a scholar of Oxford,
and had left school, and went home to board
with my close friend, who dwelt in our town:
God bless her soul! Her name was Alison.
She knew my heart and private affairs
better than our parish priest, as I may thrive!
To her I revealed all my secrets.
For whether my husband had pissed on a wall
or done something which should have cost him his life,
to her, and to another worthy wife,
and to my niece, whom I loved well,
I would have betrayed every one of his secrets.
And so I did often enough, God knows,
and that often made his face red and hot
for very shame, so that he blamed himself
for having told me so great a confidence.

And so it happened that once, in Lent
(thus many times I went to my friend's house,
for I always loved to be merry,
and to walk, in March, April, and May,
from house to house, to hear various tidings)
that Jankin the clerk and my dear friend Dame Alice
and I myself went into the fields.
My husband was at London all that Lent;
I had the better leisure to enjoy myself
and to see, and be seen by,
lusty people; how could I know how my favor
was destined to be bestowed, or where?
Therefore I made my visits to feast-eves and processions,
to sermons and these pilgrimages,
to miracle plays and to marriages,
and wore my gay scarlet clothes:
on my life, worms or moths or mites
never ate a bit of them;
and do you know why? Because they were used constantly.

Now I'll tell what happened to me.
As I was saying, we walked in the fields,

Til trewely we hadde swich daliance,
This clerk and I, that of my purveyance
I spak to him, and seyde him how that he,
If I were widwe, sholde wedde me.
For certeinly, I sey for no bobance,
Yet was I never withouten purveyance   570
Of mariage, n'of othere thinges eek:
I holde a mouses herte nat worth a leek
That hath but oon hole for to sterte to,
And if that faille, thanne is al y-do.

  I bar him on honde he hadde enchanted me;
My dame taughte me that soutiltee.
And eek I seyde I mette of him al night:
He wolde han slayn me as I lay upright
And al my bed was ful of verray blood,
But yet I hope that he shal do me good;   580
For blood bitokeneth gold, as me was taught.
And al was fals, I dremed of it right naught,
But as I folwed ay my dames lore,
As wel of this as of other thinges more.

  But now sir, lat me see, what I shal seyn?
Aha! By God, I have my tale ageyn.

  Whan that my fourthe housbond was on bere,
I weep algate, and made sory chere,
As wyves moten, for it is usage,
And with my coverchief covered my visage;   590
But for that I was purveyed of a make,
I weep but smal, and that I undertake.

  To chirche was myn housbond born amorwe
With neighebores, that for him maden sorwe;
And Janekin oure clerk was oon of tho.
As help me God, whan that I saugh him go
After the bere, me thoughte he hadde a paire
Of legges and of feet so clene and faire,
That al myn herte I yaf unto his hold.
He was, I trowe, a twenty winter old,   600
And I was fourty, if I shal seye sooth;
But yet I hadde alwey a coltes tooth.
Gat-tothed I was, and that bicam me weel:
I hadde the prente of Seinte Venus seel.
As help me God, I was a lusty oon,
And faire and riche and yong and wel bigoon;
And trewely, as myne housbondes tolde me,
I had the beste *quoniam* mighte be.

until truly this clerk and I enjoyed
such dalliance that in my foresight
I spoke to him and told him that
if I were a widow he should marry me.
For certainly (I don't say it as a boast)
I was never yet unprovided for
in marriage, and other matters too;
I hold that a mouse that has but one hole
to run to has a heart not worth a leek;
for if that should fail, then all is finished.

    I made him believe he had enchanted me;
my mother taught me that trick.
And also I said I had dreamed of him all night:
he wanted to slay me as I lay on my back,
and all my bed was full of very blood;
but yet I expected that he would bring me luck;
for blood signifies gold, as I was taught.
—And all this was false, I had dreamed none of it;
I was just following my mother's lore, as I
always did, in this as well as in other matters.

    But now sir, let me see, what am I talking about?
Aha! By God, I have my tale back again.

    When my fourth husband was on his bier,
I wept, all the same, and acted sorrowful,
as wives must, for it is customary,
and covered my face with my handkerchief;
but since I was provided with a mate,
I wept but little, that ✝ guarantee.

    My husband was brought to church in the morning,
with neighbors who mourned for him;
and Jankin our clerk was one of them.
So help me God, when I saw him walk
behind the bier, it seemed to me he had a pair
of legs and feet so neat and handsome
that I gave all my heart into his keeping.
He was, I think, twenty years old,
and I was forty, if the truth be told;
but yet I always had a colt's tooth.
I was gap-toothed,* and that became me well;
I had the print of St. Venus' seal.
So help me God, I was a lusty one,
and fair and rich and young and well off;
and truly, as my husbands told me,
I had the best *quoniam** that might be.

For certes, I am al Venerien
In felinge, and myn herte is Marcien: 610
Venus me yaf my lust, my likerousnesse,
And Mars yaf me my sturdy hardinesse.
Myn ascendent was Taur, and Mars therinne.
Allas, allas, that ever love was sinne!
I folwed ay myn inclinacioun
By vertu of my constellacioun;
That made me I coude noght withdrawe
My chambre of Venus from a good felawe.
Yet have I Martes mark upon my face,
And also in another privee place.   620
For, God so wis be my savacioun,
I ne loved never by no discrecioun,
But ever folwede myn appetyt,
Al were he short or long, or blak or whyt;
I took no kepe, so that he lyked me,
How pore he was, ne eek of what degree.

    What sholde I seye, but, at the monthes ende,
This joly clerk Jankin, that was so hende
Hath wedded me with greet solempnitee,
And to him yaf I al the lond and fee   630
That ever was me yeven therbiforе;
But afterward repented me ful sore:
He nolde suffre nothing of my list.
By God, he smoot me ones on the list,
For that I rente out of his book a leef,
That of the strook myn ere wex al deef.
Stiborn I was as is a leonesse,
And of my tonge a verray jangleresse,
And walke I wolde, as I had doon biforn,
From hous to hous, although he had it sworn;   640
For which he often tymes wolde preche,
And me of olde Romayn gestes teche,
How he Simplicius Gallus lefte his wyf,
And hir forsook for terme of al his lyf,
Noght but for open-heeded he hir say
Lokinge out at his dore upon a day.

    Another Romayn tolde he me by name,
That, for his wyf was at a someres game
Withoute his witing, he forsook hir eke.
And than wolde he upon his Bible seke   650
That ilke proverbe of Ecclesiaste,
Wher he comandeth and forbedeth faste

For certainly, my feelings all come
from Venus, and my heart from Mars:
Venus gave me my lust, my lecherousness,
and Mars gave me my sturdy hardiness,
because Taurus was in the ascendent when I was born, and
Mars was in that sign. Alas, alas, that ever love was sin!
I always followed my inclination
according to the stellar influences at my birth;
I was so made that I could not withhold
my chamber of Venus from a good fellow.
I still have the mark of Mars on my face,
and also in another private place.
For, as surely as God is my salvation,
I never had any discrimination in love,
but always followed my appetite,
be he short or tall, dark or fair;
I didn't care, so long as he pleased me,
how poor he was, nor of what rank.

What should I say, except that at the end of the month
this gay clerk Jankin, that was so pleasant,
wedded me with great ceremony,
and to him I gave all the lands and property
that had ever been given to me before;
but afterward I repented this sorely:
he would not allow anything I wanted.
By God, he hit me once on the ear
because I had torn a leaf out of his book;
as a result of that stroke, my ear became totally deaf.
I was stubborn as a lionness,
and as for my tongue, an absolute ranter;
and I'd walk, as I'd done before,
from house to house, although he'd sworn I wouldn't;
because of this he would often preach
and teach me of the deeds of ancient Romans:
how Simplicius Gallus left his wife
and forsook her for the rest of his life
just because he saw her looking out
of his door bareheaded one day.

He told me by name of another Roman
who also, because his wife was at a summer
game without his knowledge, forsook her.
And then he would seek in his Bible
for that proverb of Ecclesiasticus
where he makes a command strictly forbidding

Man shal nat suffre his wyf go roule aboute;
Than wolde he seye right thus, withouten doute:
　'Whoso that buildeth his hous al of salwes,
　And priketh his blinde hors over the falwes,
　And suffreth his wyf to go seken halwes,
　Is worthy to been hanged on the galwes.'
But al for noght; I sette noght an hawe
Of his proverbes n'of his olde sawe,   660
Ne I wolde nat of him corrected be.
I hate him that my vices telleth me,
And so do mo, God woot, of us than I.
This made him with me wood al outrely;
I nolde noght forbere him in no cas.
　Now wol I seye yow sooth, by Seint Thomas,
Why that I rente out of his book a leef,
For which he smoot me so that I was deef.
He hadde a book that gladly, night and day,
For his desport he wolde rede alway.   670
He cleped it Valerie and Theofraste,
At whiche book he lough alwey ful faste;
And eek ther was somtyme a clerk at Rome,
A cardinal, that highte Seint Jerome,
That made a book agayn Jovinian;
In whiche book eek ther was Tertulan,
Crisippus, Trotula, and Helowys,
That was abbesse nat fer fro Parys;
And eek the Parables of Salomon,
Ovydes Art, and bokes many on,   680
And alle thise wer bounden in o volume.
And every night and day was his custume,
Whan he had leyser and vacacioun
From other worldly occupacioun,
To reden on this book of wikked wyves.
He knew of hem mo legendes and lyves
Than been of gode wyves in the Bible.
For trusteth wel, it is an impossible
That any clerk wol speke good of wyves,
But-if it be of holy seintes lyves,   690
Ne of noon other womman never the mo.
Who peyntede the leoun, tel me who?
By God, if wommen hadde writen stories,
As clerkes han withinne hir oratories,
They wolde han writen of men more wikkednesse
Than all the mark of Adam may redresse.

a man to allow his wife to go roaming about;
then you could be sure he would say this:
   'Whoever builds his house of willows,
   and rides his blind horse over plowed land,
   and allows his wife to visit shrines,
   is worthy to be hanged on the gallows.'
But all for nought; I didn't care a berry
for his proverbs and old saw,
nor would I be corrected by him.
I hate that man who tells me my vices,
and so, God knows, do more of us than I.
This made him utterly furious with me;
I wouldn't give in to him in any case.
   Now I'll tell you truly, by Saint Thomas,
why I tore a leaf out of his book,
for which he hit me so that I became deaf.
He had a book that he always loved to read
in night and day to amuse himself.
He called it Valerius* and Theophrastus;
at which book he was always laughing heartily;
and also there was at some time a clerk at Rome,
a cardinal, that was called St. Jerome,
who wrote a book against Jovinian;
in this book there was also Tertulian,
Chrysippus,* Trotula,* and Heloise,*
who was an abbess not far from Paris;
and also the Parables* of Solomon,
Ovid's *Art of Love,* and many other books,
and all these were bound in one volume.
And every day and night it was his custom,
when he had leisure and could rest
from other worldly occupation,
to read in this book about wicked wives.
He knew more legends and lives of them
than there are of good wives in the Bible.
For believe me, it is an impossibility
for any clerk to speak good of wives—
unless it be of the lives of holy saints,
but never of any other woman.
Who painted the lion,* tell me who?
By God, if women had written stories,
as clerks have in their oratories,
they would have written more of men's wickedness
than all of the sex of Adam can redress.

The children of Mercurie and of Venus
Bee in hir wirking ful contrarious;
Mercurie loveth wisdom and science,
And Venus loveth ryot and dispence.   700
And, for hir diverse disposicioun,
Ech falleth in otheres exaltacioun;
And thus, God woot, Mercurie is desolat
In Pisces, wher Venus is exaltat;
And Venus falleth ther Mercurie is reysed;
Therfor no womman of no clerk is preysed.
The clerk, whan he is old, and may noght do
Of Venus werkes worth his olde sho,
Than sit he doun, and writ in his dotage
That wommen can nat kepe hir mariage!   710
    But now to purpos, why I tolde thee
That I was beten for a book, pardee.
Upon a night Jankin, that was our syre,
Redde on his book, as he sat by the fyre,
Of Eva first, that, for hir wikkednesse
Was al mankinde broght to wrecchednesse,
For which that Jesu Crist himself was slayn,
That boghte us with his herte blood agayn.
Lo, here expres of womman may ye finde,
That womman was the los of al mankinde.   720
    Tho redde he me how Sampson loste his heres:
Slepinge, his lemman kitte hem with hir sheres;
Thurgh whiche tresoun loste he bothe his yën.
    Tho redde he me, if that I shal nat lyen,
Of Hercules and of his Dianyre,
That caused him to sette himself afyre.
    No thing forgat he the care and the wo
That Socrates had with hise wyves two;
How Xantippa caste pisse upon his heed;
This sely man sat stille as he were deed;   730
He wyped his heed, namore dorste he seyn
But 'Er that thonder stinte, comth a reyn.'
    Of Phasipha, that was the quene of Crete,
For shrewednesse, him thoughte the tale swete;
Fy, spek namore—it is a grisly thing—
Of hir horrible lust and hir lyking.
    Of Clitemistra, for hir lecherye,
That falsly made hir housbond for to dye,
He redde it with ful good devocioun.
    He tolde me eek for what occasioun   740

The children of Mercury* and of Venus
are quite contrary in their ways;
Mercury loves wisdom and learning,
and Venus loves revelry and expenditure.
And, because of their diverse dispositions,
each loses power when the other is dominant;
and thus, God knows, Mercury is powerless
in the Sign of the Fish, where Venus is dominant;
and Venus falls when Mercury ascends;
therefore no woman is praised by any clerk.
The clerk, when he is old, and unable to do
any of Venus' work worth his old shoe,
then sits down and writes in his dotage
that women cannot keep their marriage vows!

But now to the purpose, as to why I was beaten,
as I told you, because of a book, for heaven's sake.
One night Jankin, who was the head of the household,
read in his book as he sat by the fire,
first, concerning Eve, that all mankind was brought
to wretchedness by her wickedness,
for which Jesus Christ himself was slain,
who redeemed us with his heart's blood.
Here you can expressly find this of woman:
that woman caused the fall of all mankind.

Then he read to me how Samson lost his hair:
while he was sleeping, his mistress cut it with her shears;
through this treason he lost both his eyes.

Then he read to me, and this is no lie,
about Hercules and his Dejanira,
who caused him to set himself on fire.

He forgot none of the sorrow and woe
that Socrates had with his two wives;
how Xantippe cast piss upon his head;
this poor man sat as still as if he were dead;
he wiped his head; he dared to say no more
than, 'Before the thunder stops, comes the rain.'

The tale of Pasiphaë,* who was the queen of Crete,
he maliciously thought sweet;
fie, speak no more—it is a grisly thing—
about her horrible lust and her preference.

Of Clytemnestra,* who because of her lechery
with falseness caused her husband's death,
he read with great devotion.

He told me also why

Amphiorax at Thebes loste his lyf;
Myn housbond hadde a legende of his wyf,
Eriphilem, that for an ouche of gold
Hath prively unto the Grekes told
Wher that hir housbonde hidde him in a place,
For which he hadde at Thebes sory grace.
  Of Lyvia tolde he me, and of Lucye;
They bothe made hir housbondes for to dye,
That oon for love, that other was for hate;
Lyvia hir housbond, on an even late,   750
Empoysoned hath, for that she was his fo.
Lucya, likerous, loved hir housbond so,
That, for he sholde alwey upon hir thinke,
She yaf him swich a maner love-drinke,
That he was deed er it were by the morwe;
And thus algates housbondes han sorwe.
  Than tolde he me how oon Latumius
Compleyned to his felawe Arrius
That in his gardin growed swich a tree,
On which he seyde how that his wyves three   760
Hanged hemself for herte despitous.
'O leve brother,' quod this Arrius,
'Yif me a plante of thilke blissed tree,
And in my gardin planted shal it be.'
  Of latter date, of wyves hath he red
That somme han slayn hir housbondes in hir bed,
And lete hir lechour dighte hir al the night
Whyl that the corps lay in the floor upright.
And somme han drive nayles in hir brayn
Whyl that they slepte, and thus they han hem slayn.   770
Somme han hem yeve poysoun in hir drinke.
He spak more harm than herte may bithinke;
And therwithal he knew of mo proverbes
Than in this world ther growen gras or herbes.
'Bet is,' quod he, 'thyn habitacioun
Be with a leoun or a foul dragoun,
Than with a womman usinge for to chyde.
Best is,' quod he, 'hye in the roof abyde
Than with an angry wyf doun in the hous;
They been so wikked and contrarious,   780
They haten that hir housbondes loveth ay.'
He seyde, 'A womman cast hir shame away,
Whan she cast of hir smok,' and forthermo,
'A fair womman, but she be chaast also,

Amphiaraus lost his life at Thebes;
my husband had a story about his wife,
Eriphyle, who for a trinket of gold
secretly told the Greeks
where her husband had hidden himself,
which is why he had sad luck at Thebes.

He told me of Livia* and of Lucilla;*
they both caused their husbands to die,
one for love and the other for hate;
Livia, late one night, poisoned
her husband, because she was his foe.
Lustful Lucilla loved her husband so
that in order to make him think of her always
she gave him a love potion of such a kind
that he was dead before morning;
and thus husbands always suffer.

Then he told me how one Latumius
complained to his friend Arrius
that in his garden there grew a tree
on which, he said, his three wives
had spitefully hanged themselves.

'O dear brother,' said this Arrius,
'give me a cutting of that blessed tree,
and it shall be planted in my garden.'

He read of wives of a later date
some of whom had slain their husbands in their beds,
and let their lechers make love to them all the night
while the corpse lay flat on the floor.
And some have driven nails into their husband's brain
while they slept, and thus slain them.
Some have given them poison in their drink.
He told of more evil than the heart can imagine;
and along with that, he knew more proverbs
than there are blades of grass or herbs in the world.

'It is better,' said he, 'to dwell
with a lion or a foul dragon
than with a woman accustomed to scold.
It is better,' said he, 'to stay high on the roof
than with an angry wife down in the house;
they are so wicked and contrary
they always hate what their husbands love.'
He said, 'A woman casts her shame away
when she casts off her smock,' and furthermore,

'A fair woman, unless she is also chaste,

Is lyk a gold ring in a sowes nose.'
Who wolde wenen, or who wolde suppose
The wo that in myn herte was, and pyne?
    And whan I saugh he wolde never fyne
To reden on this cursed book al night,
Al sodeynly three leves have I plight   790
Out of his book, right as he radde, and eke
I with my fist so took him on the cheke,
That in our fyr he fil bakward adoun.
And he up stirte as dooth a wood leoun,
And with his fist he smoot me on the heed
That in the floor I lay as I were deed.
And when he saugh how stille that I lay,
He was agast, and wolde han fled his way,
Til atte laste out of my swogh I breyde:
'O, hastow slayn me, false theef?' I seyde,   800
'And for my land thus hastow mordred me?
Er I be deed, yet wol I kisse thee.'
    And neer he cam, and kneled faire adoun,
And seyde, 'Dere suster Alisoun,
As help me God, I shal thee never smyte;
That I have doon, it is thyself to wyte.
Foryeve it me, and that I thee biseke.'
And yet eftsones I hitte him on the cheke,
And seyde, 'Theef, thus muchel am I wreke;
Now wol I dye, I may no lenger speke.'   810
But atte laste, with muchel care and wo,
We fille acorded, by us selven two.
He yaf me al the brydel in myn hond
To han the governance of hous and lond,
And of his tonge and of his hond also,
And made him brenne his book anon right tho.
And whan that I hadde geten unto me
By maistrie* al the soveraynetee,
And that he seyde, 'Myn owene trewe wyf,
Do as thee lust the terme of al thy lyf,   820
Keep thyn honour, and keep eek myn estaat,'
After that day we hadden never debaat.
God help me so, I was to him as kinde
As any wyf from Denmark unto Inde,
And also trewe, and so was he to me.
I prey to God that sit in magestee,
So blesse his soule, for His mercy dere!
Now wol I seye my tale, if ye wol here."

is like a gold ring in a sow's nose.'
Who would suppose or imagine
the woe and pain that was in my heart?
    And when I saw he would never stop
reading in this cursed book all night,
suddenly I plucked three leaves
out of his book, right as he was reading, and also
I hit him on the cheek with my fist, so
that he fell down into our fire backward.
He started up like a raging lion
and hit me on the head with his fist
so that I lay on the floor as if I were dead.
And when he saw how still I lay,
he was aghast, and would have fled away,
until at last I awoke from my swoon:
'Oh! Have you slain me, false thief?' I said,
'And have you murdered me thus for my land?
Before I die, I yet want to kiss you.'
    He came near, and kneeled down gently,
and said, 'Dear sister Alison,
so help me God, I shall never hit you;
what I have done, you are to blame for yourself.
Forgive me for it, I beseech you.'
But yet again I hit him on the cheek,
and said, 'Thief, this much I am avenged;
now I shall die, I can speak no longer.'
But at last, after much care and woe,
we fell into accord between ourselves.
He gave the bridle completely into my hand
to have control of house and land,
and also of his tongue and hand;
and I made him burn his book right then.
And when I had got for myself,
through superiority, all the sovereignty,
and he had said, 'My own true wife,
do as you wish the rest of your life,
preserve your honor, and my public position, too,'
after that day we never argued.
So God help me, I was as kind to him
as any wife from Denmark to India,
and as true, and so was he to me.
I pray to God who sits in majesty
to bless his soul, for His dear mercy's sake!
Now I'll tell my tale, if you will listen."

Biholde the wordes bitween the Somonour and the Frere

THE Frere lough, whan he hadde herd al this:
"Now, dame," quod he, "so have I joye or blis,   830
This is a long preamble of a tale!"
And whan the Somnour herde the Frere gale,
"Lo," quod the Somnour, "Goddes armes two!
A frere wol entremette him evermo.
Lo, gode men, a flye and eek a frere
Wol falle in every dish and eek matere.
What spekestow of preambulacioun?
What! amble, or trotte, or pees, or go sit doun;
Thou lettest our disport in this manere."
    "Ye, woltow so, sir Somnour?" quod the Frere,   840
"Now, by my feith, I shal, er that I go,
Telle of a somnour swich a tale or two
That alle the folk shal laughen in this place."
    "Now elles, Frere, I bishrewe thy face,"
Quod this Somnour, "and I bishrewe me,
But if I telle tales two or three
Of freres er I come to Sidingborne,
That I shal make thyn herte for to morne;
For wel I woot thy pacience is goon."
    Our Hoste cryde, "Pees, and that anoon!"   850
And seyde, "Lat the womman telle hir tale.
Ye fare as folk that dronken been of ale.
Do, dame, tel forth your tale, and that is best."
    "Al redy, sir," quod she, "right as yow lest,
If I have licence of this worthy Frere."
    "Yis, dame," quod he, "tel forth, and I wol here."

Here biginneth the Tale of the Wyf of Bathe

IN th'olde dayes of the king Arthour,
Of which that Britons speken greet honour,
Al was this land fulfild of fayerye.
The elf-queen with hir joly companye
Daunced ful ofte in many a grene mede;
This was the olde opinion, as I rede.
I speke of manye hundred yeres ago.
But now can no man see none elves mo,
For now the grete charitee and prayeres
Of limitours and othere holy freres,   10
That serchen every lond and every streem,
As thikke as motes in the sonne-beem,

Behold the words between the Summoner and the Friar

The Friar laughed, when he had heard all this:
"Now, dame," said he, "as I may have joy or bliss,
this is a long preamble to a tale!"
And when the Summoner heard the Friar exclaim,
"Lo!" said the Summoner, "By God's two arms!
A friar will always be butting in.
See, good people, a fly and a friar
will fall into every dish and also every matter.
What do you mean, talking about preambulation?
Oh, amble or trot or hold your peace, or go sit down;
you're spoiling our fun by behaving in this manner."

   "Oh, is that so, sir Summoner?" said the Friar,
"Now by my faith, before I go, I'll
tell such a tale or two about a summoner
that everyone here shall laugh."

   "Now Friar, damn your eyes,"
said this Summoner, "and damn me
if I don't tell two or three tales
about friars before I get to Sittingbourne,*
so that I shall make your heart mourn;
I can easily see that your patience is gone."

   Our Host cried "Peace! And that at once!"
And said, "Let the woman tell her tale.
You behave like people who have got drunk on ale.
Tell your tale, dame; that is best."

   "All ready, sir," said she, "just as you wish,
if I have the permission of this worthy Friar."

   "Yes, dame," said he, "tell on and I will listen."

Here begins the Wife of Bath's Tale

In the old days of King Arthur,
of whom Britons speak great honor,
this land was all filled with fairies.
The elf queen with her jolly company
danced often in many a green meadow—
this was the old belief, as I have read;
I speak of many hundred years ago.
But now no one can see elves any more,
for now the great charity and prayers
of limiters* and other holy friars,
who search every field and stream,
as thick as specks of dust in a sunbeam,

Blessinge halles, chambres, kichenes, boures,
Citees, burghes, castels, hye toures,
Thropes, bernes, shipnes, dayeryes:
This maketh that ther been no fayeryes.
For ther as wont to walken was an elf,
Ther walketh now the limitour himself,
In undermeles and in morweninges,
And seyth his Matins and his holy thinges   20
As he goth in his limitacioun.
Wommen may go saufly up and doun;
In every bush or under every tree
Ther is noon other incubus but he—
And he ne wol doon hem but dishonour.

    And so bifel it that this King Arthour
Hadde in his hous a lusty bacheler,
That on a day cam rydinge fro river;
And happed that, allone as she was born,
He saugh a mayde walkinge him biforn,   30
Of whiche mayde anon, maugree hir heed,
By verray force he rafte hir maydenheed;
For which oppressioun was swich clamour
And swich pursute unto the King Arthour,
That dampned was this knight for to be deed
By cours of lawe, and sholde han lost his heed—
Paraventure, swich was the statut tho—
But that the quene and othere ladies mo
So longe preyeden the king of grace,
Til he his lyf him graunted in the place,   40
And yaf him to the quene, al at hir wille,
To chese whether she wolde him save or spille.

    The quene thanketh the king with al hir might,
And after this thus spak she to the knight,
Whan that she saugh hir tyme, upon a day:
"Thou standest yet," quod she, "in swich array
That of thy lyf yet hastow no suretee.
I grante thee lyf if thou canst tellen me
What thing is it that wommen most desyren.
Be war, and keep thy nekke-boon from yren.   50
And if thou canst nat tellen it anon,
Yet wol I yeve thee leve for to gon
A twelfmonth and a day, to seche and lere
An answere suffisant in this matere.
And suretee wol I han, er that thou pace,
Thy body for to yelden in this place."

blessing halls, chambers, kitchens, bedrooms,
cities, towns, castles, high towers,
villages, barns, stables, dairies:
this is the reason that there are no fairies.
For where an elf was wont to walk,
there now walks the limiter himself,
in afternoons and in mornings,
and says his Matins and his holy things,
as he goes about within his limits.
Women may go up and down safely;
in every bush or under every tree
there is no other incubus but he—
and he won't do anything but dishonor to them.

It so happened that this King Arthur
had in his house a lusty bachelor,
who one day came riding from the river;
and it happened that he saw a maiden
walking before him, alone as she was born.
And from this maiden then, against her will,
and by pure force, he took her maidenhood.
Because of this violation, there was such a clamor
and such petitioning to King Arthur
that this knight was condemned to die
according to law, and should have lost his head—
it happened that such was the statute then—
except that the Queen and various other ladies
prayed to the king for grace so long
that he granted him his life on the spot,
and gave him to the queen, completely at her will,
to choose whether she would save or destroy him.

The queen thanked the king heartily,
and then spoke thus to the knight,
one day, when she saw a fitting time:
"You are still in such a position," said she,
"that you have no guarantee of your life as yet.
I will grant you life if you can tell me
what thing it is that women most desire.
Be wary, and keep your neck from the ax.
And if you cannot tell it to me now,
I will still give you leave to go
a year and a day to seek and learn
a sufficient answer in this matter.
And I want a guarantee, before you go,
that you will yield up your person in this place."

Wo was this knight and sorwefully he syketh;
But what, he may nat do al as him lyketh.
And at the laste, he chees him for to wende,
And come agayn, right at the yeres ende,　　60
With swich answere as God wolde him purveye;
And taketh his leve, and wendeth forth his weye.

He seketh every hous and every place
Wher as he hopeth for to finde grace,
To lerne what thing wommen loven most;
But he ne coude arryven in no cost
Wheras he mighte finde in this matere
Two creatures accordinge in fere.

Somme seyde wommen loven best richesse;
Somme seyde honour; somme seyde jolynesse;　　70
Somme, riche array; somme seyden, lust abedde,
And ofte tyme to be widwe and wedde.
Somme seyde that our hertes been most esed
Whan that we been y-flatered and y-plesed:
He gooth ful ny the sothe, I wol nat lye;
A man shal winne us best with flaterye,
And with attendance and with bisinesse
Been we y-lymed, bothe more and lesse.

And somme seyen that we loven best
For to be free, and do right as us lest,　　80
And that no man repreve us of our vyce,
But seye that we be wyse, and no thing nyce.
For trewely, ther is noon of us alle,
If any wight wol clawe us on the galle,
That we nil kike, for he seith us sooth;
Assay, and he shal finde it that so dooth.
For be we never so vicious withinne,
We wol been holden wyse and clene of sinne.

And somme seyn that greet delyt han we
For to ben holden stable and eek secree,　　90
And in o purpos stedefastly to dwelle,
And nat biwreye thing that men us telle.
But that tale is nat worth a rake-stelle;
Pardee, we wommen conne no thing hele;
Witnesse on Myda; wol ye here the tale?

Ovyde, amonges othere thinges smale,
Seyde Myda hadde, under his longe heres,
Growinge upon his heed two asses eres,
The whiche vyce he hidde, as he best mighte,
Ful subtilly from every mannes sighte,　　100

The knight was woeful, and he sighed sorrowfully;
but then, he could not do as he pleased.
And in the end he decided to go off,
and to come back again just at the end of the year,
with such an answer as God would provide for him;
he took his leave and went forth on his way.

He sought in every house and every place
where he hoped to find favor,
in order to learn what thing women most love;
but he reached no land where he could find
two people who were in agreement
with each other on this matter.

Some said women love riches best;
some said honor; some said amusement;
some, rich apparel; some said pleasure in bed,
and often to be widowed and remarried.
Some said that our hearts are most soothed
when we are flattered and pampered:
he came near the truth, I will not lie;
a man can win us best with flattery,
and with constant attendance and assiduity
we are ensnared, both high and low.

And some said that we love best
to be free, and do just as we please,
and to have no man reprove us for our vice,
but say that we are wise and not at all foolish.
For truly, if anyone will scratch us
on a sore spot, there is not one of us
who will not kick for being told the truth;
try it, and he who does shall find this out.
No matter how full of vice we are within,
we wish to be thought wise and clean from sin.

And some said that we take delight
in being thought reliable and able to keep a secret
and hold steadfast to a purpose
and not betray anything that people tell us.
But that idea isn't worth a rake handle;
by heaven, we women can't conceal a thing;
witness Midas; would you hear the tale?

Ovid, among other brief matters,
said Midas had two ass's ears growing
on his head under his long hair;
which evil he hid from everyone's sight
as artfully as he could,

That, save his wyf, ther wiste of it namo.
He loved hir most, and trusted hir also;
He preyede hir, that to no creature
She sholde tellen of his disfigure.

   She swoor him nay, for al this world to winne,
She nolde do that vileinye or sinne
To make hir housbond han so foul a name;
She nolde nat telle it for hir owene shame.
But nathelees, hir thoughte that she dyde
That she so longe sholde a conseil hyde;   110
Hir thoughte it swal so sore aboute hir herte
That nedely som word hir moste asterte;
And sith she dorste telle it to no man,
Doun to a mareys faste by she ran—
Til she came there, hir herte was afyre—
And, as a bitore bombleth in the myre,
She leyde hir mouth unto the water doun:
"Biwreye me nat, thou water, with thy soun,"
Quod she. "To thee I telle it, and namo:
Myn housbond hath longe asses eres two!   120
Now is myn herte all hool, now is it oute;
I mighte no lenger kepe it, out of doute."
Heer may ye se, thogh we a tyme abyde,
Yet out it moot, we can no conseil hyde.
The remenant of the tale if ye wol here,
Redeth Ovyde, and ther ye may it lere.

   This knight, of which my tale is specially,
Whan that he saugh he mighte nat come therby—
This is to seye, what wommen loven moost—
Withinne his brest ful sorweful was the goost;   130
But hoom he gooth, he mighte nat sojourne:
The day was come that hoomward moste he tourne.
And in his wey it happed him to ryde,
In al this care, under a forest syde,
Wher as he saugh upon a daunce go
Of ladies foure and twenty and yet mo;
Toward the whiche daunce he drow ful yerne,
In hope that som wisdom sholde he lerne.
But certeinly, er he came fully there,
Vanisshed was this daunce, he niste where.   140
No creature saugh he that bar lyf,
Save on the grene he saugh sittinge a wyf;
A fouler wight ther may no man devyse.
Agayn the knight this olde wyf gan ryse

so that no one knew of it except his wife.
He loved her most, and also trusted her;
he prayed her not to tell anyone
of his disfigurement.

  She swore to him that not for all the world
would she do such villainy and sin
as to give her husband so bad a name;
out of her own shame she wouldn't tell it.
But nonetheless she thought that she would die
for having to keep a secret so long;
it seemed to her that her heart swelled so painfully
some word must needs burst from her;
and since she dared not tell it to anybody,
she ran down to a marsh close by—
her heart was on fire until she got there—
and, as a bittern booms in the mire,
she laid her mouth down to the water:
"Betray me not, you water, with your sound,"
said she. "To you I tell it, and to no one else:
my husband has two long ass's ears!
Now my heart is all cured, for the secret is out!
I simply couldn't keep it any longer."
In this you can see that though we wait a time,
yet out it must come: we cannot hide a secret.
If you wish to hear the rest of the tale,
read Ovid, and there you can learn of it.

  When this knight whom my tale specially concerns
saw that he couldn't come by it—
that is to say, what women love most—
his spirit was very sorrowful within his breast;
but home he went, he might not linger:
the day was come when he must turn homeward.
And on his way, burdened with care, he happened
to ride by the edge of a forest,
where he saw more than twenty-four
ladies moving in a dance;
he drew eagerly toward that dance
in the hope that he might learn something.
But indeed, before he quite got there,
the dancers vanished, he knew not where.
He saw no living creature,
except a woman sitting on the green:
no one could imagine an uglier creature.
This old woman rose before the knight

And seyde, "Sir knight, heer forth ne lyth no wey.
Tel me what that ye seken, by your fey.
Parventure it may the bettre be;
Thise olde folk can muchel thing," quod she.

"My leve mooder," quod this knight, "certeyn,
I nam but deed, but if that I can seyn   150
What thing it is that wommen most desyre;
Coude ye me wisse, I wolde wel quyte your hyre."

"Plight me thy trouthe, heer in myn hand," quod she,
"The nexte thing that I requere thee,
Thou shalt it do, if it lye in thy might;
And I wol tell it yow er it be night."

"Have here my trouthe," quod the knight. "I grante."

"Thanne," quod she, "I dar me wel avante
Thy lyf is sauf, for I wol stonde therby,
Upon my lyf, the queen wol seye as I.   160
Lat see which is the proudeste of hem alle
That wereth on a coverchief or a calle
That dar seye nay of that I shal thee teche;
Lat us go forth withouten lenger speche."
Tho rouned she a pistel in his ere,
And bad him to be glad, and have no fere.

Whan they be comen to the court, this knight
Seyde he had holde his day, as he hadde hight,
And redy was his answere, as he sayde.
Ful many a noble wyf, and many a mayde,   170
And many a widwe, for that they ben wyse,
The quene hirself sittinge as a justyse,
Assembled been, his answere for to here;
And afterward this knight was bode appere.

To every wight comanded was silence,
And that the knight sholde telle in audience
What thing that worldly wommen loven best.
This knight ne stood nat stille as doth a best,
But to his questioun anon answerde
With manly voys, that al the court it herde: 180

"My lige lady, generally," quod he,
"Wommen desyren to have sovereyntee
As wel over hir housbond as hir love,
And for to been in maistrie him above;
This is your moste desyr, thogh ye me kille,
Doth as yow list, I am heer at your wille."

In al the court ne was ther wyf ne mayde
Ne widwe that contraried that he sayde,

and said, "Sir knight, no road lies this way.
Tell me, by your faith, what you seek for.
Perhaps it may be the better;
these old folks know many things," said she.

"Dear mother," said this knight, "certainly
I am as good as dead unless I can say
what thing it is that women most desire;
if you could tell me, I would repay your trouble well."

"Give me your promise, here upon my hand," said she,
"that you will do the next thing I require
of you, if it lies in your power,
and I will tell it to you before nightfall."
"Here is my promise," said the knight, "I grant it."

"Then," said she, "I dare to boast
that your life is safe, for I'll swear
upon my life that the queen will say as I do.
Let's see whether the proudest of all those
that wear a coverchief or headdress
dares deny what I shall teach you;
let's go on without any more talk."
Then she whispered a message in his ear,
and told him to be glad and not afraid.

When they had come to the court, this knight
said he had kept his day as he had promised,
and his answer, he said, was ready.
Many a noble wife and many a maiden,
and many a widow (since widows are so wise),
were assembled to hear his answer
with the queen herself sitting as judge;
and then the knight was ordered to appear.

Everyone was commanded to keep silence,
and the knight was commanded to tell in open assembly
what thing it is that secular women love best.
This knight did not stand in beastlike silence,
but answered to his question at once
with manly voice, so that all the court heard it:

"My liege lady," he said, "generally
women desire to have dominion
over their husbands as well as their lovers,
and to be above them in mastery;
this is your greatest desire, though you may kill me;
do as you please, I am at your will here."

In all the court there was neither wife nor maiden
nor widow who contradicted what he said,

But seyden he was worthy han his lyf.

    And with that word up stirte the olde wyf,   190
Which that the knight saugh sittinge in the grene:
"Mercy," quod she, "my sovereyn lady quene!
Er that your court departe, do me right.
I taughte this answere unto the knight;
For which he plighte me his trouthe there,
The firste thing I wolde of him requere,
He wolde it do, if it lay in his might.
Bifore the court than preye I thee, sir knight,"
Quod she, "that thou me take unto thy wyf;
For wel thou wost that I have kept thy lyf.   200
If I sey fals, sey nay, upon thy fey."

    This knight answered, "Alas and weylawey!
I woot right wel that swich was my biheste.
For Goddes love, as chees a newe requeste;
Tak al my good, and lat my body go."

    "Nay than," quod she, "I shrewe us bothe two!
For thogh that I be foul and old and pore,
I nolde for al the metal, ne for ore,
That under erthe is grave, or lyth above,
But if thy wyf I were and eek thy love."   210

    "My love?" quod he; "Nay, my dampnacioun!
Allas, that any of my nacioun
Sholde ever so foule disparaged be!"
But al for noght, the ende is this, that he
Constreyned was, he nedes moste hir wedde;
And taketh his olde wyf and gooth to bedde.

    Now wolden som men seye, paraventure,
That for my necligence I do no cure
To tellen yow the joye and al th'array
That at the feste was that ilke day.   220
To whiche thing shortly answere I shal;
I seye ther nas no joye ne feste at al,
Ther nas but hevinesse and muche sorwe;
For prively he wedded hir on the morwe,
And al day after hidde him as an oule—
So wo was him, his wyf looked so foule.

    Greet was the wo the knight hadde in his thoght,
Whan he was with his wyf abedde y-broght;
He walweth, and he turneth to and fro.
His olde wyf lay smylinge evermo,   230
And seyde, "O dere housbond, *ben'cite!*
Fareth every knight thus with his wyf as ye?

but all said he deserved to have his life.

And at that word up jumped the old woman
whom the knight had seen sitting on the green:
"Mercy," said she, "my sovereign lady queen!
Before your court depart, do right by me.
I taught this answer to the knight;
for this he gave me his promise there
that he would do the first thing
I required of him, if it lay in his power.
Before the court, then, I pray you, sir knight,"
said she, "to take me as your wife;
for well you know that I have saved your life.
If I say false, deny me, on your faith!"

The knight answered, "Alas and woe is me!
I know quite well that such was my promise.
For the love of God ask for something else;
take all my property and let my body go."

"No then," said she. "Curse the two of us!
For though I am ugly and old and poor,
I wouldn't want all the metal or ore
that is buried under the earth or lies above
unless I were your wife and your love as well."

"My love?" said he; "No, my damnation!
Alas, that any of my birth
should ever be so foully disgraced!"
But it was all for nothing; the end was this, that he
was forced to accept the fact that he must needs wed her;
and he took his old wife and went to bed.

Now some people might say, perhaps,
that out of negligence I am not bothering
to tell you about the joy and the pomp
at the feast that day,
to which objection I shall answer briefly:
I am telling you that there was no joy or feast at all,
there was nothing but gloom and much sorrow;
for he married her privately in the morning
and afterward hid himself like an owl all day—
he was so dejected because his wife looked so ugly.

Great was the woe in the knight's mind
when he was brought with his wife to bed;
he tossed and he turned to and fro.
His old wife lay smiling all the time,
and said, "O dear husband, bless my soul!
Does every knight behave with his wife as you do?

Is this the lawe of King Arthures hous?
Is every knight of his so dangerous?
I am your owene love and eek your wyf;
I am she which that saved hath your lyf;
And certes, yet dide I yow never unright.
Why fare ye thus with me this firste night?
Ye faren lyk a man had lost his wit.
What is my gilt? for Goddes love, tel me it,   240
And it shal been amended, if I may."
    "Amended?" quod this knight, "Allas, nay, nay!
It wol nat been amended never mo!
Thou art so loothly and so old also,
And therto comen of so lowe a kinde,
That litel wonder is thogh I walwe and winde.
So wolde God myn herte wolde breste!"
    "Is this," quod she, "the cause of your unreste?"
    "Ye, certainly," quod he, "no wonder is."
    "Now, sire," quod she, "I coude amende al this,   250
If that me liste, er it were dayes three,
So wel ye mighte bere yow unto me.
    But for ye speken of swich gentillesse
As is descended out of old richesse,
That therfore sholden ye be gentil men,
Swich arrogance is nat worth an hen.
Loke who that is most vertuous alway,
Privee and apert, and most entendeth ay
To do the gentil dedes that he can,
And tak him for the grettest gentil man.   260
Crist wol we clayme of him our gentillesse,
Nat of our eldres for hir old richesse:
For thogh they yeve us al hir heritage,
For which we clayme to been of heigh parage,
Yet may they nat biquethe for nothing
To noon of us hir vertuous living,
That made hem gentil men y-called be;
And bad us folwen hem in swich degree.
    Wel can the wyse poete of Florence,
That highte Dant, speken in this sentence;   270
Lo in swich maner rym is Dantes tale:
'Ful selde up ryseth by his branches smale
Prowesse of man; for God, of his goodnesse,
Wol that of him we clayme our gentillesse.'
For of our eldres may we nothing clayme
But temporel thing, that man may hurte and mayme.

Is this the law of King Arthur's house?
Is every one of his knights so cold?
I am your own love and your wife;
I am she who saved your life;
and certainly I never yet did wrong to you.
Why do you act thus with me the first night?
You act like a man who has lost his mind.
What am I guilty of? For God's sake, tell me,
and it shall be corrected, if I can manage it."

   "Corrected?" said this knight, "Alas, no, no!
It will never be corrected!
You are so loathsome and so old,
and what is more, of such low birth,
that it is little wonder if I toss and turn.
I wish to God my heart would break!"

   "Is this," said she, "the cause of your unrest?"
"Yes, certainly," said he, "it's no wonder."

   "Now, sir," said she, "I could rectify all this,
if I wanted to, before three days were up,
if you behaved yourself to me well.

   But in the matter of your speaking of such nobility
as descends from ancient wealth,
claiming that because of it you are supposed to be
noblemen—such arrogance is not worth a hen.
Find who is always the most virtuous,
privately and publicly, and who always tries hardest
to do what noble deeds he can,
and consider him the greatest nobleman.
Christ wants us to claim our nobility from him,
not from our ancestors because of their ancient wealth:
for though they give us all their heritage,
on the strength of which we claim to be of noble descent,
yet they cannot bequeath by any means
or to any of us their virtuous manner of life
which made them be called noblemen;
and which summoned us to follow them at the same level.

   Well can the wise poet of Florence
who is called Dante speak on this subject;
in this sort of rhyme is Dante's tale:
'Not oft by branches of a family tree
Does human prowess rise; for gracious God
Wants us to claim from Him nobility.'
For from our elders we may claim nothing
but perishable matter, to which man may do hurt and

Eek every wight wot this as wel as I;
If gentillesse were planted naturelly
Unto a certeyn linage, doun the lyne,
Privee and apert, than wolde they never fyne   280
To doon of gentillesse the faire offyce;
They mighte do no villeinye or vyce.

    Tak fyr, and ber it in the derkeste hous
Bitwix this and the Mount of Caucasus,
And lat men shette the dores and go thenne;
Yet wol the fyr as faire lye and brenne
As twenty thousand men mighte it biholde;
His office naturel ay wol it holde,
Up peril of my lyf, til that it dye.

    Heer may ye see wel how that genterye   290
Is nat annexed to possessioun,
Sith folk ne doon hir operacioun
Alwey, as dooth the fyr, lo, in his kinde.
For, God it woot, men may wel often finde
A lordes sone do shame and vileinye;
And he that wol han prys of his gentrye
For he was boren of a gentil hous,
And hadde hise eldres noble and vertuous,
And nil himselven do no gentil dedis,
Ne folwe his gentil auncestre that deed is,   300
He nis nat gentil, be he duk or erl;
For vileyns, sinful dedes make a cherl.
For gentillesse nis but renomee
Of thyne auncestres, for hir heigh bountee,
Which is a strange thing to thy persone.
Thy gentillesse cometh fro God allone;
Than comth our verray gentillesse of grace,
It was no thing biquethe us with our place.

    Thenketh how noble, as seith Valerius,
Was thilke Tullius Hostilius,   310
That out of povert roos to heigh noblesse.
Redeth Senek, and redeth eek Boece,
Ther shul ye seen expres that it no drede is
That he is gentil that doth gentil dedis.
And therfore, leve housbond, I thus conclude,
Al were it that myne auncestres were rude,
Yet may the hye God, and so hope I,
Grante me grace to liven vertuously;
Thanne am I gentil, whan that I biginne
To liven vertuously and weyve sinne.   320

injury. And everyone knows as well as I that
if nobility were implanted by nature
in a certain lineage, down the line of descent,
they would never cease, in private or public,
to do the fair offices of nobility;
they could do nothing shameful or evil.

Take fire, and bear it into the darkest house
from here to the Mount of Caucasus,
and let men shut the doors and go away;
yet the fire will blaze and burn as well
as if twenty thousand men were looking at it;
it will maintain its natural function always
until it dies, I'll stake my life.

By this you can easily see that nobility
is not tied to possessions,
since people do not perform their function
without variation as does the fire, according to its nature.
For, God knows, men may very often find
a lord's son committing shameful and vile deeds;
and he who wishes to have credit for his nobility
because he was born of a noble house,
and because his elders were noble and virtuous,
but will not himself do any noble deeds
or follow the example of his late noble ancestor,
he is not noble, be he duke or earl;
for villainous, sinful deeds make him a churl.
This kind of nobility is only the renown
of your ancestors, earned by their great goodness,
which is a thing apart from yourself.
Your nobility comes from God alone;
then our true nobility comes of grace,
it was in no way bequeathed to us with our station in life.

Think how noble, as Valerius says,
was that Tullius Hostilius
who rose out of poverty to high nobility.
Read Seneca, and read Boethius,* too;
there you shall see expressly that there is no doubt
that he is noble who does noble deeds.
And therefore, dear husband, I thus conclude
that even if my ancestors were low
yet God on high may—and so I hope—
grant me grace to live virtuously;
then I am noble, from the time when I begin
to live virtuously and avoid sin.

And theras ye of povert me repreve,
The hye God, on whom that we bileve,
In wilful povert chees to live his lyf;
And certes every man, mayden, or wyf
May understonde that Jesus, hevene king,
Ne wolde nat chese a vicious living.
Glad povert is an honest thing, certeyn;
This wol Senek and othere clerkes seyn.
Whoso that halt him payd of his poverte,
I holde him riche, al hadde he nat a sherte,   330
He that coveyteth is a povre wight,
For he wolde han that is nat in his might.
But he that noght hath, ne coveyteth have,
Is riche, although ye holde him but a knave.

Verray povert, it singeth proprely;
Juvenal seith of povert, 'Merily
The povre man, whan he goth by the weye,
Bifore the theves he may singe and pleye.'
Povert is hateful good, and, as I geese,
A ful greet bringer out of bisinesse;   340
A greet amender eek of sapience
To him that taketh it in pacience.
Povert is this, although it seme elenge:
Possessioun, that no wight wol chalenge.
Povert ful ofte, whan a man is lowe,
Maketh his God and eek himself to knowe.
Povert a spectacle is, as thinketh me,
Thurgh which he may his verray frendes see.
And therfore, sire, sin that I noght yow greve,
Of my povert namore ye me repreve.   350

Now, sire, of elde ye repreve me;
And certes, sire, thogh noon auctoritee
Were in no book, ye gentils of honour
Seyn that men sholde an old wight doon favour,
And clepe him fader, for your gentillesse;
And auctours shal I finden, as I gesse.

Now ther ye seye that I am foul and old,
Than drede you noght to been a cokewold;
For filthe and elde, also mote I thee,
Been grete wardeyns upon chastitee.   360
But nathelees, sin I knowe your delyt,
I shal fulfille your worldly appetyt.

Chees now," quod she, "oon of thise thinges tweye:
To han me foul and old til that I deye,

And as for the poverty you reprove me for,
high God in whom we believe
chose to live his life in willing poverty;
and certainly every man, maiden, or wife
can understand that Jesus, heaven's king,
would not choose a vicious way of life.
Contented poverty is an honorable thing, indeed;
this is said by Seneca and other learned men.
Whoever is content with his poverty
I hold to be rich, even if he hasn't a shirt.
He who covets anything is a poor man,
for he wants to have something which is not in his power.
But he who has nothing and desires nothing is rich,
although you may consider him nothing but a lowly man.

True poverty sings of its own accord;
Juvenal says of poverty, 'Merrily can
the poor man sing and joke before the
thieves when he goes by the road.'
Poverty is a good that is hated, and, I guess,
a great expeller of cares;
a great amender of knowledge, too,
to him that takes it in patience.
Poverty is this, although it seem unhealthy:
possession of that which no man will challenge.
Poverty will often, when a man is low,
make him know his God and himself as well.
Poverty is a glass, it seems to me,
through which he can see his true friends.
And therefore, sir, since I do not harm you by it,
do not reprove me for my poverty any more.

Now, sir, you reprove me for age;
but certainly, sir, aside from bookish
authority, you nobles who are honorable
say that one should honor an old person,
and call him father, for the sake of your nobility;
and I can find authors to that effect, I imagine.

Now as to the point that I am ugly and old—
then you need not dread being a cuckold;
for ugliness and age, as I may thrive,
are great wardens of chastity.
But nevertheless, since I know what pleases you,
I shall fulfill your fleshly appetite.

Choose now," said she, "one of these two things:
to have me ugly and old until I die,

And be to yow a trewe humble wyf,
And never yow displese in al my lyf;
Or elles ye wol han me yong and fair,
And take your aventure of the repair
That shal be to your hous, by cause of me,
Or in som other place, may wel be.
Now chees yourselven, whether that yow lyketh." 370

This knight avyseth him and sore syketh,
But atte laste he seyde in this manere,
"My lady and my love, and wyf so dere,
I put me in your wyse governance;
Cheseth yourself which may be most plesance,
And most honour to yow and me also.
I do no fors the whether of the two;
For as yow lyketh, it suffiseth me."

"Thanne have I gete of yow maistrye," quod she, 380
"Sin I may chese, and governe as me lest?"

"Ye certes, wyf," quod he, "I holde it best."

"Kis me," quod she, "we be no lenger wrothe;
For, by my trouthe, I wol be to yow bothe;
This is to seyn, ye, bothe fair and good.
I prey to God that I mot sterven wood
But I to yow be al so good and trewe
As ever was wyf sin that the world was newe.
And, but I be tomorn as fair to sene
As any lady, emperyce, or quene 390
That is bitwixe the est and eke the west,
Doth with my lyf and deeth right as yow lest.
Cast up the curtin, loke how that it is."

And whan the knight saugh verraily al this,
That she so fair was, and so yong therto,
For joye he hente hir in his armes two,
His herte bathed in a bath of blisse;
A thousand tyme arewe he gan hir kisse.
And she obeyed him in every thing
That mighte doon him plesance or lyking. 400

And thus they live, unto hir lyves ende,
In parfit joye; and Jesu Crist us sende
Housbondes meke, yonge, and fresshe abedde,
And grace t'overbyde hem that we wedde.
And eek I preye Jesu shorte hir lyves
That wol nat be governed by hir wyves;
And olde and angry nigardes of dispence,
God sende hem sone verray pestilence!

and be a faithful, humble wife to you,
and never displease you in all my life;
or else to have me young and fair,
and take your chances on the flocking
of people to your house because of me—
or to some other place, it may well be.
Now choose yourself, whichever you like."

The knight considered and sighed sorely,
but at last he spoke in this manner,
"My lady and my love, and wife so dear,
I put myself under your wise control;
you yourself choose which may be most pleasurable
and most honorable to you and to me also.
I don't care which of the two I get;
for whatever pleases you suffices for me."

"Then have I got mastery over you," said she,
"since I may choose and rule as I please?"

"Yes, certainly, wife," said he, "I consider that best."

"Kiss me," said she, "we won't be angry any more;
for I swear I will be both these things to you;
that is to say, both fair indeed and good.
I pray to God that I may die of madness
if I am not just as good and true to you
as ever was wife since the world began.
And, if I am not tomorrow as fair to see
as any lady, empress, or queen
between the east and the west,
do with the question of my life and death just as you wish.
Raise the curtain, and see how it is."

And when the knight actually saw all this—
that she was so fair and so young, too,
he seized her in his two arms for joy,
his heart was bathed in bliss;
he kissed her a thousand times in a row.
And she obeyed him in everything
that might give him pleasure or joy.

And thus they lived to the end of their lives
in perfect joy; and Jesu Christ send us
husbands who are meek, young, and lively in bed,
and grace to outlive those that we marry.
And also I pray Jesu to shorten the lives
of those that won't be governed by their wives;
and as for old and angry niggards of their money,
God send them soon a very pestilence.

THE MARCHANT

The Prologe of the Marchantes Tale

"Weping and wayling, care and other sorwe
I knowe ynogh, on even and a-morwe,"
Quod the Marchant, "and so doon othere mo
That wedded been. I trowe that it be so,
For wel I woot it fareth so with me.
I have a wyf, the worste that may be;
For thogh the feend to hire y-coupled were,
She wolde him overmacche, I dar wel swere.
What sholde I yow reherce in special
Hir hye malice? She is a shrewe at al.   10
Ther is a long and large difference
Bitwix Grisildis grete pacience
And of my wyf the passing crueltee.
Were I unbounden, also moot I thee,
I wolde nevere eft comen in the snare.
We wedded men live in sorwe and care—
Assaye whoso wole and he shal finde
I seye sooth, by Seint Thomas of Inde,
As for the more part—I sey nat alle:
God shilde that it sholde so bifalle.   20
A, goode sire Hoost, I have y-wedded be
Thise monthes two, and more nat, pardee;
And yet I trowe he that all his lyve
Wyflees hath been, though that men wolde him ryve
Unto the herte, ne coude in no manere
Tellen so muchel sorwe, as I now here
Coude tellen of my wyves cursednesse!"
      "Now," quod oure Hoost, "Marchaunt, so God yow blesse,
Sin ye so muchel knowen of that art,
Ful hertely I pray yow telle us part."   30
      "Gladly," quod he, "but of myn owene sore
For sory herte I telle may namore."
240

THE MERCHANT

The Prologue of the Merchant's Tale

"Weeping and wailing, care and sorrow
I know well enough, evening and morning,"
said the Merchant, "and so do many others
who are married: I believe so,
for I well know that so it goes with me.
I have a wife, the worst that can be;
for even if the devil were coupled with her
she would master him, I dare to give my oath.
Why should I repeat to you in detail
her proud malice? She is a shrew in every way.
There is a long and large difference
between Griselda's* great patience
and the surpassing cruelty of my wife.
If I were unshackled, as I may flourish
I would never get in the trap again.
We married men live in unhappiness and anxiety—
whoever wants to, let him try it, and he shall find
that, by Saint Thomas of India, I'm saying the truth
about the majority—I don't say it for all:
God forbid that it should happen that way.
Ah, good sir Host, I have been married
these two months and no more, by heaven;
and yet I think that a man who for all his life
has been without a wife could not, even if he were to be
stabbed to the heart, in any way
recount as much unhappiness as I could tell
here and now concerning my wife's cursedness!"

"Now, Merchant," said our Host, "as God may bless you,
since you have so much of that knowledge,
I pray you heartily to tell us a part of it."

"Willingly," he said, "but of my own misery
I can say no more, for heavy-heartedness."

Here biginneth the Marchantes Tale

WHYLOM ther was dwellinge in Lumbardye
A worthy knight that born was of Pavye,
In which he lived in greet prosperitee;
And sixty yeer a wyflees man was he,
And folwed ay his bodily delyt
On wommen ther as was his appetyt,
As doon thise foles that ben seculeer.*
And whan that he was passed sixty yeer—
Were it for holinesse or for dotage,
I can nat seye—but swich a greet corage   10
Hadde this knight to been a wedded man,
That day and night he dooth al that he can
T'espyen where he mighte wedded be,
Preyinge our Lord to graunten him that he
Mighte ones knowe of thilke blisful lyf
That is bitwixe an housbond and his wyf,
And for to live under that holy bond
With which that first God man and womman bond.
"Non other lyf," seyde he, "is worth a bene,
For wedlok is so esy and so clene   20
That in this world it is a paradys."
Thus seyde this olde knight that was so wys.
  And certeinly, as sooth as God is king,
To take a wyf, it is a glorious thing,
And namely whan a man is old and hoor:
Thanne is a wyf the fruit of his tresor;
Thanne sholde he take a yong wyf and a feir,
On which he mighte engendren him an heir,
And lede his lyf in joye and in solas,
Wheras thise bacheleres singe "Allas,"   30
Whan that they finden any adversitee
In love, which nis but childish vanitee.
And trewely it sit wel to be so,
That bacheleres have often peyne and wo:
On brotel ground they builde, and brotelnesse
They finde whan they wene sikernesse.
They live but as a brid or as a beste
In libertee and under non areste,
Ther as a wedded man in his estaat
Liveth a lyf blisful and ordinaat,   40
Under the yok of mariage y-bounde:
Wel may his herte in joye and blisse habounde.

Here begins the Merchant's Tale

THERE ONCE resided in Lombardy
a worthy knight whose birth was of Pavia,
where he lived in great prosperity.
He was a bachelor for sixty years,
and all that time followed fleshly pleasure
in women wherever his appetite led,
as do these fools who are not in clerical orders.
When he had passed his sixtieth year
(I cannot say whether it was for religious motive
or because he was in his dotage), this knight
felt such a strong desire to be a wedded man
that day and night he did everything he could
to discover whom he might be married to,
imploring our Lord to grant that he
might sometime come to know that blissful life
which is between a husband and his wife,
and that he might live under that holy bond
with which God first bound together man and woman.
"No other life," he said, "is worth a bean,
for wedlock is so comforting and so pure
that it is an earthly paradise."
Thus said this old knight who was so wise.

And indeed, as surely as God is our ruler,
it is a glorious thing to take a wife,
especially when a man is old and hoary:
then a wife is the best part of his treasure;
then he should take a young and beautiful wife
on whom he can engender an heir,
and lead his life in joy and in delights,
while bachelors sing another song
when they find any reverses
in the game of love, which is nothing but childish folly.
And in fact it is very suitable
that bachelors should often have pain and sorrow:
they build on unstable ground, and they shall
find instability when they expect security.
They live but as a bird or beast,
at liberty and with no control,
whereas a wedded man in his condition
lives a blissful and orderly life,
controlled in the yoke of marriage;
his heart may well be filled with joy and bliss.

For who can be so buxom as a wyf?
Who is so trewe, and eek so ententyf
To kepe him, syk and hool, as is his make?
For wele or wo, she wol him nat forsake.
She nis nat wery him to love and serve,
Thogh that he lye bedrede til he sterve.
And yet somme clerkes seyn it nis nat so,
Of whiche he Theofraste is oon of tho—   50
What force though Theofraste liste lye?
"Ne take no wyf," quod he, "for housbondrye,
As for to spare in houshold thy dispence;
A trewe servant dooth more diligence,
Thy good to kepe, than thyn owene wyf,
For she wol clayme half part al hir lyf.
And if that thou be syk, so God me save,
Thy verray frendes or a trewe knave
Wol kepe thee bet than she that waiteth ay
After thy good, and hath don many a day.   60
And if thou take a wyf unto thyn hold,
Ful lightly maystow been a cokewold."
This sentence and an hundred thinges worse
Wryteth this man, ther God his bones corse!
But take no kepe of al swich vanitee;
Deffye Theofraste and herke me.
   A wyf is Goddes yifte verraily;
Alle other maner yiftes hardily,
As londes, rentes, pasture, or commune,
Or moebles, alle ben yiftes of fortune,   70
That passen as a shadwe upon a wal.
But drede nat, if pleynly speke I shal,
A wyf wol laste and in thyn hous endure
Wel lenger than thee list, paraventure.
   Mariage is a ful gret sacrement.
He which that hath no wyf, I holde him shent:
He liveth helplees and al desolat
(I speke of folk in seculer estaat).
And herke why, I sey nat this for noght,
That womman is for mannes help y-wroght: 80
The hye God, whan he hadde Adam maked
And saugh him al allone, bely-naked,
God of his grete goodnesse seyde than,
"Lat us now make an help unto this man
Lyk to himself." And thanne he made him Eve.
Heer may ye se, and heerby may ye preve,

For who may be so obedient as a wife?
Who is so faithful and also so attentive
in watching over him, sick or healthy, as is his wife?
For better or for worse she will not forsake him.
She does not weary of loving and serving him,
even if he lies bedridden until he dies.
And yet some learned men say this is not so,
of whom Theophrastus* is one—
but what difference does it make if Theophrastus wants to
lie? "Do not take a wife for economy's sake," he said,
"so as to save expense in your household;
a faithful servant takes more trouble
to watch over your possessions than does your own wife,
for she will make a claim to half of it all her life.
And if you are sick, as God may save me,
your true friends or a faithful servant will
take better care of you than she will, who continually lies
in wait for your possessions, and has done so for many a day.
And if you take a wife into your keeping,
you may very easily become a cuckold."
This man wrote this maxim and a hundred
things worse, God curse his bones!
But pay no attention to all such foolishness;
scorn Theophrastus and listen to me.

A wife is truly a gift of God.
All other kinds of gifts, like arable lands,
revenues, pasture or pasturage rights, or
moveable goods are surely gifts of fortune,
which pass like shadows on a wall.
But, do not fear—if I am to speak plainly,
a wife will last and endure in your house
longer indeed than you perhaps wish.

Marriage is a very great sacrament.
I hold the man who has no wife to be ruined:
he lives unhelped and forsaken
(I am talking about laymen).
Listen to why—I am not saying this for nothing:
woman was created for a help to man:
God on high, having created Adam
and seeing him all alone and destitute,
then said in His great goodness,
"Let us now make a help unto this man
like himself." And then He made him Eve.
Here you may see, and hereby you may prove,

That wyf is mannes help and his confort,
His paradys terrestre and his disport.
So buxom and so vertuous is she,
They moste nedes live in unitee,   90
O flesh they been, and o flesh, as I gesse,
Hath but on herte in wele and in distresse.
    A wyf! a, Seinte Marie, *benedicite,*
How mighte a man han any adversitee
That hath a wyf? Certes, I can nat seye.
The blisse which that is bitwixe hem tweye
Ther may no tonge telle or herte thinke.
If he be povre, she helpeth him to swinke;
She kepeth his good and wasteth never a deel;
Al that hir housbonde lust hire lyketh weel;   100
She seith not ones "nay," when he seith "ye."
"Do this," seith he; "al redy, sire," seith she.
O blisful ordre of wedlok precious,
Thou art so merye, and eek so vertuous,
And so commended and appreved eek,
That every man that halt him worth a leek
Upon his bare knees oughte al his lyf
Thanken his God that him hath sent a wyf,
Or elles preye to God him for to sende
A wyf to laste unto his lyves ende,   110
For thanne his lyf is set in sikernesse.
He may nat be deceyved, as I gesse,
So that he werke after his wyves reed;
Thanne may he boldly beren up his heed,
They been so trewe and therwithal so wyse;
For which, if thou wolt werken as the wyse,
Do alwey so as wommen wol thee rede.
    Lo how that Jacob, as thise clerkes rede,
By good conseil of his moder Rebekke
Bond the kides skin aboute his nekke,   120
For which his fadres benisoun he wan.
    Lo Judith, as the storie eek telle can,
By wys conseil she Goddes peple kepte,
And slow him Olofernus whyl he slepte.
    Lo Abigayl, by good conseil how she
Saved hir housbond Nabal whan that he
Sholde han be slayn; and loke Ester also
By good conseil delivered out of wo
The peple of God, and made him Mardochee
Of Assuere enhaunced for to be.   130

that a wife is man's help and comfort,
his earthly paradise and his source of pleasure.
She is so obedient and virtuous
that by necessity they must live in unity.
They are one flesh, and, as I suppose, one flesh
has but one will, in happiness and in sorrow.

A wife! Ah, Saint Mary bless us,
How might a man have any adversity
if he has a wife? Certainly I cannot say.
No tongue may tell, or heart think,
the bliss that is between the two.
If he is poor, she helps him in his labor;
she watches over his possessions and does not waste a bit;
all that her husband desires seems desirable to her;
she does not once say "No" when he says "Yes."
"Do this," says he; "All ready, sir," says she.
O blissful order of precious wedlock,
you are so joyous, and also so virtuous,
and also so commended and approved
that every man who holds himself worth a leek
ought to thank, upon his bare knees
throughout his life, the God who has sent him a wife,
or else pray God to send him
a wife to last to the end of his life,
for then his life will be soundly based.
As I think, he may not be deceived,
if he acts according to his wife's advice;
then he may carry his head high,
wives are so faithful and at the same time so wise;
for which reason, if you would act as the wise do,
always do as women advise you.

Consider how Jacob, as learned men relate,
by the good advice of his mother Rebecca
tied the kid's skin around his neck,
whereby he won his father's blessing.

Consider Judith:* as history tells in this case, too,
she preserved God's people by wise counsel
and killed Holofernes while he slept.

Consider how Abigail* by good advice
saved her husband Nabal when he
was to be killed; and consider, too, how Esther*
by good advice delivered God's people from their suffering
and caused Mordecai
to be exalted by Ahasuerus.

Ther nis nothing in gree superlatyf,
As seith Senek, above an humble wyf.
    Suffre thy wyves tonge, as Caton bit:
She shal comande and thou shalt suffren it,
And yet she wol obeye of curteisye.
    A wyf is keper of thyn hounbondrye;
Wel may the syke man biwaille and wepe,
Ther as ther nis no wyf the hous to kepe.
I warne thee, if wisely thou wolt wirche,
Love wel they wyf as Crist loved his chirche;   140
If thou lovest thyself, thou lovest thy wyf:
No man hateth his flesh, but in his lyf
He fostreth it, and therfore bidde I thee
Cherisse thy wyf or thou shalt never thee.
Housbond and wyf, what so men jape or pleye,
Of worldly folk holden the siker weye.
They been so knit, ther may noon harm bityde,
And namely, upon the wyves syde.
    For which this Januarie, of whom I tolde,
Considered hath, inwith his dayes olde,   150
The lusty lyf, the vertuous quiete,
That is in mariage hony swete;
And for his freendes on a day he sente
To tellen hem th'effect of his entente.
    With face sad his tale he hath hem told;
He seyde, "Freendes, I am hoor and old,
And almost, God woot, on my pittes brinke;
Upon my soule somwhat moste I thinke.
I have my body folily despended;
Blessed be God, that it shal been amended!   160
For I wol be, certeyn, a wedded man,
And that anoon in al the haste I can,
Unto som mayde fair and tendre of age.
I prey yow, shapeth for my mariage
Al sodeynly, for I wol nat abyde;
And I wol fonde t'espyen, on my syde,
To whom I may be wedded hastily.
But for as muche as ye ben mo than I,
Ye shullen rather swich a thing espyen
Than I, and wher me best were to allyen.   170
    But o thing warne I yow, my freendes dere:
I wol non old wyf han in no manere;
She shal nat passe twenty yeer, certayn;
Old fish and yong flesh wolde I have ful fayn.

There is nothing of higher degree,
As Seneca says, than an humble wife.
Endure your wife's tongue, as Cato bids you:
she shall command, and you shall suffer it,
and yet she will obey you by courtesy.
A wife is the guardian of your domestic affairs;
well may the sick man wail and weep
where there is no wife to watch over the house.
I warn you: if you want to act wisely,
love your wife well, as Christ loved his church;
if you love yourself, you love your wife:
no man hates his own flesh, but during his life
he cares for it tenderly, and therefore I bid you
to cherish your wife, or you shall never prosper.
However people may joke, husband and wife
hold to the sure path for laymen.
They are so firmly knit together that no harm may arise,
particularly on the wife's side.
For these reasons, this January of whom I was telling you
considered in his latter days
the merry life and the virtuous peace
that is in honey-sweet marriage;
he sent for his friends one day
to tell them the outcome of his design.
He told them his tale with sober face;
he said, "Friends, I am white-haired and old,
and almost, God knows, at the brink of my grave;
I must give a little thought to my soul.
I have expended my body in folly;
blessed be God that this shall be corrected!
For I will be married,
and that as fast as I can,
to some fair maiden of tender age.
I entreat you, plan for my marriage
hastily, for I don't want to wait;
and I on my side will try to search out
whom I may be married to quickly.
But because there are more of you, you are likely
to discern more quickly than I such a possibility,
and where it would be best for me to ally myself.
But I warn you of one thing, dear friends:
I won't have any kind of old wife;
she shall not be over twenty, for certain;
I would very willingly have old fish but fresh meat.

Bet is, " quod he, "a pyk than a pikerel;
And bet than old boef is the tendre veel:
I wol no womman thritty yeer of age—
It is but bene-straw and greet forage.
And eek thise olde widwes, God it woot,
They conne so muchel craft on Wades boot,   180
So muchel broken harm whan that hem leste,
That with hem sholde I never live in reste.
For sondry scoles maketh sotile clerkis;
Womman of manye scoles half a clerk is.
But certeynly a yong thing may men gye,
Right as men may warm wex with handes plye.
Wherfore I sey yow pleynly, in a clause,
I wol non old wyf han right for this cause.
For if so were I hadde swich mischaunce
That I in hire ne coude han no plesaunce,   190
Thanne sholde I lede my lyf in avoutrye,
And go streight to the devel whan I dye;
Ne children sholde I none upon hire geten,
Yet were me levere houndes hadde me eten
Than that myn heritage sholde falle
In straunge hand; and this I tell yow alle:
I dote nat, I woot the cause why
Men sholde wedde, and forthermore woot I
Ther speketh many a man of mariage,
That woot namore of it than woot my page   200
For whiche causes man sholde take a wyf:
If he ne may nat liven chast his lyf,
Take him a wyf with greet devocioun,
By cause of leveful procreacioun
Of children, to th'onour of God above,
And nat only for paramour or love;
And for they sholde lecherye eschue,
And yelde hir dette whan that it is due;
Or for that ech of hem sholde helpen other
In meschief, as a suster shal the brother,   210
And live in chastitee ful holily—
But sires, by your leve, that am nat I,
For God be thanked, I dar make avaunt,
I fele my limes stark and suffisaunt
To do al that a man bilongeth to;
I woot myselven best what I may do.
Though I be hoor, I fare as dooth a tree
That blosmeth er that fruyt y-woxen be;

A pike* is better than a pickerel," he said,
"but tender veal is better than old beef.
I don't want any woman thirty years of age;
that's nothing but straw and coarse fodder.
And besides, God knows, these old widows
have so much skill in Wade's* boat—
can cause so much vexation when they want to—
that I should never live in peace with them.
Studying in different schools makes cunning scholars:
a woman who has been at many schools is half a scholar.
But one may certainly guide a young thing,
just as one may ply warm wax with the hands.
Therefore I say to you plainly and briefly
that for just this cause I won't take an old wife.
For if it were to happen that I had such a misfortune
as not to be able to take any pleasure in my wife,
then I should lead my life in adultery
and go straight to the devil when I die.
Nor should I engender any children upon her,
yet I would rather have had dogs eat me
than to have my inheritance fall
into the hands of strangers; and to all of you I say this:
I am not doting; I know why
we should marry, and furthermore I know
that many a man speaks of marriage
who knows no more than my page does
of the reasons for which man should take a wife:
if a man cannot live his life chastely,
let him take himself a wife with great devoutness
for the sake of lawful procreation
of children to the honor of God above,
and not simply for sexual pleasure or love;
and let him do this because, also, they should eschew lechery
and pay their debt to each other when it is due;
or let him take a wife because one should help the other
in tribulation, as a sister should help her brother,
and live in chastity with great holiness—
but by your leave, sirs, I am not in the latter class,
for, God be thanked, I dare to boast that
I feel my limbs to be strong and competent
to do all that belongs to a man;
I myself know best what I can do.
Although I am white-haired, I fare like a tree
that blossoms before the fruit has grown;

And blosmy tree nis neither drye ne deed:
I fele me nowher hoor but on myn heed; 220
Myn herte and alle my limes been as grene
As laurer thurgh the yeer is for to sene.
And sin that ye han herd al myn entente,
I prey yow to my wil ye wol assente."
    Diverse men diversely him tolde
Of mariage manye ensamples olde:
Somme blamed it, somme preysed it, certeyn;
But atte laste, shortly for to seyn,
As al day falleth altercacioun
Bitwixen freendes in disputisoun, 230
Ther fil a stryf bitwixe his bretheren two,
Of which that oon was cleped Placebo;
Justinus soothly called was that other.
    Placebo seyde, "O Januarie brother,
Ful litel nede hadde ye, my lord so dere,
Conseil to axe of any that is here;
But that ye been so ful of sapience
That yow ne lyketh, for your heighe prudence,
To weyven fro the word of Salomon;
This word seyde he unto us everichon: 240
'Wirk alle thing by conseil,' thus seyde he,
'And thanne shaltow nat repenten thee.'
But though that Salomon spak swich a word,
Myn owene dere brother and my lord,
So wisly God my soule bringe at reste,
I hold your owene conseil is the beste.
For brother myn, of me tak this motyf:
I have now been a court-man al my lyf,
And, God it woot, though I unworthy be,
I have stonden in ful greet degree 250
Abouten lordes of ful heigh estaat,
Yet hadde I never with noon of hem debaat;
I never hem contraried, trewely;
I woot wel that my lord can more than I;
What that he seith, I holde it ferme and stable;
I seye the same or elles thing semblable.
A ful gret fool is any conseillour,
That serveth any lord of heigh honour,
That dar presume, or elles thenken it
That his conseil sholde passe his lordes wit. 260
Nay, lordes been no foles, by my fay.
Ye han yourselven shewed heer today

a blossoming tree is neither dry nor dead:
I feel gray nowhere except on my head;
my heart and all my limbs seem as green
as laurel looks throughout the year.
Now, since you have heard my full purpose,
I pray that you will assent to my desire."

Diverse men advised him diversely with many
ancient stories to illustrate their points about marriage:
it is sure than some gave it blame, others gave it praise;
but at last (to speak briefly)
as altercation constantly occurs
between friends in dispute,
an argument arose between his two brothers,
of whom one was called Placebo
and the other was in truth named Justinus.

Placebo said, "O brother January,
you had little need, my lord so dear,
to ask advice of anyone who is here;
it was only that you are so full of wisdom
that in your exalted prudence it does not please you
to depart from the proverb of Solomon.
He pronounced this maxim for each of us:
'Do everything by advice,' thus he said,
'and then you shall not repent of your action.'
But although Solomon uttered such a proverb,
my dear brother and my lord,
as surely as I hope God may bring my soul to peace,
I hold that your own counsel is the best.
For, brother mine, take this policy from me:
I have now been a courtier all my life,
and God knows, although I am unworthy,
I have stood in a very superior rank
in attendance on lords of very high estate,
yet I never argued with them;
truly, I never contradicted them;
I know well that my lord knows more than I;
whatever he says, I hold it to be firm and established.
I say the same or else something like it.
Any counsellor is a great fool
who, serving a lord of great honor,
dares to presume, or else to think,
that his advice should be better than his lord's wisdom.
No, lords are no fools, by my faith.
You yourself have manifested here today

So heigh sentence, so holily and weel,
That I consente and conferme everydeel
Youre wordes alle and youre opinioun.
By God, ther nis no man in al this toun,
Ne in Itaille, that coude bet han sayd:
Crist halt him of this conseil wel apayd.
And trewely it is an heigh corage
Of any man that stapen is in age   270
To take a yong wyfl by my fader kin,
Your herte hangeth on a joly pin!
Dooth now in this matere right as yow leste,
For finally I holde it for the beste."

    Justinus, that ay stille sat and herde,
Right in this wyse he to Placebo answerde:
"Now, brother myn, be pacient, I preye,
Sin ye han seyd, and herkneth what I seye.

    Senek amonges othere wordes wyse
Seith that a man oghte him right wel avyse   280
To whom he yeveth his lond or his catel;
And sin I oghte avyse me right wel
To whom I yeve my good awey fro me,
Wel muchel more I oghte avysed be
To whom I yeve my body for alwey.
I warne yow wel, it is no childes pley
To take a wyf withouten avysement.
Men moste enquere—this is myn assent—
Wher she be wys, or sobre, or drokelewe,
Or proud, or elles otherweys a shrewe;   290
A chidestere, or wastour of thy good,
Or riche, or poore, or elles mannish wood—
Al be it so that no man finden shal
Noon in this world that trotteth hool in al,
Ne man ne beest swich as men coude devyse;
But nathelees, it oghte y-nough suffise
With any wyf, if so were that she hadde
Mo gode thewes than hir vyces badde;
And al this axeth leyser for t'enquere.
For God it woot, I have wept many a tere   300
Ful prively sin I have had a wyf:
Preyse whoso wole a wedded mannes lyf,
Certein I finde in it but cost and care,
And observances, of alle blisses bare.
And yet, God woot, my neighebores aboute,
And namely of wommen many a route,

such noble sentiments in so holy and good a fashion
that I agree with and confirm in every part
all your words and your opinion.
By God, there isn't a man in all this town,
or in all Italy, who could have said better:
Christ holds himself well pleased with this plan,
and, truly, it shows a fine spirit
in any man who is advanced in age
to take a young wife! By my father's race,
your heart is taking a merry way!
Do now just as you wish in this matter,
for, finally, I consider that best."

Justinus, who all this time had sat still and listened,
answered Placebo in just this way:
"Now, my brother, I pray you to be patient,
since you have had your say, and listen to what I shall say.
Among his other wise proverbs, Seneca
says that a man ought to consider right well
to whom he is giving his land or his riches;
and since I ought to consider right well
to whom I am giving away my goods,
all the more ought I consider
to whom I am giving my body forever.
I give you firm warning, it is no child's play
to take a wife without deliberation.
One must inquire, in my opinion,
whether she is discreet, or sober, or inclined to drink,
or proud, or shrewish in other ways;
whether she is a chider or a waster of your goods,
or rich, or poor, or inclined to unwomanly rages—
although it is true that no man shall find
any in the world that runs soundly in every respect,
neither man nor beast such as could be imagined;
but nevertheless, it ought to be enough
in the case of any wife, if she has
more good qualities than evil vices;
and all this demands leisure for inquiry.
For, God knows, I have wept many a tear
in secret since I have had a wife:
let who so will praise a married man's life,
I certainly find in it only cost and misery,
and duties, devoid of every bliss.
And yet, God knows, my neighbors roundabout,
and especially many a host of women,

Seyn that I have the moste stedefast wyf,
And eek the mekeste oon that bereth lyf—
But I wot best wher wringeth me my sho.
Ye mowe, for me, right as yow lyketh do;   310
Avyseth yow—ye been a man of age—
How that ye entren into mariage,
And namely with a yong wyf and a fair.
By him that made water, erthe, and air,
The yongeste man that is in al this route
Is bisy ynogh to bringen it aboute
To han his wyf allone. Trusteth me,
Ye shul nat plesen hire fully yeres three—
This is to seyn, to doon hir ful plesaunce:
A wfy axeth ful many an observaunce.   320
I prey yow that ye be nat yvel apayd."
    "Wel," quod this Januarie, "and hastow sayd?
Straw for thy Senek and for thy proverbes!
I counte nat a panier ful of herbes
Of scole-termes; wyser men than thow,
As thou hast herd, assenteden right now
To my purpose; Placebo, what sey ye?"
    "I seye it is a cursed man," quod he,
"That letteth matrimoigne, sikerly."
And with that word they rysen sodeynly,   330
And been assented fully that he sholde
Be wedded whanne him list and wher he wolde.

    Heigh fantasye and curious bisinesse
Fro day to day gan in the soule impresse
Of Januarie aboute his mariage.
Many fair shap and many a fair visage
Ther passeth thurgh his herte night by night.
As whoso toke a mirour polished bright,
And sette it in a commune market-place,
Thanne sholde he see ful many a figure pace   340
By this mirour; and in the same wyse
Gan Januarie inwith his thoght devyse
Of maydens whiche that dwelten him bisyde.
He wiste nat wher that he mighte abyde:
For if that oon have beautee in hir face,
Another stant so in the peples grace
For hir sadnesse and hir benignitee,
That of the peple grettest voys hath she;
And some were riche and hadden badde name.
But nathelees, bitwixe ernest and game,   350

say that I have the most steadfast wife,
and also the meekest one, alive.
But I know best where my shoe pinches me.
You may do what you want for my part;
but you are a man of age—consider
that you are entering into marriage,
and, particularly, with a young, pretty wife.
By Him Who made the water, earth and air,
the youngest man in this group
has enough trouble
to keep his wife to himself. Believe me,
you shall not please her for as much as three years—
that is to say, please her fully:
a wife requires much to be performed.
Please don't be annoyed."

"Well," said this January, "and have you finished?
A straw for your Seneca and for your proverbs!
I don't give a basket of greens
for pedantries; wiser men than you,
as you heard, just now assented
to my intention; Placebo, what do you say?"

"I say," he said, "that it's an abominable man
who hinders matrimony, surely."
And at that word they abruptly ended their sitting,
and were in full agreement that January should
be married when he liked and to whomever he wanted.

Lofty fancies and minute solicitude
from day to day made their imprint upon the soul
of January concerning his marriage.
Many fair shapes and many a pretty face
passed through his heart night by night.
As, if anyone took a brightly polished mirror
and set it in a public market place,
he would then see many figures passing
by his mirror, so in the same fashion
January in his thoughts commenced to muse
about girls who lived near him.
He didn't know where he might rest:
for if one of them had a beautiful face,
another was so established in popular favor
for her sobriety and benevolence
that she had the majority's voice;
and some were rich, and had an evil name.
But nevertheless, partly for sober reasons, partly for lighter

He atte laste apoynted him on oon,
And leet alle othere from his herte goon,
And chees hir of his owene auctoritee—
For Love is blind al day and may nat see.
And whan that he was in his bed y-broght,
He purtreyed in his herte and in his thoght
Hir fresshe beautee and hir age tendre,
Hir myddel smal, hir armes longe and sclendre,
Hir wyse governaunce, hir gentillesse,
Hir wommanly beringe and hir sadnesse.   360
And whan that he on hire was condescended,
Him thoughte his chois mighte nat ben amended.
For whan that he himself concluded hadde,
Him thoughte ech other mannes wit so badde,
That inpossible it were to replye
Agayn his chois: this was his fantasye.
His freendes sente he to at his instaunce,
And preyed hem to doon him that plesaunce
That hastily they wolden to him come:
He wolde abregge hir labour alle and some;   370
Nedeth namore for him to go ne ryde;
He was apoynted ther he wolde abyde.

  Placebo cam, and eek his freendes sone,
And alderfirst he bad hem alle a bone,
That noon of hem none argumentes make
Agayn the purpos which that he hath take;
Which purpos was plesant to God, seyde he,
And verray ground of his prosperitee.

  He seyde ther was a mayden in the toun,
Which that of beautee hadde greet renoun;   380
Al were it so she were of smal degree,
Suffyseth him hir youthe and hir beautee;
Which mayde he seyde he wolde han to his wyf,
To lede in ese and holinesse his lyf.
And thanked God that he mighte han hire al,
That no wight his blisse parten shal;
And preyde hem to labouren in this nede,
And shapen that he faille nat to spede;
For thanne, he seyde, his spirit was at ese.
"Thanne is," quod he, "no thing may me displese,   390
Save o thing priketh in my conscience,
The which I wol reherce in youre presence.
  I have," quod he, "herd seyd ful yore ago
Ther may no man han parfite blisses two—

ones, he at last settled on one
and let all the others pass from his heart,
and chose her on his own authority—
for Love is ever blind and cannot see.
When he was conveyed to bed,
he pictured in his heart and mind
her fresh beauty and tender age,
her slim waist, her long, slender arms,
her discreet behavior, her genteel courtesy,
her womanly bearing, and her steadfastness.
And when he had determined on her,
he thought that his choice might not be improved on
For when he himself had come to a decision,
he thought that every other man's wit was so lacking
that it would be impossible to object
to his choice: this was his delusion.
He sent urgently to his friends
and asked them to do him the pleasure
of coming to him hastily:
he would shorten all their labors;
he no longer needed to walk or to ride;
he had determined where he would rest.

   Soon Placabo came, and his other friends as well,
and first of all January made a request of all of them
that no one would make any arguments
against the design which he had adopted;
which design he said was pleasing to God
and the very basis of his own welfare.

   He said that there was a girl in the town
who had a great reputation for beauty;
althugh she was of low estate,
her youth and beauty were enough for him;
which girl, he said, he wanted to have for wife
so as to lead his life in comfort and holiness.
And he thanked God that he might have her completely
so that no man might share in his bliss;
and he asked them to do their offices in this matter
and arrange things so that he should not fail to gain his
end; for then, he said, his spirit would be at rest.
"Then," he said, "nothing can displease me,
except for one thing that pricks my conscience,
which I shall relate in your presence.

   I have heard it said long ago," he remarked,
"that no man may have two kinds of perfect bliss—

This is to seye, in erthe and eek in hevene.
For though he kepe him fro the sinnes sevene,
And eek from every branche of thilke tree,
Yet is ther so parfit felicitee
And so greet ese and lust in mariage,
That ever I am agast now in myn age   400
That I shal lede now so mery a lyf,
So delicat, withouten wo and stryf,
That I shal have myn hevene in erthe here.
For sith that verray hevene is boght so dere
With tribulacioun and greet penaunce,
How sholde I thanne, that live in swich plesaunce
As alle wedded men doon with hir wyvis,
Come to the blisse ther Crist eterne on lyve is?
This is my drede, and ye, my bretheren tweye,
Assoileth me this questioun, I preye."   410
     Justinus, which that hated his folye,
Answerde anonright in his japerye;
And for he wolde his longe tale abregge,
He wolde noon auctoritee allegge,
But seyde, "Sire, so ther be noon obstacle
Other than this, God of his heigh miracle
And of his mercy may so for yow wirche,
That, er ye have youre right of holy chirche,
Ye may repente of wedded mannes lyf,
In which ye seyn ther is no wo ne stryf.   420
And elles, God forbede but he sente
A wedded man him grace to repente
Wel ofte rather than a sengle man.
And therfore, sire, the beste reed I can:
Dispeire yow noght, but have in your memorie,
Paraunter she may be your purgatorie:
She may be Goddes mene and Goddes whippe!
Thanne shal youre soule up to hevene skippe
Swifter than dooth an arwe out of the bowe.
I hope to God, herafter shul ye knowe   430
That their nis no so greet felicitee
In mariage, ne nevere mo shal be,
That you shal lette of your savacioun,
So that ye use, as skile is and resoun,
The lustes of youre wyf attemprely,
And that ye plese hir nat too amorously,
And that ye kepe yow eek from other sinne.
My tale is doon, for my wit is thinne.

that is to say, on earth and in heaven as well.
For even if he keep himself from the seven* deadly sins,
and every subbranch of that tree,
yet there is such perfect felicity
and such great comfort and joy in marriage
that here in my old age I am continually afraid
that I shall now have so merry a life,
one of such delight, without sorrow and conflict,
that I shall have my heaven here upon earth.
For since true heaven is purchased so dearly,
with tribulation and heavy penance,
how then should I, who live in such pleasure
as all married men have with their wives,
come to that bliss where Christ lives eternally?
This is my fear, and you, my two brothers,
please resolve this question for me."

    Justinus, who despised his folly,
answered immediately in his derisive way;
and because he wanted to cut short his long tale,
he would not cite authorities
but said, "Sir, if there is no obstacle
other than this, God with his miraculous power
and mercy may so arrange for you
that, before having your final due of holy church,
you may repent of the life of a married man,
in which you say there is no sorrow or conflict.
Put it another way: God forbid but that he should send
the grace of frequent repentance sooner to a married man
than he should to a single man.
And therefore, sir, the best advice I can give is
not to despair, but to keep in mind
that perhaps a wife may be your purgatory:
she may be God's means and God's scourge!
Then your soul shall skip up to heaven
more swiftly than an arrow from the bow.
I expect, by God, that hereafter you will learn
there is no such great felicity
in marriage, nor evermore shall be,
as would keep you from your salvation,
if, as is reasonable, you enjoy
the pleasures of your wife moderately,
and if you do not delight her too amorously,
and if you keep yourself from other sin.
My tale is told, for my wit is slight.

Beth nat agast herof, my brother dere,
But lat us waden out of this matere.   440
The Wyf of Bathe, if ye han understonde,
Of mariage which ye have on honde
Declared hath ful wel in litel space.
Fareth now wel; God have yow in his grace."

And with this word this Justin and his brother
Han take hir leve, and ech of hem of other.
For whan they saw that it moste nedes be,
They wroghten so, by sly and wys tretee,
That she this mayden, which that Maius highte,
As hastily as evere that she mighte,   450
Shal wedded be unto this Januarie.
I trowe it were too longe you to tarie
If I you tolde of every scrit and bond
By which that she was feffed in his lond,
Or for to herknen of hir riche array;
But finally y-comen is the day
That to the chirche bothe be they went
For to receyve the holy sacrement.

Forthcomth the preest with stole aboute his nekke,
And bad hire be lyk Sarra and Rebekke   460
In wisdom and in trouthe of mariage,
And seyde his orisons as is usage,
And croucheth hem, and bad God sholde hem blesse,
And made al siker ynogh with holinesse.

Thus been they wedded with solempnitee.
And at the feste sitteth he and she
With other worthy folk upon the deys.
Al ful of joye and blisse is the paleys,
And ful of instruments and of vitaille,
The moste deyntevous of al Itaille.   470
Biforn hem stoode instruments of swich soun,
That Orpheus, ne of Thebes Amphioun
Ne maden nevere swich a melodye.

At every cours thanne cam loud minstralcye,
That nevere tromped Joab, for to here,
Nor he Theodomas, yet half so clere
At Thebes whan the citee was in doute.
Bacus the wyn hem shinketh al aboute,
And Venus laugheth upon every wight,
For Januarie was bicome hir knight,   480
And wolde bothe assayen his corage
In libertee and eek in mariage;

Don't be afraid of this, dear brother,
but let us leave this subject.
The Wife of Bath, if you have understood,
has pronounced very well and briefly on this matter
of marriage which we have in hand.
Now farewell, God have you in his grace."
    And at this word Justinus and his brother
took their leave of him and of each other.
When they saw it had to be,
they so arranged, by clever and prudent negotiations,
that this girl, who was named Maius,
should, as hastily as ever she could,
be married to January.
I believe it would delay you too long
if I told you of every writ and bond
by which she was endowed with his land,
or if you were to hear of her rich array,
but finally the day came
when they both went to church
to receive the holy sacrament.
The priest came forth with his stole about his neck
and enjoined her to be like Sarah and Rebecca
in prudence and faithfulness in marriage,
and said his prayers according to custom, and signed
them with the cross, and bade that God should bless them,
and made everything secure enough with holiness.
    Thus they were married with ceremony,
and at the feast he and she sat
with other worthy folk on the dais.
The palace was brimming with joy and bliss
and filled with provisions and food,
the most delicious in all Italy.
Before them were instruments of such sweetness
that neither Orpheus* nor Amphion of Thebes
ever made such melody.
    At every course there came such loud music
that, to listen to it, neither Joab*
nor Thiodamas* at Thebes, when the fate of the city
was in doubt, trumpeted even half so splendidly.
Bacchus poured the wine out all around,
and Venus smiles on every man,
for January had become her knight
and willed to try his mettle
not only in liberty but also in marriage;

And with hir fyrbrond in hir hand aboute
Daunceth biforn the bryde and al the route.
And certeinly, I dar right wel seyn this,
Ymenëus, that god of wedding is,
Saugh never his lyf so mery a wedded man.
Hold thou thy pees, thou poete Marcian,
That wrytest us that ilke wedding murie
Of hire Philologye and him Mercurie,   490
And of the songes that the Muses songe—
Too smal is bothe thy penne and eek thy tonge
For to descryven of this mariage.
Whan tendre youthe hath wedded stouping age,
Ther is swich mirthe that it may nat be writen;
Assayeth it yourself, than may ye witen
If that I lye or noon in this matere.

   Maius, that sit with so benigne a chere,
Hire to biholde it semed fayëryë—
Quene Ester loked never with swich an yë   500
On Assuer, so meke a look hath she—
I may yow nat devyse al hir beautee,
But thus muche of hir beautee telle I may,
That she was lyk the brighte morwe of May,
Fulfild of alle beautee and plesaunce.

   This Januarie is ravisshed in a traunce
At every time he loked on hir face;
But in his herte he gan hir to manace
That he that night in armes wolde hir streyne
Harder than ever Paris dide Eleyne.   510
But nathelees yet hadde he greet pitee
That thilke night offenden hire moste he,
And thoughte, "Allas, O tendre creature,
Now wolde God ye mighte wel endure
Al my corage, it is so sharp and kene;
I am agast ye shul it nat sustene—
But God forbede that I dide al my might!
Now wolde God that it were woxen night,
And that the night wolde lasten everemo.
I wolde that al this peple were ago."   520
And finally he doth al his labour,
As he best mighte, savinge his honour,
To haste hem fro the mete in subtil wyse.

   The tyme cam that reson was to ryse,
And after that men daunce and drinken faste,
And spyces al aboute the hous they caste,

and with her firebrand in her hand
she danced about before the bride and all the company.
And certainly I may hazard to say this,
that Hymen, who is god of weddings,
never in his life saw so merry a wedded man.
Hold your peace, you poet Martianus,*
who created for us that merry wedding
of Philology and Mercury,
and wrote about the songs the Muses sang—
too limited are both your pen and tongue
to describe this marriage.
When tender youth has wedded stooping age,
there is such merriment that it may not be written;
try it yourself, then you may know
whether or not I am lying about this matter.

   It seemed like magic to look on
Maius, she sat with so gracious a countenance—
so meek a look she had that Queen Esther never
gazed with such an eye on Ahasuerus.
I cannot describe all her beauty to you,
but I may tell this much—
that she was like a bright May morning,
filled with all beauty and delight.

   January was ravished away into a trance
every time he looked upon her face;
but in his heart he commenced to threaten
that he would constrain her that night in his arms
more violently than Paris ever did Helen.
Nevertheless, he felt great pity that
he would have to assail her that night,
and thought, "Alas, tender creature,
now would to God that you might easily endure
all my vigor, it is so sharp and keen;
I am fearful that you will not sustain it—
but God forbid that I should do all I can!
Now would God that it had grown to night,
and that the night would last forever.
I wish that all these people were gone."
Finally, as best he could, he did what he
might, saving his honor as a host,
to hasten them unostentatiously from the food.

   The time came when it was proper to rise,
and after that they danced and drank deep,
and cast spices all about the house,

And ful of joye and blisse is every man—
All but a squyer, highte Damian,
Which carf biforn the knight ful many a day:
He was so ravisshed on his lady May   530
That for the verray peyne he was ny wood;
Almost he swelte and swowned ther he stood,
So sore hath Venus hurt him with hir brond,
As that she bar it daunsinge in hir hond.
And to his bed he wente him hastily.
Namore of him as at this tyme speke I,
But ther I lete him wepe ynough and pleyne,
Til fresshe May wol rewen on his peyne.
    O perilous fyr that in the bedstraw bredeth!
O famulier foo, that his servyce bedeth!   540
O servant traitour, false hoomly hewe,
Lyk to the naddre in bosom, sly, untrewe!
God shilde us alle from your aqueyntaunce!
O Januarie, dronken in plesaunce
In mariage, see how thy Damian,
Thyn owene squyer and thy borne man,
Entendeth for to do thee vileinye!
God graunte thee thyn hoomly fo t'espye,
For in this world nis worse pestilence
Than hoomly foo al day in thy presence.   550
    Parfourned hath the sonne his ark diurne;
No lenger may the body of him sojurne
On th'orisonte as in that latitude.
Night with his mantel that is derk and rude
Gan oversprede the hemisperie aboute,
For which departed is this lusty route
Fro Januarie, with thank on every syde.
Hom to hir houses lustily they ryde,
Whereas they doon hir thinges as hem leste,
And whan they sye hir tyme, goon to reste.   560
Sone after that, this hastif Januarie
Wolde go to bedde—he wolde no lenger tarie.
He drinketh ipocras, clarree, and vernage
Of spyces hote, t'encresen his corage;
And many a letuarie hadde he ful fyn,
Swiche as the cursed monk dan Constantyn
Hath writen in his book *De Coitu:*
To eten hem alle he nas no-thing eschu.
And to his privee freendes thus seyde he,
"For Goddes love, as sone as it may be,   570

and every man was full of joy and contentment—
all but a squire named Damian,
who had carved before the knight for many a day:
he was so ravished with his lady May
that for the very pain he was nearly mad;
he almost languished and fainted where he stood,
so painfully had Venus wounded him with her brand
as she bore it in her hand while she danced.
Hastily he took to his bed.
I speak no more of him at this time,
but leave him there weeping and grieving his fill
until fresh May will take pity on his suffering.

O perilous fire that grows within the bedding!
O family foe, who proffers his service!
O traitorous servant, false household menial,
sly and treacherous like an adder in the bosom!
God defend us all from knowing you!
O January, drunk with the pleasures
of marriage, see how Damian,
your own squire, born your man,
aims to do you a foul deed!
God grant you the boon of discerning your domestic foe,
for there is no worse plague in this world
than a household foe continually in your presence.

The sun had run his daily arc;
no longer might his sphere linger
on the horizon in that latitude.
Night with his harsh, dark mantle
began to overspread the whole hemisphere of the sky,
so that this merry crowd left
January, with thanks on every side.
They rode home merrily to their houses
where they minded their business as they wished,
and when they saw their time, went to bed.
Soon afterward this urgent January
wanted to go to bed—he would wait no longer.
He drank cordials and wine
containing hot spices to increase his ardor;
and he had many a concentrated medicine,
such as the accursed monk master Constantinus*
has written of in his book *De coitu;*
he did not scruple in the least to eat them all.
He spoke thus to his intimate friends,
"For the love of God, as soon as possible

Lat voyden al this hous in curteys wyse."
And they han doon right as he wol devyse.
Men drinken and the travers drawe anon;
The bryde was broght abedde as stille as stoon.
And whan the bed was with the preest y-blessed,
Out of the chambre hath every wight him dressed.
And Januarie hath faste in armes take
His fresshe May, his paradys, his make;
He lulleth hire, he kisseth hir ful ofte
With thikke bristles of his berd unsofte,   580
Lyk to the skin of houndfish, sharp as brere
For he was shave al newe in his manere,
He rubbeth hir aboute hir tendre face,
And seyde thus, "Allas, I moot trespace
To you, my spouse, and you gretly offende
Er tyme come that I wil doun descende.
But nathelees, considereth this," quod he,
"Ther nis no werkman, whatsoevere he be,
That may bothe werke wel and hastily;
This wol be doon at leyser parfitly.   590
It is no fors how longe that we pleye:
In trewe wedlok coupled be we tweye,
And blessed be the yok that we been inne,
For in our actes we mowe do no sinne;
A man may do no sinne with his wyf,
Ne hurte himselven with his owene knyf;
For we han leve to pleye us by the lawe."
Thus laboureth he till that the day gan dawe,
And than he taketh a sop in fyn clarree,
And upright in his bed thanne sitteth he;   600
And after that he sang ful loude and clere,
And kiste his wyf and made wantoun chere:
He was al coltish, ful of ragerye,
And ful of jargon as a flekked pye.
The slakke skin aboute his nekke shaketh,
Whyl that he sang, so chaunteth he and craketh.
But God woot what that May thoughte in hir herte
Whan she him saugh up sittinge in his sherte,
In his night-cappe, and with his nekke lene—
She preyseth nat his pleying worth a bene.   610
Thanne seide he thus, "my reste wol I take;
Now day is come I may no lenger wake."
And doun he leyde his heed, and sleep til pryme.
And afterward whan that he saugh his tyme

clear this house in a courteous way."
And they did just as he wanted to contrive.
They drank a toast and then drew the curtains;
the bride was brought to bed as still as stone.
And when the bed had been blessed by the priest,
everyone went out of the room.
January took close in his arms
his fresh May, his paradise, his mate;
he soothed her, he kissed her again and again;
he rubbed about her tender face
with the thick bristles of his harsh beard,
like a dogfish's skin, sharp as briar
(for he was newly shaven according to his custom);
he said, "Alas, I must do you injury,
my spouse, and great offense
before the time comes when I shall come down.
Nevertheless, consider this," he said,
"there is no workman, whatever kind he is,
who may work both well and in haste;
this shall be done at leisure perfectly.
It makes no difference how long we are at play:
we two are coupled in faithful wedlock,
and blessed be our yoke,
for in our acts we may do no sin;
a man can do no sin with his wife,
any more than he will hurt himself with his own knife;
for we have leave by law to take our pleasure."
Thus he labored until day dawned,
and then he ate a sop of bread in fine wine,
and then he sat up in bed;
and after that he sang loud and clear,
and kissed his wife, and behaved wantonly:
he was very frisky, brimful of dalliance,
and full of chatter as a magpie.
The slack skin around his neck shook
as he sang, he trilled and croaked so much,
But God knows what May thought in her heart
when she saw him sitting up in his nightshirt
and nightcap, with his lean neck—
she didn't think his diversions worth a bean.
Then he said, "I'll take my rest;
now day is come, I can't stay awake any longer."
And he laid his head down and slept until nine in the
morning. Afterward, when the time seemed right to him,

Up ryseth Januarie. But fresshe May
Heeld hir chambre unto the fourthe day,
As usage is of wyves for the beste,
For every labour somtyme moot han reste,
Or elles longe may he nat endure—
This is to seyn, no lyves creature,   620
Be it of fish, or brid, or beest, or man.

Now wol I speke of woful Damian
That languissheth for love, as ye shul here;
Therefore I speke to him in this manere:
I seye, "O sely Damian, allas,
Answere to my demaunde as in this cas:
How shaltow to thy lady fresshe May
Telle thy wo? She wole alwey seye nay;
Eek if thou speke, she wol thy wo biwreye.
God be thyn help, I can no bettre seye."   630

This syke Damian in Venus fyr
So brenneth that he dyeth for desyr,
For which he putte his lyf in aventure.
No lenger mighte he in this wyse endure,
But prively a penner gan he borwe,
And in a lettre wroot he al his sorwe,
In manere of a compleynt or a lay,
Unto his faire fresshe lady May;
And in a purs of silk, heng on his sherte,
He hath it put and leyde it at his herte.   640

The mone that, at noon, was, thilke day
That Januarie hath wedded fresshe May,
In two of Taur, was into Cancre gliden:
So longe hath Maius in hir chambre biden,
As custume is unto thise nobles alle:
A bryde shal nat eten in the halle
Til dayes foure or three dayes atte leste
Y-passed been; than lat hir go to feste.
The fourthe day compleet fro noon to noon,
Whan that the heighe masse was y-doon,   650
In halle sit this Januarie, and May
As fresh as is the brighte someres day.
And so bifel how that this gode man
Remembred him upon this Damian,
And seyde, "Seinte Marie! how may this be
That Damian entendeth nat to me?
Is he ay syk, or how may this bityde?"
His squyeres whiche that stoden ther bisyde

he got up. But fresh May
kept her chamber until the fourth day,
as the custom is of wives, all for the best,
for every laborer must have rest some time,
or otherwise he cannot last long—
that is to say, any creature alive,
whether it is fish or bird or beast or man.

Now I will speak of woeful Damian,
who languishes for love as you shall hear;
therefore I speak to him thus:
I say, "O poor Damian, alas,
answer my question about this matter:
how shall you tell your sorrow to your lady,
fresh May? She will always deny you;
also, if you speak, she will disclose your sorrow.
God be your help; I have no better answer."

Sick Damian so burned in Venus'
fire that he died for desire,
for which cause he risked his life.
He could not last any longer in this fashion,
but secretly he borrowed a pencase
and wrote all his sorrow in a letter,
in the manner of a complaint or poem,
to his fair, fresh lady May;
and he put it in a purse of silk
that hung on his shirt, and laid it over his heart.

The moon, which at noon on the day
that January married fresh May was
two degrees inside the sign of the Bull, had glided into the
Crab: Maius had stayed thus long in her chamber,
as the custom is among noble people:
a bride must not eat in the hall
until four, or at least three, days
have passed; then let her go to the feast.
The fourth full day, running from noon to noon,
when High Mass was finished,
January and May sat in the hall;
she was as fresh as a bright summer day.
And it so happened that this good man
bethought him of Damian,
and said, "Saint Mary! How may it be
that Damian does not attend on me?
Is he sick all this time, or how may it happen?"
His squires, who stood nearby,

Excused him by cause of his siknesse,
Which letted him to doon his bisinesse: 660
Noon other cause mighte make him tarie.
    "That me forthinketh," quod this Januarie.
"He is a gentil squyer, by my trouthe.
If that he deyde, it were harm and routhe.
He is as wys, discreet, and as secree
As any man I woot of his degree,
And thereto manly and eek servisable,
And for to been a thrifty man right able.
But after mete as sone as ever I may,
I wol myself visyte him, and eek May,   670
To doon him al the confort that I can."
And for that word him blessed every man,
That of his bountee and his gentillesse
He wolde so conforten in siknesse
His squyer—for it was a gentil dede.
"Dame," quod this Januarie, "tak good hede,
At after mete ye with your wommen alle,
Whan ye han been in chambre out of this halle,
That alle ye go see this Damian;
Doth him disport—he is a gentil man—   680
And telleth him that I wol him visyte,
Have I no thing but rested me a lyte;
And spede yow faste, for I wol abyde
Til that ye slepe faste by my syde."
And with that word he gan to him to calle
A squyer that was marchal of his halle,
And tolde him certeyn thinges what he wolde.
    This fresshe May hath streight hir wey y-holde
With alle hir wommen unto Damian.
Doun by his beddes syde sit she than,   690
Confortinge him as goodly as she may.
This Damian, whan that his tyme he say,
In secree wise his purs, and eek his bille,
In which that he y-writen hadde his wille,
Hath put into hir hand withouten more,
Save that he syketh wonder depe and sore,
And softely to hir right thus seyde he,
"Mercy, and that ye nat discovere me,
For I am deed if that this thing be kid."
This purs hath she inwith hir bosom hid,   700
And wente hir wey—ye gete namore of me.
But unto Januarie y-comen is she,

excused him on the grounds of illness,
which kept him from performing his duties:
no other reason might keep him back.
   "I regret that," said January.
"He is a gentle squire, by my faith!
If he died, it would be a loss and a pity.
He is as prudent, discreet, and trusty
as any man I know of his rank,
and in addition manly and ready to give service,
and quite capable of being a successful man.
But after dinner, just as soon as I may,
I will visit him myself, and May will, too,
to give him all the comfort that I can."
And at this speech every man blessed him
for being thus willing in his goodness and courtesy
to give to his squire comfort
in sickness; it was a courteous deed.
"Madame," said January, "be sure that
after dinner when you have left this hall
and been in your chamber, you and all
your women go see Damian;
cheer him up; he is a well-bred man—
and tell him that I will visit him
when I have rested just a little;
and go quickly, for I will be waiting
until you come to bed close by my side."
And thereupon he called to him
a squire who was the major-domo in his hall
and told him what he wanted done about certain matters.
   Fresh May took her way with all
her women straight to Damian.
She then sat down by his bedside,
comforting him as kindly as she could.
When Damian saw his opportunity,
he secretly put into her hand his purse,
and also his note, in which he had written
his desire. He did this without explanation,
except that he sighed most deeply and bitterly,
and whispered to her just thus,
"Your mercy! Do not reveal me,
for I am dead if this thing is made known."
She hid the purse in her bosom
and went her way—you get no more from me.
She came to January,

That on his beddes syde sit ful softe.
He taketh hir and kisseth hire ful ofte,
And leyde him doun to slepe, and that anon.
She feyned hire as that she moste gon
Ther as ye woot that every wight moot nede;
And whan she of this bille hath taken hede,
She rente it al to cloutes atte laste
And in the privee softely it caste.   710

   Who studieth now but faire fresshe May?
Adoun by olde Januarie she lay,
That sleep til that the coughe hath him awaked.
Anon he preyde hire strepen hire al naked;
He wolde of hir, he seyde, han som plesaunce,
And seyde hir clothes dide him encombraunce,
And she obeyeth, be hire lief or looth.
But lest that precious folk be with me wrooth,
How that he wroghte I dar not to yow telle,
Or whether hir thoughte it paradys or helle;   720
But here I lete hem werken in hir wyse
Til evensong rong, and that they moste aryse.

   Were it by destinee or aventure,
Were it by influence or by nature,
Or constellacion, that in swich estat
The hevene stood that tyme fortunat
As for to putte a bille of Venus werkes
(For alle thing hath tyme, as seyn thise clerkes)
To any womman, for to gete hir love,
I can nat seye; but grete God above,   730
That knoweth that non act is causelees,
He deme of al, for I wol holde my pees.
But sooth is this, how that this fresshe May
Hath take swich impression that day,
For pitee of this syke Damian,
That from hir herte she ne dryve can
The remembrance for to doon him ese.
"Certeyn," thoghte she, "whom that this thing displese
I rekke noght. For here I him assure
To love him best of any creature,   740
Though he namore hadde than his sherte."
Lo, pitee renneth sone in gentil herte!

   Heer may ye se how excellent franchyse
In wommen is whan they hem narwe avyse.
Som tyrant is, as ther be many oon,
That hath an herte as hard as any stoon,

who was sitting very comfortably on the side of his bed.
He embraced her and kissed her again and again,
and at once lay down to sleep.
She pretended that she had to go
where you know everyone must;
and when she had perused the note,
she finally tore it to shreds
and threw it quietly in the privy.

   Who ponders now but fresh and pretty May?
She lay down by old January,
who slept until his cough awakened him.
Then he asked her to strip naked;
he would, he said, have some pleasure from her,
and, he said, her clothes hampered him.
She obeyed, whether it was agreeable to her or loathsome.
But lest fastidious people would be angry with me,
I dare not tell you how he acted
or whether she thought it paradise or hell; but here
I leave them conducting themselves in their fashion
until the bell for evensong rang and they had to get up.

   Whether it was by destiny or chance,
by occult influence or by nature,
or by astrological influence—so that, being in such a
position, the heavens were at that time at a point
favorable for presenting a petition of Venus' works
to any woman in order to get her love
(everything has its time, say these learned men),
I do not know; but let great God above,
who knows no act is without a cause,
judge all, for I will hold my peace.
But the truth is that fresh May
was that day so impressed
with pity for sick Damian
that she could not drive from her heart
the thought of comforting him.
"Indeed," she thought, "I do not care whom this matter
displeases, for here I promise
to love him best of all,
even if he had no more than his shirt."
Behold, pity* soon arises in the gentle heart!

   Here you may see what excellent generosity
there is in women when they take careful thought.
There is some tyrant (there are many such)
who has a heart as hard as any stone

Which wolde han lete him sterven in the place
Wel rather than han graunted him hir grace,
And hem rejoysen in hir cruel pryde
And rekke nat to been an homicyde.   750
   This gentil May, fulfilled of pitee,
Right of hir hande a lettre made she,
In which she graunteth him hir verray grace:
Ther lakketh noght but only day and place
Wher that she mighte unto his lust suffyse,
For it shall be right as he wol devyse.
And whan she saugh hir time upon a day
To visite this Damian goth May,
And sotilly this lettre doun she threste
Under his pilwe: rede it if him leste.   760
She taketh him by the hand and harde him twiste
So secrely that no wight of it wiste,
And bad him been al hool; and forth she wente
To Januarie whan that he for hir sente.
   Up ryseth Damian the nexte morwe:
Al passed was his siknesse and his sorwe.
He kembeth him, he preyneth him and pyketh,
He dooth al that his lady lust and lyketh.
And eek to Januarie he gooth as lowe
As evere dide a dogge for the bowe.   770
He is so plesant unto every man—
For craft is al, whoso that do it can—
That every wight is fayn to speke him good;
And fully in his lady grace he stood.
Thus lete I Damian aboute his nede,
And in my tale forth I wol procede.
   Somme clerkes holden that felicitee
Stant in delyt, and therefore certeyn he
This noble Januarie, with al his might
In honest wyse as longeth to a knight,   780
Shoop him to live ful deliciously:
His housinge, his array as honestly
To his degree was maked as a kinges.
Amonges othere of his honest thinges,
He made a gardin walled al with stoon;
So fair a gardin woot I nowher noon,
For out of doute I verraily suppose
That he that wroot the Romance of the Rose
Ne coude of it the beautee wel devyse;
Ne Priapus ne mighte nat suffyse—   790

and who would have left him dying where he lay
sooner than have granted him her favor;
such ones would rejoice in their cruel pride
and do not scruple to be murderers.

This gentle May, filled with pity,
wrote a letter in her own hand
in which she granted him her authentic favor:
nothing lacked but time and place
in which she might satisfy his desire,
for it was to be just as he should arrange.
And one day, when she saw her opportunity,
May went to visit Damian,
and cunningly she thrust the letter down
under his pillow: let him read it if he wants.
She took him by the hand and wrung it hard,
so secretly that no one knew of it,
and told him to get well; and forth she went
to January when he sent for her.

Damian got up the next morning:
his sickness and his depression were all over.
He combed his hair, he preened himself, he tidied up,
he did everything that pleased his lady.
And also to January he was as obedient and humble
as a well-trained hunting dog.
He was so pleasant to every man
—for craft is everything, if you can manage it—
that everyone was glad to speak well of him;
and he stood fully in his lady's favor.
Thus I leave Damian busy about his needs,
and I shall proceed with my tale.

Some learned men hold that felicity
consists in sensuous pleasure, and for that end
noble January certainly contrived with all his might
to live most delightfully in honorable fashion
as befits a knight:
his buildings, his finery were
made as honorably for their rank as a king's.
Among other honorable possessions of his,
he had built a garden, walled on all sides with stone;
I do not know of so fair a garden anywhere else,
for beyond doubt I truly believe
that he who wrote the *Romance* of the Rose*
could not suitably describe the beauty of it;
nor might Priapus suffice—

Though he be god of gardins—for to telle
The beautee of the gardin, and the welle
That stood under a laurer alwey grene.
Ful ofte tyme he Pluto and his quené
Proserpina and al hir fayërye
Disporten hem and maken melodye
Aboute that welle, and daunced, as men tolde.
This noble knight, this Januarie the olde,
Swich deintee hath in it to walke and pleye
That he wol no wight suffren bere the keye   800
Save he himself; for of the smale wiket
He bar alwey of silver a cliket,
With which whan that him leste he it unshette.
And whan he wolde paye his wyf hir dette
In somer seson, thider wolde he go,
And May his wyf, and no wight but they two;
And thinges whiche that were nat doon abedde,
He in the gardin parfourned hem and spedde.
And in this wyse many a merye day
Lived this Januarie and fresshe May.   810
But worldly joye may nat alwey dure
To Januarie, ne to no creature.
    O sodeyn hap, o thou Fortune instable,
Lyk to the scorpion so deceivable,
That flaterest with thyn heed when thou wolt stinge,
Thy tayl is deeth, thurgh thyn enveniminge!
O brotil joye, o swete venim queynte!
O monstre, that so subtilly canst peynte
Thy yiftes under hewe of stedfastnesse,
That thou deceyvest bothe more and lesse!   820
Why hastow Januarie thus deceyved,
That haddest him for thy fulle frend receyved?
And now thou hast biraft him bothe his yën,
For sorwe of which desyreth he to dyen.
    Allas, this noble Januarie free,
Amidde his lust and his prosperitee,
Is woxen blind, and that al sodeynly.
He wepeth and he wayleth pitously;
And therwithal the fyr of jalousye,
Lest that his wyf sholde falle in som folye,   830
So brente his herte that he wolde fayn
That som man bothe hire and him had slayn;
For neither after his deeth nor in his lyf
Ne wolde he that she were love ne wyf,

although he is god of gardens—to tell
the beauty of the garden and of its well,
which lay beneath an ever-green laurel tree.
Frequently Pluto* and his queen
Proserpina and all their fairy crew
played and sang
and danced around that well, as we are told.
This noble knight, old January,
took such delight in strolling and disporting himself there
that he would allow no one to carry the key
except himself; for the narrow wicket gate
he always carried a small key of silver
with which he opened the gate when he wanted.
And when, in the summer, he wanted to pay
his wife her debt, he and May would
go there, no one except those two;
and things that were not done in bed
he successfully performed in the garden.
For many a merry day January
and fresh May lived in this fashion.
But worldly joy may not always last
for January, or for any other created being.

   O chance, unbargained for, O unstable Fortune,
deceitful as the scorpion,*
you flatter with your head when you intend to sting;
your tail is death by your poisoning!
O brittle joy! O sweet, subtle venom!
O monster, who can so cleverly color
your gifts with the hue of constancy
that you deceive both great and small!
Why have you, who had accepted January fully
as your friend, thus deceived him?
Now you have robbed him of the sight of both his eyes,
for sorrow at which he desires to die.

   Alas, this noble, generous January,
in the midst of his pleasure and well-being,
became blind, and without any warning.
He wept and wailed piteously,
and, besides, the fire of jealousy,
for fear that his wife would fall into some folly,
so burned his heart that he would have been glad
if someone had slain both her and himself;
for no more after his death than in his life
did he want her to be either paramour or wife;

But evere live as widwe in clothes blake,
Soul as the turtle that hath lost hir make.
But atte laste, after a monthe or tweye,
His sorwe gan aswage, sooth to seye;
For whan he wiste it may noon other be,
He paciently took his adversitee—   840
Save out of doute he may nat forgoon
That he nas jalous everemore in oon;
Which jalousye it was so outrageous
That neither in halle, n'in noon other hous,
Ne in noon other place, neverthemo,
He nolde suffre hire for to ryde or go,
But if that he hadde hand on hire alway;
For which ful ofte wepeth fresshe May,
That loveth Damian so benignely
That she moot outher dyen sodeynly,   850
Or elles she moot han him as hire leste;
She wayteth whan hir herte wolde breste.

   Upon that other syde Damian
Bicomen is the sorwefulleste man
That evere was, for neither night ne day
Ne mighte he speke a word to fresshe May,
As to his purpos, of no swich matere,
But if that Januarie moste it here,
That hadde an hand upon hire evermo;
But nathelees, by wryting to and fro   860
And privee signes, wiste he what she mente,
And she knew eek the fyn of his entente.

   O Januarie, what mighte it thee availle
Though thou mightest see as fer as shippes saille?
For also good is blind deceyved be
As to be deceyved whan a man may see.
Lo Argus, which that hadde an hondred yën,
For al that evere he coude poure or pryen,
Yet was he blent, and God wot so ben mo
That wenen wisly that it be nat so.   870
Passe over is an ese, I sey namore.

   This fresshe May that I spak of so yore,
In warme wex hath emprented the cliket
That Januarie bar of the smale wiket,
By which into his gardin ofte he wente.
And Damian, that knew al hir entente,
The cliket countrefeted prively—
Ther nis namore to seye, but hastily

he wanted her to live ever after as a widow in black,
alone as the dove that has lost her mate.
But at last, after a month or two,
his sorrow began to be assuaged, if the truth be known;
for when he knew it could not be otherwise,
he took his adversity in patience—
except, beyond doubt, that he could not forego
being constantly jealous;
this jealousy was so excessive
that even in his hall, or any other house,
or any other place
he would not allow her to go in any manner
unless he always had a hand on her;
on this account fresh May often wept;
she loved Damian so cordially
that either she must have him as she wished
or suddenly die: she stood
in expectation of the time when her heart would break.

    On the other side Damian
became the most sorrowful man
that ever was, for neither night nor day
might he speak a word of any matter
to fresh May concerning his purpose
without January's having to hear it,
who had his hand on her always.
Nevertheless, by writing back and forth
and by secret signs, he knew what she thought,
and she, too, knew the goal of his intention.

    O January, what might it avail you
if you could see as far as ship can sail?
It is just as well to be deceived when one is blind
as to be deceived when one may see.
Consider Argus, who had a hundred eyes:
no matter how intently he could peer and pry,
he was still hoodwinked; and, God knows, so are others
who think that it is surely not so.
Letting the matter drop is a relief; I say no more.

    This fresh May, whom I first mentioned so long ago,
took in warm wax an imprint of the key
carried by January for the narrow wicket gate
by which he so often entered his garden.
Damian, who knew all her plan,
secretly made a copy of the key—
there is no more to say except that shortly

Som wonder by this cliket shal bityde.
Which ye shul heren if ye wole abyde.   880
    O noble Ovyde, ful sooth seystou, God woot,
What sleighte is it, thogh it be long and hoot,
That he nil finde it out in som manere!
By Piramus and Tesbee may men lere;
Thogh they were kept ful longe streite overal,
They been accorded, rouninge thurgh a wal,
Ther no wight coude han founde out swich a sleighte.
    But now to purpos: er that dayes eighte
Were passed, er the monthe of Juil, bifil
That Januarie hath caught so greet a wil—   890
Thurgh egging of his wyf—him for to pleye
In his gardin, and no wight but they tweye,
That in a morwe unto his May seith he,
"Rys up, my wyf, my love, my lady free;
The turtles vois is herd, my douve swete;
The winter is goon with alle his reynes wete.
Com forth now with thyn eyën columbyn.
How fairer been thy brestes than is wyn!
The gardin is enclosed al aboute:
Com forth, my whyte spouse; out of doute,   900
Thou hast me wounded in myn herte. O wyf,
No spot of thee ne knew I al my lyf.
Com forth and lat us taken our disport;
I chees thee for my wyf and my confort."
    Swiche olde lewed wordes used he.
On Damian a signe made she
That he sholde go biforn with his cliket:
This Damian thanne hath opened the wiket,
And in he stirte, and that in swich manere
That no wight mighte it see neither y-here;   910
And stille he sit under a bush anoon.
    This Januarie, as blind as is a stoon,
With Maius in his hand and no wight mo,
Into his fresshe gardin is ago,
And clapte to the wiket sodeynly.
    "Now, wyf," quod he, "here nis but thou and I,
That art the creature that I best love.
For, by that Lord that sit in heven above,
Levere ich hadde to dyen on a knyf
Than thee offende, trewe dere wyf.   920
For Goddes sake, thenk how I thee chees,
Noght for no coveityse, doutelees,

some miracle will happen because of this key,
which you shall hear if you will wait.

O noble Ovid,* God knows you speak truth in saying
that, whatever trick it is, though it take time and sweat,
love will find it out somehow!
One may learn this by the example of Pyramus and Thisbe;
although they were long guarded closely on all sides, they
came to an understanding by whispering through a wall,
where no one else could have discovered such a trick.

But now back to the story: before eight days
had passed in the month before July, it happened
that January fell into so strong a desire
(through his wife's urging) to dally
in his garden with no one there but the two of them,
that one morning he said to May,
"Rise up, my wife, my love, my gracious lady;
the voice* of the turtle is heard, my sweet dove;
the winter is past, with its wet rain;
now come away, with your eyes like those of the dove.
Thy breasts are fairer than wine!
The garden is enclosed all about:
come away, my lily-white spouse; beyond doubt
you have ravished my heart, O wife,
I knew no fault in thee all my life.
Come forth, and let us take our pleasure;
I choose you out for my wife and my comfort."

He made use of such old, wanton speeches as this.
She made a sign to Damian
to go in advance with his key:
Damian then opened the wicket
and went in quickly, in such fashion
that no one might see or hear him;
and then he sat still beneath a bush.

January, blind as a stone,
with May held by his hand and no one else,
went into his fresh garden
and slammed the wicket shut quickly.

"Now, wife," he said, "here is no one but you and me,
and you are the creature whom I love best.
By the Lord who sits in heaven above,
I would rather die by the knife
than do you any injury, faithful dear wife.
Think, for God's sake, how I chose you—
not for avarice, surely,

But only for the love I had to thee.
And though that I be old, and may nat see,
Beth to me trewe, and I wol telle yow why.
Three thinges, certes, shul ye winne ther-by:
First, love of Crist, and to yourself honour,
And al myn heritage, toun and tour—
I yeve it yow: maketh chartres as yow leste;
This shal be doon tomorwe er sonne reste, 930
So wisly god my soule bringe in blisse.
I prey yow first in covenant ye me kisse;
And thogh that I be jalous, wyte me noght.
Ye been so depe enprented in my thoght,
That whan that I considere youre beautee,
And therwithal the unlykly elde of me,
I may nat, certes, thogh I sholde dye,
Forbere to been out of youre companye
For verray love; this is withouten doute.
Now kis me, wyf, and lat us rome aboute." 940
This fresshe May, whan she thise wordes herde,
Benignely to Januarie answerde,
But first and forward she bigan to wepe.
"I have," quod she, "a soule for to kepe
As wel as ye, and also myn honour,
And of my wyfhod thilke tendre flour,
Which that I have assured in youre hond
Whan that the preest to yow my body bond;
Wherfore I wole answere in this manere,
By the leve of yow, my lord so dere: 950
I prey to God that nevere dawe the day
That I ne sterve as foule as womman may,
If ever I do unto my kin that shame,
Or elles I empeyre so my name,
That I be fals. And if I do that lak,
Do strepe me, and putte me in a sak,
And in the nexte river do me drenche:
I am a gentil womman and no wenche.
Why speke ye thus? but men ben ever untrewe,
And wommen have repreve of yow ay newe. 960
Ye han non other contenance, I leve,
But speke to us of untrust and repreve."
And with that word she saugh wher Damian
Sat in the bush, and coughen she bigan,
And with hir finger signes made she
That Damian sholde climbe upon a tree

but only for the love I felt for you.
And though I am old and cannot see,
be true to me; I shall tell you why you should.
By doing so you shall certainly win three things:
Christ's love, honor to yourself,
and all my inheritance, town and castle—
I give it to you: make charters for it as you wish;
this shall be done tomorrow before sundown,
as surely as I hope God may bring my soul to joy.
I ask you first to seal this covenant with a kiss;
and although I am jealous, don't blame me for it.
You have made so deep an impression on my mind
that, when I consider your beauty
and, with it, my unsuitable age,
certainly I cannot, though I should die,
bear for very love to be out of your company;
this is beyond doubt.
Now kiss me, wife, and let us stroll here and there."

    When fresh May had heard these words,
she answered January graciously,
but first of all she began to weep.
"I have," she said, "a soul to save
as well as you do, and also my honor
and the tender flower of my womanhood
which I entrusted to your hands
when the priest bound my body to you;
therefore I will answer in this manner,
by your leave, my dear lord:
I pray God that the day may never dawn
when I do not die as disgracefully as a woman can
if I ever do such shame to my family
or so mar my name
as to be false. And if I commit that sin,
have me stripped, and put in a sack,
and drowned in the nearest river:
I am a gentlewoman and no wanton.
Why do you talk this way? But men are always unfaithful,
and women have reproof from you ever anew.
I believe you have no face to put upon your faults
except to talk to us of unfaithfulness and reproof."

    At that word she saw where Damian
was sitting beneath the bush, and she began to cough
and made signs with her finger
to him to climb up into a tree

That charged was with fruit; and up he wente,
For verraily he knew al hir entente,
And every signe that she coude make,
Wel bet than Januarie, hir owene make,   970
For in a lettre she hadde told him al
Of this matere how he werchen shal.
And thus I lete him sitte upon the pyrie,
And Januarie and May rominge myrie.

   Bright was the day, and blew the firmament;
Phebus hath of gold his stremes doun sent
To gladen every flour with his warmnesse.
He was that tyme *in Geminis,* as I gesse,
But litel fro his declinacioun
Of Cancer, Jovis exaltacioun.   980
And so bifel, that brighte morwe-tyde,
That in that gardin in the ferther syde
Pluto, that is king of fayërye,
And many a lady in his compaignye,
Folwinge his wyf, the quene Proserpina,
Which that he ravisshed out of Etna
Whyl that she gadered floures in the mede—
In Claudian ye may the stories rede,
How in his grisly carte he hire fette—
This king of fairye thanne adoun him sette   990
Upon a bench of turves fresh and grene,
And right anon thus seyde he to his quene:
   "My wyf," quod he, "ther may no wight seye nay;
Th'experience so preveth every day
The treson whiche that wommen doon to man.
Ten hondred thousand tales tellen I can
Notable of your untrouthe and brotilnesse.
O Salomon, wys and richest of richesse,
Fulfild of sapience and of worldly glorie,
Ful worthy been thy wordes to memorie   1000
To every wight that wit and reson can—
Thus preiseth he yet the bountee of man:
'Amonges a thousand men yet fond I oon,
But of wommen alle fond I noon.'
Thus seith the king that knoweth youre wikkednesse.
And Jesus *filius Syrak,* as I gesse,
Ne spekech of yow but selde reverence.
A wilde fyr and corrupt pestilence
So falle upon your bodies yet tonight!
Ne see ye nat this honurable knight?   1010

that was full of fruit; and up he went,
for indeed he knew all her mind
and every sign that she could make
much better than January, her own husband,
for she had told him in a letter everything
concerning how he should go about this matter.
I leave him thus sitting in the pear tree,
and January and May strolling about happily.

The day was bright and the sky was blue;
Phoebus had sent down his golden rays
to gladden every flower with his warmth.
He was at that time in the sign of the Twins, as I judge,
only a little way from his northernmost declination
in the sign of Cancer, which sign is Jupiter's exaltation.
It so happened that sunny morning
that on the further side of that garden were
Pluto, who is the king of fairyland,
and many a lady in his company
following his wife, Queen Proserpina,
whom he had ravished away from Mount Aetna
while she was gathering flowers in the meadow—
you can read the story in Claudian*
of how he fetched her in his horrible chariot;
this king of fairies sat down
on a bench of fresh green turf
and then said to his queen:

"My wife, no one may contradict this;
experience proves every day
the treachery which women commit against men.
I can tell ten hundred thousand stories
which are remarkable for your infidelity and fickleness.
O Solomon, wise, most abounding in riches,
full of knowledge and wordly glory,
your words are very worthwhile to commit to mind
for everyone who recognizes wisdom and reason—
thus he still praises the goodness of man:
'Among a thousand men I yet found one,
but among all women I found none.'
Thus speaks the king who knows your wickedness.
And Jesus* son of Sirach, as I believe,
seldom speaks well of you.
May wildfire and a destroying pestilence
yet fall upon your bodies this night!
Don't you see this honorable knight?

By-cause, allas, that he is blind and old,
His owene man shal make him çokewold.
Lo wher he sit, the lechour, in the tree!
Now wol I graunten of my magestee
Unto this olde, blinde worthy knight
That he shal have ayeyn his eyen sight,
Whan that his wyf wolde doon him vileinye;
Than shal he knowen al hir harlotrye,
Both in repreve of hir and othere mo." –
"Ye shal," quod Proserpyne. "Wol ye so?   1020
Now, by my modres sires soule I swere
That I shal yeven hire suffisant answere,
And alle wommen after for hir sake,
That, though they be in any gilt y-take,
With face bold they shulle hemself excuse,
And bere hem doun that wolden hem accuse:
For lakke of answer noon of hem shal dyen.
Al hadde man seyn a thing with bothe his yën,
Yit shul we wommen visage it hardily,
And wepe, and swere, and chyde subtilly,   1030
So that ye men shul been as lewed as gees—
What rekketh me of youre auctoritees?
    I woot wel that this Jew, this Salomon,
Fond of us wommen foles many oon;
But though that he ne fond no good womman,
Yet hath ther founde many another man
Wommen ful trewe, ful gode, and vertuous.
Witnesse on hem that dwelle in Cristes hous:
With martirdom they preved hir constance.
The Romayn gestes maken remembrance   1040
Of many a verray, trewe wyf also.
But sire, ne be nat wrooth, al be it so,
Though that he seyde he fond no good womman,
I prey yow, take the sentence of the man:
He mente thus, that in sovereyn bontee
Nis noon but God, but neither he ne she.
    Ey, for verray God, that nis but oon,
What make ye so muche of Salomon?
What though he made a temple, Goddes hous?
What though he were riche and glorious?   1050
So made he eek a temple of false goddis:
How mighte he do a thing that more forbode is?
Pardee, as faire as ye his name emplastre,
He was a lechour and an ydolastre;

Because he is blind and old, alas,
his own servant is to cuckold him.
Look where he sits, the lecher, in the tree!
Now I will in my majesty make the grant
to this old, blind, worthy knight
that he shall recover his eyesight
when his wife does him shame;
then he shall know all her harlotry,
in reproof both of her and of others."

"Shall you?" said Proserpina. "Do you want to do that?
Now, by the soul of my mother's father I swear
that I shall give a good enough answer to her,
and to all women thereafter, for her sake,
so that, even if they are taken in the guilty act,
they shall boldfacedly give an excuse for themselves
and bear down those that would accuse them:
none of them shall die for lack of an answer.
Even if a man has seen a thing with both his eyes,
yet shall we women face it out confidently
and weep, and take our oath and scold deviously,
so that you men will be as ignorant as geese—
what do I care about your authorities?

I certainly know that this Jew, this Solomon,
found many a fool among us women;
but even if he didn't find any good woman,
many another man has found
very faithful, good, and virtuous ones.
Take witness on those of them who dwell in Christ's abode:
they proved their constancy by martyrdom.
The stories of Rome also make mention
of many a true, faithful wife.
But, sir, don't be angry, even though this is the way it is;
although Solomon said that he found no good woman,
I pray you, take the man's meaning:
he meant this, that in the matter of sovereign goodness
there is no one but God in Trinity.

Ah, by the one true God,
why do you make so much of Solomon?
What if he made a temple, a house of God?
What if he was rich and glorious?
So he made a temple of false gods, too:
how could he do a thing that is more forbidden?
By heaven, no matter how you whitewash his reputation,
he was a lecher and an idolater;

And in his elde he verray God forsook.
And if that God ne hadde, as seith the book,
Y-spared him for his fadres sake, he sholde
Have lost his regne rather than he wolde.
I sette right noght of al the vileinye,
That ye of wommen wryte, a boterflye.   1060
I am a womman, nedes moot I speke,
Or elles swelle til myn herte breke.
For sithen he seyde that we been jangleresses,
As evere hool I moote brouke my tresses,
I shal nat spare for no curteisye
To speke him harm that wolde us vileinye."

    "Dame," quod this Pluto, "be no lenger wrooth;
I yeve it up. But sith I swoor myn ooth
That I wolde graunten him his sighte ageyn,
My word shal stonde, I warne yow certeyn.   1070
I am a king: it sit me noght to lye."

    "And I," quod she, "a queene of fayërye:
Hir answere shal she have, I undertake.
Lat us namore wordes heerof make.
Forsoothe, I wol no lenger yow contrarie."

    Now lat us turne agayn to Januarie,
That in the gardin with his faire May
Singeth ful merier than the papejay,
"Yow love I best, and shal, and other noon."
So longe aboute the aleyes is he goon   1080
Til he was come agaynes thilke pyrie,
Wher as this Damian sitteth ful myrie
An heigh among the fresshe leves grene.

    This fresshe May, that is so bright and shene,
Gan for to syke and seyde, "Allas, my syde!
Now sire," quod she, "for ought that may bityde,
I moste han of the peres that I see,
Or I moot dye, so sore longeth me
To eten of the smale peres grene.
Help, for hir love that is of hevene quene!   1090
I telle yow wel, a womman in my plyt
May han to fruit so greet an appetyt
That she may dyen but she of it have."

    "Allas," quod he, "that I ne hadde heer a knave
That coude climbe! Allas, allas," quod he,
"For I am blind!" "Ye, sire, no fors," quod she:
"But wolde ye vouche sauf, for Goddes sake,
The pyrie inwith youre armes for to take

and in his old age he forsook the true God.
And, as the book says, if God hadn't
spared him for his father's sake, he would
have lost his rule sooner than he wanted.
I don't give a butterfly for all
the shame that you write about women.
I am a woman, I have to speak,
or else swell until my heart bursts.
Since he said that we are idle talkers,
as ever I hope to possess my tresses unshorn I shall not,
for the sake of any courteous forbearance, refrain
from speaking harm of this man who wished shame upon us."

    "My lady," said Pluto, "don't be angry any longer;
I give up. But since I swore an oath
that I would give him back his sight,
my word shall stand, I warn you for a certainty.
I am a king: it does not suit me to lie."

    "And I," she said, "a queen of faery:
she shall have her answer, I guarantee it.
Let us have no more words about this.
Truly, I won't contradict you any longer."

    Now let us turn to January again,
who sang more merrily than a parrot
in the garden with his pretty May,
"I love you best, and always shall, and no other."
He walked around the paths far enough
to come up to that pear tree
where Damian was sitting happily
on high, among the fresh green leaves.

    Fresh May, who was so bright and shining,
began to sigh, and said, "Alas, my side!
Now, sir," she said, "no matter what happens,
I must have some of the pears that I see,
or I must die, I have so strong a longing
to eat some of the small green pears.
Help, for the love of her who is heaven's queen!
I tell you indeed, a woman in my condition
may have so great an appetite for fruit
that she may die unless she gets some."
"Alas," he said, "that I don't have a young manservant here
that could climb! Alas, alas," he said,
"that I am blind." "Yea, sir, it doesn't matter," she said:
"but if you would deign, for God's sake,
to put your arms around the pear tree

(For wel I woot that ye mistruste me),
Thanne sholde I climbe wel ynogh," quod she,   1100
"So I my foot mighte sette upon your bak."

"Certes," quod he, "thereon shal be no lak,
Mighte I yow helpen with myn herte blood."
He stoupeth doun, and on his bak she stood,
And caughte hir by a twiste, and up she gooth.
Ladies, I preye yow that ye be nat wrooth;
I can nat glose, I am a rude man.
And sodeynly anon this Damian
Gan pullen up the smok, and in he throng,
    And whan that Pluto saugh this grete wrong,   1110
To Januarie he gaf agayn his sighte,
And made him see as wel as evere he mighte.
And whan that he hadde caught his sighte agayn,
Ne was ther nevere man of thing so fayn.
But on his wyf his thoght was everemo:
Up to the tree he caste his eyen two,
And saugh that Damian his wyf had dressed
In swich manere it may nat been expressed,
But if I wolde speke uncurteisly;
And up he yaf a roring and a cry,   1120
As doth the moder whan the child shal dye.
"Out! help! allas! harrow!" he gan to crye,
"O stronge lady store, what dostow?"

    And she answerde, "Sire, what eyleth yow?
Have pacience and reson in youre minde.
I have yow holpe on bothe your eyen blinde.
Up peril of my soule, I shal nat lyen,
As me was taught, to hele with your yën,
Was no thing bet to make yow to see
Than strugle with a man upon a tree: 1130
God woot I dide it in ful good entente."

    "Strugle!" quod he, "Ye, algate in it wente!
God yeve yow bothe on shames deeth to dyen!
He swyved thee—I saugh it with myne yën,
And elles be I hanged by the hals."

    "Thanne is," quod she, "my medicyne al fals;
For certeinly if that ye mighte see,
Ye wolde nat seyn thise wordes unto me;
Ye han som glimsing and no parfit sighte."

    "I see," quod he, "as wel as evere I mighte,   1140
Thonked be God, with bothe myne eyen two,
And by my trouthe, me thoughte he dide thee so."

(for I well know that you don't trust me),
then I would climb well enough," she said,
"provided that I might put my foot on your back."

"Certainly," he said, "you should not lack
if I could help you with my heart's blood."
He stooped down, and she stood on his back
and caught hold of a branch, and up she went.
Ladies, I ask you not to be angry with me;
I cannot gloss, I am a blunt man.
Without warning, then, this Damian
pulled up the smock, and in he thrust.

When Pluto saw this great wrong,
he restored January's sight,
and made him see as well as he ever could.
And when he had got his sight back,
there was never another man so glad of anything.
But his thoughts continued to dwell on his wife:
he cast his two eyes up to the tree,
and saw that Damian had managed his wife
in such a way as may not be expressed
unless I would speak discourteously;
and he gave a roar and cry
like a mother's when her child is on the point of death.
"Alas! Help, thief!" he cried.
"Outrageous, gross woman, what are you doing?"

And she answered, "Sir, what ails you?
Be patient and reasonable.
I have given help to your two blind eyes.
On my soul, I shall not lie:
as I was taught, there was nothing better
to heal your eyes with and give you vision
than to struggle with a man in a tree:
God knows, I meant well."

"Struggle!" said he, "yes, but it went in!
God give you both to die a shameful death!
He plumbed you—I saw it with my eyes;
else let me be hanged by the neck."

"Then," said she, "my medicine is all false;
for if you could see, certainly
you would not utter these words to me;
you have some glimmering but no perfect sight."

"I see," he said, "as well as I ever could,
with both my eyes, thanked be God,
and by my faith, I thought he handled you that way."

"Ye maze, maze, gode sir," quod she.
"This thank have I for I have maad yow see;
Allas," quod she, "that evere I was so kinde!"
    "Now, dame," quod he, "lat al passe out of minde.
Com doun, my lief, and if I have missayd,
God help me so as I am yvel apayd.
But, by my fader soule, I wende han seyn
How that this Damian had by thee leyn,   1150
And that thy smok had leyn upon his brest."
    "Ye, sire," quod she, "ye may wene as yow lest;
But, sire, a man that waketh out of his sleep,
He may nat sodeynly wel taken keep
Upon a thing, ne seen it parfitly,
Till that he be adawed verraily;
Right so a man that longe hath blind y-be
Ne may nat sodeynly so wel y-see,
First whan his sighte is newe come ageyn,
As he that hath a day or two y-seyn.   1160
Til that your sighte y-satled be a whyle,
Ther may ful many a sighte yow bigyle.
Beth war, I preye yow; for, by hevene king,
Ful many a man weneth to seen a thing,
And it is al another than it semeth:
He that misconceyveth, he misdemeth."
And with that word she leep doun fro the tree.
    This Januarie, who is glad but he?
He kisseth hire and clippeth hir ful ofte,
And on hir wombe he stroketh hire ful softe,   1170
And to his palays hoom he hath hire lad.
Now, gode men, I praye yow to be glad.
Thus endeth here my tale of Januarie.
God blesse us and his moder Seinte Marie.

"You are dazed, dazed, good sir," she said.
"This is the thanks I get for having made you see;
alas," she said, "that I was ever so kind!"

"Now, my lady," he said, "let everything be forgotten.
Come down, my dear, and if I have misspoken
God help me in respect to my being ill-pleased.
But, on my father's soul, I thought I saw
that Damian was lying by you
and that your smock lay on his breast."

"Yea, sir," she said, "you may think as you wish;
but, sir, a man that wakes from his sleep
cannot suddenly grasp
a thing, or see it perfectly,
until he is really awake;
just so, a man who has been blind for a long time
may not immediately see as well
at first when his sight has just recently returned
as a man that has seen for a day or two.
Until your sight has settled for a while,
many a view may fool you.
Be cautious, I implore you; for, by the heavenly Ruler,
many a man thinks he is seeing something,
and it is completely different from what it seems to be.
Whoever misapprehends, misjudges."
And so saying she jumped down from the tree.

Who was happy but January?
He kissed her and hugged her again and again,
he stroked her body very gently,
and he led her home to his palace.
Now, good people, I ask you to be satisfied.
Thus ends here my tale of January.
God and his mother Saint Mary bless us

THE FRANKELEYNS TALE

In Armorik, that called is Britayne,
Ther was a knight that loved and dide his payne
To serve a lady in his beste wyse;
And many a labour, many a greet empryse
He for his lady wroghte er she were wonne,
For she was oon the faireste under sonne,
And eek thereto come of so heigh kinrede
That wel unnethes dorste this knight, for drede,
Telle hir his wo, his peyne, and his distresse.
But atte laste, she, for his worthinesse,   10
And namely for his meke obeysaunce,
Hath swich a pitee caught of his penaunce
That prively she fil of his accord
To take him for hir housbonde and hir lord,
Of swich lordshipe as men han over hir wyves;
And for to lede the more in blisse hir lyves,
Of his free wil he swoor hir as a knight
That never in all his lyf he, day ne night,
Ne sholde upon him take no maistrye
Agayn hir wil, ne kythe hir jalousye,   20
But hir obeye and folwe hir wil in al
As any lovere to his lady shal;
Save that the name of soveraynetee,
That wolde he have for shame of his degree.
   She thanked him, and with ful greet humblesse
She seyde, "Sire, sith of your gentillesse
Ye profre me to have so large a reyne,
Ne wolde never God bitwixe us tweyne,
As in my gilt, were outher werre or stryf.
Sir, I wol be your humble trewe wyf,   30
Have heer my trouthe, til that myn herte breste."
Thus been they bothe in quiete and in reste.
   For o thing, sires, saufly dar I seye:
That frendes everich other moot obeye,
If they wol longe holden companye.
Love wol nat ben constreyned by maistrye;
Whan maistrie comth, the god of love anon
Beteth hise winges, and farewel—he is gon.

THE FRANKLIN'S TALE

IN ARMORICA, which is called Brittany,
there was a knight who loved a lady and took pains
to serve her as best he could;
and he performed many a labor, many a great enterprise,
for her, before she was won,
for she was one of the fairest under the sun,
and also she came of such a noble family
that, for fear, this knight scarcely dared
tell her his woe, his pain, and his distress.
But at last, because of his great worth,
and particularly because of his meek obedience,
she took such pity on his suffering
that privately she agreed
to take him for her husband and her lord—
in such lordship as men have over their wives;
and in order that they might lead their lives together the
more blissfully, of his free will he swore to her as a knight
that never in all his life, by day or night,
would he take an authoritarian role over her
against her will, nor show jealousy to her,
but would obey her and always follow her will in all things,
as any lover ought to his lady;
except that he wanted to have the title of sovereignty:
that he wanted for the sake of the dignity of his position.
   She thanked him, and with great humility
she said, "Sir, since in your courtesy
you offer me so free a rein,
God forbid that there should ever be between us two,
through my fault, any quarrel or strife.
Sir, I will be your humble, true wife,
I give you my pledge, until my heart stops beating."
Thus they were both in peace and accord.
   For there is one thing, sirs, I can safely say:
that those bound by love must obey each other
if they are to keep company long.
Love will not be constrained by mastery;
when mastery comes, the god of love at once
beats his wings, and farewell—he is gone.

Love is a thing as any spirit free;
Wommen of kinde desiren libertee,   40
And nat to ben constreyned as a thral;
And so doon men, if I sooth seyen shal.
Loke who that is most pacient in love,
He is at his avantage al above.
Pacience is an heigh vertu certeyn,
For it venquisseth, as thise clerkes seyn,
Thinges that rigour sholde never atteyne.
For every word men may nat chyde or pleyne.
Lerneth to suffre, or elles, so moot I goon,
Ye shul it lerne wherso ye wole or noon.   50
For in this world, certein, ther no wight is
That he ne dooth or seith somtyme amis.
Ire, siknesse, or constellacioun,
Wyn, wo, or chaunginge of complexioun*
Causeth ful ofte to doon amis or speken.
On every wrong a man may nat be wreken;
After the tyme, moste be temperaunce
To every wight that can on governaunce.
And therfore hath this wyse worthy knight,
To live in ese, suffrance hir bihight,   60
And she to him ful wisly gan to swere
That never sholde ther be defaute in here.

    Heer may men seen an humble wys accord:
Thus hath she take hir servant and hir lord,
Servant in love and lord in mariage;
Thanne was he bothe in lordship and servage.
Servage? Nay, but in lordshipe above,
Sith he hath bothe his lady and his love;
His lady, certes, and his wyf also,
The which that lawe of love acordeth to.   70
And whan he was in this prosperitee,
Hoom with his wyf he gooth to his contree,
Nat fer fro Penmark, ther his dwelling was,
Wheras he liveth in blisse and in solas.

    Who coude telle but he hadde wedded be
The joye, the ese, and the prosperitee
That is bitwixe an housbonde and his wyf?
A yeer and more lasted this blisful lyf,
Til that the knight of which I speke of thus,
That of Kayrrud was cleped Arveragus,   80
Shoop him to goon and dwelle a yeer or tweyne
In Engelond, that cleped was eek Briteyne,

Love is a thing as free as any spirit;
women naturally desire liberty,
and not to be constrained like slaves;
and so do men, if I shall tell the truth.
See who is the most patient in love:
he has the greatest advantage.
Patience is surely a great virtue,
for it vanquishes, as these scholars say,
things that rigor would never manage.
One cannot scold or complain at every word.
Learn to endure patiently, or else, as I live and breathe,
you shall learn it whether you want to or not.
For certainly there is no one in this world
who doesn't sometimes do or say something amiss.
Anger, sickness, or planetary influences,
wine, sorrow, or changing of the balance of humors
often causes one to do or speak amiss.
A man cannot be avenged for every wrong;
according to the occasion, everyone who knows
how to manage himself must use temperance.
And therefore this wise, worthy knight, in order to
live in comfort, promised her forbearance,
and she wisely gave her promise to him
that there would never be any lack of it on her part.

Here one may see a humble, wise agreement:
she has thus accepted her servant and her lord,
servant in love and lord in marriage;
he was, then, both in lordship and in servitude.
Servitude? No, but in the higher state of lordship,
since he had both his lady and his love;
his lady, certainly, and his wife too,
which is in accordance with the law of love.
And when he was in this happy state,
he went home with his wife to his own country,
not far from Penmarch, where his home was,
and there he lived in bliss and happiness.

Who could tell, unless he had been married,
the joy, the comfort, and the happiness
there is between a husband and his wife?
This blissful life lasted for a year and more,
until the knight of whom I am speaking,
who was called Arveragus of Kerru,*
prepared to go and stay a year or two
in England, which was also called Britain,*

To seke in armes worship and honour—
For al his lust he sette in swich labour—
And dwelled ther two yeer, the book seith thus.
  Now wol I stinte of this Arveragus,
And speken I wole of Dorigene his wyf,
That loveth hir housbonde as hir hertes lyf.
For his absence wepeth she and syketh,
As doon thise noble wyves whan hem lyketh.   90
She moorneth, waketh, wayleth, fasteth, pleyneth;
Desyr of his presence hir so distreyneth
That al this wyde world she sette at noght.
Hir frendes, whiche that knewe hir hevy thoght,
Conforten hir in al that ever they may;
They prechen hir, they tell hir night and day,
That causelees she sleeth hirself, allas;
And every confort possible in this cas
They doon to hir with al hir bisinesse,
Al for to make hir leve hir hevinesse.   100
  By proces, as ye knowen everichoon,
Men may so longe graven in a stoon
Til som figure therinne emprented be.
So longe han they conforted hir til she
Receyved hath, by hope and by resoun,
Th'emprenting of hir consolacioun,
Thurgh which hir grete sorwe gan aswage;
She may nat alwey duren in swich rage.
  And eek Arveragus, in al this care,
Hath sent hir lettres hoom of his welfare,   110
And that he wol come hastily agayn;
Or elles hadde this sorwe hir herte slayn.
  Hir freendes sawe hir sorwe gan to slake,
And preyed hir on knees, for Goddes sake,
To come and romen hir in companye,
Awey to dryve hir derke fantasye.
And finally she graunted that requeste;
For wel she saugh that it was for the beste.
  Now stood hir castel faste by the see,
And often with hir freendes walketh she   120
Hir to disporte upon the bank an heigh,
Wheras she many a ship and barge seigh
Seilinge hir cours wheras hem liste go;
But thanne was that a parcel of hir wo,
For to hirself ofte "Allas!" seith she,
"Is ther no ship of so manye as I see

to seek glory and honor at arms—
for all his joy was in such feats—
and he stayed there two years, as the book says.

Now I will stop talking of this Arveragus,
and speak of Dorigen his wife,
who loved her husband as her own heart's life.
On account of his absence she wept and sighed,
as these noble wives do when they please.
She mourned, lost sleep, wailed, fasted, lamented;
desire for his presence so afflicted her
that she cared nothing for all this wide world.
Her friends, who knew her distress of mind,
comforted her in every way they could;
they preached to her, night and day they told her
that she was killing herself without cause, alas;
and they diligently gave her
every possible comfort in this situation,
all in order to make her stop grieving.

In due process of time, as you all know,
one may scrape on a stone so long
that some figure is imprinted there.
They comforted her so long that she
received, through hope and reason,
the imprint of their consolation,
through which her great sorrow began to diminish;
she could not go on forever in such grief.

And also, while she was in this sorrow, Arveragus
had sent her letters home assuring her of his welfare
and saying that he would return quickly;
otherwise this sorrow would have slain her heart.

Her friends saw her sorrow began to abate,
and prayed her on their knees for the love of God
to come and stroll about with them,
to drive away her dark fantasies.
And finally she granted that request,
for she saw well that it was for the best.

Now her castle stood close by the sea,
and often she walked with her friends
to amuse herself high up on the precipitous coast.
From there she saw many a ship and barge
sailing their courses, wherever they chose to go;
but then that added to her sorrow,
for she often said to herself, "Alas,
is there no ship of the many I see

Wol bringen hom my lord? Thanne were myn herte
Al warisshed of his bittre peynes smerte."
  Another tyme ther wolde she sitte and thinke
And caste hir eyen dounward fro the brinke;   130
But whan she saugh the grisly rokkes blake,
For verray fere so wolde hir herte quake
That on hir feet she mighte hir noght sustene.
Thanne wolde she sitte adoun upon the grene
And pitously into the see biholde,
And seyn right thus, with sorweful sykes colde:
  "Eterne God, that thurgh thy purveyaunce
Ledest the world by certein governaunce,
In ydel, as men seyn, ye nothing make;
But, Lord, thise grisly feendly rokkes blake,   140
That semen rather a foul confusioun
Of werk than any fair creacioun
Of swich a parfit wys God and a stable,
Why han ye wroght this werk unresonable?
For by this werk, south, north, ne west, ne eest,
Ther nis y-fostered man, ne brid, ne beest;
It dooth no good, to my wit, but anoyeth.
See ye nat, Lord, how mankinde it destroyeth?
An hundred thousand bodies of mankinde
Han rokkes slayn, al be they nat in minde,   150
Which mankinde is so fair part of thy werk
That thou it madest lyk to thyn owene merk.
Thanne semed it ye hadde a greet chiertee
Toward mankinde; but how thanne may it be
That ye swiche menes make it to destroyen,
Which menes do no good, but ever anoyen?
I woot wel clerkes wol seyn, as hem leste,
By arguments, that al is for the beste,
Though I ne can the causes nat y-knowe.
But thilke God that made wind to blowe,   160
As kepe my lord! This my conclusioun;
To clerkes lete I al disputisoun.
But wolde God that alle thise rokkes blake
Were sonken into helle for his sake!
Thise rokkes sleen myn herte for the fere."
Thus wolde she seyn, with many a pitous tere.
  Hir freendes sawe that it was no disport
To romen by the see, but disconfort;
And shopen for to pleyen somwher elles.
They leden hir by riveres and by welles,   170

which will bring home my lord? Then my heart would be
all healed of its keen and bitter pain."

Another time she would sit there thinking,
and direct her eyes down from the cliff edge;
but when she saw the grisly black rocks,
her heart would quake so for pure fear
that she couldn't keep on her feet.
Then she would sit down on the grass
and piteously look at the sea,
and say, with sorrowful, bitter sighs,

"Eternal God, Who through Your providence
guides the world with sure control,
men say You make nothing in vain;
but, Lord, these grisly, hostile black rocks,
which seem to be a vile, confused work
rather than any fair creation
of a God so perfect, wise, and stable—
why have You made this unreasonable thing?
For neither south, north, west, nor east
does this work help man, bird, or beast;
to my mind it does harm, not good.
Don't you see, Lord, how it destroys mankind?
Rocks have slain a hundred thousand men,
although out of memory,
and mankind is so fair a part of Your work
that You made it in Your own image.
At that time, it seemed that You had a great charity
toward mankind; but how then may it be
that You create such means to destroy it,
which means do no good, but always do harm?
I know quite well learned men will say, as they like,
with arguments, that all is for the best,
although I cannot know the causes.
But may the God that made the winds to blow
keep my lord safe! This is my conclusion;
to learned men I leave all argument.
But would to God that all these black rocks
were sunk into hell for his sake!
These rocks destroy my heart with fear."
Thus, with many a piteous tear, she would speak.

Her friends saw that it was no diversion
for her to roam by the sea, but a discomfort;
and they arranged to amuse themselves elsewhere.
They led her by rivers and wells,

And eek in othere places delitables;
They dauncen and they pleyen at ches and tables.
  So on a day, right in the morwe-tyde,
Unto a gardin that was ther bisyde,
In which that they hadde maad hir ordinaunce
Of vitaille and of other purveyaunce,
They goon and pleye hem al the longe day.
And this was on the sixte morwe of May,
Which May had peynted with his softe shoures
This gardin ful of leves and of floures;   180
And craft of mannes hand so curiously
Arrayed hadde this gardin, trewely,
That never was ther gardin of swich prys,
But if it were the verray paradys.
Th' odour of floures and the fresshe sighte
Wolde han maked any herte lighte
That ever was born, but if to gret siknesse
Or to gret sorwe helde it in distresse,
So ful it was of beautee with pleasaunce.
At after-dinner gonne they to daunce,   190
And singe also, save Dorigen allone,
Which made alwey hir compleint and hir mone,
For she ne saugh him on the daunce go,
That was hir housbonde and hir love also.
But nathelees she moste a tyme abyde,
And with good hope lete hir sorwe slyde.
  Upon this daunce, amonges othere men,
Daunced a squyer biforen Dorigen
That fressher was and jolyer of array,
As to my doom, than is the monthe of May.   200
He singeth, daunceth, passinge any man
That is, or was, sith that the world bigan.
Therwith he was, if men sholde him discryve,
Oon of the beste faringe man on lyve:
Yong, strong, right vertuous, and riche and wys,
And wel biloved, and holden in gret prys.
And shortly, if the sothe I tellen shal,
Unwiting of this Dorigen at al,
This lusty squyer, servant to Venus,
Which that y-cleped was Aurelius,   210
Hadde loved hir best of any creature
Two yeer and more, as was his aventure,
But never dorste he tellen hir his grevaunce;
Withouten coppe he drank al his penaunce.

and in other delightful places too;
they danced and they played at chess and backgammon.
     So one day, early in the morning,
they went to a garden that was close by,
in which they had made their arrangements
for food and other supplies,
and enjoyed themselves all day long.
This was on the sixth morning of May,
and May, with his soft showers, had painted
this garden full of leaves and flowers;
and the craft of man's hand had so skillfully
set out this garden that there
really never was one so precious,
unless it were paradise itself.
The scent and the fresh sight of flowers
would have lightened any heart
that ever was born, unless too great sickness
or too great sorrow held it in distress,
it was so full of beauty and pleasure.
After dinner they went on to dance,
and sing too, save only Dorigen,
who mourned and lamented constantly
because she couldn't see among the dancers him
who was her husband and also her love.
But nonetheless she had to remain a while,
and, hopefully, let her sorrow slip away.
     Among other men in this dance,
a squire danced before Dorigen
who was fresher and gayer in his attire,
in my opinion, than the month of May.
He sang and danced surpassing anyone
that is or was since the world began.
Besides, he was, if one should describe him,
one of the handsomest men alive:
young, strong, right virtuous, and rich and prudent,
and well-loved, and held in great esteem.
And, if I am to tell the truth, in brief it was this:
completely without Dorigen's knowledge
the lusty squire, who was called Aurelius,
as a servant of Venus had loved Dorigen
best of any creature for more than two years,
as it chanced to fall to his lot;
but he never dared tell her his sorrow;
he drank up all his penance without a cup.

He was despeyred, no thing dorste he seye,
Save in his songes somwhat wolde he wreye
His wo, as in a general compleynyng:
He seyde he lovede, and was biloved no thing;
Of swich matere made he manye layes,
Songes, compleintes, roundels, virelayes,   220
How that he dorste nat his sorwe telle,
But languissheth, as a furie dooth in helle;
And dye he moste, he seyde, as dide Ekko
For Narcisus, that dorste nat telle hir wo.
In other manere than ye here me seye
Ne dorste he nat to hir his wo biwreye,
Save that, paraventure, som tyme at daunces,
Ther yonge folk kepen hir observaunces,
It may wel be he loked on hir face
In swich a wyse as man that asketh grace;   230
But no thing wiste she of his entente.
Nathelees, it happed, er they thennes wente,
By cause that he was hir neighebour
And was a man of worship and honour,
And hadde y-knowen him of tyme yore,
They fille in speche; and forthe, more and more,
Unto his purpos drough Aurelius,
And whan he saugh his tyme, he seyde thus:
   "Madame," quod he, "by God that this world made,
So that I wiste it mighte your herte glade,   240
I wolde that day that your Arveragus
Wente over the see, that I, Aurelius,
Hadde went ther never I sholde have come agayn;
For wel I woot my service is in vayn.
My gerdon is but bresting of myn herte.
Madame, reweth upon my peynes smerte,
For with a word ye may me sleen or save;
Heer at your feet God wolde that I were grave!
I ne have as now no leyser more to seye;
Have mercy, swete, or ye wol do me deye!"   250
   She gan to loke upon Aurelius:
"Is this your wil," quod she, "and sey ye thus?
Never erst," quod she, "ne wiste I what ye mente.
But now, Aurelie, I knowe your entente,
By thilke God that yaf me soule and lyf,
Ne shal I never been untrewe wyf
In word ne werk, as fer as I have wit:
I wol ben his to whom that I am knit;

He was in despair; he dared say nothing,
except that in his songs he would disclose
his woe somewhat, as in a general lament:
he said he loved, and was not at all beloved;
of such matter he made many lays,
songs, complaints, roundelays, virelays—
about how he dared not tell his sorrow,
but languished, as a fury does in hell;
and he must die, he said, as Echo,
who dared not tell her woe, did for Narcissus.
In other ways than you have heard me say
he did not dare reveal his woe to her;
except that, perhaps, sometimes at dances,
where young folks perform their devotions,
it may well be he looked into her face
in the manner of a man who asks for favor;
but she knew nothing of his intention.
Nonetheless, before they went from the garden it happened
that, since he was her neighbor
and was a man of reputation and honor
and she had known him from long ago,
they fell into conversation; and Aurelius
drew nearer and nearer to his purpose;
and when he saw an opportunity he spoke as follows: -

   "Madame," said he, "by God that made this world,
if I knew that it might gladden your heart,
I wish that on that day when your Arveragus
went over the sea, I, Aurelius,
had gone where I should never have returned again;
for well I know my service is in vain.
My reward is only heartbreak.
Madame, have pity on my bitter pains,
for with a word you can slay or save me;
would to God I were buried here at your feet!
I have no leisure now to say more;
have mercy, sweet, or you will cause my death."
   She looked at Aurelius:
"Is this what you want," said she, "and do you say thus?
Never before," she said, "did I know what you had in mind.
But now that I know your intention, Aurelius,
by that God that gave me soul and life,
I will never be an unfaithful wife
in word or deed, as far as I can manage:
I will be his to whom I am knit;

Tak this for fynal answer as of me."
But after that in pley thus seyde she: 260
"Aurelie," quod she, "by heighe God above,
Yet wolde I graunte yow to been your love,
Sin I yow see so pitously complayne:
Loke what day that endelong Britayne
Ye remoeve alle the rokkes, stoon by stoon,
That they ne lette ship ne boot to goon—
I seye, whan ye han maad the coost so clene
Of rokkes that ther nis no stoon y-sene,
Thanne wol I love yow best of any man;
Have heer my trouthe in al that ever I can."   270
"Is ther non other grace in yow?" quod he.
"No, by that Lord," quod she, "that maked me!
For wel I woot that it shal never bityde.
Lat swiche folies out of your herte slyde.
What deyntee sholde a man han in his lyf
For to go love another mannes wyf,
That hath hir body whan so that him lyketh?"
      Aurelius ful ofte sore syketh;
Wo was Aurelie, whan that he this herde,
And with a sorweful herte he thus answerde: 280
      "Madame," quod he, "this were an inpossible!
Thanne moot I dye of sodein deth horrible."
And with that word he turned him anoon.
Tho come hir othere freendes many oon
And in the aleyes romeden up and doun,
And no thing wiste of this conclusioun,
But sodeinly bigonne revel newe
Til that the brighte sonne loste his hewe;
For th'orisonte hath reft the sonne his light—
This is as muche to seye as it was night.   290
And hoom they goon in joye and in solas,
Save only wrecche Aurelius, allas!
He to his hous is goon with sorweful herte;
He seeth he may nat fro his deeth asterte.
Him semed that he felt his herte colde;
Up to the hevene his handes he gan holde,
And on his knowes bare he sette him doun,
And in his raving seyde his orisoun—
For verray wo out of his wit he breyde.
He niste what he spak, but thus he seyde;   300
With pitous herte his pleynt hath he bigonne
Unto the goddes, and first unto the sonne:

take this for my final answer."
But after that she spoke playfully:

"Aurelius," said she, "by high God above,
yet I would like to consent to be your love,
since I see you so piteously complain:
look to the day that along the length of Brittany
you remove all the rocks, stone by stone,
so that they do not hinder any ship or boat from sailing—
I say, when you have so cleared the coast
of rocks that there is no stone to be seen,
then I will love you best of any man;
here is my word of honor as firm as can be."
"Will you not grant me favor otherwise?" he asked.
"No," she said, "by that God that made me!
For well I know that it shall never happen.
Let such follies slide from your heart.
What kind of joy can a man have in life
if he goes and loves the wife of another man,
who has her body whenever he pleases?"

Aurelius sighed sorely again and again;
woeful was he when he had heard this,
and with a sorrowful heart he answered,
"Madame, this is an impossibility!
I must, then, die a sudden and horrible death."
And with those words he turned away at once.
Then came many of her other friends
and they strolled up and down the paths,
but they knew nothing of this conversation;
quickly they began new revelry,
lasting until the bright sun faded;
for the horizon had bereft the sun of his light—
this is as much as to say it was night.
And home they went in joy and delight,
save only wretched Aurelius, alas!
He went to his house with a sorrowful heart;
he saw that he could not escape his death,
it seemed to him he felt his heart grow cold;
he held his hands up to heaven
and set himself down on his bare knees,
and in his raving said his prayers—
he was going out of his mind with pure grief.
He did not know what he spoke, but this is what he said;
with piteous heart he began his complaint
to the gods, and first to the sun:

He seyde, "Appollo, god and governour
Of every plaunte, herbe, tree and flour,
That yevest, after thy declinacioun,
To ech of hem his tyme and his sesoun,
As thyn herberwe chaungeth lowe or hye,
Lord Phebus, cast thy merciable yë
On wrecche Aurelie, which that am but lorn.
Lo, lord! My lady hath my deeth y-sworn   310
Withoute gilt, but thy benignitee
Upon my dedly herte have some pitee!
For wel I woot, lord Phebus, if yow lest,
Ye may me helpen, save my lady, best.
Now voucheth sauf that I may yow devyse
How that I may been holpe and in what wyse.

    Your blisful suster, Lucina the shene,
That of the see is chief godesse and quene—
Though Neptunus have deitee in the see,
Yet emperesse aboven him is she: 320
Ye knowen wel, lord, that right as hir desyr
Is to be quiked and lighted of your fyr,
For which she folweth yow ful bisily,
Right so the see desyreth naturelly
To folwen hir, as she that is goddesse
Bothe in the see and riveres more and lesse.
Wherfore, lord Phebus, this is my requeste—
Do this miracle, or do myn herte breste—
That now, next at this opposicioun,
Which in the signe shal be of the Leoun,   330
As preyeth hir so greet a flood to bringe
That fyve fadme at the leeste it overspringe
The hyeste rokke in Armorik Briteyne,
And lat this flood endure yeres tweyne;
Thanne certes to my lady may I seye:
'Holdeth your heste, the rokkes been aweye.'

    Lord Phebus, dooth this miracle for me:
Preye hir she go no faster cours than ye;
I seye, preyeth your suster that she go
No faster cours than ye thise yeres two   340
Thanne shal she been evene atte fulle alway,
And spring-flood laste bothe night and day.
And, but she vouche-sauf in swiche manere
To graunte me my sovereyn lady dere,
Prey hir to sinken every rok adoun
Into hir owene derke regioun

He said, "Apollo, god and ruler
of every plant, herb, tree and flower,
who give to each of them its time and its season
according to your position—
as your dwelling changes, low or high—
lord Phoebus, cast your merciful eyes
on wretched Aurelius, who is but lost.
See, lord, my lady has sworn my death,
although I am guiltless, unless your beneficence
have some pity on my dying heart!
For well I know, lord Phoebus, that if you wish
you, next to my lady, can help me best.
Allow me to tell you now
how I can be helped, and in what way.

Concerning your blissful sister, Lucina* the bright,
who is chief goddess and queen of the sea
(although Neptune has dominion of the sea,
yet she is empress above him),
you know well, lord, that just as her desire
is to be quickened and lighted by your fire
(for which reason she follows you constantly),
just so the sea naturally desires
to follow her, as the goddess who rules
both the sea and the rivers, greater and less.
Therefore, lord Phoebus, this is my request—
perform this miracle, or let my heart break—
when you are next in opposition,
in the sign of the Lion,
pray her to bring so great a flood
that at the very least it shall rise five fathoms
over the highest rock in Armorican Brittany,
and let this flood last two years;
then certainly I can say to my lady,
'Keep your promise, the rocks are gone.'

Lord Phoebus, perform this miracle for me:
pray her to go no faster a course than you;
I say pray your sister to make
no faster a course than you for these two years:
then she will always be just at the full,
and spring tide shall last both day and night.
And, unless she will deign to grant
me my dear sovereign lady in this way,
pray her to sink every rock down
into her own dark region

Under the ground, ther Pluto dwelleth inne,
Or nevere mo shal I my lady winne.
Thy temple in Delphos wol I barefoot seke;
Lord Phebus, see the teres on my cheke,   350
And of my peyne have som compassioun,"
And with that word in swowne he fil adoun,
And longe tyme he lay forth in a traunce.
    His brother, which that knew of his penaunce,
Up caughte him and to bedde he hath him broght.
Dispeyred in this torment and this thoght
Lete I this woful creature lye;
Chese he, for me, whether he wol live or dye.
    Arveragus, with hele and greet honour,
As he that was of chivalrye the flour,   360
Is comen hoom, and othere worthy men.
O blisful artow now, thou Dorigen,
That hast thy lusty housbonde in thyne armes,
The fresshe knight, the worthy man of armes,
That loveth thee as his owene hertes lyf.
No thing list him to been imaginatyf
If any wight had spoke, whyl he was oute,
To hire of love; he hadde of it no doute.
He noght entendeth to no swich matere,
But daunceth, justeth, maketh hir good chere;   370
And thus in joye and blisse I lete hem dwelle,
And of the syke Aurelius wol I telle.
    In langour and in torment furious
Two yeer and more lay wrecche Aurelius,
Er any foot he mighte on erthe goon;
Ne confort in this tyme hadde he noon,
Save of his brother, which that was a clerk:
He knew of al this wo and al this werk.
For to non other creature certeyn
Of this matere he dorste no word seyn;   380
Under his brest he bar it more secree
Than ever dide Pamphilus for Galathee.
His brest was hool withoute for to sene,
But in his herte ay was the arwe kene;
And wel ye knowe that of a sursanure
In surgerye is perilous the cure,
But men mighte touche the arwe or come therby.
His brother weep and wayled prively,
Til atte laste him fil in remembraunce
That whiles he was at Orliens in Fraunce,   390

under the ground, where Pluto dwells,
or I shall nevermore win my lady.
Barefoot I will seek out your temple in Delphos;
lord Phoebus, see the tears on my cheek,
and have some compassion on my pain."
And with those words he fell down in a swoon,
and for a long time he lay in a trance.

His brother, who knew of his suffering,
picked him up and brought him to bed.
I shall let this woeful creature lie
despairing in this torment and these imaginings;
let him choose, for my part, whether he will live or die.

Arveragus, with prosperity and great honor,
came home as the flower of chivalry,
and other worthy men with him.
Ah, Dorigen, you are blissful now,
with your lusty husband in your arms—
the vigorous knight, the valiant man of arms,
who loves you as his own heart's life.
He wasn't inclined to worry about
whether anyone had spoken to her of love
while he was gone; he had no doubts about it.
He paid no attention to such matters,
but danced, jousted, and entertained her;
and thus I leave them in joy and bliss,
and will tell you about the sick Aurelius.

In languor and furious torment
wretched Aurelius lay for more than two years
before he could walk a foot;
nor did he have any comfort in this time,
except from his brother, a scholar,
who knew of his woe and the whole business.
Of course Aurelius didn't dare say a word
about this matter to any other creature;
he bore his love more secretly within his breast
than Pamphilus ever did for Galathea.*
To outward appearance his heart was whole,
but within his breast the sharp arrow remained;
and as you well know, in surgery the cure of
a superficially healed wound is perilous
unless you can touch the arrow and get at it.
His brother wept and wailed in secret,
until at last he happened to remember
that while he was at Orleans in France,

As yonge clerkes that been likerous
To reden artes that been curious
Seken in every halke and every herne
Particuler sciences for to lerne,
He him remembred that, upon a day,
At Orliens in studie a book he say
Of magik naturel, which his felawe,
That was that tyme a bacheler of lawe,
Al were he ther to lerne another craft,
Had prively upon his desk y-laft;   400
Which book spak muchel of the operaciouns
Touchinge the eighte and twenty mansiouns
That longen to the mone, and swich folye,
As in our dayes is nat worth a flye;
For holy chirches feith in our bileve
Ne suffreth noon illusion us to greve.
And whan this book was in his remembraunce,
Anon for joye his herte gan to daunce,
And to himself he seyde prively,
"My brother shal be warisshed hastily;   410
For I am siker that ther be sciences
By whiche men make diverse apparences
Swiche as thise subtile tregetoures pleye.
For ofte at festes have I wel herd seye
That tregetours withinne an halle large
Have maad come in a water and a barge,
And in the halle rowen up and doun.
Somtyme hath semed come a grim leoun;
And somtyme floures springe as in a mede;
Somtyme a vyne, and grapes whyte and rede;   420
Somtyme a castel, al of lym and stoon;
And whan hem lyked, voyded it anoon.
Thus semed it to every mannes sighte.
   Now thanne conclude I thus, that if I mighte
At Orliens som old felawe y-finde
That hadde this mones mansions in minde,
Or other magik naturel above,
He sholde wel make my brother han his love;
For with an apparence a clerk may make
To mannes sighte that alle the rokkes blake   430
Of Britaigne weren y-voyded everichon,
And shippes by the brinke comen and gon,
And in swich forme enduren a day or two;
Thanne were my brother warisshed of his wo.

where young scholars who lust
to learn occult arts
seek in every nook and cranny
to learn esoteric sciences—
he remembered that one day
while studying at Orleans he saw a book
about natural* magic, which his comrade,
who was at that time a bachelor of law,
had privately left on his desk,
although he was there to learn another skill;
this book said much about the operations
concerning the twenty-eight mansions
of the moon, and such folly
as is not worth a fly nowadays;
for Holy Church's faith, which is in our Creed,
does not allow such illusions to grieve us.
And when he remembered this book,
at once his heart began to dance for joy,
and he said to himself secretly,
"My brother shall be quickly cured;
for I am sure that there are sciences
by means of which illusions can be made
such as these clever conjurers produce.
For I have indeed heard that at feasts
conjurers have often caused water
to come into a great hall, with a barge
that rowed up and down in the room.
Sometimes a grim lion has seemed to come;
and sometimes flowers spring up as in a meadow;
sometimes a vine, and grapes, white and red;
sometimes a castle, all of limestone and rock;
and when they pleased, the conjurers made everything vanish
immediately. Thus it seemed to every man's sight.

Now then, I conclude that if I could
find some old comrade at Orleans
who knew the mansions of the moon,
or other higher natural magic,
he would indeed arrange for my brother to have his love;
for with an illusion a learned man can make
it seem to men's sight that all the black rocks
of Brittany have disappeared—every one—
and that ships are coming and going by the brink;
this can last a day or two;
then my brother would be cured of his woe.

Thanne moste she nedes holden hir biheste,
Or elles he shal shame hir atte leste."
    What sholde I make a lenger tale of this?
Unto his brotheres bed he comen is,
And swich confort he yaf him for to gon
To Orliens that he up stirte anon,   440
And on his wey forthward thanne is he fare,
In hope for to ben lissed of his care.
    Whan they were come almost to that citee,
But if it were a two furlong or three,
A yong clerk rominge by himself they mette,
Which that in Latin thriftily hem grette,
And after that he seyde a wonder thing:
"I know," quod he, "the cause of your coming";
And er they ferther any fote wente
He tolde hem al that was in hir entente.   450
    This Briton clerk him asked of felawes
The whiche that he had knowe in olde dawes;
And he answerde him that they dede were,
For which he weep ful ofte many a tere.
    Doun of his hors Aurelius lighte anon,
And with this magicien forth is he gon
Hoom to his hous, and maden hem wel at ese.
Hem lakked no vitaille that mighte hem plese;
So wel arrayed hous as ther was oon
Aurelius in his lyf saugh never noon.   460
    He shewed him, er he wente to sopeer,
Forestes, parkes ful of wilde deer;
Ther saugh he hertes with hir hornes hye,
The gretteste that ever were seyn with yë.
He saugh of hem an hondred slayn with houndes,
And somme with arwes blede of bittre woundes.
He saugh, whan voided were thise wilde deer,
Thise fauconers upon a fair river
That with hir haukes han the heron slayn.
Tho saugh he knightes justing in a playn;   470
And after this, he dide him swich plesaunce
That he him shewed his lady on a daunce
On which himself he daunced, as him thoughte.
And whan this maister, that this magik wroughte,
Saugh it was tyme, he clapte his handes two,
And farewel—al our revel was ago.
And yet remoeved they never out of the hous
Whyl they saugh al this sighte merveillous,

Dorigen would have to keep her promise,
or else he will at least shame her."

Why should I make a longer tale of this?
He came to his brother's bed
and gave him such encouragement to go
to Orleans that Aurelius got up at once,
and then started forth on his way
hoping to be released from his sorrow.

When they had come almost to that city,
only about two or three furlongs from it,
they met a young scholar walking by himself
who greeted them properly in Latin,
and after that he said a remarkable thing:
"I know," said he, "the cause of your coming";
and before they went a foot further
he told them everything they had in mind.

The clerk from Brittany asked him about friends
whom he had known in old days;
and he answered that they were dead,
which made the brother weep many a tear.

Aurelius alighted from his horse quickly,
and went with this magician, who took them
home to his house and made them most comfortable.
They lacked no food that might please them;
Aurelius had never in his life seen
a house as well provided as this one was.

Before he went to supper, the magician showed him
forests and parks full of wild deer;
there he saw harts with their tall horns,
the largest that were ever seen.
He saw a hundred of them slain by hounds,
and some bled with cruel wounds from arrows.
He saw, when these wild deer had disappeared,
falconers on the bank of a beautiful river
who had killed a heron with their hawks.
Then he saw knights jousting on a plain;
and after this, the magician gave him the pleasure
of seeing his lady in a dance
in which he himself danced, as it seemed to him.
And when the master who had made this magic
saw it was time, he clapped his two hands
and farewell—all our revel was gone.
And yet they had never moved out of the house
while they saw all this marvelous sight,

But in his studie, theras his bookes be,
They seten stille, and no wight but they three.   480
   To him this maister called his squyer,
And seyde him thus: "Is redy our soper?
Almost an houre it is, I undertake,
Sith I yow bad our soper for to make,
Whan that thise worthy men wenten with me
Into my studie, theras my bookes be."
   "Sire," quod this squyer, "whan it lyketh yow,
It is al redy, though ye wol right now."
"Go we thanne soupe," quod he, "as for the beste;
This amorous folk som-tyme mote han hir reste."   490
   At after-soper fille they in tretee
What somme sholde this maistres gerdon be
To remoeven alle the rokkes of Britayne,
And eek from Gerounde to the mouth of Sayne.
   He made it straunge, and swoor, so God him save,
Lasse than a thousand pound he wolde nat have,
Ne gladly for that somme he wolde nat goon.
   Aurelius, with blisful herte anoon,
Answered thus, "Fy on a thousand pound!
This wyde world, which that men seye is round,   500
I wolde it yeve, if I were lord of it.
This bargayn is ful drive, for we ben knit.
Ye shal be payed trewely, by my trouthe!
But loketh now, for no necligence or slouthe,
Ye tarie us heer no lenger than tomorwe."
   "Nay," quod this clerk, "have heer my feith to borwe."
   To bedde is goon Aurelius whan him leste,
And wel ny al that night he hadde his reste;
What for his labour and his hope of blisse,
His woful herte of penaunce hadde a lisse.   510
   Upon the morwe, whan that it was day,
To Britaigne toke they the righte way,
Aurelius and this magicien bisyde,
And been descended ther they wolde abyde;
And this was, as thise bokes me remembre,
The colde frosty seson of Decembre.
   Phebus wax old and hewed lyk latoun,
That in his hote declinacioun
Shoon as the burned gold with stremes brighte;
But now in Capricorn adoun he lighte,   520
Wheras he shoon ful pale, I dar wel seyn.
The bittre frostes, with the sleet and reyn,

but had sat still in his study, where his books were,
and no one else but the three of them.

This master called his squire to him
and spoke to him thus: "Is our supper ready?
It is almost an hour, I'm sure,
since I told you to make our supper;
it was then that these worthy men went with me
into my study, where my books are."

"Sir," said the squire, "when it pleases you—
it is all ready, even if you want it right now."
"Then let us go and eat," said he, "as it is best;
these amorous folk must sometime have their rest."

After supper they fell to bargaining
about what sum this master's reward should be
for removing all the rocks of Brittany
and also from the Gironde to the mouth of the Seine.

He made difficulties, and swore, as God might save him,
he would not have less than a thousand pounds—
nor would he go gladly for that sum.

Aurelius, then, with a blissful heart,
answered, "Fie on a thousand pounds!
If I were lord of this wide world,
which is said to be round, I would give it.
This bargain is fully driven, for we are agreed.
You shall be faithfully paid, on my honor!
But now see that you don't, through negligence or sloth,
cause us to tarry here any longer than tomorrow."

"No," said this clerk, "I give you my word."

Aurelius went to bed in due time,
and he had his rest almost all that night;
what with his labor and his hope of bliss,
his troubled heart had some release from suffering.

In the morning, when it was day,
they took the direct road to Brittany,
Aurelius and this magician beside him,
and dismounted when they had arrived at their journey's
end; and this was, as the books remind me,
the cold, frosty season of December.

Phoebus grew old and brassy-colored;
in his hot position he had
shone with bright rays like burnished gold,
but now he lighted down in Capricorn,
where I dare indeed to say he shone quite pale.
The bitter frosts, with the sleet and rain,

Destroyed hath the grene in every yerd.
Janus sit by the fyr with double berd,
And drinketh of his bugle-horn the wyn;
Biforn him stant braun of the tusked swyn,
And "Nowell" cryeth every lusty man.
　　Aurelius, in al that ever he can,
Doth to his maister chere and reverence,
And preyeth him to doon his diligence   530
To bringen him out of his peynes smerte,
Or with a swerd that he wolde slitte his herte.
　　This subtil clerk swich routhe had of this man
That night and day he spedde him that he can,
To wayten a tyme of his conclusioun;
This is to seye, to make illusioun,
By swich an apparence or jogelrye
(I ne can no termes of astrologye)
That she and every wight sholde wene and seye
That of Britaigne the rokkes were aweye,   540
Or elles they were sonken under grounde.
So atte laste he hath his tyme y-founde
To maken his japes and his wrecchednesse
Of swich a supersticious cursednesse.
His tables Toletanes forth he broght
Ful wel corrected, ne ther lakked noght,
Neither his collect ne his expans yeres,
Ne his rotes ne his othere geres,
As been his centres and his arguments,
And his proporcionels convenients   550
For his equacions in every thing;
And, by his eighte spere in his wirking,
He knew ful wel how fer Alnath was shove
Fro the heed of thilke fixe Aries above
That in the ninthe speere considered is;
Ful subtilly he calculed al this.
　　Whan he hadde founde his firste mansioun,
He knew the remenant by proporcioun,
And knew the arysing of his mone weel,
And in whos face and terme and every deel,   560
And knew ful weel the mones mansioun
Acordaunt to his operacioun,
And knew also his othere observaunces
For swiche illusiouns and swiche meschaunces
As hethen folk useden in thilke dayes;
For which no lenger maked he delayes,

have destroyed the green in every yard.
Janus* with his double beard sits by the fire
and drinks the wine from his wild ox horn;
before him stands flesh of the tusked swine,
and every lusty man cries out, "Nowell!"

Aurelius honored and entertained his master
in every way he could,
and begged him to do his utmost
to bring him out of his bitter pains;
otherwise he would stab himself in the heart with a sword.

The clever clerk had such pity for this man
that night and day he hurried as best he could
to find a time for his purpose;
that is to say, to make an illusion,
by such an apparition or jugglery—
I don't know any astrological terms—
that Dorigen and everyone else would both think and say
that all the rocks of Brittany were gone,
or else that they had sunk under the ground.
So at last he found his time
to do his tricks and this superstitiously
wicked, wretched business.
He brought out his astronomical tables of Toledo,*
properly corrected; nothing was lacking,
neither his collect nor his expanse* years,
nor his roots* nor his other gear,
such as his centers* and his arguments
and his tables of proportions
for all his equations of all kinds;
and by the precession of the eighth sphere he well
knew how far Alnath (in the head of the Ram) had moved
from the head of the theoretical, fixed Ram higher up,
which is considered to be in the ninth sphere;
he calculated all this most skillfully.

When he had found the first position of the moon,
he knew the rest by the use of proportion,
and understood well the arising of the moon
and in which planet's face and term, and everything else,
and he knew quite well the position of the moon
which was in accordance with his purpose,
and also knew the other rules
for illusions and such mischief
as was practiced by heathen folk in those days;
so that now he made no further delay,

But thurgh his magik, for a wyke or tweye,
It semed that alle the rokkes were aweye.
  Aurelius, which that yet despeired is
Wher he shal han his love or fare amis,   570
Awaiteth night and day on this miracle;
And whan he knew that ther was noon obstacle,
That voided were thise rokkes everichon,
Doun to his maistres feet he fil anon,
And seyde, "I woful wrecche, Aurelius,
Thanke yow, lord, and lady myn Venus,
That me han holpen fro my cares colde";
And to the temple his wey forth hath he holde,
Wheras he knew he sholde his lady see.
And whan he saugh his tyme, anon right he,   580
With dredful herte and with ful humble chere,
Salewed hath his sovereyn lady dere:
  "My righte lady," quod this woful man,
"Whom I most drede and love as I best can,
And lothest were of al this world displese,
Nere it that I for yow have swich disese
That I moste dyen heer at your foot anon,
Noght wolde I telle how me is wo bigon;
But certes outher moste I dye or pleyne;
Ye slee me giltelees for verray peyne.   590
But of my deeth thogh that ye have no routhe,
Avyseth yow, er that ye breke your trouthe.
Repenteth yow, for thilke God above,
Er ye me sleen by cause that I yow love.
For madame, wel ye woot what ye han hight—
Nat that I chalange any thing of right
Of yow my sovereyn lady, but your grace;
But in a gardin yond, at swich a place,
Ye woot right wel what ye bihighten me;
And in myn hand your trouthe plighten ye   600
To love me best, God woot, ye seyde so,
Al be that I unworthy be therto.
Madame, I speke it for the honour of yow,
More than to save myn hertes lyf right now;
I have do so as ye comanded me,
And if ye vouche-sauf, ye may go see.
Doth as yow list, have your biheste in minde,
For quik or deed, right ther ye shal me finde;
In yow lyth al, to do me live or deye,
But wel I woot the rokkes been aweye."   610

but through his magic, for a week or two
it seemed that all the rocks were gone.

Aurelius, who was still in despair over
whether he would have his love or not,
waited night and day for this miracle;
and when he knew that there was no obstacle,
that every one of these rocks had disappeared,
he fell down at his master's feet at once
and said, "I, Aurelius, woeful wrētch,
thank you, lord, and my lady Venus,
who have helped me from my bitter cares":
and he took his way to the temple,
where he knew he would see his lady.
As soon as he saw an opportunity,
with fearful heart and a humble manner he
greeted his dear and sovereign lady:

"My own true lady," this woeful man said,
"Whom I most fear and love as best I can,
and would be of all this world most loath to displease:
if I were not so sick with love for you
that I am dying here at your feet,
I would tell you nothing of how woebegone I am;
but indeed, I shall die if I do not speak;
you kill me with pain, innocent as I am.
But although you have no pity on my death,
consider before you break your promise.
Repent, for the sake of God above,
before you slay me because I love you.
For, madame, well you know what you promised—
not that I claim anything as a right
from you, my sovereign lady, except your grace;
but in a garden yonder, at such a place,
you know right well what you promised me;
putting your hand in mine, you plighted your word
to love me best; God knows you said so,
although I am unworthy of it.
Madame, I speak it for the sake of your honor
more than to save my heart's life at this moment;
I have done as you commanded me,
and if you will, you can go and see.
Do as you please, have your pledge in mind,
for you shall find me, alive or dead, right there;
it is up to you, to make me live or die:
but well I know that the rocks are gone."

He taketh his leve, and she astonied stood;
In al hir face nas a drope of blood.
She wende never han come in swich a trappe:
"Allas!" quod she, "that evere this sholde happe!
For wende I never, by possibilitee,
That swich a monstre or merveille mighte be;
It is agayns the proces of nature."
And hoom she gooth a sorweful creature.
For verray fere unnethe may she go:
She wepeth, wailleth, al a day or two,   620
And swowneth, that it routhe was to see;
But why it was to no wight tolde she,
For out of toune was goon Arveragus.
But to hirself she spak, and seyde thus,
With face pale and with ful sorweful chere,
In hir compleynt, as ye shal after here:

"Allas," quod she, "on thee, Fortune, I pleyne,
That unwar wrapped hast me in thy cheyne;
For which t'escape woot I no socour
Save only deeth or elles dishonour;   630
Oon of thise two bihoveth me to chese.
But natheless, yet have I lever lese
My lyf than of my body have a shame,
Or knowe myselven fals, or lese my name,
And with my deth I may be quit, ywis.
Hath ther nat many a noble wyf, er this,
And many a mayde y-slayn hirself, allas,
Rather than with hir body doon trespas?

Yis, certes, lo, thise stories beren witnesse;
Whan thretty tyraunts, ful of cursednesse,   640
Hadde slayn Phidoun in Athenes, atte feste,
They comanded his doghtres for t'areste,
And bringen hem biforn hem in despyt
Al naked, to fulfille hir foul delyt,
And in hir fadres blood they made hem daunce
Upon the pavement, God yeve hem mischaunce!
For which thise woful maydens, ful of drede,
Rather than they wolde lese hir maydenhede,
They prively ben stirt into a welle,
And dreynte hemselven, as the bokes telle.   650

They of Messene lete enquere and seke
Of Lacedomie fifty maydens eke,
On whiche they wolden doon hir lecherye;
But was ther noon of al that companye

He took his leave, and she stood astonished;
in all her face there was not a drop of blood.
She had never expected to fall into such a trap:
"Alas," she said, "that ever this should happen!
For I never imagined it possible
that such a freak or marvel could be;
it is against the process of nature."
And she went home, a sorrowful creature.
She could scarcely walk for dread:
she wept, she wailed, all through a day or two,
and swooned so that it was pitiful to see;
but she told no one why this was,
for Arveragus had gone out of town.
But she spoke to herself, with a pale face
and most sorrowful expression, saying
in her lament, as you shall hear:

"Alas, I complain against you, Fortune,
who have tied me, all unwary, in your chain,
from which I know of no way to escape
except only death or else dishonor;
I must choose one of these two.
But nevertheless, I would still rather lose
my life than be shamed in my body,
or know myself false, or lose my good name;
and with my death I can be freed, indeed.
Has not many a noble wife before this—
and many a maiden—slain herself, alas,
rather than sin with her body?

Yes, surely; see, these stories bear witness;
when thirty tyrants, full of wickedness,
had slain Phidon* at a feast in Athens,
they commanded his daughters to be arrested
and brought before them for scorn,
all naked, to fulfill their foul delight;
and they made them dance on the pavement
in their father's blood—God give them misfortune!
And so these woeful maidens, full of fear,
jumped secretly into a well
and drowned themselves rather than lose
their virginity, as the books tell us.

The men of Messene also sought out
fifty maidens of Lacedaemonia,
on whom they wished to work their lechery;
but there was none of all that group

That she nas slayn, and with a good entente
Chees rather for to dye than assente
To been oppressed of hir maydenhede.
Why sholde I thanne to dye been in drede?
  Lo, eek, the tiraunt Aristoclides,
That loved a mayden heet Stimphalides,   660
Whan that hir fader slayn was on a night,
Unto Dianes temple goth she right
And hente the image in hir handes two,
Fro which image wolde she never go.
No wight ne mighte hir handes of it arace,
Til she was slayn right in the selve place.
Now sith that maydens hadden swich despyt
To been defouled with mannes foul delyt,
Wel oghte a wyf rather hirselven slee
Than be defouled, as it thinketh me.   670
  What shal I seyn of Hasdrubales wyf,
That at Cartage birafte hirself hir lyf?
For whan she saugh that Romayns wan the toun,
She took hir children alle and skipte adoun
Into the fyr, and chees rather to dye
Than any Romayn dide hir vileinye.
  Hath nat Lucresse y-slayn hirself, allas,
At Rome whan that she oppressed was
Of Tarquin, for hir thoughte it was a shame
To liven whan that she hadde lost hir name?   680
  The sevene maydens of Milesie also
Han slayn hemself for verray drede and wo
Rather than folk of Gaule hem sholde oppresse.
Mo than a thousand stories, as I gesse,
Coude I now telle as touchinge this matere.
  Whan Habradate was slayn, his wyf so dere
Hirselven slow, and leet hir blood to glyde
In Habradates woundes depe and wyde,
And seyde, 'My body, at the leeste way,
Ther shal no wight defoulen, if I may.'   690
  What sholde I mo ensamples heerof sayn,
Sith that so manye han hemselven slayn
Wel rather than they wolde defouled be?
I wol conclude that it is bet for me
To sleen myself than been defouled thus.
I wol be trewe unto Arveragus,
Or rather sleen myself in som manere,
As dide Demociones doghter dere,

that was not slain, choosing with a good intent
to die rather than consent
to be ravished of her maidenhood.
Why then should I be afraid to die?

   Consider, too, the tyrant Aristoclides,
who loved a maiden called Stymphalis;
when her father was slain one night,
she went right to Diana's temple
and seized the image in her two hands;
she would never go from this image.
No one could tear her hands from it
until she was slain right in that same place.
Now since maidens were so reluctant
to be defiled with man's foul delight,
a wife surely ought to slay herself rather
than be defiled, it seems to me.

   What shall I say of Hasdrubal's wife,
who took her own life at Carthage?
For when she saw the Romans win the town,
she took all her children and jumped down
into the fire, and chose to die rather
than have any Roman dishonor her.

   Did not Lucrece slay herself, alas,
at Rome when she was ravished
by Tarquin, since she thought it was shameful
to live when she had lost her good name?

   Also the seven maidens of Miletus
slew themselves for very fear and woe,
rather than have the men of Gaul ravish them.
I could tell more than a thousand stories,
I believe, touching this matter.

   When Abradates was slain, his dear wife
slew herself, and let her blood flow
into Abradates' deep, wide wounds,
and said, 'My body, at least,
shall be defiled by no one, if I can help it.'

   Why should I recite more examples of this,
since so many have slain themselves
rather than be defiled?
I shall conclude that it is better for me
to slay myself than to be so defiled.
I will be true to Arveragus,
or else slay myself in some way,
as Demotion's dear daughter did

By cause that she wolde nat defouled be.
  O Cedasus, it is ful greet pitee   700
To reden how thy doghtren deyde, allas,
That slowe hemself for swich maner cas.
  As greet a pitee was it, or wel more,
The Theban mayden that for Nichanore
Hirselven slow, right for swich maner wo.
  Another Theban mayden dide right so;
For oon of Macedonie hadde hir oppressed,
She with hir deeth hir maydenhede redressed.
  What shal I seye of Nicerates wyf,
That for swich cas birafte hirself hir lyf?   710
  How trewe eek was to Alcebiades
His love, that rather for to dyen chees
Than for to suffre his body unburied be!
  Lo which a wyf was Alceste," quod she.
"What seith Omer of gode Penalopee?
Al Grece knoweth of hir chastitee.
  Pardee, of Laodomya is writen thus,
That whan at Troye was slayn Protheselaus
No lenger wolde she live after his day.
  The same of noble Porcia telle I may;   720
Withoute Brutus coude she nat live,
To whom she hadde al hool hir herte yive.
  The parfit wyfhod of Arthemesye
Honoured is thurgh al the Barbarye.
  O Teuta queene, thy wyfly chastitee
To alle wyves may a mirour be.
  The same thing I seye of Biliea,
Of Rodogone and eek Valeria."
  Thus pleyned Dorigene a day or tweye,
Purposinge ever that she wolde deye.   730
But nathelees, upon the thridde night
Hom cam Arveragus, this worthy knight,
And asked hir why that she weep so sore,
And she gan wepen ever lenger the more.
  "Allas!" quod she, "that evere was I born!
Thus have I seyd," quod she, "thus have I sworn—"
And told him al as ye han herd bifore;
It nedeth nat reherce it yow namore.
  This housbond with glad chere in freendly wyse
Answerde and seyde as I shal yow devyse: 740
"Is ther oght elles, Dorigen, but this?"
  "Nay, nay," quod she, "God help me so as wis;

because she didn't want to be defiled.

O Scedasus, it is very pitiful
to read how your daughters died, alas,
who slew themselves in such a case.

Just as pitiful, or even more so,
was the Theban maiden who slew herself
because of Nicanor, in just this sort of trouble.

Another Theban maiden did just the same;
because a Macedonian had ravished her,
she avenged her maidenhood with her death.
What shall I say of Nicerates' wife,
who took her own life in such a case?
How true, also, was the beloved of
Alcibiades, who chose to die rather
than allow his body to lie unburied!

See what a wife Alcestis was," said she.
"What does Homer say of good Penelope?
All Greece knows of her chastity.

By heaven, it is written of Laodamia
that when Protesilaus was killed at Troy
she would no longer live after his death.
I can say the same of noble Portia;
she could not live without Brutus,
to whom she had given her whole heart.
The perfect wifehood of Artemisia
is honored in all barbarian countries.

O Teuta, queen, your wifely chastity
should be a mirror to all wives.
I say the same thing of Bilia,
of Rhodogone and Valeria too."

Thus Dorigen lamented a day or two,
resolving always that she would die.
But nevertheless, on the third night
Arveragus, the worthy knight, came home,
and asked her why she wept so sorely,
and she began to weep all the more.

"Alas," said she, "that ever I was born!
I have said this," she said, "I have sworn thus—"
and told him everything as you have heard before;
there is no need to repeat it to you.

Cheerfully and amicably this husband
answered as I shall tell you:
"Is there anything else, Dorigen, but this?"

"No, no," she said, "God help me indeed;

This is to muche, and it were Goddes wille."
"Ye, wyf," quod he, "lat slepen that is stille;
It may be wel, paraventure, yet today.
Ye shul your trouthe holden, by my fay!
For God so wisly have mercy upon me,
I hadde wel lever y-stiked for to be,
For verray love which that I to yow have,
But if ye sholde your trouthe kepe and save.   750
Trouthe is the hyeste thing that man may kepe."
But with that word he brast anon to wepe,
And seyde, "I yow forbede, up peyne of deeth,
That nevere whyl thee lasteth lyf ne breeth,
To no wight tell thou of this aventure.
As I may best, I wol my wo endure,
Ne make no contenance of hevinesse,
That folk of yow may demen harm or gesse."
    And forth he cleped a squyer and a mayde:
"Goth forth anon with Dorigen," he sayde,   760
"And bringeth hir to swich a place anon."
They take hir leve and on hir wey they gon,
But they ne wiste why she thider wente.
He nolde no wight tellen his entente.
    Paraventure an heep of yow, ywis,
Wol holden him a lewed man in this,
That he wol putte his wyf in jupartye;
Herkneth the tale, er ye upon hir crye.
She may have bettre fortune than yow semeth;
And whan that ye han herd the tale, demeth.   770
    This squyer which that highte Aurelius,
On Dorigen that was so amorous,
Of aventure happed hir to mete
Amidde the toun, right in the quikkest strete,
As she was boun to goon the wey forth right
Toward the gardin theras she had hight;
And he was to the gardinward also,
For wel he spyed whan she wolde go
Out of hir hous to any maner place.
But thus they mette, of aventure or grace;   780
And he saleweth hir with glad entente,
And asked of hir whiderward she wente.
    And she answerde half as she were mad,
"Unto the gardin, as myn housbond bad,
My trouthe for to holde, allas, allas!"
    Aurelius gan wondren on this cas,

this is too much, even if it were divinely intended."

"Now, wife," he said, "let sleeping dogs lie;
perhaps all may yet be well this day.
You shall keep your promise, by my faith!
For as surely as I pray God to have mercy on me,
I would rather be stabbed,
because of the true love I have for you,
than have you fail to keep your word of honor.
Honor is the highest thing that man can hold."
But at that word he burst into tears,
and said, "I forbid you, on pain of death,
ever, while life or breath lasts,
to tell anyone of this misadventure.
As best I can, I will endure my woe,
nor will I show a sorrowful countenance
so that people could guess or think harm of you."

And he called a squire and a maid:
"Go out with Dorigen now," he said,
"and bring her to such a place at once."
They took their leave and went their way,
but they didn't know why she was going there.
He wouldn't tell anyone his intention.

Perhaps many of you, indeed,
will hold him to be a stupid man in this,
to put his wife in jeopardy;
listen to the tale, before you condemn her.
She may have better luck than you think;
and when you have heard the tale, you can judge.

This squire who was called Aurelius,
who was so enamored of Dorigen,
happened to meet her by chance
in the middle of the town, right in the busiest street,
as she was off to go straight
toward the garden as she had promised;
and he was also going toward the garden,
for he watched closely to see when she would go
out of her house to any sort of place.
But they met thus, whether by chance or luck;
and he greeted her hopefully,
and asked her where she was going.

And she answered, as if she were half mad,
"To the garden, as my husband ordered,
to keep my promise, alas, alas!"
Aurelius was astonished at this,

And in his herte hadde greet compassioun
Of hir and of hir lamentacioun,
And of Arveragus, the worthy knight,
That bad hir holden al that she had hight,   790
So looth him was his wyf sholde breke hir trouthe;
And in his herte he caughte of this greet routhe,
Consideringe the beste on every syde,
That fro his lust yet were him lever abyde
Than doon so heigh a cherlish wrecchednesse
Agayns franschyse and alle gentillesse;
For which in fewe wordes seyde he thus:
    "Madame, seyth to your lord Arveragus,
That sith I see his grete gentillesse
To yow, and eek I see wel your distresse,   800
That him were lever han shame (and that were routhe)
Than ye to me sholde breke thus your trouthe,
I have wel lever ever to suffre wo
Than I departe the love bitwix yow two.
I yow relesse, madame, into your hond
Quit every serement and every bond
That ye han maad to me as heerbiforn,
Sith thilke tyme which that ye were born.
My trouthe I plighte, I shal yow never repreve
Of no biheste; and here I take my leve,   810
As to the treweste and the beste wyf
That ever yet I knew in al my lyf.
But every wyf be war of hir biheste:
On Dorigene remembreth atte leste.
Thus can a squyer doon a gentil dede
As well as can a knight, withouten drede."
    She thonketh him upon hir knees al bare,
And hoom unto hir housbond is she fare,
And tolde him al as ye han herd me sayd;
And be ye siker, he was so weel apayd   820
That it were inpossible me to wryte;
What sholde I lenger of this cas endyte?
    Arveragus and Dorigene his wyf
In sovereyn blisse leden forth hir lyf.
Never eft ne was ther angre hem bitwene;
He cherisseth hir as though she were a quene,
And she was to him trewe for evermore.
Of thise two folk ye gete of me namore.
    Aurelius, that his cost hath al forlorn,
Curseth the tyme that ever he was born: 830

and in his heart had great compassion
for her and her lamentation,
and for Arveragus, the worthy knight,
who had ordered her to hold to all she had pledged,
because he was so loath to have his wife break her promise;
in his heart he felt great pity for this,
and considering what was best on all sides, thought
that now he would rather abstain from his pleasure
than do such a very churlish, wretched deed
against generosity and all nobility;
for which reason he spoke in a few words as follows:
    "Madame, say to your lord Arveragus
that since I see his great nobility
to you, and since I well see your distress also,
and that he would rather suffer shame (which would be a
pity) than have you break your word to me,
I would rather suffer sorrow always
than divide the love between you two.
Into your hand, madame, I release,
as being discharged, every oath and every bond
that you have before now made to me,
since the time when you were born.
I give you my word of honor, I shall never reprove you
about any promise; and here I take my leave
as of the truest and the best wife
that I ever yet knew in all my life.
But every wife should be careful of what she promises,
and remember Dorigen, at least.
Thus a squire can do a courteous deed
as well as a knight can, certainly."
    She thanked him on her knees,
and went home to her husband,
and told him all, as you have heard me tell it;
and you can be sure he was so well pleased
that it would be impossible for me to describe;
why should I write of this matter any longer?
    Arveragus and Dorigen his wife
led their life in sovereign bliss.
Never hereafter was there anger between them;
he cherished her as though she were a queen,
and she was true to him for evermore.
Of these two folks you'll get no more of me.
    Aurelius, whose expenditure had been all in vain,
cursed the time that ever he was born:

"Allas," quod he, "allas that I bihighte
Of pured gold a thousand pound of wighte
Unto this philosophre! How shal I do?
I see namore but that I am fordo.
Myn heritage moot I nedes selle,
And been a begger; heer may I nat dwelle,
And shamen al my kinrede in this place,
But I of him may gete bettre grace.
But nathelees, I wol of him assaye
At certeyn dayes, yeer by yeer, to paye,   840
And thanke him of his grete curteisye;
My trouthe wol I kepe, I wol nat lye."

    With herte soor he gooth unto his cofre
And broghte gold unto this philosophre,
The value of fyve hundred pound, I gesse,
And him bischeth, of his gentillesse,
To graunte him dayes of the remenaunt,
And seyde, "Maister, I dar wel make avaunt,
I failed never of my trouthe as yit;
For sikerly my dette shal be quit   850
Towardes yow, however that I fare
To goon a-begged in my kirtle bare.
But wolde ye vouche-sauf, upon suretee,
Two yeer or three for to respyten me,
Thanne were I wel; for elles moot I selle
Myn heritage: ther is namore to telle."

    This philosophre sobrely answerde,
And seyde thus, whan he thise wordes herde:
"Have I nat holden covenant unto thee?"
"Yes, certes, wel and trewely," quod he.
"Hastow nat had thy lady as thee lyketh?"
"No, no," quod he, and sorwefully he syketh.
"What was the cause? Tel me if thou can."
Aurelius his tale anon bigan,
And tolde him al, as ye han herd bifore;
It nedeth nat to yow reherce it more.

    He seide, "Arveragus, of gentillesse,
Hadde lever dye in sorwe and in distresse
Than that his wyf were of hir trouthe fals."
The sorwe of Dorigen he tolde him als,   870
How looth hir was to been a wikked wyf,
And that she lever had lost that day hir lyf,
And that hir trouthe she swoor thurgh innocence:
She never erst hadde herd speke of apparence.

"Alas," said he, "alas that I promised
a thousand pounds weight of pure gold
to this philosopher! What shall I do?
I see nothing more than that I am undone.
I must needs sell my heritage
and be a beggar; I can't remain here
and shame all my kindred in this place,
unless I can get more forbearance from him.
But nevertheless, I'll propose to pay him
at fixed dates, year by year,
and thank him for his great courtesy;
I will keep my promise, I will not be false."

With a sore heart he went to his money box
and brought gold to this philosopher,
the value of five hundred pounds, I judge,
and begged him, of his courtesy,
to grant him time to pay the rest,
and said, "Master, I can boast
that I never failed to keep my word as yet;
for surely my debt to you shall be
discharged, even if it means I must
go begging in my shirt.
But if you would grant, on security,
two or three years of respite to me,
then it would be well for me; for otherwise I must sell
my inheritance: there is no more to say."

The philosopher answered seriously,
and spoke as follows, when he heard those words,
"Have I not kept my covenant with you?"
"Yes, certainly, well and truly," said Aurelius.
"Have you not had your lady as you wished?"
"No, no," said he, and he sighed sorrowfully.
"What was the reason? Tell me, if you can."
Aurelius then began his story,
and told him all, as you have heard before;
there is no need to repeat it to you.

He said, "Arveragus, in his nobility,
would rather die in sorrow and distress
than have his wife be false to her word."
He also told him of the sorrow of Dorigen,
how loath she was to be a wicked wife,
and that she would rather have lost her life that day,
and that she had sworn her oath in innocence:
she had never before heard of illusions;

"That made me han of hir so greet pitee;
And right as frely as he sente hir me,
As frely sente I hir to him ageyn.
This al and som, ther is namore to seyn."

    This philosophre answerde, "Leve brother,
Everich of yow dide gentilly til other.   880
Thou art a squyer, and he is a knight;
But God forbede, for His blisful might,
But if a clerk coude doon a gentil dede
As wel as any of yow, it is no drede!
    Sire, I relesse thee thy thousand pound,
As thou right now were cropen out of the ground,
Ne never er now ne haddest knowen me.
For sire, I wol nat take a peny of thee
For al my craft, ne noght for my travaille.
Thou hast y-payed wel for my vitaille;   890
It is ynogh, and farewel, have good day":
And took his hors, and forth he gooth his way.

    Lordinges, this question thanne wol I aske now:
Which was the moste free,* as thinketh yow?
Now telleth me, er that ye ferther wende.
I can namore, my tale is at an ende.

"That made me have such great pity for her
that just as freely as he sent her to me,
as freely I sent her back to him.
This is the sum of it, there is no more to say."

   "Dear brother," answered the philosopher,
"each of you acted nobly toward the other.
You are a squire and he is a knight;
but God in his blissful might forbid
that a clerk could not do as noble a deed
as any of you, never fear!

   Sir, I release you of your thousand pounds,
as if you had just crept out of the ground
and had never known me before now.
For, sir, I will not take a penny from you
for all my art, or anything for my labor.
You have paid well for my food;
it is enough, and farewell, I bid you good day":
and he took his horse and went off on his way.

   My lords, I would now like to ask you this question:
which was the most generous, as it seems to you?
Now tell me, before you go any further.
I know no more, my tale is at an end.

THE PARDONER

"Thou bel amy, thou Pardoner," he seyde,
"Tel us some mirthe or japes right anon."
"It shall be doon," quod he, "by Seint Ronyon!
But first," quod he, "heer at this ale-stake
I wol both drinke and eten of a cake."
   But right anon thise gentils gonne to crye,
"Nay, let him telle us of no ribaudye;
Tel us som moral thing, that we may lere
Som wit, and thanne wol we gladly here."
"I graunte, y-wis," quod he, "but I mot thinke   10
Upon som honest thing whyl that I drinke."

The Prologe of the Pardoners Tale

Radix malorum est Cupiditas: Ad Thimotheum, sexto.

"LORDINGS," quod he, "in chirches whan I preche,
I peyne me to han an hauteyn speche
And ringe it out as round as gooth a belle,
For I can al by rote that I telle.
My theme is alwey oon, and ever was—
'*Radix malorum est Cupiditas.*'
First I pronounce whennes that I come,
And than my bulles shewe I, alle and somme.
Our lige lordes seel on my patente,
That shewe I first, my body to warente,   10
That no man be so bold, ne preest ne clerk,
Me to destourbe of Cristes holy werk;
And after that than telle I forth my tales,
Bulles of popes and of cardinales,
Of patriarkes, and bishoppes I shewe;
And in Latyn I speke a wordes fewe,
To saffron with my predicacioun,
And for to stire hem to devocioun.
Than shewe I forth my longe cristal stones,
Y-crammed ful of cloutes and of bones;   20

THE PARDONER

Words of the Host to the Pardoner

"You pretty boy, you Pardoner," he said,
"tell us some merry stories or jokes right now."
"It shall be done," said he, "by Saint Ronyon!
But first," he said, "I'll have a drink
and eat a cake at this alehouse sign."
    But right away the gentlefolk cried out,
"No, don't let him tell us any ribaldry;
tell us some moral thing, so that we can learn
something worthwhile, and then we shall gladly listen."
"I grant it, certainly," said he, "but I must think
up some decent thing while I drink."

The Prologue of the Pardoner's Tale

The love of money is the root of all evil: I Timothy 6:10

"My lords," said he, "when I preach in church
I take pains to have a haughty speech,
and ring it out as roundly as a bell,
for I know by heart all that I tell.
My theme is always the same, and ever was—
'Radix* malorum est cupiditas.'
First I announce where I come from,
and then I show my papal bulls, each and every one.
The papal seal is on my patent—
I show that first, to safeguard my person,
so that no man, priest or clerk, shall be so bold
as to hinder me from Christ's holy work;
and after that I tell my tales;
I show bulls of popes, cardinals,
patriarchs, and bishops;
and I speak a few words in Latin,
to give color and flavor to my preaching,
and to stir them to devotion.
Then I bring out my long glass jars,
crammed full of rags and bones;

339

Reliks been they, as wenen they echoon.
Than have I in latoun a sholder-boon
Which that was of an holy Jewes shepe.
'Good men,' seye I, 'tak of my wordes kepe;
If that this boon be wasshe in any welle,
If cow, or calf, or sheep, or oxe swelle
That any worm hath ete or worm y-stonge,
Tak water of that welle, and wash his tonge,
And it is hool anon; and forthermore,
Of pokkes and of scabbe and every sore   30
Shal every sheep be hool, that of this welle
Drinketh a draughte. Tak kepe eek what I telle:
If that the good-man that the bestes oweth
Wol every wike, er that the cok him croweth,
Fastinge, drinken of this welle a draughte,
As thilke holy Jewe our eldres taughte,
His bestes and his stoor shal multiplye.
And, sirs, also it heleth jalousye;
For, though a man be falle in jalous rage,
Let maken with this water his potage,   40
And never shal he more his wyf mistriste,
Though he the sooth of hir defaute wiste,
Al had she taken preestes two or three.

    Heer is a miteyn eek that ye may see.
He that his hond wol putte in this miteyn,
He shal have multiplying of his greyn,
Whan he hath sowen, be it whete or otes,
So that he offre pens, or elles grotes.

    Good men and wommen, o thing warne I yow:
If any wight be in this chirche now   50
That hath doon sinne horrible, that he
Dar nat, for shame, of it y-shriven be,
Or any womman, be she yong or old,
That hath y-maad hir housbond cokewold,
Swich folk shul have no power ne no grace
To offren to my reliks in this place.
And who-so findeth him out of swich blame,
He wol com up and offre in goddes name,
And I assoille him by the auctoritee
Which that by bulle y-graunted was to me.'   60

    By this gaude have I wonne, yeer by yeer,
An hundred mark sith I was Pardoner.
I stonde lyk a clerk in my pulpet,
And whan the lewed peple is doun y-set,

these are relics—as they all suppose.
Then I have a shoulderbone, set in
metal, from a holy Jew's sheep.
'Good men,' say I, 'take heed of my words;
if this bone is washed in any well,
and then if a cow, or calf, or sheep, or ox should swell
because of eating a worm, or being stung by one,
take water from that well, and wash its tongue,
and it shall be cured at once; and furthermore,
every sheep that drinks a draft from this well
shall be cured of pox and of scabs and every other kind of
sore. Pay attention to this also:
if the farmer who owns the beasts
will, fasting, and before the cock crows,
take a drink from this well,
as this holy Jew taught our ancestors,
his beasts and his stock shall multiply.
And, sirs, it also cures jealousy;
for, though a man may have fallen into a jealous rage,
let his soup be made with this water, and then
he shall never more mistrust his wife,
although he may know the fact of her sin,
and even if she had taken two or three priests as lovers.

　Here is a mitten, too, that you can see.
He who puts his hand in this mitten
shall have his grain multiply
when he has sown, be it wheat or oats,
providing he offers pence or groats.

　Good men and women, I warn you of one thing:
if there is anyone now in this church
who has committed a sin so horrible that he
dare not, for shame, be shriven of it,
or any woman, be she young or old,
who has made her husband a cuckold,
such folk shall have no power or grace
to make an offering to my relics here.
But whoever finds himself free from such faults
will come up and make an offering in God's name,
and I absolve him by the authority
which was granted to me by this bull.'

　By this trick I have won, year after year,
a hundred marks since I became a Pardoner.
I stand like a learned man in my pulpit,
and when the ignorant people have sat down,

I preche, so as ye han herd bifore,
And telle an hundred false japes more.
Than peyne I me to strecche forth the nekke,
And est and west upon the peple I bekke,
As doth a dowve sitting on a berne.
Myn hondes and my tonge goon so yerne   70
That it is joye to see my bisinesse.
Of avaryce and of swich cursednesse
Is al my preching, for to make hem free
To yeve her pens, and namely unto me;
For my entente is nat but for to winne,
And no thing for correccioun of sinne.
I rekke never, whan that they ben beried,
Though that her soules goon a-blakeberied!
For certes, many a predicacioun
Comth ofte tyme of yvel entencioun;   80
Som for plesaunce of folk and flaterye,
To been avaunced by ipocrisye,
And som for veyne glorie, and som for hate.
For, whan I dar non other weyes debate,
Than wol I stinge him with my tonge smerte
In preching, so that he shal nat asterte
To been defamed falsly, if that he
Hath trespased to my brethren or to me.
For, though I telle noght his propre name,
Men shal wel knowe that it is the same   90
By signes and by othere circumstances.
Thus quyte I folk that doon us displesances;
Thus spitte I out my venim under hewe
Of holynesse, to seme holy and trewe.
    But shortly myn entente I wol devyse:
I preche of no thing but for coveityse.
Therfor my theme is yet, and ever was
'Radix malorum est cupiditas.'
Thus can I preche agayn that same vyce
Which that I use, and that is avaryce.   100
But, though myself be gilty in that sinne,
Yet can I maken other folk to twinne
From avaryce, and sore to repente.
But that is nat my principal entente.
I preche no thing but for coveityse;
Of this matere it oughte ynogh suffyse.
    Than telle I hem ensamples many oon
Of olde stories, longe tyme agoon:

I preach, as you have just heard,
and tell a hundred other falsehoods.
Then I take pains to stretch out my neck
and nod east and west at the people,
like a dove sitting on a barn.
My hands and my tongue go so fast
that it is a joy to see my busy activity.
All my preaching is about avarice
and such cursed sins, in order to make them
give freely of their pennies—namely, to me;
for my intention is to win money,
not at all to cast out sins.
I don't care, when they are buried,
if their souls go a-blackberrying!
Certainly, many a sermon
proceeds from an evil intention;
some are intended to please and flatter folk,
to gain advancement through hypocrisy,
and some are for vanity, and some for hate.
For when I do not dare to argue any other way,
then I will sting my opponent smartly with my tongue
in preaching, so that he can't escape
being falsely defamed, if he
has offended my brethren or me.
For, though I don't tell his proper name,
people will easily know it is he
by signs and other circumstances.
Thus I repay folk that displease us;
thus I spit out my venom under the color
of holiness, to seem holy and true.

But I shall explain my intention briefly:
I preach for no cause but covetousness.
Therefore my theme is still, and ever was,
'Radix malorum est cupiditas.'
Thus I can preach against the same vice
which I practice, and that is avarice.
But, though I myself am guilty of that sin,
yet I can make other folk turn
from avarice, and repent sorely.
But that is not my principal intention.
I preach for no reason except covetousness;
but that ought to be enough of this matter.

Then I give them many instances
from old stories of long ago:

For lewed peple loven tales olde;
Swich thinges can they wel reporte and holde.   110
What, trowe ye, that whyles I may preche,
And winne gold and silver for I teche,
That I wol live in povert wilfully?
Nay, nay, I thoghte it never trewely!
For I wol preche and begge in sondry londes;
I wol not do no labour with myn hondes,
Ne make baskettes and live thereby,
Because I wol nat beggen ydelly.
I wol non of the apostles counterfete;
I wol have money, wolle, chese, and whete,   120
Al were it yeven of the povrest page,
Or of the povrest widwe in a village,
Al sholde hir children sterve for famyne.
Nay! I wol drinke licour of the vyne
And have a joly wenche in every toun.
But herkneth, lordings, in conclusioun;
Your lyking is that I shall telle a tale.
Now have I dronke a draughte of corny ale,
By God, I hope I shal yow telle a thing
That shal, by resoun, been at your lyking.   130
For, though myself be a ful vicious man,
A moral tale yet I yow telle can,
Which I am wont to preche, for to winne.
Now holde your pees, my tale I wol beginne."

Here biginneth the Pardoners Tale

In Flaundres whylom was a companye
Of yonge folk that haunteden folye,
As ryot, hasard, stewes, and tavernes,
Whereas, with harpes, lutes, and giternes,
They daunce and pleye at dees bothe day and night,
And ete also and drinken over hir might,   140
Thurgh which they doon the devel sacrifyse
Within that develes temple, in cursed wyse,
By superfluitee abhominable;
Hir othes been so grete and so dampnable
That it is grisly for to here hem swere:
Our blissed Lordes body they to-tere—
Hem thoughte Jewes rente him noght y-nough.
And ech of hem at otheres sinne lough.

for ignorant people love old tales;
such things they can easily repeat and remember.
What! Do you think that while I can preach
and win gold and silver for my teaching,
that I will intentionally live in poverty?
No, no, I certainly never considered that!
For I will preach and beg in various lands;
I will not labor with my hands,
or live by making baskets
in order to keep from being an idle beggar.
I don't want to imitate any of the apostles;
I want to have money, wool, cheese, and wheat,
even if it is given by the poorest page,
or the poorest widow in a village,
although her children die of starvation.
No! I will drink liquor of the vine
and have a jolly wench in every town.
But listen, my lords, in conclusion;
your wish is for me to tell a tale.
Now that I have had a drink of strong ale,
by God, I hope that I shall tell you something
that shall, with good reason, be to your liking.
For although I am myself a very vicious man,
yet I can tell you a moral tale,
which I am accustomed to preach for profit.
Now hold your peace, I will begin my tale."

Here begins the Pardoner's Tale

IN FLANDERS once there was a company
of young folk, who devoted themselves to such follies
as riotous living, gambling, brothels, and taverns,
where, with harps, lutes, and guitars
they danced and played at dice day and night,
and also ate and drank more than they could handle;
and thus they offered sacrifices to the devil
within the devil's temple, in a cursed manner,
through abominable overindulgence;
their oaths were so great and so damnable
that it was grisly to hear them swear:
they tore our blessed Lord's body to pieces—
it seemed to them that the Jews had not torn him enough.
And each of them laughed at the others' sins.

And right anon than comen tombesteres
Fetys and smale, and yonge fruytesteres,   150
Singers with harpes, baudes, wafereres,
Whiche been the verray develes officeres
To kindle and blowe the fyr of lecherye
That is annexed unto glotonye;
The Holy Writ take I to my witnesse
That luxurie is in wyn and dronkenesse.
    Lo, how that dronken Lot unkindely
Lay by his doghtres two, unwitingly;
So dronke he was, he niste what he wroghte.
    Herodes, who-so wel the stories soghte,   160
Whan he of wyn was replet at his feste,
Right at his owene table he yaf his heste
To sleen the Baptist John ful giltelees.
    Senek seith eek a good word doutelees:
He seith he can no difference finde
Bitwix a man that is out of his minde
And a man which that is dronkelewe,
But that woodnesse, y-fallen in a shrewe,
Persevereth lenger than doth dronkenesse.
O glotonye, ful of cursednesse!   170
O cause first of our confusioun!
O original of our dampnacioun,
Til Crist had boght us with his blood agayn!
Lo, how dere, shortly for to sayn,
Aboght was thilke cursed vileinye:
Corrupt was al this world for glotonye!
    Adam our fader, and his wyf also,
Fro Paradys to labour and to wo
Were driven for that vyce, it is no drede;
For whyl that Adam fasted, as I rede,   180
He was in Paradys; and whan that he
Eet of the fruyt defended on the tree,
Anon he was out cast to wo and peyne.
O glotonye, on thee wel oghte us pleyne!
O, wiste a man how many maladyes
Folwen of excesse and of glotonyes,
He wolde been the more mesurable
Of his diete, sittinge at his table.
Allas! The shorte throte, the tendre mouth,
Maketh that Est and West, and North and South,   190
In erthe, in eir, in water men to swinke
To gete a glotoun deyntee mete and drinke!

And then would come dancing girls,
graceful and dainty, and young girls selling fruit,
singers with harps, bawds, girls with cakes—
all truly the devil's agents
to kindle and blow the fire of lechery
that is closely attached to gluttony;
I take Holy Writ to my witness
that lechery comes from wine and drunkenness.

    Look how drunken Lot unnaturally
lay by his two daughters unwittingly;
he was so drunk he didn't know what he was doing.

    Herod (as anyone who has read the story knows),
when he was full of wine at his feast,
right at his own table, gave his order
to slay John the Baptist, who was entirely guiltless.

    Seneca, too, undoubtedly has a good saying:
he states that he can find no difference
between a man who is out of his mind
and one who is drunk,
except that madness, occuring in an ill-natured man,
lasts longer than drunkenness does.
O gluttony, full of cursedness!
O first cause of our ruin!
O origin of our damnation,
until Christ had redeemed us with his blood!
Lo, how dearly, in short,
was this cursed villainy paid for;
this whole world was corrupted through gluttony.

    Adam our father, and his wife, too,
were driven from Paradise to labor and woe
because of that vice—there is no doubt about it;
for while Adam fasted, as I read,
he was in Paradise; and when he
ate of the forbidden fruit on the tree,
he was at once cast out to woe and pain.
O gluttony, we certainly ought to complain against you!
Oh, if a man knew how many maladies
follow from excess and gluttony,
he would be more temperate
in his diet when he sits at his table.
Alas! The short throat, the sensitive mouth,
make men labor east and west and north
and south, in earth, in air, and in water,
to get a glutton dainty food and drink.

Of this matere, O Paul, wel canstow trete:
"Mete unto wombe, and wombe eek unto mete,
Shal God destroyen bothe," as Paulus seith.
Allas, a foul thing is it, by my feith,
To seye this word, and fouler is the dede,
Whan man so drinketh of the whyte and rede
That of his throte he maketh his privee
Thurgh thilke cursed superfluitee.   200
    The Apostel weping seith ful pitously,
"Ther walken many of which yow told have I,
I seye it now weping with pitous voys,
That they been enemys of Cristes croys,
Of whiche the ende is deeth, wombe is her god."
O wombe! O bely! O stinking cod,
Fulfild of donge and of corrupcioun!
At either ende of thee foul is the soun.
How greet labour and cost is thee to finde!
Thise cokes, how they stampe, and streyne, and grinde,   210
And turnen substaunce into accident,
To fulfille al thy likerous talent!
Out of the harde bones knokke they
The mary, for they caste noght awey
That may go thurgh the golet softe and swote;
Of spicerye, of leef, and bark, and rote
Shal been his sauce y-maked by delyt,
To make him yet a newer appetyt.
But certes, he that haunteth swich delyces
Is deed whyl that he liveth in tho vyces.   220
    A lecherous thing is wyn, and dronkenesse
Is ful of stryving and of wrecchednesse.
O dronke man, disfigured is thy face,
Sour is thy breeth, foul artow to embrace,
And thurgh thy dronke nose semeth the soun
As though thou seydest ay "Sampsoun, Sampsoun";
And yet, God wot, Sampsoun drank never no wyn.
Thou fallest as it were a stiked swyn;
Thy tonge is lost, and al thyn honest cure;
For dronkenesse is verray sepulture   230
Of mannes wit and his discrecioun.
In whom that drinke hath dominacioun,
He can no conseil kepe, it is no drede.
Now kepe yow fro the whyte and fro the rede,
And namely fro the whyte wyn of Lepe
That is to selle in Fish-strete or in Chepe;

Of this matter, Paul, well can you treat:
"Meats for the belly, and the belly for meats:
but God shall destroy both it and them," as Saint Paul says.
Alas, it is a foul thing, by my faith,
to say this word, and the deed is fouler,
when a man so drinks of white and red wine
that he makes his throat into his privy
through this cursed overindulgence.

    The Apostle says, weeping piteously,
"For many walk, of whom I have told you often,
and now tell you even weeping,
that they are the enemies of the cross of Christ:
whose end is destruction, whose God is their belly."
O stomach! O belly! O stinking bag,
filled with dung and corruption!
At either end of you the sound is foul.
How much labor and cost it takes to provide for you!
These cooks, how they pound, and strain, and grind,
and turn substance into accident,*
to please your gluttonous appetite!
They knock the marrow out of the hard bones,
for they throw away nothing
that may go softly and sweetly through the gullet;
with spices, of leaf and bark and root,
his sauces shall be made for deliciousness,
to whet a yet keener appetite.
But certainly, he who is accustomed to such delicacies
is dead while he lives in those vices.

    Wine is a lecherous thing, and drunkenness
is full of quarreling and wretchedness.
O drunken man, your face is disfigured,
your breath is sour, you are foul to embrace,
and through your drunken nose a sound seems to come
as if you were always saying "Samson, Samson";
and yet, God knows, Samson never drank any wine.
You fall as if you were a stuck pig;
your tongue is lost, and all your self-respect;
for drunkenness is truly the tomb
of man's wit and discretion.
When drink dominates a man,
he cannot keep secrets—no fear that he can!
Now guard yourself against the white and the red,
and particularly against the white wine of Lepe
that is sold in Fishstreet and Cheapside;

This wyn of Spayne crepeth subtilly
In othere wynes, growing faste by,
Of which ther ryseth swich fumositee
That whan a man hath dronken draughtes three,   240
And weneth that he be at hoom in Chepe,
He is in Spayne, right at the toune of Lepe,
Nat at the Rochel, ne at Burdeux toun;
And thanne wol he seye, "Sampsoun, Sampsoun."

But herkneth, lordings, a word, I yow preye,
That alle the sovereyn actes, dar I seye,
Of victories in the Olde Testament
Thurgh verray God, that is omnipotent,
Were doon in abstinence and in preyere;
Loketh the Bible and ther ye may it lere.   250

Loke, Attila, the grete conquerour,
Deyde in his sleep, with shame and dishonour,
Bledinge ay at his nose in dronkenesse;
A capitayn shoulde live in sobrenesse.
And over al this, avyseth yow right wel
What was comaunded unto Lamuel—
Nat Samuel, but Lamuel, seye I—
Redeth the Bible, and finde it expresly
Of wyn-yeving to hem that han justyse.
Namore of this, for it may wel suffyse.   260

And now that I have spoke of glotonye,
Now wol I yow defenden hasardrye.
Hasard is verray moder of lesinges,
And of deceite, and cursed forsweringes,
Blaspheme of Crist, manslaughtre, and wast also
Of catel and of tyme; and forthermo,
It is repreve and contrarie of honour
For to ben holde a commune hasardour.
And ever the hyer he is of estaat,
The more is he holden desolaat.   270
If that a prince useth hasardrye,
In alle governaunce and policye
He is, as by commune opinioun,
Y-holde the lasse in reputacioun.

Stilbon, that was a wys embassadour,
Was sent to Corinthe, in ful greet honour,
Fro Lacidomie, to make hir alliaunce.
And whan he cam, him happede, par chaunce,
That alle the grettest that were of that lond,
Pleyinge atte hasard he hem fond.   280

this wine of Spain creeps subtly
into other wines, growing nearby,
from which there then rise such heady fumes
that when a man has taken three drinks,
and thinks he is at home in Cheapside,
he is in Spain, right at the town of Lepe,
not at La Rochelle nor at Bordeaux;
and then he will say, "Samson, Samson."

But listen, my lords, to one fact, I pray:
that all the great actions, I may say,
in the victories of the Old Testament,
by the true God, Who is omnipotent,
were performed in abstinence and prayer;
look in the Bible, and you can learn it there.

Look how Attila, the great conquerer,
died in his sleep, shamefully and dishonorably,
bleeding from his nose in drunkenness;
a captain should live soberly.
And besides this, consider well
what Lemuel* was told—
not Samuel, but Lemuel, I mean—
read the Bible, and find what is expressly
stated about serving wine to those who administer justice.
No more of this, for what has been said should be enough.

And now that I have spoken of gluttony,
next I shall warn you against gambling.
Gambling is the very mother of lies,
and of deceit, and of cursed perjuries,
of blasphemy of Christ, of manslaughter, and also of waste
of property and time; and furthermore,
it is a reproof and a dishonor
to be considered a common gambler.
The higher such a man may be in rank,
the more abandoned he is held to be.
If a prince gambles,
in all matters of rule and policy
he is, by general opinion,
the less esteemed.

Stillbon, who was a wise ambassador,
was sent in great pomp to Corinth
from Sparta, to make an alliance between them.
When he arrived, it happened by chance
that he found all the greatest men
of the land gambling.

For which, as sone as it mighte be,
He stal him hoom agayn to his contree,
And seyde, "Ther wol I nat lese my name;
Ne I wol nat take on me so greet defame
Yow for to allye unto none hasardours.
Sendeth othere wyse embassadours;
For, by my trouthe, me were lever dye
Than I yow sholde to hasardours allye.
For ye that been so glorious in honours
Shul nat allyen yow with hasardours   290
As by my wil, ne as by my tretee."
This wyse philosophre thus seyde he.
   Loke eek that to the king Demetrius
The king of Parthes, as the book seith us,
Sente him a paire of dees of gold in scorn,
For he hadde used hasard therbiforn;
For which he heeld his glorie or his renoun
At no value or reputacioun.
Lordes may finden other maner pley
Honeste ynogh to dryve the day awey.   300
   Now wol I speke of othes false and grete
A word or two, as olde bokes trete.
Gret swering is a thing abhominable,
And false swering is yet more reprevable.
The heighe God forbad swering at al,
Witnesse on Mathew; but in special
Of swering seith the holy Jeremye,
"Thou shalt swere sooth thyn othes, and nat lye,
And swere in dome and eek in rightwisnesse";
But ydel swering is a cursednesse.   310
Bihold and see that in the firste table
Of heighe Goddes hestes honurable
How that the seconde heste of him is this—
"Tak nat my name in ydel or amis."
Lo, rather he forbedeth swich swering
Than homicyde or many a cursed thing;
I seye that, as by ordre, thus it stondeth;
This knowen that his hestes understondeth,
How that the second heste of God is that.
And forther over, I wol thee telle al plat   320
That vengeance shal nat parten from his hous
That of his othes is to outrageous.
"By Goddes precious herte, and by his nayles,
And by the blode of Crist, that is in Hayles,

For this reason, as soon as possible
he stole home again to his country,
and said, "I don't want to lose my good name there;
nor will I take upon myself such a great dishonor
as to ally you with gamblers.
Send other wise ambassadors;
for I swear I would rather die
than ally you with gamblers.
For you who are so famous for your honors
shall not be allied with gamblers
by my will, or by my treaty."
Thus said this wise philosopher.

Look, too, how the King of the Parthians,
as the book tells us, sent in scorn
to King Demetrius a pair of golden dice,
because he had practiced gambling before;
therefore the Parthian held Demetrius' glory and renown
as of no value or repute.
Lords may find other kinds of amusement
decent enough to while away the day.

Now I will speak a word or two of
false and strong oaths, as ancient books treat of the subject.
Hard swearing is an abominable thing,
and false swearing is more reprehensible yet.
High God forbade swearing entirely—
witness Saint Matthew; and, in particular,
the holy Jeremiah says of swearing,
"And thou shalt swear
in truth, in judgment, and in rightousness";
but idle swearing is a sin.
Behold, and see that in the first table
of high God's honorable commandments,
the second* of the commandments is this—
"Thou shalt not take the name of the Lord thy God in vain."
Lo, he forbids such swearing before
homicide or many another cursed sin;
I tell you that it stands in this order;
anyone who understands his commandments knows
that this is the second commandment of God.
And furthermore, I will tell you flat
that vengeance shall not forsake the house
of the man who is outrageous in his oaths.
"By God's precious heart, and by his nails,
and by the blood of Christ that is at Hayles,*

Seven is my chaunce, and thyn is cink and treye;
By Goddes armes, if thou falsly pleye,
This dagger shal thurghout thyn herte go—
This fruyt cometh of the bicched bones two:
Forswering, ire, falsenesse, homicyde.
Now, for the love of Crist that for us dyde,   330
Lete your othes, bothe grete and smale;
But, sirs, now wol I telle forth my tale.

THISE ryotoures three, of whiche I telle,
Longe erst er pryme rong of any belle,
Were set hem in a taverne for to drinke;
And as they satte, they herde a belle clinke
Biforn a cors, was caried to his grave;
That oon of hem gan callen to his knave:
"Go bet," quod he, "and axe redily,
What cors is this that passeth heer forby;   340
And look that thou reporte his name wel."
  "Sir," quod this boy, "it nedeth never-a-del.
It was me told, er ye cam heer, two houres;
He was, pardee, an old felawe of youres,
And sodeynly he was y-slayn tonight,
Fordronke, as he sat on his bench upright;
Ther cam a privee theef men clepeth Deeth,
That in this contree al the peple sleeth,
And with his spere he smoot his herte a-two,
And wente his wey withouten wordes mo.   350
He hath a thousand slayn this pestilence:
And, maister, er ye come in his presence,
Me thinketh that it were necessarie
For to be war of swich an adversarie;
Beth redy for to mete him evermore.
Thus taughte me my dame, I sey namore."
"By Seinte Marie," seyde this taverner,
"The child seith sooth, for he hath slayn this yeer,
Henne over a myle, within a greet village,
Both man and womman, child and hyne, and page.   360
I trowe his habitacioun be there;
To been avysed greet wisdom it were,
Er that he dide a man a dishonour."
"Ye, Goddes armes," quod this ryotour,
"Is it swich peril with him for to mete?
I shal him seke by wey and eek by strete,

seven is my chance, and yours is five and three;
by God's arms, if you cheat
this dagger shall go through your heart"—
this fruit comes of the two cursed bones:
perjury, ire, falsehood, homicide.
Now, for the love of Christ who died for us,
leave off your oaths, both great and small;
but, sirs, now I will tell my tale.

These three rakes I am telling about,
long before any bell had rung for morning service,
had sat themselves in a tavern to drink;
and as they sat, they heard a bell clink
before a corpse which was being carried to its grave;
one of them called to his serving boy:
"Go quickly," said he, "and ask at once
whose corpse this is that passes by here;
and look to it that you report his name correctly."

"Sir," said the boy, "there is no need at all for that.
It was told to me two hours before you came here.
He was, indeed, an old companion of yours,
and last night he was suddenly slain,
as he sat upright on his bench, very drunk;
there came a stealthy thief men call Death,
who slays all the people in this country,
and with his spear he smote the man's heart in two,
and went on his way without a word.
He has slain a thousand during this pestilence:
and, master, before you come in his presence,
it seems to me it is necessary
to be wary of such an adversary;
always be ready to meet him.
Thus my mother taught me, I say no more."
"By Saint Mary," said the tavern keeper,
"The child tells the truth, for this year Death has slain
both man and woman, child and laborer and page,
in a large village over a mile hence.
I believe he must live there;
it would be wise to be wary,
before he does harm to you."
"Yea, by God's arms," said the rake,
"Is it so dangerous to meet him?
I shall seek him in the highways and byways,

I make avow to Goddes digne bones!
Herkneth, felawes, we three been al ones;
Lat ech of us holde up his hond til other,
And ech of us bicomen otheres brother,   370
And we wol sleen this false traytour Deeth;
He shal be slayn, which that so many sleeth,
By Goddes dignitee, er it be night."
　　Togidres han thise three hir trouthes plight
To live and dyen ech of hem for other,
As though he were his owene y-boren brother.
And up they sterte al dronken, in this rage,
And forth they goon towardes that village
Of which the taverner had spoke biforn,
And many a grisly ooth than han they sworn,   380
And Cristes blessed body they to-rente—
Deeth shal be deed, if that they may him hente.
　　Whan they han goon nat fully half a myle,
Right as they wolde han troden over a style,
An old man and a povre with hem mette.
This olde man ful mekely hem grette,
And seyde thus: "Now, lordes, God yow see!"
　　The proudest of thise ryotoures three
Answerde agayn, "What, carl, with sory grace,
Why artow al forwrapped save thy face?   390
Why livestow so longe in so greet age?"
　　This olde man gan loke in his visage,
And seyde thus: "For I ne can nat finde
A man, though that I walked into Inde,
Neither in citee nor in no village,
That wolde chaunge his youthe for myn age;
And therfore moot I han myn age stille,
As longe time as it is Goddes wille.
　　Ne Deeth, allas, ne wol nat han my lyf;
Thus walke I, lyk a restelees caityf,   400
And on the ground, which is my modres gate,
I knokke with my staf, bothe erly and late,
And seye, 'Leve moder, leet me in!
Lo, how I vanish, flesh, and blood, and skin!
Allas, whan shul my bones been at reste?
Moder, with yow wolde I chaunge my cheste,
That in my chambre longe tyme hath be,
Ye, for an heyre clout to wrappe me!'
But yet to me she wol nat do that grace,
For which ful pale and welked is my face.   410

I vow by God's worthy bones!
Listen, comrades, we three are all of one mind;
let each of us hold up his hand to the other two,
and each of us become the others' brother,
and we will slay this false traitor Death;
he shall be slain, who slays so many,
on God's honor, before night falls."

Together these three pledged their word of honor
to live and die each for the other,
as though each were the other's own brother born.
And up they jumped in their drunken rage,
and went forth toward that village
which the taverner had spoken of before;
many a grisly oath they then swore,
and they tore Christ's blessed body to pieces—
Death shall be dead, if they can catch him.

When they had gone not quite half a mile,
just as they were about to step over a stile,
a poor old man met them.
This old man greeted them meekly,
and said, "Now, lords, God protect you."

The proudest of these three rakes
answered, "What, fellow, bad cess to you!
Why are you all wrapped up except for your face?
Why do you live so long, in such old age?"

The old man looked into his face
and said, "Because even if I walked to India
I could not find a man,
either in city or in village,
who would exchange his youth for my age;
and therefore I must still keep my age
for as long as it is God's will.

Nor, alas, will Death take my life;
so I walk like a restless prisoner,
and on the ground, which is my mother's gate,
I knock with my staff, both early and late,
and say, 'Dear mother, let me in!
Lo, how I fade away, flesh and blood and skin!
Alas, when shall my bones be at rest?
Mother, I would gladly exchange my chest,
which has been in my chamber such a long time,
for a haircloth winding sheet to wrap myself in!'
But still she will not do me that favor,
and that is why my face is pale and withered.

But, sirs, to yow it is no curteisye
To speken to an old man vileinye,
But he trespasse in worde, or elles in dede.
In Holy Writ ye may your-self wel rede,
'Agayns an old man, hoor upon his heed,
Ye sholde aryse'; wherfor I yeve yow reed,
Ne dooth unto an old man noon harm now,
Namore than ye wolde men dide to yow
In age, if that ye so longe abyde;
And God be with yow, wher ye go or ryde. 420
I moot go thider as I have to go."
   "Nay, olde cherl, by God, thou shalt nat so,"
Seyde this other hasardour anon;
"Thou partest nat so lightly, by Seint John!
Thou spak right now of thilke traitour Deeth,
That in this contree alle our frendes sleeth.
Have heer my trouthe, as thou art his aspye,
Tel wher he is, or thou shalt it abye,
By God, and by the holy sacrament!
For soothly thou art oon of his assent 430
To sleen us yonge folk, thou false theef!"
   "Now, sirs," quod he, "if that yow be so leef
To finde Deeth, turne up this croked wey,
For in that grove I lafte him, by my fey,
Under a tree, and ther he wol abyde;
Nat for your boost he wol him no thing hyde.
See ye that ook? Right ther ye shul him finde.
God save yow, that boghte agayn mankinde,
And yow amende!"—thus seyde this olde man.
And everich of thise ryotoures ran 440
Til he cam to that tree, and ther they founde
Of florins fyne of golde y-coyned rounde
Wel ny an eighte busshels, as hem thoughte.
No lenger thanne after Deeth they soughte,
But ech of hem so glad was of that sighte,
For that the florins been so faire and brighte,
That doun they sette hem by this precious hord.
The worste of hem he spake the firste word.
   "Brethren," quod he, "tak kepe what I seye;
My wit is greet, though that I bourde and pleye. 450
This tresor hath fortune unto us yiven
In mirthe and jolitee our lyf to liven,
And lightly as it comth, so wol we spende.
Ey, Goddes precious dignitee, who wende

But, sirs, it is not courteous of you
to speak rudely to an old man,
unless he injures you by word or deed.
You can read for yourself in Holy Writ,
'Thou shalt rise up before
the hoary head'; therefore I advise you,
do not do harm to an old man now
any more than you would wish others to do to you
in old age, if you live until then;
and God be with you, wherever you walk or ride.
I must go where I have to go."

   "No, old rogue, by God you shall not,"
said another of the gamblers then;
"You aren't going to get away so easily, by Saint John!
You spoke just now of this traitor Death,
who slays all our friends in this country.
Take my promise: since you are his spy,
you had better tell where he is, or you shall pay for it,
by God and by the holy sacrament!
For truly you are one of his party, agreed
to slay us young folk, you false thief!"

   "Well, sirs," he answered, "if you are so eager
to find Death, turn up this crooked path,
for by my faith I left him in that grove,
under a tree, and there he will stay;
your boasting won't make him hide himself at all.
Do you see that oak? You shall find him right there.
May God, who redeemed mankind, save
and amend you!" Thus said the old man.
And every one of the rakes ran
until he came to that tree; and there they found
almost eight bushels, it seemed,
of fine round florins coined of gold.
Then they did not seek for Death any longer;
each of them was so glad at the sight,
since the florins were so fair and bright,
that they sat themselves down by this precious hoard.
The worst of them spoke first.

   "Brothers," he said, "pay attention to what I say;
my wits are keen, although I joke and fool.
Fortune has given us this treasure
so that we can live our life in mirth and jollity,
and lightly as it came, so will we spend it.
Eh, God's honor! Who would have guessed

Today that we sholde han so fair a grace?
But mighte this gold be caried fro this place
Hoom to myn hous, or elles unto youres—
For wel ye woot that al this gold is oures—
Than were we in heigh felicitee.
But trewely, by daye it may nat be;　　　　　460
Men wolde seyn that we were theves stronge,
And for our owene tresor doon us honge.
This tresor moste y-caried be by nighte,
As wysly and as slyly as it mighte.
Wherfore I rede that cut among us alle
Be drawe, and lat see wher the cut wol falle;
And he that hath the cut, with herte blythe
Shal renne to the toune, and that ful swythe,
And bringe us breed and wyn ful prively.
And two of us shul kepen subtilly　　　　　470
This tresor wel; and, if he wol nat tarie,
Whan it is night, we wol this tresor carie
By oon assent whereas us thinketh best."
That oon of hem the cut broughte in his fest,
And bad hem drawe, and loke wher it wol falle;
And it fil on the yongeste of hem alle;
And forth toward the toun he wente anon.
And also sone as that he was gon,
That oon of hem spak thus unto that other:
"Thou knowest wel thou art my sworne brother;　　460
Thy profit wol I telle thee anon.
Thou woost wel that our felawe is agon;
And heer is gold, and that ful greet plentee,
That shal departed been among us three.
But natheles, if I can shape it so
That it departed were among us two,
Hadde I nat doon a freendes torn to thee?"
　That other answerde, "I noot how that may be;
He woot how that the gold is with us tweye.
What shal we doon? What shal we to him seye?"　　490
　"Shal it be conseil?" seyde the firste shrewe;
"And I shal tellen thee, in wordes fewe,
What we shal doon, and bringe it wel aboute."
　"I graunte," quod that other, "out of doute,
That, by my trouthe, I wol thee nat biwreye."
　"Now," quod the firste, "thou woost wel we be tweye,
And two of us shul strenger be than oon.
Look whan that he is set, that right anoon

that we should have such good luck today?
But if this gold could be carried from this place
home to my house, or else to yours—
for you know, of course, that all this gold is ours—
then we should be happy as can be.
But, certainly, it cannot be done by day;
people would say that we were bold thieves,
and hang us for our own treasure.
This treasure must be carried by night,
as cunningly and slyly as possible.
Therefore I suggest that we all draw
lots, and see where the lot will fall;
and he whose lot it is shall cheerfully
and quickly run to the town,
and secretly bring us bread and wine.
Two of us shall craftily guard
this treasure well; and, if he does not tarry,
we will carry this treasure when it is night
wherever we all agree is best."
The speaker brought the straws in his fist,
and told them to draw, and see where the lot would fall;
it fell to the youngest of them all,
and he went off toward the town at once.
As soon as he was gone,
the first one spoke thus to the other:
"You know well you are my sworn brother;
I am about to tell you something to your advantage.
You know that our companion is gone;
and here is gold—a great deal of it—
that is to be divided among us three.
Nevertheless, if I could manage it so
that it was divided among us two,
wouldn't I have done you a friendly turn?"

The other answered, "I don't know how that can be;
he knows that the gold is with us two.
What shall we do? What shall we say to him?"

"Will you keep a secret?" said the first villain;
"If so, I shall tell you, in a few words,
what we shall do, and bring it off safely."

"I promise," said the other, "you needn't doubt,
that, on my word, I will not betray you."

"Now," said the first, "you know well we are two,
and two of us will be stronger than one.
Watch for when he sits down; right away

Arys as though thou woldest with him pleye;
And I shal ryve him thurgh the sydes tweye   500
Whyl that thou strogelest with him as in game,
And with thy dagger look thou do the same;
And than shal al this gold departed be,
My dere freend, bitwixen me and thee;
Than may we bothe our lustes al fulfille,
And pleye at dees right at our owene wille."
And thus acorded been thise shrewes tweye
To sleen the thridde, as ye han herd me seye.

This yongest, which that wente unto the toun,
Ful ofte in herte he rolleth up and doun   510
The beautee of thise florins newe and brighte.
"O Lord!" quod he, "If so were that I mighte
Have al this tresor to myself allone,
Ther is no man that liveth under the trone
Of God that sholde live so mery as I!"
And atte laste the feend, our enemy,
Putte in his thought that he shold poyson beye,
With which he mighte sleen his felawes tweye—
For why the feend fond him in swich lyvinge,
That he had leve him to sorwe bringe;   520
For this was outrely his fulle entente,
To sleen hem bothe, and never to repente.
And forth he gooth, no lenger wolde he tarie,
Into the toun, unto a pothecarie,
And preyed him, that he him wolde selle
Som poyson, that he mighte his rattes quelle;
And eek ther was a polcat in his hawe,
That, as he seyde, his capouns hadde y-slawe,
And fayn he wolde wreke him, if he mighte,
On vermin, that destroyed him by nighte.   530

The pothecarie answerde, "and thou shalt have
A thing that, also God my soule save,
In al this world ther nis no creature,
That ete or dronke hath of this confiture
Noght but the mountance of a corn of whete,
That he ne shal his lyf anon forlete;
Ye, sterve he shal, and that in lasse whyle
Than thou wolt goon a paas nat but a myle;
This poyson is so strong and violent."

This cursed man hath in his hond y-hent   540
This poyson in a box, and sith he ran
Into the nexte strete, unto a man,

get up, as if you wanted to play a prank on him;
and I shall stab him through from one side to the other
while you struggle with him as if in fun,
and with your dagger see to it that you do the same;
then, my dear friend, all this gold shall be
divided between you and me;
then we may both satisfy all our desires
and play at dice just as we wish."
And thus these two villains agreed
to slay the third, as you have heard me say.

The youngest, who was going to the town,
kept revolving in his heart
the beauty of the bright, new florins.
"Oh Lord!" he said, "If only I might
have all this treasure to myself alone,
there is no man living beneath the throne
of God who would live as merrily as I!"
And at last, the fiend, our enemy,
put it in his thoughts that he should buy poison
with which he might slay his two comrades—
since the fiend found his manner of living such
that he had leave to bring him to sorrow;
for this was plainly the youth's full intention,
to slay them both, and never to repent.
And on he went, he would tarry no longer,
into the town, to an apothecary,
and entreated the man to sell him
some poison, so that he might kill his rats;
and also, he said, there was a polecat
in his yard that had slain his capons,
and he wanted to revenge himself, if he could,
on the vermin·that brought destruction on him by night.

The apothecary answered, "You shall have
such a poison that, as God may save my soul,
there is no creature in all this world
which, if it eats or drinks of this mixture
no more than the amount of a grain of wheat,
will not lose his life at once;
yes, he shall die, and that in less time
than it would take you to walk a mile,
this poison is so strong and violent."

The cursed man took the box of poison
in his hand, and then he ran
to a man in the next street,

And borwed of him large botels three;
And in the two his poyson poured he;
The thridde he kepte clene for his drinke,
For al the night he shoop him for to swinke
In caryinge of the gold out of that place.
And whan this ryotour with sory grace
Had filled with wyn his grete botels three,
To his felawes agayn repaireth he.　　　　　　　　　550
　　What nedeth it to sermone of it more?
For right as they had cast his deeth bifore,
Right so they han him slayn, and that anon.
And whan that this was doon, thus spak that oon:
"Now lat us sitte and drinke, and make us merie,
And afterward we wol his body berie."
And with that word it happed him, par cas,
To take the botel ther the poyson was,
And drank, and yaf his felawe drinke also,
For which anon they storven bothe two.　　　　　　　560
　　But, certes, I suppose that Avicen
Wroot never in no canon ne in no fen
Mo wonder signes of empoisoning
Than hadde thise wrecches two, er hir ending.
Thus ended been thise homicydes two,
And eek the false empoysoner also.
　　O cursed sinne, of alle cursednesse!
O traytours homicyde, o wikkednesse!
O glotonye, luxurie, and hasardrye!
Thou blasphemour of Crist with vileinye　　　　　570
And othes grete, of usage and of pryde!
Allas, mankinde, how may it bityde,
That to thy Creatour which that thee wroghte,
And with his precious herte-blood thee boghte,
Thou art so fals and so unkinde, allas!
　　Now, goode men, God forgeve yow your trespas,
And ware yow fro the sinne of avaryce.
Myn holy pardoun may yow alle waryce,
So that ye offre nobles or sterlinges,
Or elles silver broches, spones, ringes.　　　　　580
Boweth your heed under this holy bulle!
Cometh up, ye wyves, offreth of your wolle!
Your name I entre heer in my rolle anon;
Into the blisse of hevene shul ye gon;
I yow assoile, by myn heigh power,
Yow that wol offre, as clene and eek as cleer

and borrowed three large bottles from him;
in two of them he poured his poison;
the third he kept clean for his own drink,
for he planned to work all night
carrying the gold away from that place.
And when this rascal—bad cess to him—
had filled his three big bottles with wine,
he returned again to his comrades.

What need is there to preach more about it?
For exactly as they had planned his death before,
just so they slew him, and that at once.
And when this was done, the first one said,
"Now let us sit and drink, and make merry,
and afterward we will bury his body."
And at that word, he happened, by chance,
to take a bottle which had poison in it,
and drank, and gave his comrade a drink too,
so that they both soon died.

But certainly, I suppose that Avicenna
never wrote in any canon of medicine, or any part of one,
more astonishing symptoms of poisoning
that these two wretches suffered before their end.
Thus were these two homicides finished,
and the false poisoner too.

O cursed sin, full of evil!
O homicidal traitors, O wickedness!
O gluttony, lechery, and gambling!
You villainous blasphemer of Christ
with great oaths, coming from habit and from pride!
Alas, mankind, how may it happen
that to your Creator that made you
and redeemed you with his precious heart's blood
you are so false and so unnatural, alas!

Now, good men, God forgive you your sin,
and keep you from the sin of avarice.
My holy pardon can save you all,
providing you offer nobles or sterling coins,
or else silver brooches, spoons, or rings.
Bow your head under this holy bull!
Come up, you wives, offer some of your wool!
I will enter your name here in my roll at once;
you shall enter into the bliss of heaven;
I absolve you by my high power—
you that will make offerings—as clean and pure

As ye were born; and, lo, sirs, thus I preche.
And Jesu Crist, that is our soules leche,
So graunte yow his pardon to receyve;
For that is best; I wol yow nat deceyve. 590

The Epilogue

"But sirs, o word forgat I in my tale:
I have relikes and pardon in my male
As faire as any man in Engelond,
Whiche were me yeven by the Popes hond.
If any of yow wol, of devocioun,
Offren, and han myn absolucioun,
Cometh forth anon, and kneleth heer adoun,
And mekely receyveth my pardoun:
Or elles, taketh pardon as ye wende,
Al newe and fresh at every miles ende, 600
So that ye offren alwey newe and newe
Nobles and pens which that be gode and trewe.
It is an honour to everich that is heer
That ye mowe have a suffisant pardoneer
T'assoille yow, in contree as ye ryde,
For aventures which that may bityde.
Peraventure ther may falle oon or two
Doun of his hors, and breke his nekke atwo.
Look which a seuretee is it to yow alle
That I am in your felaweship y-falle, 610
That may assoille yow, bothe more and lasse,
Whan that the soule shal fro the body passe.
I rede that our Hoste heer shal biginne,
For he is most envoluped in sinne.
Com forth, sir Hoste, and offre first anon,
And thou shalt kisse the reliks everichon,
Ye, for a grote! Unbokel anon thy purs."
"Nay, nay," quod he, "than have I Cristes curs!
Lat be," quod he, "it shal nat be, so thee'ch!
Thou woldest make me kisse thyn olde breech, 620
And swere it were a relik of a seint,
Thogh it were with thy fundement depeint!
But by the croys which that Seint Eleyne fond,
I wolde I hadde thy coillons in myn hond
In stede of relikes or of seintuarie;
Lat cutte hem of, I wol thee helpe hem carie;

as you were born. And lo, sirs, thus I preach.
And Jesus Christ, who is physician of our souls,
grant that you receive his pardon;
for that is best; I will not deceive you.

The Epilogue

"But sirs, I forgot one thing in my tale.
I have in my pouch relics and pardons,
as fine as those of any other man in England,
which were given to me by the Pope's own hand.
If any of you wish, out of devotion,
to make an offering and have my absolution,
come forth now, and kneel down here,
and meekly receive my pardon:
or else take a pardon as you go on your way,
all new and fresh at the end of every mile,
just so that you offer ever anew
nobles and pennies which are good and genuine.
It is an honor to everyone here
that you may have a competent pardoner
to absolve you, as you ride through the country,
for occasions which may arise.
Perhaps one or two of you
may fall from your horses and break your necks.
Look what a safeguard it is to all of you
that I have fallen in with your company,
since I can absolve you, high and low,
when your soul shall pass from your body.
I recommend that our Host here should begin,
for he is the most enveloped in sin.
Come forth, sir Host, and make the first offering now,
and you shall kiss every one of the relics.
Yes, for a groat! Unbuckle your purse at once."
    "No, no," said he, "I would rather be damned of Christ!
Let be," he said, "it shall not be, as I hope to thrive!
You would make me kiss your old breeches,
and swear they were the relic of a saint,
though they were stained by your fundament!
But by the cross which Saint Helena found,
I wish I had your testicles in my hand
instead of relics or reliquaries;
Let them be cut off, I'll help you carry them;

They shul be shryned in an hogges tord."
   This Pardoner answerde nat a word;
So wrooth he was, no word ne wolde he seye.
   "Now," quod our Host, "I wol no lenger pleye   630
With thee, ne with noon other angry man."
But right anon the worthy Knight bigan,
Whan that he saugh that al the peple lough,
"Namore of this, for it is right ynough;
Sir Pardoner, be glad and mery of chere;
And ye, sir Host, that been to me so dere,
I prey yow that ye kisse the Pardoner.
And Pardoner, I prey thee, drawe thee neer,
And, as we diden, lat us laughe and pleye."
Anon they kiste, and riden forth hir weye.   640

they shall be enshrined in a hog's turd."
The Pardoner answered not a word;
he was so angry he wouldn't say anything.
"Now," said our Host, "I won't joke with you
any more, or with any other angry man."
But right away the worthy Knight began,
when he saw all the people laughing,
"No more of this, for it is quite enough.
Sir Pardoner, be of a glad and merry temper;
and you, sir Host, who are so dear to me,
I beg you to kiss the Pardoner.
And Pardoner, I pray you, draw near;
let us laugh and have fun as we did before."
Then they kissed each other, and rode forth on their way.

THE PRIORESSE

The Prologe of the Prioresses Tale

O LORD, oure Lord, thy name how merveillous
Is in this large worlde y-sprad—quod she—
For noght only thy laude precious
Parfourned is by men of dignitee,
But by the mouth of children thy bountee
Parfourned is, for on the brest soukinge
Som tyme shewen they thyn heryinge.

Wherfore in laude, as I best can or may,
Of thee and of the whyte lilye flour
Which that thee bar, and is a mayde alway,   10
To telle a storie I wol do my labour—
Nat that I may encresen hir honour,
For she hirself is honour, and the rote
Of bountee, next hir Sone, and soules bote.

O moder Mayde, O mayde Moder free!
O bussh unbrent, brenninge in Moyses sighte,
That ravishedest doun fro the deitee,
Thurgh thyn humblesse, the goost that in th'alighte,
Of whos vertu, whan he thyn herte lighte,
Conceived was the Fadres sapience: 20
Help me to telle it in thy reverence.

Lady, thy bountee, thy magnificence,
Thy vertu, and thy grete humilitee
Ther may no tonge expresse in no science;
For somtyme, Lady, er men praye to thee,
Thou goost biforn of thy benignitee,
And getest us the light, of thy preyere,
To gyden us unto thy Sone so dere.

My conning is so wayk, O blisful Quene,
For to declare thy grete worthinesse,   30
That I ne may the weighte nat sustene,
But as a child of twelf month old, or lesse,
That can unnethes any word expresse,

370

THE PRIORESS

The Prologue of the Prioress's Tale

O Lord our Governor, how marvelous is your name,
spread through this wide world—she said—
for not only is your precious praise
celebrated by worthy men,
but by the mouths of children your bounty
is expressed: suckling at the breast
sometimes they show forth your praise.

Therefore in praise (as best I know or can)
of you and of the white lily flower
who bore you, and is forever a virgin,
I shall take pains to tell a story—
not so that I may increase her honor,
for she herself is honor, and next to her son
the root of bounty and the help of souls.

O mother-maid, O gracious maiden-mother,
O bush unconsumed, burning in Moses' sight,
who ravished down from the deity,
by your humility, the Spirit who alighted within you,
of whose power, when he made light your heart,
the Wisdom of the Father was conceived:
help me to tell my tale in reverence of you.

Lady, your bounty, your glory,
your power, and your great humility
no tongue has knowledge to express;
for sometimes, Lady, before men pray to you,
you go before in your benignity
and get us by your prayer the light
to guide us to your dear Son.

My skill is so weak, O blessed Queen,
to declare your great worth,
that I cannot sustain the weight of my burden;
it is with me as with a child of twelve months or less,
who can express scarcely a word;

Right so fare I, and therfore I yow preye,
Gydeth my song that I shall of yow seye.

Here biginneth the Prioresses Tale

Ther was in Asie, in a greet citee,
Amonges Cristen folk, a Jewerye,
Sustened by a lord of that contree
For foule usure and lucre of vilanye,
Hateful to Crist and to his companye;   40
And thurgh the strete men mighte ryde or wende,
For it was free, and open at either ende.

A litel scole of Cristen folk ther stood
Doun at the ferther ende, in which ther were
Children an heep, y-comen of Cristen blood,
That lerned in that scole yeer by yere
Swich maner doctrine as men used there;
This is to seyn, to singen and to rede,
As smale children doon in hir childhede.

Among thise children was a widwes sone,   50
A litel clergeon, seven yeer of age,
That day by day to scole was his wone,
And eek also, whereas he saugh th'image
Of Cristes moder, hadde he in usage,
As him was taught, to knele adoun and seye
His *Ave Marie*, as he goth by the weye.

Thus hath this widwe hir litel sone y-taught
Our blisful Lady, Cristes moder dere,
To worshipe ay, and he forgat it naught,
For sely child wol alday sone lere;
But ay whan I remembre on this matere,
Seint Nicholas stant ever in my presence,
For he so yong to Crist did reverence.

This litel child, his litel book lerninge,
As he sat in the scole at his prymer,
He *Alma redemptoris* herde singe,
As children lerned hir antiphoner;
And, as he dorste, he drough him ner and ner,
And herkned ay the wordes and the note,
Til he the firste vers coude al by rote.   70

therefore I pray you,
guide the song that I shall sing of you.

Here begins the Prioress's Tale

In a great city in Asia there was,
among the Christian folk, a community of Jews,
maintained by the lord of that country
for purposes of foul usury and filthy lucre,
hateful to Christ and his followers;
and through their street people might ride or walk,
for it was free and open at either end.

A little Christian school stood there,
down at the farther end, in which were
many children of Christian blood,
who learned in the school year by year
such subjects as were customary there;
that is to say, to sing and read,
as small children do in their childhood.

Among these children was a widow's son,
a little scholar seven years of age,
who day by day was wont to go to school;
and also, whenever he saw the image
of Christ's mother, he would customarily,
as he had been taught, kneel down and say
his *Ave Maria,* on his way.

Thus the widow had taught her little son
always to worship our blissful Lady,
Christ's dear Mother, and he did not forget it,
for an innocent child will always learn quickly;
but whenever I think about this subject,
Saint Nicholas always comes to my mind,
since he did reverence to Christ so young.

This little child studied his little book:
as he sat in the school reading his primer,
he heard *Alma* redemptoris* being sung,
as older children learned their anthem books;
and, as much as he dared, he drew nearer and nearer
and listened to the words and notes
until he knew the first verse all by heart.

Noght wiste he what this Latin was to seye,
For he so yong and tendre was of age;
But on a day his felaw gan he preye
T'expounden him this song in his langage,
Or telle him why this song was in usage;
This preyde he him to construe and declare
Ful ofte tyme upon his knowes bare.

His felaw, which that elder was than he,
Answerde him thus: "This song, I have herd seye,
Was maked of our blisful Lady free, 80
Hir to salue, and eek hir for to preye
To been our help and socour whan we deye.
I can no more expounde in this matere;
I lerne song, I can but smal grammere."

"And is this song maked in reverence
Of Cristes moder?" seyde this innocent;
"Now certes, I wol do my diligence
To conne it al, er Cristemasse is went;
Though that I for my prymer shal be shent,
And shal be beten thryës in an houre, 90
I wol it conne, Our Lady for to honoure."

His felaw taughte him homward prively,
Fro day to day, til he coude it by rote,
And than he song it wel and boldely
Fro word to word, acording with the note;
Twyës a day it passed thurgh his throte,
To scoleward and homward whan he wente;
On Cristes moder set was his entente.

As I have seyd, throughout the Jewerye
This litel child, as he cam to and fro, 100
Ful merily than wolde he singe, and crye
O Alma redemptoris everemo.
The swetnes hath his herte perced so
Of Cristes moder, that, to hir to preye,
He can nat stinte of singing by the weye.

Our firste fo, the serpent Sathanas,
That hath in Jewes herte his waspes nest,
Up swal, and seide, "O Hebraik peple, allas!
Is this to yow a thing that is honest,

He knew not at all what this Latin meant,
since he was of so young and tender an age;
but one day he asked his comrade
to explain the song to him in his own language,
or tell him why this song was sung;
on his bare knees he begged him many times
to translate and explain this.

His comrade, who was older than he,
answered him thus: "This song, I have heard said,
was composed about our blissful gracious Lady,
to greet her, and also to pray her
to be our help and succor when we die.
I can explain no more about it;
I am learning to sing, I know very little Latin grammar."

"And is this song written in reverence
of Christ's mother?" said this innocent;
"Now certainly, I will try diligently
to learn it all before Christmas has gone by;
even if I shall be punished for neglecting my primer
and shall be beaten three times in an hour,
I will learn it, to honor Our Lady."

Day by day his comrade taught it to him secretly
on the way home, until he knew it by heart,
and then he sang it well and boldly
word for word according with the tune;
twice a day it issued from his throat,
on the way to school and on the way home;
his heart was set on Christ's mother.

As I have said, this little child, as he
went to and fro through the ghetto,
would sing most merrily, and cry
O Alma redemptoris constantly.
The sweetness of Christ's mother had so
pierced his heart that, in order to pray to her,
he could not stop singing on his way.

Our first foe, the serpent Satan,
who has his wasp's nest in the hearts of Jews,
swelled up, and said, "O Hebrew people, alas!
Is this a thing that is seemly to you,

That swich a boy shal walken as him lest   110
In your despyt, and singe of swich sentence,
Which is agayn your lawes reverence?"

Fro thennes forth the Jewes han conspyred
This innocent out of this world to chace;
An homicyde thereto han they hyred,
That in an aley hadde a privee place;
And as the child gan forby for to pace,
This cursed Jew him hente and heeld him faste,
And kitte his throte, and in a pit him caste.

I seye that in a wardrobe they him threwe   120
Whereas these Jewes purgen hir entraille.
O cursed folk of Herodes al newe,
What may your yvel entente yow availle?
Mordre wol out, certein, it wol nat faille,
And namely ther th'onour of God shal sprede,
The blood out cryeth on your cursed dede.

O martir, souded to virginitee,
Now maystou singen, folwing ever in oon
The whyte lamb celestial—quod she—
Of which the grete evangelist, Seint John,   130
In Pathmos wroot, which seith that they that goon
Biforn this lamb, and singe a song al newe,
That never fleshly wommen they ne knewe.

This povre widwe awaiteth al that night
After hir litel child, but he cam noght;
For which, as sone as it was dayes light,
With face pale of drede and bisy thoght,
She hath at scole and elleswher him soght,
Til finally she gan so fer espye
That he last seyn was in the Jewerye.   140

With modres pitee in hir brest enclosed,
She gooth, as she were half out of hir minde,
To every place wher she hath supposed
By lyklihede hir litel child to finde;
And ever on Cristes moder meke and kinde
She cryde, and atte laste thus she wroghte:
Among the cursed Jewes she him soghte.

that such a boy should walk as it pleases him
in contempt of you, and sing of such a doctrine,
which is contrary to the reverence due to your laws?"

Thenceforth the Jews conspired
to hunt this innocent out of this world;
for this purpose they hired a murderer,
who had a hiding place in an alley;
and when the child was passing by,
this cursed Jew seized him and held him fast,
and cut his throat, and cast him into a pit.

I tell you they threw him into a privy
where these Jews purged their entrails.
O folk of Herod cursed yet again,
what can your evil intent avail you?
Murder will out, certainly, it will not fail,
especially when the honor of God shall thereby be increased;
the blood cries out on your cursed deed.

O martyr consecrated to virginity,
now you may sing, ever following
the white lamb of heaven—she said—
of which the great evangelist Saint John
wrote in Patmos, saying that they who walk
before this lamb, and sing a new song,
never knew women carnally.

This poor widow waited all that night
for her little child, but he did not come;
therefore, as soon as it was daylight,
with the pale face of dread and a disturbed mind,
she looked for him at school and elsewhere,
until finally she got so far as to discern
that he was last seen in the ghetto.

With a mother's fear in her breast,
she went, as if she were half out of her mind,
to every place where she supposed
it likely to find her little child;
and ever she called upon Christ's mother,
so meek and kind, who at last led her
to look for him among the cursed Jews.

She frayneth and she preyeth pitously
To every Jew that dwelte in thilke place,
To tell hir, if hir child wente oght forby.   150
They seyde nay; but Jesu, of his grace,
Yaf in hir thought, inwith a litel space,
That in that place after hir sone she cryde,
Wher he was casten in a pit bisyde.

O grete God, that parfournest thy laude
By mouth of innocents, lo heer thy might!
This gemme of chastitee, this emeraude,
And eek of martirdom the ruby bright,
Ther he with throte y-corven lay upright,
He *Alma redemptoris* gan to singe   160
So loude that al the place gan to ringe.

The Cristen folk, that thurgh the strete wente,
In coomen, for to wondre upon this thing,
And hastily they for the provost sente;
He cam anon withouten tarying,
And herieth Crist that is of heven king,
And eek his moder, honour of mankinde;
And after that, the Jewes leet he binde.

This child with pitous lamentacioun
Up taken was, singing his song alway;   170
And with honour of greet processioun
They carien him unto the nexte abbay.
His moder swowning by the bere lay;
Unnethe might the peple that was there
This newe Rachel bringe fro his bere.

With torment and with shamful deth echon
This provost dooth thise Jewes for to sterve
That of this mordre wiste, and that anon;
He nolde no swich cursednesse observe.
Yvel shal have, that yvel wol deserve.   180
Therfor with wilde hors he dide hem drawe,
And after that he heng hem by the lawe.

Upon his bere ay lyth this innocent
Biforn the chief auter, whyl masse laste,
And after that, the abbot with his covent
Han sped hem for to burien him ful faste;

She asked and she begged piteously
of every Jew that dwelled in that place
to tell her if her child had gone by at all.
They said no, but Jesu of his grace
put it in her mind, after a little while,
to call out for her son in the place
next to which he was cast in a pit.

O great God, Who manifest your praise
by the mouths of innocents, behold here thy might!
This gem of chastity, this emerald,
the ruby bright of martyrdom also,
there as he lay with his throat cut, his face upturned,
he began to sing *Alma redemptoris*
so loudly that all the place rang with it.

The Christian folk who were going through this street
came in to marvel at this thing,
and they hastily sent for the provost;
he came at once without tarrying,
and praised Christ who is king of heaven,
and his mother too, honor of mankind;
and after that he had the Jews bound.

This child was taken up with piteous lamentation,
continually singing his song,
and with full processional honor
they carried him to the nearest abbey.
His mother lay swooning by the bier;
the people there could scarcely
bring this latter-day Rachel from it.

With torment and with shameful death
this provost put every one of the Jews that
knew of this murder to death, and that at once;
he would not countenance any such cursedness.
Evil shall get what it deserves.
Therefore he had them drawn with wild horses,
and after that he hanged them according to law.

This innocent still lay upon his bier
before the high altar, while Mass lasted,
and after that, the abbot with his convent
diligently made haste to bury him.

And whan they holy water on him caste,
Yet spak this child, whan spreynd was holy water,
And song *O Alma redemptoris mater!*

This abbot, which that was an holy man   190
As monkes been, or elles oghten be,
This yonge child to conjure he bigan,
And seyde, "Oh dere child, I halse thee,
In vertu of the Holy Trinitee,
Tel me what is thy cause for to singe,
Sith that thy throte is cut, to my seminge?"

"My throte is cut unto my nekke-boon,"
Seyde this child, "and, as by wey of kinde,
I sholde have deyed, ye, longe tyme agoon,
But Jesu Crist, as ye in bokes finde,   200
Wil that his glorie laste and be in minde;
And, for the worship of his moder dere,
Yet may I singe *O Alma* loude and clere.

"This welle of mercy, Cristes moder swete,
I lovede alwey, as after my connnige;
And whan that I my lyf sholde forlete,
To me she cam, and bad me for to singe
This antem verraily in my deyinge,
As ye han herd, and, whan that I had songe,
Me thoughte, she leyde a greyn upon my tonge.   210

"Wherfor I singe, and singe I moot certeyn
In honour of that blisful mayden free,
Til fro my tonge of-taken is the greyn;
And afterward thus seyde she to me,
'My litel child, now wol I fecche thee
Whan that the greyn is fro thy tonge y-take;
Be nat agast, I wol thee nat forsake.'"

This holy monk, this abbot, him mene I,
His tonge out caughte and took awey the greyn,
And he yaf up the goost ful softely.   220
And whan this abbot had this wonder seyn,
His salte teres trikled doun as reyn,
And gruf he fil al plat upon the grounde,
And stille he lay as he had been y-bounde.

And when they cast holy water on him,
still this child spoke, when the holy water had been
sprinkled, and sang *O Alma redemptoris mater!*

The abbot, who was a holy man,
as monks are (or else ought to be),
began to entreat this young child,
and said, "O dear child, I beseech thee,
by the power of the holy Trinity,
tell me what causes you to sing,
for your throat has been cut, as far as I can see."

"My throat is cut through to the neck bone,"
said this child, "and by the law of nature
I should have died—indeed, long ago;
but Jesu Christ, as you will find in books,
desires that his glory last and be kept in mind;
and, for the honor of his dear mother,
yet shall I sing *O Alma* loud and clear.

I always loved this well of mercy,
Christ's mother sweet, as best I could;
and when I was about to lose my life,
she came to me, and truly told me to sing
this anthem as I died,
as you have heard, and when I had sung,
it seemed to me she laid a grain upon my tongue.

Therefore I sing, and certainly must go on singing
in honor of that blissful gracious maiden,
until the grain is taken from my tongue;
and afterward she said to me,
'My little child, now I will fetch you
when the grain is taken from your tongue;
do not be afraid, I will not forsake you.'"

This holy monk, this abbot (him I mean),
pulled out the tongue and took away the grain,
and quietly the child gave up the ghost.
When the abbot had seen this miracle,
his salt tears trickled down like rain,
and he fell flat upon the ground
and lay as still as if he had been bound.

The covent eek lay on the pavement
Weping, and herien Cristes moder dere,
And after that they ryse, and forth ben went,
And toke awey this martir fro his bere,
And in a tombe of marbul stones clere
Enclosen they his litel body swete;   230
Ther he is now, God leve us for to mete.

O yonge Hugh of Lincoln, slayn also
With cursed Jewes, as it is notable
(For it nis but a litel whyle ago),
Preye eek for us, we sinful folk unstable,
That, of his mercy, God so merciable
On us his grete mercy multiplye,
For reverence of his moder Marye. Amen.

The rest of the monks also lay on the floor,
weeping and praising Christ's dear mother,
and after that they rose and went forth,
taking this martyr from his bier,
and they enclosed his sweet little body
in a tomb of shining marble;
where he is now, God grant that we may meet.

O young Hugh* of Lincoln, also slain
by cursed Jews, as everyone knows
(for it was but a little while ago),
pray for us unstable sinful folk,
that of His mercy God so merciful will
multiply His great mercy toward us,
for reverence of his mother Mary. Amen.

THE NONNES PREESTES TALE

A POVRE widwe, somdel stape in age,
Was whylom dwelling in a narwe cotage,
Bisyde a grove, stonding in a dale.
This widwe, of which I telle yow my tale,
Sin thilke day that she was last a wyf,
In pacience ladde a ful simple lyf,
For litel was hir catel and hir rente;
By housbondrye of swich as God hir sente
She fond hirself and eek hir doghtren two.
Three large sowes hadde she, and namo,   10
Three kyn, and eek a sheep that highte Malle.
Ful sooty was hir bour and eek hir halle,
In which she eet ful many a sclendre meel.
Of poynaunt sauce hir neded never a deel:
No deyntee morsel passed thurgh hir throte;
Hir dyete was accordant to hir cote.
Repleccioun ne made hir never syk;
Attempree dyete was al hir phisyk,
And exercyse, and hertes suffisaunce.
The goute lette hir nothing for to daunce,   20
N'apoplexye shente nat hir heed;
No wyn ne drank she, neither whyt ne reed:
Hir bord was served most with whyt and blak,
Milk and broun breed, in which she fond no lak;
Seynd bacoun, and somtyme an ey or tweye,
For she was as it were a maner deye.

    A yerd she hadde, enclosed al aboute
With stikkes, and a drye dich withoute,
In which she hadde a cok, hight Chauntecleer:
In al the land of crowing nas his peer.   30
His vois was merier than the mery orgon
On messe-dayes that in the chirche gon;
Wel sikerer was his crowing in his logge
Than is a clokke, or an abbey orlogge.
By nature knew he ech ascencioun
Of equinoxial in thilke toun;
For whan degrees fiftene were ascended,
Thanne crew he, that it mighte nat ben amended.

THE NUN'S PRIEST'S TALE

A POOR widow, somewhat advanced in age,
once dwelt in a humble cottage
beside a grove in a valley.
This widow whom I am telling you about
had patiently lived a simple life
since the day that she lost her husband.
Her property and her income were meager;
by frugal management of such as God gave her
she supported herself, and her two daughters as well.
She had three large sows (no more),
three cows, and, besides, a sheep named Molly.
Grimed with soot was her bedchamber and hall,
in which she ate many a scanty meal.
She had no need at all of sharp sauce;
no dainty morsel went down her throat—
her diet accorded with her condition in life.
Overeating never made her sick;
a temperate diet, exercise,
and a contented heart were her only medicine.
Gout didn't in the least hinder her from dancing,
nor did apoplexy ever hurt her head.
She drank no wine—neither white nor red;
her board was more likely to be set with white and black—
milk and dark bread, of which she found no lack—
broiled bacon and sometimes an egg or two,
for she was something of a dairywoman.
    She had a farmyard, enclosed
with paling and a dry ditch.
In the yard she had a cock named Chauntecleer:
in all the land he had no equal in crowing.
His voice was merrier than the merry organ
that plays in the church on holy days,
and in his dwelling his crowing was more dependable
than any clock, even the great one of an abbey.
He knew by instinct the daily
movement of the heavens,
for when they had moved fifteen degrees
he crowed in a way that could not be bettered.

His comb was redder than the fyn coral,
And batailed, as it were a castel wal.   40
His bile was blak, and as the jeet it shoon;
Lyk asur were his legges and his toon;
His nayles whytter than the lilie flour,
And lyk the burned gold was his colour.
This gentil cok hadde in his governaunce
Sevene hennes, for to doon al his plesaunce,
Whiche were his sustres and his paramours,
And wonder lyk to him as of colours;
Of which the faireste hewed on hir throte
Was cleped faire damoysele Pertelote.   50
Curteys she was, discreet, and debonaire,
And compaignable, and bar hirself so faire,
Sin thilke day that she was seven night old,
That trewely she hath the herte in hold
Of Chauntecleer, loken in every lith;
He loved hir so that wel was him therwith.
But such a joye was it to here hem singe,
Whan that the brighte sonne gan to springe,
In swete accord, "My lief is faren in londe."
For thilke tyme, as I have understonde,   60
Bestes and briddes coude speke and singe.

And so bifel that in a daweninge,
As Chauntecleer among his wyves alle
Sat on his perche, that was in the halle,
And next him sat this faire Pertelote,
This Chauntecleer gan gronen in his throte,
As man that in his dreem is drecched sore.
And whan that Pertelote thus herde him rore,
She was agast, and seyde, "O herte dere,
What eyleth yow, to grone in this manere?   70
Ye been a verray sleper, fy, for shame!"
And he answerde and seyde thus, "Madame,
I pray yow that ye take it nat agrief.
By God, me mette I was in swich meschief
Right now, that yet myn herte is sore afright.
Now God," quod he, "my swevene recche aright,
And keep my body out of foul prisoun!
Me mette how that I romed up and doun
Withinne our yerde, whereas I saugh a best,
Was lyk an hound, and wolde han maad arest   80
Upon my body, and wolde han had me deed.
His colour was bitwixe yelwe and reed;

His comb was redder than fine coral,
and crenellated like a castle wall;
his bill was black and shone like jet;
his legs and toes were like azure;
his nails whiter than the lily;
and his color like the burnished gold.
This courtly cock had at his command
seven hens to do his pleasure.
They were his sisters and his paramours,
and marvelously like him in coloring;
of them the one with the most beautifuly colored throat
was called the fair damsel Pertelote:
she was courteous, discreet, debonaire,
and companionable, and she conducted herself so
handsomely that since the day she was seven
nights old she had truly held the heart
of Chauntecleer bound and captive.
He loved her so much that all was well with him.
But what a joy it was to hear them,
when the bright sun began to rise, singing
"My love has gone away" in sweet harmony—
for at that time, as I understand,
beasts and birds could speak and sing.

   It befell one morning at dawn,
as Chauntecleer was sitting on his perch
in the hall among all his wives,
and as Pertelote sat next to him,
that he began to groan in his throat,
like a man who is sorely troubled in his dream.
And when Pertelote heard him roaring this way,
she was aghast, and said, "Dear heart,
what ails you to groan in this manner?
You're a great sleeper, aren't you?—Fie, for shame!"
And he answered thus: "Madame,
I pray you not to take it amiss.
By God, I dreamed I was in such mischief
just now that my heart is still sore afraid.
Now may God," he said, "help to interpret my dream
correctly, and keep my body from foul captivity!
I dreamed that I was roaming up and down
in our yard, when I saw a beast
that was like a dog and that wanted to seize
my body and kill me.
His color was between yellow and red,

And tipped was his tail, and bothe his eres,
With blak, unlyk the remenant of his heres;
His snowte smal, with glowinge eyen tweye.
Yet of his look for fere almost I deye;
This caused me my groning, doutelees."

"Avoy!" quod she, "Fy on yow, hertelees!
Allas!" quod she, "For by that God above,
Now han ye lost myn herte and al my love;   90
I can nat love a coward, by my feith.
For certes, what so any womman seith,
We alle desyren, if it mighte be,
To han housbondes hardy, wyse,* and free,
And secree, and no nigard, ne no fool,
Ne him that is agast of every tool,
Ne noon avauntour, by that God above!
How dorste ye seyn for shame unto your love
That any thing mighte make yow aferd?
Have ye no mannes herte, and han a berd?   100
Allas, and conne ye been agast of swevenis?
Nothing God wot, but vanitee in sweven is.
Swevenes engendren of replecciouns,
And ofte of fume, and of complecciouns,
Whan humours been to habundant in a wight.
Certes this dreem, which ye han met to-night,
Cometh of the grete superfluitee
Of youre rede *colera*, pardee,
Which causeth folk to dreden in hir dremes
Of arwes, and of fyr with rede lemes,   110
Of grete bestes, that they wol hem byte,
Of contek, and of whelpes grete and lyte;
Right as the humour of malencolye
Causeth ful many a man in sleep to crye
For fere of blake beres or boles blake,
Or elles, blake develes wole hem take.
Of othere humours coude I telle also
That werken many a man in sleep ful wo;
But I wol passe as lightly as I can.

Lo Catoun, which that was so wys a man,   120
Seyde he nat thus, 'Ne do no fors of dremes'?
Now, sire," quod she, "whan we flee fro the bemes,
For Goddes love, as tak som laxatyf;
Up peril of my soule and of my lyf,
I counseille yow the beste, I wol nat lye,
That bothe of colere and of malencolye

and his tail and both his ears were tipped
with black, unlike the rest of his coat.
His snout was small and he had two glowing eyes.
I am still almost dying for fear of the look of him.
This caused my groaning, doubtless."

"Avaunt!" she said, "Fie on you, faint heart!
Alas," she said, "for, by God above,
now you have lost my heart and all my love.
I cannot love a coward, by my faith.
For certainly, whatever any woman says,
we all desire, if it might be,
to have husbands who are bold, prudent, and generous,
and discreet*—neither niggards nor fools
nor someone who is frightened of every weapon,
nor a boaster, by God above!
How dare you for shame say to your love
that anything might make you afraid?
Have you no man's heart, and yet you have a man's beard?
Alas, and can you be afraid of dreams?
Nothing but nonsense is in dreams, God knows!
Dreams come from overeating,
and often from flatulence, and from temperamental
dispositions when humors are too abundant in a man.
Certainly this dream which you had this night
comes from the great superfluity
of your red choler,
which causes folk in their dreams to dread
arrows and fire with red flames,
or huge beasts that want to bite them,
and strife, and dogs great and small—
just as the humor of melancholy
causes full many a man to cry out in sleep
either for fear of black bears and black bulls
or else because he thinks that black devils want to seize
him. I could tell of other humors, too,
that work woe to many a man in sleep,
but I want to pass over as lightly as I can.

Look at Cato, who was so wise a man—didn't he
pronounce on the subject thus: 'Pay no attention to dreams'?
Now sir," said she, "when we fly down from the beams,
take some laxative, for the love of God.
On peril of my life and soul,
I am counseling you for the best; I don't want to deceive
you: you should purge yourself of both choler

Ye purge yow; and for ye shul nat tarie,
Though in this toun is noon apothecarie,
I shal myself to herbes techen yow,
That shul ben for your hele, and for your prow;   130
And in our yerd tho herbes shal I finde,
The whiche han of hir propretee, by kinde,
To purgen yow binethe and eek above.
Forget not this, for Goddes owene love!
Ye been ful colerik of complexioun.*
Ware the sonne in his ascencioun
Ne fynde yow nat repleet of humours hote:
And if it do, I dar wel leye a grote
That ye shul have a fevere terciane,
Or an agu, that may be youre bane.   140
A day or two ye shul have digestyves
Of wormes, er ye take your laxatyves
Of lauriol, centaure, and fumetere,
Or elles of ellebor, that groweth there,
Of catapuce, or of gaytres beryis,
Of erbe yve growing in our yerd, ther mery is;
Pekke hem up right as they growe, and ete hem in.
Be mery, housbond, for your fader kin!
Dredeth no dreem; I can say yow namore."

    "Madame," quod he, "*graunt mercy* of your lore.   150
But nathelees, as touching daun Catoun,
That hath of wisdom swich a greet renoun,
Though that he bad no dremes for to drede,
By God, men may in olde bokes rede
Of many a man more of auctoritee
Than ever Catoun was, so mote I thee,
That al the revers seyn of his sentence,
And han wel founden by experience
That dremes ben significaciouns,
As wel of joye as tribulaciouns   160
That folk enduren in this lyf present.
Ther nedeth make of this noon argument;
The verray preve sheweth it in dede.

    Oon of the gretteste auctours that men rede
Seith thus, that whylom two felawes wente
On pilgrimage, in a ful good entente;
And happed so, thay come into a toun,
Wheras ther was swich congregacioun
Of peple, and eek so streit of herbergage
That they ne founde as muche as o cotage   170

and melancholy; and in order to keep you from dallying—
there is, after all, no apothecary in this town—
I myself shall teach you about herbs
that will work for your health and profit,
and in our yard I shall find those herbs
which by nature have properties
to purge you below, and above, too.
Don't forget this, for God's own love!
You are of a very choleric temperament;
beware lest the sun in his ascension
find you overfull of hot humors;
if it does, I'll venture to bet a groat
that you will have a tertian fever
or an ague that may be your bane.
You shall have digestives of worms
for a day or two before you take your laxatives
of spurge-laurel, centaury, fumitory,
or else of hellebore growing down there,
of caper-spurge or of berries of the gaytree,
and of ground ivy growing in our pleasant yard.
Peck them up right as they grow and swallow them down.
Be merry, husband, for the honor of your father's family!
Dread no dream; I can say no more to you."

"Madame" said he, "I thank you for your lore.
But nevertheless, in regard to Master Cato,
who had such a great reputation for wisdom:
although he said not to dread dreams,
you can, by God, read in ancient books
of many a man of more authority
than ever Cato was, as I hope to thrive,
who says just the opposite of his opinion,
and has found by experience
that dreams are signs
of joy as well as of tribulations
that people endure in this present life.
There is no need to make an argument of this;
real experience shows it clearly.

One of the greatest authors men read
says thus: once two friends went
on a pilgrimage, with very pious intentions;
it happened that they came into a town
where there was such a press
of people and such a shortage of lodgings
that they didn't find so much as a cottage

In which they bothe mighte y-logged be.
Wherfor thay mosten, of necessitee,
As for that night, departen compaignye;
And ech of hem goth to his hostelrye,
And took his logging as it wolde falle.
That oon of hem was logged in a stalle,
Fer in a yerd, with oxen of the plough;
That other man was logged wel ynough,
As was his aventure or his fortune,
That us governeth alle as in commune.   180
     And so bifel that, longe er it were day,
This man mette in his bed, theras he lay,
How that his felawe gan upon him calle,
And seyde, 'Allas, for in an oxes stalle
This night I shal be mordred ther I lye.
Now help me, dere brother, er I dye;
In alle haste com to me,' he sayde.
This man out of his sleep for fere abrayde;
But whan that he was wakned of his sleep,
He turned him, and took of this no keep;   190
Him thoughte his dreem nas but a vanitee.
Thus twyës in his sleping dremed he.
And atte thridde tyme yet his felawe
Cam, as him thoughte, and seide, 'I am now slawe;
Bihold my blody woundes, depe and wyde!
Arys up erly in the morwe-tyde,
And at the west gate of the toun,' quod he,
'A carte ful of dong ther shaltow see,
In which my body is hid ful prively;
Do thilke carte aresten boldely.   200
My gold caused my mordre, sooth to sayn';
And tolde him every poynt how he was slayn,
With a ful pitous face, pale of hewe.
And truste wel, his dreem he fond ful trewe;
For on the morwe, as sone as it was day,
To his felawes in he took the way;
And whan that he cam to this oxes stalle,
After his felawe he bigan to calle.
     The hostiler answered him anon,
And seyde, 'Sire, your felawe is agon;   210
As sone as day he wente out of the toun.'
This man gan fallen in suspecioun,
Remembring on his dremes that he mette,
And forth he goth, no lenger wolde he lette,

in which they could both be lodged.
Therefore they found that they must, of necessity,
part company for that night;
and each of them went to a hostelry,
and took his lodging as his luck might fall.
One of them was lodged in a stall,
far away in a barnyard, with the plow oxen;
the other man was lodged well enough,
as was his luck or fortune,
which governs all of us equally.

It so happened that long before it was day
the second man dreamed as he lay in his bed
that his comrade called to him,
and said, 'Alas, for tonight
I shall be murdered where I lie in an ox's stall.
Now help me, dear brother, before I die;
come to me in all haste,' he said.
The man started up out of his sleep for fear;
but when he was awake
he turned over and took no notice of this;
he thought the dream was only nonsense.
He dreamed thus twice in his sleep.
Yet a third time his friend
came, as it seemed to him, and said, 'I have now been
slain; behold my bloody wounds, deep and wide!
Get up early tomorrow morning,
and at the west gate of the town,' he said,
'you shall see a cart full of dung,
in which my body is secretly hidden;
stop that cart boldly.
My gold was the cause of my murder, it is true';
and with a piteous, pale face
he told his friend every detail of how he was slain.
And believe me, the friend found that his dream was true;
for on the next day, as soon as it was light,
he made his way to his companion's inn,
and when he came to the ox's stall
he began to call for his comrade.

The innkeeper answered him quickly,
and said, 'Sir, your companion is gone:
as soon as it was day he went out of the town.'
The man became suspicious,
remembering the dreams he had had,
and he went immediately

Unto the west gate of the toun, and fond
A dong-carte, wente as it were to donge lond,
That was arrayed in the same wyse
As ye han herd the dede man devyse;
And with an hardy herte he gan to crye
Vengeaunce and justice of this felonye: 220
'My felawe mordred is this same night,
And in this carte he lyth gapinge upright.
I crye out on the ministres,' quod he,
'That sholden kepe and reulen this citee;
Harrow! Allas! Her lyth my felawe slayn!'
What sholde I more unto this this tale sayn?
The peple out sterte and caste the cart to grounde,
And in the middel of the dong they founde
The dede man, that mordred was al newe.

O blisful God, that art so just and trewe!   230
Lo, how that thou biwreyest mordre alway!
Mordre wol out, that see we day by day.
Mordre is so wlatsom and abhominable
To God, that is so just and resonable,
That he ne wol nat suffre it heled be;
Though it abyde a yeer, or two, or three,
Mordre wol out, this my conclusioun.
And right anoon, ministres of that toun
Han hent the carter, and so sore him pyned,
And eek the hostiler so sore engyned,   240
That thay biknewe hir wikkednesse anoon,
And were anhanged by the nekke-boon.

Here may men seen that dremes been to drede.
And certes, in the same book I rede,
Right in the nexte chapitre after this—
I gabbe nat, so have I joye or blis—
Two men that wolde han passed over see,
For certeyn cause, into a fer contree,
If that the wind ne hadde been contrarie;
That made hem in a citee for to tarie,   250
That stood ful mery upon an haven-syde.
But on a day, agayn the even-tyde,
The wind gan chaunge, and blew right as hem leste.
Jolif and glad they wente unto hir reste,
And casten hem ful erly for to saille.
But to that oo man fil a greet mervaille:
That oon of hem, in sleping as he lay,
Him mette a wonder dreem, agayn the day;

to the west gate of the town, where he found
a dung cart, which looked as if it were on the way to spread
dung on the land, that was in the same state
as the dead man had described;
so with a bold heart he cried out
for vengeance and justice for this felony:
'My friend was murdered tonight,
and in this cart he lies dead on his back.
I call upon the authorities,' he said,
'who are supposed to guard and rule this city;
Help! Alas, my comrade lies here slain!'
What more should I add to this story?
The people rushed out and turned the cart over,
and in the middle of the dung they found
the dead man, who had just been murdered.
O blissful God, who art so just and true!
Lo, how you always reveal murder!
Murder will out; that we see day by day.
Murder is so loathsome and abominable
to God, who is so just and reasonable,
that he will not suffer it to be concealed;
though it may wait a year, or two or three,
murder will out, this is my conclusion.
—And right away officials of that town
seized the carter, and tortured him so sorely,
and also the innkeeper, whom they racked,
that these soon acknowledged their wickedness,
and were hanged by the neck.

Thus one can see that dreams are to be dreaded.
And, certainly, I read in the same book,
right in the next chapter after this—
I'm not making it up, as I hope for joy or bliss—
of two men who would have crossed the sea
for a certain reason, to a distant country,
if the wind had not been unfavorable;
that made them wait in a city
which was pleasantly located by a harborside.
But one day, toward evening,
the wind changed and blew just as they wanted.
They went to their rest joyfully,
planning to sail early the next day.
But a great wonder befell one of the men:
as he lay sleeping,
he had a marvelous dream, toward daybreak;

Him thoughte a man stood by his beddes syde,
And him comaunded that he sholde abyde,   260
And seyde him thus, 'If thou tomorwe wende,
Thou shalt be dreynt; my tale is at an ende.'
He wook, and tolde his felawe what he mette,
And preyde him his viage for to lette;
As for that day, he preyde him to abyde.
His felawe, that lay by his beddes syde,
Gan for to laughe, and scorned him ful faste.
'No dreem,' quod he, 'may so myn herte agaste
That I wil lette for to do my thinges.
I sette not a straw by thy dreminges,   270
For swevenes been but vanitees and japes.
Men dreme alday of owles or of apes,
And eke of many a mase therwithal;
Men dreme of thing that never was ne shal.
But sith I see that thou wolt heer abyde,
And thus forsleuthen wilfully thy tyde,
God wot it reweth me; and have good day.'
And thus he took his leve and wente his way.
But er that he hadde halfe his cours y-seyled,
Noot I nat why, ne what mischaunce it eyled,   280
But casuelly the shippes botme rente,
And ship and man under the water wente
In sighte of othere shippes it byside
That with hem seyled at the same tyde.
And therfor, faire Pertelote so dere,
By swiche ensamples olde maistow lere
That no man sholde been to reccheleees
Of dremes, for I sey thee douteleees
That many a dreem ful sore is for to drede.
    Lo, in the lyf of Seint Kenelm I rede—   290
That was Kenulphus sone, the noble king
Of Mercenrike—how Kenelm mette a thing
A lyte er he was mordred, on a day;
His mordre in his avisioun he say.
His norice him expouned every del
His sweven, and bad him for to kepe him wel
For traisoun; but he nas but seven yeer old,
And therfore litel tale hath he told
Of any dreem, so holy was his herte.
By God, I hadde lever than my sherte   300
That ye had rad his legende as have I.
Dame Pertelote, I sey yow trewely,

it seemed to him a man stood by his bedside
and ordered him to wait,
and said to him, 'If you sail tomorrow,
you will be drowned; that's all I have to say.'
He woke up, and told his comrade what he had dreamed,
and begged him to delay his voyage;
he asked him to wait another day.
His friend, who lay in the next bed,
laughed, and scorned him thoroughly.
'No dream,' he said, 'can so dismay my heart
that I will put off going about my business.
I don't care a straw for your dreams,
for dreams are nothing but illusions and frauds.
Men are always dreaming of owls or apes,
and other bewildering nonsense;
men dream of things that never were and never shall be.
But since I see you intend to stay here,
and thus willfully waste your tide,
God knows I'm sorry; and good day to you.'
And thus he took his leave and went his way.
But before he had sailed half his course—
I don't know why, or what was the trouble with it—
but accidentally the ship's bottom was split,
and ship and man sank
in the sight of other ships alongside,
which had sailed with them on the same tide.
And therefore, fair Pertelote so dear,
by such ancient examples you may learn
that no man should be too heedless
of dreams, for I tell you that without
a doubt many a dream is sorely to be dreaded.

  Lo, I read in the life of Saint Kenelm
(who was the son of Kenulphus, the noble king
of Mercia) how Kenelm dreamed something
one day, a little before he was murdered;
he saw his murder in a vision.
His nurse explained his dream to him
completely, and warned him to guard himself well
against treason; but he was only seven years old,
and therefore he set little store
by any dream, his heart was so holy.
By God, I'd give my shirt
to have had you read his legend as I have.
Dame Pertelote, I tell you truly

Macrobeus, that write th'avisioun
In Affrike of the worthy Cipioun,
Affermeth dremes, and seith that they been
Warning of thinges that men after seen.
    And forthermore, I pray yow loketh wel
In th'Olde Testament, of Daniel,
If he held dremes any vanitee.
Reed eek of Joseph, and ther shul ye see   310
Wher dremes ben somtyme (I sey nat alle)
Warning of thinges that shul after falle.
Loke of Egipt the king, daun Pharao,
His bakere and his boteler also,
Wher they ne felte noon effect in dremes.
Whoso wol seken actes of sondry remes
May rede of dremes many a wonder thing.
    Lo Cresus, which that was of Lyde king,
Mette he nat that he sat upon a tree,
Which signified he sholde anhanged be?   320
Lo heer Andromacha, Ectores wyf,
That day that Ector sholde lese his lyf
She dremed on the same night biforn
How that the lyf of Ector sholde be lorn,
If thilke day he wente into bataille;
She warned him, but it mighte nat availle;
He wente for to fighte nathelees,
But he was slayn anoon of Achilles.
But thilke tale is al to long to telle,
And eek it is ny day, I may nat dwelle.   330
Shortly I seye, as for conclusioun,
That I shal han of this avisioun
Adversitee; and I seye forthermore
That I ne telle of laxatyves no store,
For they ben venimous, I woot it wel;
I hem defye, I love hem never a del.
    Now let us speke of mirthe, and stinte al this;
Madame Pertelote, so have I blis,
Of o thing God hath sent me large grace;
For whan I see the beautee of your face—   340
Ye ben so scarlet reed about your yën—
It maketh al my drede for to dyen;
For, also siker as *In principio,*
Mulier est hominis confusio;
Madame, the sentence of this Latin is,
'Womman is mannes joye and al his blis.'

that Macrobius,* who wrote the vision
of the worthy Scipio in Africa,
affirms the truth of dreams, and says that they are
warnings of things that men perceive afterward.

And furthermore, I beg you to look carefully
in the Old Testament, at the story of Daniel,
and see if he held dreams to be any nonsense.
Read of Joseph, too, and there you shall see
whether dreams are sometimes (I don't say *all* of them)
warnings of things that shall happen later.
Look at the king of Egypt, Lord Pharaoh,
and his butler and baker, too,
and see if they found no effect in dreams.
Whoever studies the history of various realms
may read many marvelous things about dreams.

Look at Croesus, who was king of Lydia;
didn't he dream that he sat in a tree,
which meant that he would be hanged?
There is Andromache, Hector's wife;
on the very night before the day that Hector
was to lose his life, she dreamed
of how his life would be lost
if he went into battle that day;
she warned him, but it was of no avail;
he went to fight anyway,
but was soon slain by Achilles.
But that story is all too long to tell,
and also it is nearly day, I mayn't tarry.
Briefly, I say in conclusion,
that this vision means I shall have
some adversity; and I say furthermore
that I set no store by laxatives,
for they are venomous, I know it well;
I defy them, I don't like them a bit.

Now let us speak of pleasant things, and stop all this;
Madame Pertelote, as I hope for bliss,
in one respect God has shown me great favor;
for when I see the beauty of your face—
you are so scarlet red about your eyes—
it destroys all my dread;
for it is just as certain as *In* principio*,
Mulier* est hominis confusio;
Madame, the meaning of this Latin is,
'Woman is man's joy and all his bliss.'

For whan I fele a-night your softe syde,
Albeit that I may nat on you ryde,
For that our perche is maad so narwe, alas!
I am so ful of joye and of solas
That I defye bothe sweven and dreem."   350
And with that word he fley doun fro the beem,
For it was day, and eek his hennes alle;
And with a chuk he gan hem for to calle,
For he had founde a corn, lay in the yerd.
Royal he was, he was namore aferd;
He fethered Pertelote twenty tyme,
And trad as ofte, er that it was pryme.
He loketh as it were a grim leoun,
And on his toos he rometh up and doun;   360
Him deyned not to sette his foot to grounde.
He chukketh, whan he hath a corn y-founde,
And to him rennen thanne his wyves alle.
Thus royal, as a prince is in his halle,
Leve I this Chauntecleer in his pasture;
And after wol I telle his aventure.
    Whan that the month in which the world bigan,
That highte March, whan God first maked man,
Was complet, and passed were also,
Sin March bigan, thritty dayes and two,   370
Bifel that Chauntecleer, in al his pryde,
His seven wyves walking by his syde,
Caste up his eyen to the brighte sonne,
That in the signe of Taurus hadde y-ronne
Twenty degrees and oon, and somwhat more;
And knew by kynde, and by noon other lore,
That it was pryme, and crew with blisful stevene.
"The sonne," he sayde, "is clomben up on hevene
Fourty degrees and oon, and more, ywis.
Madame Pertelote, my worldes blis,   380
Herkneth thise blisful briddes how they singe,
And see the fresshe floures how they springe;
Ful is myn herte of revel and solas."
But sodeinly him fil a sorweful cas;
For ever the latter ende of joye is wo.
God woot that worldly joye is sone ago;
And if a rethor coude faire endyte,
He in a cronique saufly mighte it wryte,
As for a sovereyn notabilitee.
Now every wys man, lat him herkne me;   390

For at night when I feel your soft side,
although I cannot ride on you
since our perch was made so narrow, alas!—
I am so full of joy and delight
that I defy nightmares and dreams."
And with those words he flew down from the beam,
and so did all his hens, for it was day;
and with a chuck he called for them
since he had found a bit of grain lying in the yard.
He was regal, no longer afraid;
he feathered Pertelote twenty times
and rode her as often, before midmorning.
He looked like a grim lion,
as he roamed to and fro on tiptoes;
he did not deign to set his foot on the ground.
He chucked when he had found a grain,
and then his wives all ran to him.
Thus I leave this Chauntecleer to his dinner,
royal as a prince in his hall,
and next I will tell of his adventure.

    When the month that is called March,
in which the world began and God first made man,
was over, and when, in addition, since the
beginning of March thirty-two days had passed,
it befell that Chauntecleer, in all his pride,
with his seven wives walking by his side,
cast up his eyes to the bright sun,
which had passed through somewhat more
than twenty-one degrees in the sign of Taurus;
he knew by instinct, and by no other lore,
that it was nine o'clock, and crowed with a blissful voice.
"The sun," he said, "has indeed climbed up the heavens
forty-one degrees and a fraction.
Madame Pertelote, my earthly bliss,
listen to how the blissful birds sing,
and see how the fresh flowers spring up;
my heart is full of joy and content."
But suddenly a sad mischance befell him;
for the latter end of joy is ever woe.
God knows that worldly joy is soon gone;
and a rhetorician who could write well
might safely put this in a chronicle
as a notable maxim.
Now let every wise man listen to me;

This storie is also trewe, I undertake,
As is the book of Launcelot de Lake,
That wommen holde in ful gret reverence.
Now wol I torne agayn to my sentence.
   A col-fox, ful of sly iniquitee,
That in the grove hadde woned yeres three,
By heigh imaginacioun forncast,
The same night thurghout the hegges brast
Into the yerd, ther Chauntecleer the faire
Was wont, and eek his wyves, to repaire;   400
And in a bed of wortes still he lay
Til it was passed undern of the day,
Wayting his tyme on Chauntecleer to falle,
As gladly doon thise homicydes alle,
That in awayt liggen to mordre men.
O false mordrer, lurking in thy den!
O newe Scariot, newe Genilon!
False dissimilour, O Greek Sinon,
That broghtest Troye al outrely to sorwe!
O Chauntecleer, acursed be that morwe   410
That thou into that yerd flough fro the bemes:
Thou were ful wel y-warned by thy dremes
That thilke day was perilous to thee.
But what that God forwoot mot nedes be,
After the opinioun of certeyn clerkis.
Witnesse on him that any perfit clerk is,
That in scole is gret altercacioun
In this matere, and greet disputisoun,
And hath ben of an hundred thousand men.
But I ne can not bulte it to the bren   420
As can the holy doctour Augustyn,
Or Boëce, or the bishop Bradwardyn,
Whether that Goddes worthy forwiting
Streyneth me nedely for to doon a thing
(Nedely clepe I simple necessitee);
Or elles, if free choys be graunted me
To do that same thing, or do it noght,
Though God forwoot it, er that it was wroght;
Or if his witing streyneth nevere a del
But by necessitee condicionel.   430
I wol not han to do of swich matere;
My tale is of a cok, as ye may here,
That took his counseil of his wyf, with sorwe,
To walken in the yerd upon that morwe

this story is just as true, I guarantee,
as the book of Lancelot du Lac,
which women hold in such high regard.
Now I will turn again to my theme.
    A fox with black markings, full of sly iniquity,
who had lived in the wood three years,
that same night (as was destined by divine planning)
burst through the hedges
into the yard where noble Chauntecleer
and his wives were wont to repair;
and he lay quietly in a bed of cabbages
until midmorning had passed,
biding his time to fall on Chauntecleer,
as all these homicides usually do,
who lie in wait to murder men.
O false murderer, lurking in your den!
O new Iscariot, new Ganelon!*
False dissembler, Greek Sinon,
who brought Troy utterly to sorrow!
O Chauntecleer, accursed be that day
when you flew into that yard from the beams:
you were well warned by your dreams
that this day was perilous to you.
But what God foresees must needs be,
according to the opinion of certain clerks.
Any learned clerk will bear witness
that in the schools there is much altercation
and dispute about this matter,
it has been debated among a hundred thousand men.
But I cannot sift the grain from the chaff in this matter,
as the holy doctor Augustine can,
or Boethius or Bishop Bradwardine:*
whether God's worthy foreknowledge
constrains me to do a thing
(by "constraint" I refer to simple* necessity);
or else, whether I am granted free choice
to do that same thing or not to do it,
though God foresaw it before it was done;
or whether his foreknowledge doesn't constrain at all
except by conditional necessity.
I won't have anything to do with such matters;
my tale is about a cock, as you can hear,
who, unfortunately, took advice from his wife
to walk in the yard the day after

That he had met the dreem that I yow tolde.
Wommennes counseils been ful ofte colde;
Wommannes counseil broughte us first to wo,
And made Adam fro paradys to go,
Theras he was ful mery, and wel at ese.
But for I noot to whom it mighte displese   440
If I counseil of wommen wolde blame,
Passe over, for I seyde it in my game.
Rede auctours, wher they trete of swich matere,
And what thay seyn of wommen ye may here.
Thise been the cokkes wordes, and nat myne;
I can noon harm of no womman divyne.

Faire in the sond, to bathe hir merily,
Lyth Pertelote, and alle hir sustres by,
Agayn the sonne; and Chauntecleer so free
Song merier than the mermayde in the see;   450
For Phisiologus seith sikerly
How that they singen wel and merily.
And so bifel that as he caste his yë
Among the wortes on a boterflye,
He was war of this fox that lay ful lowe.
Nothing ne liste him thanne for to crowe,
But cryde anon, "Cok, cok," and up he sterte,
As man that was affrayed in his herte.
For naturelly a beest desyreth flee
Fro his contrarie, if he may it see,   460
Though he never erst had seyn it with his yë.

This Chauntecleer, whan he gan him espye,
He wolde han fled, but that the fox anon
Seyde, "Gentil sire, allas, wher wol ye gon?
Be ye affrayed of me that am your freend?
Now certes, I were worse than a feend
If I to yow wolde harm or vileinye.
I am nat come your counseil for t'espye;
But trewely, the cause of my cominge
Was only for to herkne how that ye singe.   470
For trewely ye have as mery a stevene
As eny aungel hath that is in hevene;
Therwith ye han in musik more felinge
Than hadde Boëce, or any that can singe.
My lord your fader (God his soule blesse!)
And eek your moder, of hir gentilesse,
Han in myn hous y-been, to my gret ese;
And certes, sire, ful fayn wolde I yow plese.

he had had the dream I told you about.
Women's counsel is often baneful;
woman's counsel brought us first to woe,
and caused Adam to leave Paradise,
where he had been merry and well at ease.
But since I don't know whom it might displease
If I disparage the counsel of women,
overlook that, for I said it in sport.
Read the authorities where they treat of such matters,
and you'll hear what they say about women;
these are the cock's words, and not mine;
I can't find any harm in any woman.

    Pertelote lay in the sand, merrily
bathing in the sun, and all
her sisters with her; noble Chauntecleer
sang more merrily than a mermaid in the sea
(for Physiologus* says reliably
that mermaids sing well and merrily).
And it happened that as he cast his eye
on a butterfly among the cabbages,
he became aware of the fox who was lying low there.
He had no desire to crow then,
but cried at once, "Cok, cok," and started up
like a man terrified in his heart,
for a beast instinctively wants to flee
from his natural enemy, if he should see it,
although he may never before have seen it with his eyes.

    This Chauntecleer, when he saw the fox,
would have fled, but the fox at once
said, "Gentle sir, alas, where are you going?
Are you afraid of me, your friend?
Now certainly, I would be worse than a fiend
if I wished to harm or dishonor you.
I didn't come to spy on your secrets;
but truly, the reason I came
was only to hear how you sing.
For indeed you have as merry a voice
as any angel in heaven;
and moreover you have more feeling for music
than had Boethius, or any other singer.
My lord your father (God bless his soul!)
and your gentle mother
have been at my house, to my great pleasure;
and certainly, sir, I would gladly entertain you.

But for men speke of singing, I wol saye,
So mote I brouke wel myn eyen tweye,   480
Save yow, I herde never man so singe
As dide your fader in the morweninge;
Certes, it was of herte, al that he song.
And for to make his voys the more strong,
He wolde so peyne him that with bothe his yën
He moste winke, so loude he wolde cryen,
And stonden on his tiptoon therwithal,
And strecche forth his nekke long and smal.
And eek he was of swich discrecioun
That ther nas no man in no regioun   490
That him in song or wisdom mighte passe.
I have wel rad in daun Burnel the Asse,
Among his vers, how that ther was a cok,
For that a preestes sone yaf him a knok
Upon his leg whyl he was yong and nyce,
He made him for to lese his benefyce.
But certeyn, ther nis no comparisoun
Bitwix the wisdom and discrecioun
Of youre fader, and of his subtiltee.
Now singeth, sire, for seinte charitee: 500
Let see, conne ye your fader countrefete?"
This Chauntecleer his winges gan to bete,
As man that coude his tresoun nat espye,
So was he ravisshed with his flaterye.

    Allas, ye lordes, many a fals flatour
Is in your courtes, and many a losengeour,
That plesen yow wel more, by my feith,
Than he that soothfastnesse unto yow seith.
Redeth Ecclesiaste of flaterye;
Beth war, ye lordes, of hir trecherye.   510

    This Chauntecleer stood hye upon his toos,
Strecching his nekke, and heeld his eyen cloos,
And gan to crowe loude for the nones;
And daun Russel the fox sterte up at ones
And by the gargat hente Chauntecleer,
And on his bak toward the wode him beer,
For yet ne was ther no man that him sewed.
O Destinee, that mayst nat been eschewed!
Allas, that Chauntecleer fleigh from the bemes!
Allas, his wyf ne roghte nat of dremes!   520
And on a Friday fil al this mechaunce.
O Venus, that art goddesse of plesaunce,

But speaking of singing, I will say,
as I hope to enjoy the use of my two eyes,
that, except for you, I never heard anyone sing
the way your father did in the morning;
certainly all that he sang came from the heart.
And to make his voice the stronger,
he would exert himself so much that he had
to close both his eyes, he would crow so loudly,
and stand on his tiptoes at the same time,
and stretch forth his long, slender neck.
And also he was so judicious
that there was no one anywhere
who could surpass him in song or wisdom.
I have, indeed, read in the book of Sir Brunellus* the Ass,
among its verses, that there was once a cock:
because a priest's son who was young and foolish
gave him a knock on his leg, the cock
caused him to lose a benefice.
But certainly there is no comparison
between his cleverness and the wisdom
and discretion of your father.
Now sing, sir, for holy charity:
let's see, can you imitate your father?"
Chauntecleer began to beat his wings
like a man who could not see the treason which threatened
him, he was so ravished by the fox's flattery.

   Alas, you lords, in your courts are many
false flatterers and deceivers
who please you much more, by my faith,
than he who tells you the truth.
Read what Ecclesiasticus says of flattery;
beware, you lords, of their treachery.

   Chauntecleer stood high on his toes,
stretching his neck out; he held his eyes closed,
and then began to crow very loudly;
and Sir Russel the fox started up at once
and seized Chauntecleer by the throat,
and carried him on his back toward the woods,
for as yet no one was pursuing him.
O Destiny, who may not be eschewed!
Alas, that Chauntecleer flew from the beams!
Alas, that his wife didn't believe in dreams!
And on a Friday fell all this misfortune.
O Venus, who are goddess of pleasure,

Sin that thy servant was this Chauntecleer,
And in thy service dide al his poweer,
More for delyt, than world to multiplye,
Why woldestow suffre him on thy day to dye?
O Gaufred, dere mayster soverayn,
That, whan thy worthy king Richard was slayn
With shot, compleynedest his deth so sore,
Why ne hadde I now thy sentence and thy lore,   530
The Friday for to chyde, as diden ye?
For on a Friday soothly slayn was he.
Than wolde I shewe yow how that I coude pleyne
For Chauntecleres drede and for his peyne.

    Certes, swich cry ne lamentacioun
Was never of ladies maad whan Ilioun
Was wonne, and Pirrus with his streite swerd,
Whan he hadde hent King Priam by the berd,
And slayn him, as saith us *Eneydos*,
As, maden alle the hennes in the clos   540
Whan they had seyn of Chauntecleer the sighte.
But sovereynly dame Pertelote shrighte
Ful louder than dide Hasdrubales wyf
Whan that hir housbond hadde lost his lyf,
And that the Romayns hadde brend Cartage;
She was so ful of torment and of rage
That wilfully into the fyr she sterte,
And brende hirselven with a stedfast herte.
O woful hennes, right so cryden ye
As, whan that Nero brende the cittee   550
Of Rome, cryden senatoures wyves,
For that hir housebondes losten alle hir lyves;
Withouten gilt this Nero hath hem slayn.
Now wol I torne to my tale agayn:
    This sely widwe and eek hir doghtres two
Herden thise hennes crye and maken wo,
And out at dores sterten they anoon,
And syen the fox toward the grove goon,
And bar upon his back the cok away;
And cryden, "Out!" "Harrow!" and "Weylawey!"   560
"Ha, ha, the fox!" and after him they ran,
And eek with staves many another man;
Ran Colle our dogge, and Talbot and Gerland,
And Malkin with a distaf in hir hand;
Ran cow and calf, and eek the verray hogges,
For-fered for berking of the dogges

since Chauntecleer was your servant
and did all that he could in your service,
more for delight than to multiply the world's beings,
why would you allow him to die on your day?
O Geoffrey,* dear sovereign master,
who lamented the death of your worthy
King Richard so sorely when he was shot,
why don't I now have your expressive wisdom and learning,
to chide the Friday, as you did?
(For, truly, he was slain on a Friday.)
Then I would show you how I could mourn
for Chauntecleer's dread and pain.

    Certainly, never was made such a cry and lamentation
by the Trojan ladies when Ilion
was won, and Pyrrhus with his unsparing sword
had taken king Priam by the beard
and slain him (the *Aeneid* tells us),
as made all the hens in the yard
when they had seen the sight of Chauntecleer.
But chiefly Dame Pertelote shrieked—
much louder than did Hasdrubal's wife
when her husband had lost his life
and the Romans had burned Carthage
(that lady was so full of torment and rage
that she threw herself into the fire of her own will
and burned herself with a steadfast heart).
O woeful hens, just so cried you
as, when Nero burned the city of
Rome, the senators' wives cried,
because their husbands had all lost their lives;
Nero had them slain, innocent as they were.
Now I will turn to my tale again.

    This poor widow, and her two daughters, too,
heard the hens cry and lament,
and they quickly rushed outdoors
and saw the fox go toward the grove,
bearing away the cock on his back;
and they cried, "Out! Help, woe, alas!
Hah, hah, the fox!" and they ran after him,
and many others followed with staves in hand;
out ran Colle our dog, and Talbot and Garland,
and Malkin with a distaff in her hand;
cow and calf ran, and even the hogs,
they were so frightened by the barking of the dogs

And shouting of the men and wimmen eke;
They ronne so hem thoughte hir herte breke.
They yelleden as feendes doon in helle;
The dokes cryden as men wolde hem quelle;   570
The gees for fere flowen over the trees;
Out of the hyve cam the swarm of bees—
So hidous was the noyse, a, *benedicite!*
Certes, he Jakke Straw and his meynee
Ne made never shoutes half so shrille
Whan that they wolden any Fleming kille,
As thilke day was maad upon the fox.
Of bras thay broghten bemes, and of box,
Of horn, of boon, in whiche they blewe and pouped,
And therwithal thay shryked and they houped;   580
It semed as that heven sholde falle.
Now, gode men, I pray yow herkneth alle!
    Lo, how Fortune turneth sodeinly
The hope and pryde eek of hir enemy!
This cok, that lay upon the foxes bak,
In al his drede unto the fox he spak,
And seyde, "Sire, if that I were as ye,
Yet sholde I seyn, as wis God helpe me,
'Turneth agayn, ye proude cherles alle!
A verray pestilence upon yow falle!   590
Now am I come unto this wodes syde,
Maugree your heed, the cok shal heer abyde;
I wol him ete in feith, and that anon.' "
The fox answerde, "In feith, it shal be don,"
And as he spak that word, al sodeinly
This cok brak from his mouth deliverly,
And heighe upon a tree he fleigh anon.
And whan the fox saugh that he was y-gon,
"Allas!" quod he, "O Chauntecleer, allas!
I have to yow," quod he, "y-doon trespas,   600
In as muche as I maked yow aferd
Whan I yow hente and broghte out of the yerd;
But, sire, I dide it in no wikke entente;
Com doun, and I shal telle yow what I mente.
I shal seye sooth to yow, God help me so."
"Nay than," quod he, "I shrewe us bothe two,
And first I shrewe myself, bothe blood and bones,
If thou bigyle me ofter than ones.
Thou shalt namore thurgh thy flaterye
Do me to singe and winke with myn yë.   610

and the shouting of the men and women;
they ran so that they thought their hearts would break.
They yelled like fiends in hell;
the ducks cried out as if they were going to be killed;
the geese, terrified, flew over the trees;
the swarm of bees came out of the hive—
so hideous was the noise, God bless us!
Surely even Jack* Straw and his throng
never gave shouts half so shrill
when they wanted to kill a Fleming
as were uttered that day at the fox.
They brought trumpets of brass and of boxwood,
of horn and of bone, on which they blew and tooted,
and at the same time they shrieked and whooped;
it seemed as if heaven should fall.
Now good men, I pray you all listen!

See how Fortune suddenly reverses
the hope and pride of their enemy!
This cock, who lay on the fox's back,
spoke in all his dread to the fox,
and said, "Sir, if I were as you,
I would say, so help me God,
'Turn again, all you silly fools!
A pox upon you!
Now that I have come to the edge of the wood,
in spite of you the cock shall stay here;
in faith, I will eat him, and right now at that.' "
The fox answered, "In faith, it shall be done,"
and the moment he spoke those words, the cock
nimbly broke away from his mouth,
and immediately flew high up into a tree.
And when the fox saw that he was gone,
he said, "Alas, O Chauntecleer, alas!
I have wronged you," he said,
"inasmuch as I frightened you
when I took you and brought you out of the yard;
but, sir, I did it with no wicked intent;
come down, and I shall tell you what I meant.
I shall tell you the truth, so help me God."
"No indeed," said the cock, "may we both be damned,
but may I be damned first, both blood and bones
if you beguile me more than once.
No more shall you, through your flattery,
get me to close my eyes and sing.

For he that winketh whan he sholde see,
Al wilfully, God lat him never thee!"
"Nay," quod the fox, "but God yeve him meschaunce
That is so undiscreet of governaunce
That jangleth whan he sholde holde his pees."
      Lo, swich it is for to be recchelees,
And necligent, and truste on flaterye.
But ye that holden this tale a folye,
As of a fox, or of a cok and hen,
Taketh the moralitee, good men.   620
For Seint Paul seith that al that writen is
To our doctryne it is y-write, ywis.
Taketh the fruyt, and lat the chaf be stille.
      Now, gode God, if that it be thy wille,
As seith my Lord, so make us alle good men;
And bringe us to his heighe blisse. Amen.

For he who knowingly blinks when he should see,
God let him never thrive!"
"No," said the fox, "but God give him misfortune
who is so indiscreet in his conduct
as to jabber when he should hold his peace."

    Lo, this is what it is like to be careless
and negligent, and to trust in flattery.
But you that think this tale is a trifle
about a fox, or a cock and a hen:
accept the moral, good people.
For Saint Paul says that all that is written
is certainly written for our learning.
Take the fruit, and let the chaff alone.
Now, gracious God, if it be your will,
as my Lord says, make us all good men;
and bring us to his exalted bliss. Amen.

GLOSSARY

All entries are alphabetized under the word immediately preceding the asterisk in the text.

Note on Biblical quotations: As far as possible, Chaucer's quotations from the Bible in this translation follow the wording of the King James version. But we have followed Chaucer where he paraphrases, or suits his own translation to his particular purposes.

Abigail—The story is in *I Samuel* 25. She apologized to David for her husband's misdeeds. When Nabal learned of this, he died—possibly of chagrin; Abigail then married David.

accident—"turn substance into accident" means to give new qualities to substance; a loose and ironic use of the terms of scholastic philosophy.

Actaeon—A hunter who angered Diana by gazing on her naked; she therefore turned him into a stag, and he was devoured by his own hunting dogs.

Aesculapius—Legendary founder of the science of medicine. The other names which follow in the *General Prologue* are the authorities revered by medieval medicine, ranging from ancient Greece to Chaucer's own day.

Alma redemptoris—A hymn to the Virgin.

Almagest—Ptolemy's astronomical treatise (2nd cent. A.D.); often used, however, for any other book on astronomy, as well as various works attributed to Ptolemy. The Wife of Bath's quotations will not be found in the *Almagest*.

Amor vincit omnia—"Love conquers all things."

Angelus ad virginem—A hymn on the Annuciation; the King's Tune, mentioned in the following line of *The Miller's Tale*, was probably a popular song.

Apostle—(*Pardoner's Tale*, Wife of Bath's Prologue) St. Paul.

Argus—Juno set hundred-eyed Argus to guard Io, beloved of Jupiter and transformed into a cow because of Juno's jealousy. Mercury, sent by Jupiter, sang all hundred eyes to sleep and killed Argus.

arts course—The first stage of university education, the trivium.

Boethius (480?–524?)—Author of *The Consolation of Philosophy*, one of the best-known books of the Middle Ages; it was translated into English by Chaucer, among others. His treatise on music was also well known.

Bradwardine (d. 1349)—Like Boethius, an authority on the difficult theological issues of predestination and free will.

Britain—In Middle English the words for Britain and Brittany are often identical.

Brunellus the Ass—A medieval Latin satirical poem.

Cadmus—Cadmus and Amphion were founders of Thebes.

Callisto—A nymph of Diana who was seduced by Jupiter; Diana turned her into a bear. She was later made the constellation Arctos, the Great Bear—not, as Chaucer has it, the North Star—by Jupiter.

Caracalla—Marcus Aurelius Antoninus Caracalla, Roman emperor murdered in 217 A.D.

Cato—Dionysius Cato (3rd or 4th cent.). A book of proverbs which was used as a primer for schoolchildren was attributed to him.

centers—Parts of an astrolabe. *Argument* is a term for a mathematical variable used in astrology.

chough—This bird was supposed to tell husbands of their wives' infidelities.

Chrysippus—St. Jerome mentions him as an antifeminist.

Cithaeron—Confused by Chaucer with Venus' island of Cythera.

Claudian—Claudius Claudianus (4th cent.), author of an epic poem on the rape of Proserpine.

clerk—A learned man; a student or former student of a university, candidate for the priesthood or a man in holy orders. The modern words "clergy" and "cleric" are, of course, related; but in the Middle Ages anyone of extensive education would be called a clerk and would be likely to be in minor orders, although not necessarily a priest.

Clytemnestra—Wife of the Greek hero Agamemnon. She and her lover, Aegisthus, murdered Agamemnon when he returned from the Trojan War.

complexioun—An individual's temperament or disposition, as determined by the proportions of the four humors (*q.v.*) in his constitution.

Constantinus—Constantinus Afer (11th cent.), author of the work on coitus mentioned further on in *The Merchant's Tale.*

curfew—Probably 8 P.M.

Daphne—Daphne, whose name Chaucer spelled "Dane" (hence the line cautioning the reader that this is not Diana), was a nymph who was turned into a laurel tree, at her own wish, to escape the pursuit of Apollo.

discreet—This and "nor a boaster," further on in *The Nun's Priest's Tale,* are in reference to favors bestowed by a lady. Pertelote refers to the code of chivalric love service, as between a knight and his beloved. Cf. *privee.*

Dunmow—At Dunmow in Essex a flitch of bacon is awarded annually to a couple who have lived a year without quarreling.

Esther—Heroine of the Biblical *Book of Esther.*

expanse years—The magician had tables showing the movements of the planets over both longer and shorter periods (collect and expanse years).

expulsive power—The "expulsive, or animal power," in medieval medicine, was one of three "virtues" thought to control life: the natural, situated in the liver; the vital, centering in the heart; and the animal, in the muscles. The muscles had "expulsive" power, and should have driven out poisons from the "natural virtue."

First Mover—That is, God. This speech is based on several passages in Boethius' *Consolation of Philosophy* (6th cent.).

Franklin—A wealthy landowner, in the class just below the gentry.

fre—generous; *fredom*, generosity of spirit.

Galathea—Pamphilus and Galathea are lovers in a medieval Latin poetic dialogue.

Ganelon—The traitor of *The Song of Roland;* like Judas Iscariot and Sinon, a byword for treachery.

gap-toothed—With teeth set far apart; apparently this was thought to be a sign of an amorous disposition.

gentil—Noble, well-bred.

gentilesse—a key concept for Chaucer; generosity, fellow-feeling, fairness. Associated twice by Chaucer with Christian virtue. Usual overtones of aristocratic "gentility" are repudiated by Chaucer, at least rhetorically.

Geoffrey—Geoffroi de Vinsauf, author of a treatise on poetry (12th cent.) containing, as an example of lamentation, a poem on the death of Richard I.

Griselda's great patience—Griselda is the patient wife about whom the Clerk had told a tale.

Hayles—Abbey in Gloucestershire at which a phial of Christ's blood was supposedly preserved.

Heloise (12th cent.)—Her love affair with the scholar Abelard was a well-known medieval scandal.

hende—Pleasant, courteous; possibly ready to hand, handy; sly or clever.

Hercules—Hercules' wife, Dejanira, believing that he was about to desert her, gave him a shirt which she thought was a love charm; it burned him so badly that he killed himself.

"hereos"—Illness caused by love, Eros.

Herod—In medieval English plays, Herod shows his rage by exaggerated language and contortions.

hour—Briefly, an "hour" was assigned to each planet (and to the deity for which it was named), starting with the planet for which the day was named. On the basis of this astrological calculation, the twenty-third "hour" from sunrise on Sunday would belong to Venus. The first "hour" from sunrise on Monday belonged to Diana (as in English, so in Latin, Monday is named after the moon, whose goddess is Diana). The fourth hour from this sunrise belongs to Mars. These hours were called "unequal" because, under this system, the period from sunrise to sunset, or from sunset to sunrise, was divided into twelve hours, no matter how long or short the period was at different times of year.

Hugh of Lincoln—A medieval saint; a child supposedly killed by Jews.

humor—The four humors were fluids supposed to control health and disposition: blood, phlegm, choler (yellow bile), and melancholy (black bile). Each was supposed to be a different combination of the four qualities, hot, cold, moist, and dry; for example the sanguine humor, blood, was hot and moist. Ailments were thought to be caused by an imbalance of these humors.

Idleness—The gatekeeper of the garden of love in the *Romance of the Rose, q.v.*

In principio—Opening words of Gospel according to St. John: "the beginning [was the Word]." *Nun's Priest's Tale:* this is equivalent to saying, "It's the gospel truth." However, a further play or words may be intended: woman has been man's downfall from the beginning—that is, a reference to Eve.

Jack Straw—One of the leaders of the Peasants' Revolt of 1381. Competition for jobs made Flemings unpopular.

Janus—The Roman god of doorways and of beginnings and endings was portrayed as having two faces—one looking forward and one backward. The month of January is named for him; he symbolizes the coming of the New Year after the winter solstice and the Christmas season.

Jesus son of Sirach—*Ecclesiasticus* is attributed to him.

Joab—In *2 Samuel* 2:28. A follower of David whose trumpet stopped a battle.

Judith—The *Book of Judith* is one of the Apocrypha.

Juno—Juno was an enemy to Thebes because of Jupiter's liasons with at least two women of the Theban royal house.

Kerru—A town in Brittany.

Lamech—Said to be the first to have more than one wife; also a murderer. *Genesis* 4:19-23.

Lemuel—King Lemuel, mentioned in *Proverbs* 31:1. His mother told him that kings should not drink.

limiters—Friars licensed to beg in a certain area—like the Friar of the pilgrimage.

lion—Refers to a fable of Aesop in which a lion, shown a scene in which a man is killing a lion, points out that a leonine artist might have depicted the opposite situation.

Livia—A member of the Roman imperial family who poisoned her husband, Drusus, for her lover, Sejanus.

Lucilia—Wife of the poet Lucretius, who misjudged the properties of an aphrodisiac.

Lucina—One of the names of Diana, as goddess of the moon; usually (as in *The Knight's Tale*) in her function as a goddess of childbirth.

Macrobius—Macrobius' commentary (ca. 400) on Cicero's *Dream of Scipio* was a well-known compendium of medieval dream lore. Chauntecleer is mistaken in stating that Macrobius wrote the *Dream of Scipio* itself.

maistrie—Skill or superiority; mastery; in marriage, control of one partner by the other.

Martianus—Martianus Capella (5th cent.), author of an allegorical Latin poem on the marriage of Philology and Mercury.

martyr—St. Thomas à Becket, murdered at Canterbury Cathedral in 1170.

Maurus—St. Maurus (d. 565) and St. Benedict (d. 544) were authors of monastic rules.

Medea and Circe—Figures in classical narrative whose enchantments, connected with love, harmed others. Circe turned men into beasts.

Meleager—Killed the Calydonian boar, sacred to Diana, and was destroyed by her.

Mercury—Mercury was considered to be the god (and planet) of science and philosophy, and therefore of clerks (q.v.).

Middelburg—Wool trade with the Continent was carried on between Orwell in Suffolk and Middelburg in the Netherlands.

Mulier est hominis confusio—Woman is man's ruin.

natural magic—Magic based on astrology, as against "black magic."

night—"Sunday night before daybreak": the night after Sunday; that is, early Monday morning.

noble—A gold coin.

Orpheus—The music of the mythological figures Orpheus and Amphion had magic effects.

Ovid (d. 17? A.D.)—Ovid's Latin poems *The Art of Love* and *Metamorphoses* were particularly well known in the Middle Ages. The story of Pyramus and Thisbe is one of many stories Chaucer takes from the *Metamorphoses*.

Parables of Solomon—*The Book of Proverbs*.

Pasiphaë—Pasiphaë was in love with a bull, who fathered the famous Minotaur, half bull and half man.

Pater Noster—Our Father; opening words of the Lord's Prayer.

Phidon—Oddly enough, this story and the others which follow in *The Franklin's Tale* are all to be found in the antifeminist tract by St. Jerome mentioned in the Wife of Bath's Prologue.

Physiologus—A Latin bestiary, or work of mainly fanciful natural history with moral interpretations.

pike, pickerel—It used to be supposed that the pickerel was a younger, and the pike an older, example of the same species of fish.

Pilate's voice—Pilate was a great ranter in some of the medieval mystery plays.

pity soon arises in the gentle heart—This line is almost identical in *The Knight's Tale* and *The Merchant's Tale*—where its use is obviously ironic.

Pluto—God of the underworld. *Knight's Tale, Franklin's Tale:* his queen, Proserpina, was sometimes thought of as an aspect of Diana. *Merchant's Tale:* here Chaucer presents the classical god and goddess of the underworld as king and queen of fairyland—which is not without precedent in the Middle Ages.

privee—Private; secretive; discreet. Note reappearance of this and following word in different senses throughout *Miller's Tale*.

privetee—private affairs.

Puella and Rubeus—Designs made up of dots, which look much like constellations of stars; used in the method of divination called geomancy.

Questio quid juris—"The question is, what part of the law?" A phrase the Summoner would have often heard in court.

quoniam—Like *belle chose,* a word for pudendum.

Radix malorum est cupiditas—The love of money is the root of all evil.

Romance of the Rose (13th cent.)—An allegorical poem which was very popular in the Middle Ages. Many of the details of the Temple of Venus in *The Knight's Tale* are drawn from it. The first part of the poem centers around a walled garden of love.

rood-beam—A beam which divides the chancel from the nave of a church; on it a rood (crucifix) was generally placed.

roots—Tables for making astrological calculations.

Rouncivalle—A hospital in London, supported as a branch of the convent of Our Lady of Roncesvalles in Spain. Apparently there were repeated exposures of unauthorized "pardoners" claiming the right to sell pardons to support this hospital.

Saturn—In astrology Saturn was "cold," the most malign of the planets. Chaucer and others combine mythological and astrological aspects of Saturn.

scorpion—Medieval natural history tells us that the scorpion charms her victim with her head, then stings with her tail.

second commandment—This is the third of the commandments according to the Protestant manner of dividing them.

seculeer—Referring to either the secular clergy (as opposed to the regular clergy—those, like monks, living under a rule or *regula*) or the laity. It has sometimes been supposed that Chaucer used this word at a time when he intended *The Merchant's Tale* to be told by the Monk or Friar. But the word may be used ironically, signifying that the nonsecular are just as frail as the secular.

seven deadly sins—The seven deadly sins, frequently mentioned in medieval (and later) literature, are pride, envy, anger, sloth, avarice, gluttony, and lechery.

significavit—A writ which transferred an offender from the ecclesiastical to the civil authorities for punishment.

simple necessity—Inevitably predestined action; as opposed to conditional necessity, which allows for exercise of free will.

Sittingbourne—A town forty miles from London on the way to Canterbury.

St. Paul's—Lawyers were often consulted in the porch of this cathedral in London.

tables of Toledo—Term going back to tables prepared by an Arab astronomer in Spain in the eleventh century.

Thebaid—The *Thebaid* of Statius (d. A.D. 96) is one of Chaucer's sources for *The Knight's Tale;* however, his main source was Boccaccio's *Teseida.* The scene of Emily's prayer is in Boccaccio, but not in Statius.

Theophrastus—Author of an antifeminist work.

Thiodamas—A legendary Theban seer whose invocation was followed by trumpeting.

Trotula—A woman doctor. Possibly she is mentioned here because she was the author of works dealing with sexual matters.

Turnus—Unsuccessful suitor for Lavinia in Vergil's *Aeneid;* killed by Aeneas.

Valerius—A Roman historian, not be confused with the "Valerius and Theophrastus" mentioned in the Wife's prologue.

Valerius and Theophrastus—The *Letter of Valerius* is an antifeminist work, as are the works of Theophrastus, St. Jerome, and Tertullian mentioned by the Wife of Bath.

voice of the turtle—The turtledove. This speech is, of course, paraphrased from the Song of Solomon.

Wade's boat—Wade was a legendary hero, but the relevance of his boat is not known; it may have been magical.

wife (Noah's)—A comic feature in English religious plays (mystery plays) was Noah's inability to get his wife on board the ark.

window (St. Paul's)—Intricate tooled designs resembling the windows in St. Paul's Cathedral.

worthy—Brave; or distinguished in whatever field it may apply to. A knight and a wife would obviously be "worthy" in different ways.

BIBLIOGRAPHY

("C." is Chaucer; "pb" means "also available in paperback.")

Texts, bibliography, notes, criticisms: F. N. Robinson, *The Works* . . . , 2nd ed., 1957; E. T. Donaldson, *C.'s Poetry, An Anthology* . . . , 1958; A. C. Baugh, *C.'s Major Poetry*, 1963.

Biography: M. Chute, *Geoffrey C. of England*, 1946 (pb).

Specific critical works: R. D. French, *A C. Handbook*, 2nd ed., 1947; W. F. Bryan and G. Dempster, *Sources and Analogues of C.'s Canterbury Tales*, 1941, 1958. M. Bowden, *A Commentary on the General Prologue* . . . , 1948 (background of pilgrims); W. C. Curry, *C. and the Mediaeval Sciences*, rev. 1960; D. D. Griffith, *Bibliography of C.*, 1955 (references therein to other bibliographies).

General critical works ("Chaucer" prominent in title): H. S. Bennett, 1947; D. S. Brewer, 1953; B. H. Bronson, 1960; G. K. Chesterton, 1932; N. Coghill, 1949; G. L. Kittredge, 1915; W. W. Lawrence, 1950; E. Legouis, 1913; J. L. Lowes, 1934 (pb); K. Malone, 1951; J. M. Manly, 1926; C. Muscatine, 1957; H. R. Patch, 1939; R. Preston, 1952; R. K. Root, rev. 1922; P. V. D. Shelly, 1940; J. Speirs, 1951; J. S. P. Tatlock, 1950; also C. S. Lewis, *The Allegory of Love*, 1936 (pb); R. M. Lumiansky, *Of Sondry Folk*, 1955.

Paperback collections of articles on C.: ed. by R. J. Schoeck and Taylor, 1960; ed. by E. C. Wagenknecht, 1959; also *Discussions of the Canterbury Tales*, ed. by C. J. Owen, 1961.

Bantam Book Catalog

Here's your up-to-the-minute listing of over 1,400 titles by your favorite authors.

This illustrated, large format catalog gives a description of each title. For your convenience, it is divided into categories in fiction and non-fiction—gothics, science fiction, westerns, mysteries, cookbooks, mysticism and occult, biographies, history, family living, health, psychology, art.

So don't delay—take advantage of this special opportunity to increase your reading pleasure.

Just send us your name and address and 50¢ (to help defray postage and handling costs).